RECONCILING FRANCE AGAINST DEMOCRACY

Reconciling France against Democracy

The Croix de Feu and the Parti Social Français, 1927–1945

SEAN KENNEDY

McGill-Queen's University Press
Montreal & Kingston • London • Ithaca

© McGill-Queen's University Press 2007

ISBN 978-0-7735-3205-2

Legal deposit second quarter 2007
Bibliothèque nationale du Québec

Printed in Canada on acid-free paper

This book has been published with the help of a grant from the
Canadian Federation for the Humanities and Social Sciences,
through the Aid to Scholarly Publications Programme, using
funds provided by the Social Sciences and Humanities Research
Council of Canada. Funding has also been received from the
University of New Brunswick.

McGill-Queen's University Press acknowledges the support of the
Canada Council for the Arts for our publishing program. We also
acknowledge the financial support of the Government of Canada
through the Book Publishing Industry Development Program
(BDIDP) for our publishing activities.

Library and Archives Canada Cataloguing in Publication

Kennedy, Sean, 1969–
    Reconciling France against democracy: the Croix de feu and
the Parti social français, 1927–1945 / Sean Kennedy.

Includes bibliographical references and index.
ISBN 978-0-7735-3205-2

1. Croix de feu (Organization: France)–History. 2. Parti social
français–History. 3. La Rocque, François de, 1886–1946.
4. France–Politics and government–1914–1940. 5. France–
Politics and government–1940–1945. 6. Conservatism–France–
History–20th century. I. Title.

DC361.K45 2007   944.081'5   C2006-905346-4

Typeset by Jay Tee Graphics Ltd. in Sabon 10/13

Contents

Tables

Acknowledgments

This book, which began as a doctoral dissertation at York University, has been a long time in the making, and I have received much support along the way. Without a doctoral fellowship from the Social Sciences and Humanities Research Council of Canada and financial support from the J.W. Pickersgill Fellowship of the Government of Newfoundland and Labrador, it would have been impossible for me to undertake research in France. Additional research trips for this project were funded with the generous support of the University of New Brunswick's Department of History and the Research Travel Award of the Society for French Historical Studies. Funds from UNB's History Department, the Vice-President Research, and the Faculty of Arts Busteed Publication Fund and a grant from the Humanities and Social Sciences Federation of Canada with funds from the Social Sciences and Humanities Research Council of Canada have supported the publication of this book.

In France Gilles de La Rocque, now deceased, graciously allowed me to consult the Fonds de La Rocque, held at the Archives Nationales, as well as the Archives d'Histoire Contemporaine in Paris and the records of the PSF's Nord federation in Lille. I am indebted to a large number of archivists and librarians in France for guiding me through their collections and the process of obtaining *dérogations*, and for facilitating what were sometimes brief visits. I would particularly like to thank Odile Gaultier-Voituriez at the Archives d'Histoire Contemporaine for helping to orient me during my first research trip to France. Personnel at the British Public Record Office and the US National Archives in Washington helped me to locate relevant documents. The interlibrary loan staff of, first, York University and then the University of New Brunswick located many sources on my behalf.

I completed my dissertation under the supervision of William D. Irvine. Bill suggested this topic to me and was an outstanding supervisor; he has continued to provide advice and support in years since I completed it. The other members of my examining committee – Bettina Bradbury, George Comninel, Adrian Shubert, Harvey Simmons, and John Hellman of McGill University – supplied excellent feedback. Since I came to UNB in 1999, my colleagues in the Department of History have indulged my interest in the French far right and provided constant encouragement. While my debt to all of them is great, I must especially thank Peter Kent, who read the manuscript in its entirety and provided valuable comments. The intelligence and enthusiasm of the students I have taught, especially in my courses relating to French history and to fascism, have been inspiring. Among scholars of the French right, I have benefited from conversations with Serge Berstein, Joel Blatt, Samuel Goodfellow, Samuel Kalman, Albert Kéchichian, Laurent Kestel, Cheryl Koos, Diane Labrosse, Paul Mazgaj, Geoff Read, Daniella Sarnoff, David Schalk, and Robert Soucy. As the references for this book attest, my debt to other scholars is considerable, notwithstanding interpretational differences. At McGill-Queen's University Press, Kyla Madden, editor, and Joan McGilvray, coordinating editor, have been very positive, insightful, and effective in helping the manuscript through the various stages of publication. They have also been very patient. The book has benefited greatly from Elizabeth Hulse's skilled copy-editing. I am indebted to the anonymous readers for the press, who provided detailed, thoughtful, and constructive commentary on the manuscript. Any errors or shortcomings are of course my own.

I would like to thank Duke University Press for permission to reproduce material from my article "The Croix de Feu, the Parti Social Français, and the Politics of Aviation, 1931–1939," *French Historical Studies* 23:2 (2000): 373–99, and Oxford University Press for permission to reproduce material from my article "Accompanying the Marshal: La Rocque and the Progrès Social Français under Vichy," *French History* 15 (2001): 186–213.

Over the years I have spent working on the Croix de Feu, friends and family have always been ready to listen. To John Bingham and Barbara Clow, John FitzGerald, Stephen Henderson, Ross Leckie and Kathryn Taglia, and James Muir, my sincere thanks. My parents, Theresa and Michael, have always been enthusiastic about this project, for which I am indebted.

My wife, Lisa, has encouraged my academic life since we were undergraduates and has endured long absences, cluttered apartments and offices, and bouts of second-guessing over revisions. She has never ceased to amaze me with her energy, wit, ability to adapt, and willingness to provide support. This book is dedicated to her.

Abbreviations

ADP	Auxiliaires de la Défense Passive
CFTC	Confédération Française des Travailleurs Chrétiens
CGT	Confédération Générale du Travail
CNIP	Centre National des Indépendants et Paysans
EVP	Équipes Volantes de Propagande
FFCF	Fils et Filles des Croix de Feu
FN	Front National
LICA	Ligue Internationale contre l'Antisémitisme
LPF	Ligue Patriotique des Françaises
MRP	Mouvement Républicain Populaire
MSF	Mouvement Social Français
PCF	Parti Communiste Français
PDP	Parti Démocrate Populaire
PPF	Parti Populaire Français
PRL	Parti Républicain de la Liberté
PRNS	Parti Républicain National et Social
PSF	Parti Social Français
RF	Réconciliation Française
RGR	Rassemblement des Gauches Républicaines
RNAS	Rassemblement National d'Action Sociale
RPF	Rassemblement du Peuple Français
SFIO	Section Française de l'Internationale Ouvrière
SOL	Service d'Ordre Légionnaire
SPES	Société de Préparation et d'Education Sportive
SPF	Syndicats Professionnels Français
UDSR	Union Démocratique et Socialiste de la Résistance
UNC	Union Nationale des Combattants

UNR   Union pour la Nouvelle République
USR   Union Socialiste Républicaine
VN   Volontaires Nationaux

Map of France. From T.B. Smith, *Creating the Welfare State in France* (McGill-Queen's University Press, 2003). Reproduced with permission.

Croix de Feu members in Paris, 6 February 1934 (Roger-Viollet, 4472–11)

François de La Rocque, 1932 (Roger-Viollet, 9021–2)

Croix de Feu members march past La Rocque and Mermoz, Paris, May 1935
(Roger-Viollet, 2508–2)

The Croix de Feu marching in Paris, 14 July 1935 (Roger-Viollet, 2508–3)

The Croix de Feu marching on Bastille Day, 14 July 1935
(Roger-Viollet, 1304–2)

Police charging PSF counter-demonstrators at a meeting of the PCF, Parc des
Princes, 6 October 1936 (Roger-Viollet, 950–10)

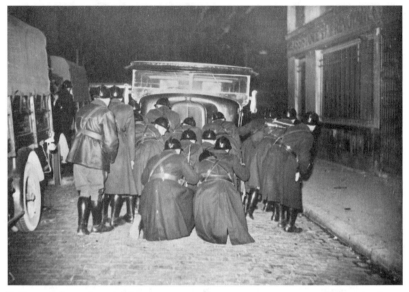

Police confront Popular Front counter-demonstrators at a PSF film screening, Clichy, 16 March 1937 (Roger-Viollet, 2192–13)

La Rocque on trial for reconstituting the Croix de Feu, Paris, December 1937 (Roger-Viollet, 3645–13)

RECONCILING FRANCE AGAINST DEMOCRACY

Introduction

I saw La Rocque only once, very early one October morning in 1936, in the passageway of the train that was carrying me back from Biarritz. A short, pale, rather flabby fellow, he was standing outside the door of his sleeping compartment, between two bodyguards, watching the sun come up. After that, he came to the dining car to have his café au lait and smoke a pipe. I concluded that he was not a threat to the Republic.

These are the reflections of Édouard Daladier, France's prime minister from April 1938 to February 1940, concerning François de La Rocque, leader of the Croix de Feu and subsequently the Parti Social Français (PSF). Daladier wrote this passage while both men were captives of the Third Reich in 1944. Having already made clear that he found his former political opponent anything but threatening, over the following months in prison Daladier softened his attitude further. Yet at this time he still believed that "La Rocque wanted to create a national movement and assume power legally, with the idea of instituting an authoritarian, corporatist state."[1]

Daladier's remarks thus convey contradictory impressions. On the one hand, he was dismissive; indeed, if his remarks in 1944 accurately reflect his impressions in October 1936, then he was discounting La Rocque as a threat to the democratic Third Republic at a time when his Communist and Socialist allies in the Popular Front were strongly convinced otherwise. That very month, in fact, thousands of PSF members had clashed with police as they protested the holding of a mass rally by the Communists, since their own meeting scheduled for that day had been banned. The fracas culminated in La Rocque and his colleagues being charged with reconstituting the Croix de Feu, which itself had been dissolved by Léon Blum's Popular Front government only months before on the grounds that it was a paramilitary organization which posed a threat to French democracy. Daladier believed, at least in retrospect, that such fears were overblown. But at the same time he conceded that La Rocque and his supporters had vast ambitions, seeking to alter the political and social system in profound ways. Moreover, they had an unprecedented support base for those ambitions. With the Croix de Feu having reached a membership of over half a million members by 1936 and the PSF over one million by 1938, these organizations surpassed in scale all their rivals and opponents.

In many ways, Daladier's terse remarks encapsulate the major concerns of both contemporaries and historians as far as the Croix de Feu and the PSF are concerned. What did these movements wish to achieve? Should their political demeanour be regarded as essentially benign or ultimately sinister? Was the scope of their ambitions for France matched by their political skills, or did La Rocque and his followers ultimately lack determination and substance?

On the face of it, an overview of these organizations evokes ambivalent responses to such questions. The Croix de Feu developed into an enormous movement with a threatening stance, but the fact that it failed to take power raises questions about how fearsome it really was. To be sure, the organization developed a potent message. It preached a nationalist revival inspired by the myth of a country unified in war between 1914 and 1918. La Rocque and his colleagues believed that this experience of "national reconciliation" could serve as the foundation of a new order. A renovated France would be rid of destructive political sectarianism, class conflict, and internal enemies. The movement also intimated that it could use force to achieve its objectives. Indeed, it first gained truly national prominence in the wake of the riots of 6 February 1934, when it marched, along with a number of other groups, on the Chamber of Deputies and skirmished with the police. Subsequently, the Croix de Feu expanded rapidly, and it was deemed by the Popular Front to be the most dangerous of its far-right opponents. By 1936 its huge membership participated in a wide range of ancillary organizations, gathering diverse segments of the French population into a variegated social network. Yet this seemingly formidable instrument was unable to prevent the Popular Front from winning the elections held that year and it submitted to dissolution by the Blum government, to the great consternation of some of its militants. La Rocque was accused of being weak, even a traitor.

But La Rocque was far from finished. Preparations had been made to create a new movement in advance of the anticipated dissolution. When the PSF was launched in the summer of 1936, it soon recovered much of the Croix de Feu's membership as well as new supporters. Organizationally, though, it was distinct from its predecessor. Whereas the Croix de Feu had been a movement that had political ambitions but not a corresponding electoral infrastructure, the PSF was a bona fide party. This shift was necessary since the Popular Front had banned the Croix de Feu and other nationalist organizations, but it also reflected a desire to have a more direct impact on political life. In some ways the PSF was an even greater success than its forerunner. It attracted perhaps twice as many supporters, and its associational life had more texture; it offered an ever-widening range of cultural, recreational, and social service networks and tried to reach out to French society beyond the movement. Such activities still provoked alarm amongst a broad spectrum of opinion; La Rocque's opponents noted that the PSF continued to denounce them in vehement terms and still engaged in threatening mobilizations, at least until renewed threats of dissolution curtailed such displays.

But while the PSF was in some ways a resounding success, the new party also encountered difficulties. The timing of and circumstances surrounding its formation meant that it had a limited parliamentary presence. Some of its energies were diverted into the courts as a result of its leaders being charged with reconstituting the Croix de Feu. Relations with other right-wing formations proved troublesome, at times dismal. Fierce competition for pre-eminence among nationalists culminated in yet another legal battle when former premier André Tardieu accused La Rocque – a man who prided himself on being beholden to no one – of taking money from the government in the early 1930s. Above all, the reorientation of the French political system in a conservative direction, under the aegis of Édouard Daladier, at the end of the decade seemed to deny the PSF political space. Following the defeat of 1940, the movement faced an ostensibly more propitious environment; after all, the Vichy regime's slogan, "Work, Family, Nation," was appropriated from it. The PSF, however, believed that it had been marginalized well before La Rocque and scores of its cadres were arrested by the Germans in 1943. Thus, while the PSF was able to attract considerable support, it had been unable to translate this into power. The structures and evolution of the republican political system in the 1930s hampered its progress, and under Vichy it was consigned to isolation.

As this overview suggests, the Croix de Feu and the PSF had an intensely nationalist agenda. Beyond that, however, there have some sharp interpretational differences concerning these movements, particularly with respect to how they should be classified. The present work offers its own perspective on that issue, but also seeks to provide a more comprehensive account of La Rocque and his followers. While analyzing the goals and political valence of the Croix de Feu and the PSF, it is equally concerned with exploring the associational life of these movements and the various strategies they pursued to achieve political power and transform France. In doing so, it assesses why their quest for political power ended in failure, but also considers how they shaped French political culture during the 1930s and thereafter.

The Croix de Feu and the PSF are the subjects of a growing historiography, but it is the issue of deciding whether or not they should be considered fascist that has dominated the interpretive agenda. On one side of the divide, former militants and members of La Rocque's family contend that he was a patriot whose actions were informed by Christian principles. The movements he led, they argue, were constructive in nature, seeking to renovate a nation in crisis. They assert that the charge of fascism is partisan and unfounded.[2] A number of historians, while adopting a more critical and detached stance, broadly share this view. In this regard, René Rémond's interpretation, as developed in his study of right-wing traditions in France, has proven extremely influential. Rémond does not doubt that La Rocque had political ambitions, but he questions whether there was anything in the Croix de Feu's vague program that could not be reconciled with a reform of republican institutions or that distinguished it from the traditional right. The fact that, following its dissolution, the Croix de Feu was transformed into the PSF, which accepted the Third Republic, suggests to Rémond that La Rocque's intentions had been relatively moderate all along. Ultimately, the PSF, by taking a segment of opinion hitherto hostile to democracy and reconciling it to the latter in the context of a mass party organization, foreshadowed postwar Gaullism.[3]

Rémond's concise analysis has had a formative impact upon much subsequent scholarship. Operating within his interpretive framework, a range of studies have provided information on the Croix de Feu and the PSF in various regions of France.[4] A particularly extensive contribution was made by Philippe Machefer, whose publications offer valuable information about the programs, membership, and activities of La Rocque's followers.[5] Machefer highlights the unsavoury features of the Croix de Feu and the PSF to a greater extent than Rémond; he notes parallels between their outlook and the clerical authoritarianism practised in countries such as Portugal at the time and points to antisemitism on the part of the PSF during the Vichy era. Nevertheless, he agrees with Rémond that before the war the PSF was integrating into the republican system. Some English-language scholars share this outlook. Gareth Howlett's 1985 thesis, for instance, which draws extensively upon La Rocque's papers and develops fresh insights on the tactics of these movements, concludes they seemed radical in form but were essentially moderate in substance.[6]

Jacques Nobécourt's exhaustively researched biography of La Rocque develops a similar interpretation in depth. He sees his subject as a "Christian nationalist" who tried to heal the divisions afflicting France. Though Nobécourt admits that La Rocque had his flaws, he concludes that he never impugned "democracy as a system of government nor the Republic as a regime."[7] This was the case even before the Croix de Feu was transformed into the PSF. While Nobécourt sees the dissolution of 1936 as a significant rupture in the history of the movement, his primary concern is to show that it was an unfair act of retribution by the Popular Front government. A prominent theme of his biography is that the French left conducted a vicious and cynical slander campaign against La Rocque which had a lasting impact. His study also examines the fate of the PSF during the Second World War in great detail, arguing that La Rocque opposed Vichy in important ways. Nobécourt concludes that the PSF leader was victimized by both the left and the right during this period. Imprisoned by the Nazis, he was unlawfully detained after the war at the behest of de Gaulle's provisional government.

Further recent scholarship also supports the notion that the Croix de Feu and the PSF evolved in a moderate direction. Albert Kéchichian concedes that in its early years the Croix de Feu situated itself on the far right, but he argues that La Roque's final goal was to de-politicize a bitterly divided country through a moral mobilization of civil society. Jean-Paul Thomas, who has conducted detailed research into the PSF's membership, finds continuities between it and Charles de Gaulle's Rassemblement du Peuple Français (RPF), which was active from 1947 until 1955. Through painstaking analysis, Thomas has convincingly argued that the PSF was the largest political movement in modern French history, with as many as 1.2 million members on the eve of the Second World War.[8] He also sees merit in the claim that the PSF foreshadowed postwar Gaullism. He has discovered that after 1945 a significant number of La Rocque's former supporters rallied to de Gaulle and that the geographic profiles of the PSF and the RPF were similar.[9]

Depictions of La Rocque and his supporters, to the effect that while evincing some disturbing characteristics, they ultimately served to pioneer democratic, mass conservative politics in France, have been critiqued by a growing number of historians. As part of a broader effort to demonstrate that French fascism was a significant phenomenon, Robert Soucy argues that both the Croix de Feu and the PSF were fascist movements. In their hatred of democrats, Communists, and decadence, he maintains, they shared the predilections of other European fascists. Though conceding that La Rocque moderated his rhetoric from time to time, especially after the foundation of the PSF in 1936, Soucy interprets this shift as a tactical response to changed circumstances.[10] To the end, he insists, La Rocque and his supporters were determined foes of the Third Republic. In a related vein, William Irvine contends that many of the arguments used to show that the Croix de Feu was not fascist do not accord with the actual experiences of Italian Fascism and German Nazism. For instance, the argument that La Rocque was not a fascist because he was too legalistic – namely, that he eventually adopted the parliamentary road by transforming the Croix de Feu into a formal party – overlooks the fact that Mussolini and Hitler did much the same thing.[11]

Irvine's and Soucy's arguments have won supporters. For example, in his study of fascism in interwar Alsace, Samuel Goodfellow maintains that while it tried to appear more moderate than other elements of the far right, the PSF espoused a fascist transformation of French society. It called for an authoritarian state and the organization of the economy along corporatist lines. Zeev Sternhell, an influential scholar of French fascism, had long dismissed La Rocque as a mere conservative but has recently revised his view. He now asserts that the efforts of the Croix de Feu and the PSF to synthesize ultra-nationalism with a consideration of the social question were typical of the third way between Marxism and capitalism preached by fascists.[12]

Conversely, Kevin Passmore's endorsement of the revisionist view that both the Croix de Feu and the PSF were fascist, as developed in his study of the right in the Rhône and a series of articles, is only partial.[13] In his view, while the Croix de Feu mobilized many people who normally supported conservatives, it also embodied a genuine radicalism, fed by a visceral hostility towards traditional elites for their shortcomings. This stance made the movement both authoritarian and populist; the fact that it projected its world view through paramilitarism, he concludes, made it fascist. Passmore thus shares the view of Irvine and

Soucy as far as the Croix de Feu is concerned, but his reasons for doing so are distinctive. Moreover, he also contends that the dissolution of 1936 and the creation of the PSF represented a true rupture. Compared to its predecessor, the PSF placed more emphasis upon electoral success, and it gradually abandoned paramilitarism. Though at the end of the 1930s it still displayed authoritarian features, Passmore suggests that had the war not intervened, the PSF might have become a more conventional conservative party.

Clearly, the debate over the fascist character of the Croix de Feu and the PSF has become increasingly sophisticated, even though a consensus remains elusive. But as several participants in the debate have noted, these movements can be studied from other perspectives. Irvine observes that whether or not the Croix de Feu and the PSF should be considered fascist is central to the debate over the significance of fascism in interwar France; if La Rocque and his followers are exempted from the fascist category, then the significance of fascism in France is considerably diminished. But Irvine also emphasizes the intrinsic importance of understanding a mass political movement that erupted on the political landscape of the 1930s: "Is it not more important simply to give the formation the serious scholarly study it deserves?" Similarly, in his article on women's social work activities in the Croix de Feu and the PSF, Passmore endorses studying these organizations, along with other movements of the French right, in relation to a range of historical problems "without necessarily bracketing the question of fascism."[14]

Indeed, a number of scholars of the French far right have recently called for a shift in emphasis. While there is now much criticism of the view advanced by Rémond and others that the Croix de Feu and the PSF were essentially benign in their goals, there is also skepticism about an overarching focus upon labelling these organizations. The political sociologist Michel Dobry strongly criticizes the belief that interwar France was allergic to fascism. But when it comes to studying the far right, he downplays the importance of taxonomy and stresses, for instance, the mutability of political movements and the affinities between traditional conservatives and fascists. In his view, the issue of whether or not movements such as the Croix de Feu and the PSF should be considered fascist "does not constitute the sole, or even the principal, research question."[15] Dobry's outlook is shared by Didier Leschi, who emphasizes La Rocque's efforts to distinguish his followers from other ultra-nationalist movements and thereby secure a broader base of support.[16] Brian Jenkins, editor of a collection of essays on the inter-war far right, concludes that the controversy over French fascism has grown sterile. While endorsing the view that the Croix de Feu posed a serious threat to democracy, he suggests that given the lack of a consensus definition of fascism, it might be more profitable to develop comparisons with specific cases such as German Nazism or Italian Fascism.[17] The renowned historian of Vichy France Robert Paxton has turned his attention to the study of fascism, but he is also wary of classifying movements with excessive precision.[18] In his analysis of Henry Dorgères's Greenshirts, who competed with La Rocque for support in the French countryside during the 1930s, he concludes that in studying the far right it is more profitable for the historian to focus on contexts and processes than rigid categories.[19]

In relation to previous scholarship, the present work seeks to locate the Croix de Feu and the PSF on the spectrum of interwar European politics, but without becoming preoccupied with categorization. It concentrates upon situating them in the political culture of interwar France and assessing their tactics in dealing with their foes on the left and competitors on the right. It considers how they embodied and disseminated in a concrete way, to a substantial proportion of the French populace, the integral nationalist solutions they offered as panaceas for their country's problems. I contend that the Croix de Feu and the PSF are best understood as authoritarian nationalist movements which consistently sought to recast France fundamentally, and that they displayed adaptability in facing the various challenges which they encountered. In the process, they both reflected and contributed importantly to a sea change in interwar French political culture which ultimately – though not inevitably – manifested itself in the Vichy regime's National Revolution.

In developing this interpretation, I draw upon the rich scholarship on Europe's interwar far right. One of the main tenets of much recent work in this field is that fascism must be understood as one member of a large political family. Fascists coexisted and often cooperated with right-wing authoritarians and conservatives who shared many of their concerns; the boundaries between these categories were blurred. But whereas interwar authoritarians and conservatives tended to prize hierarchy and a paternalist social order, fascists were more willing to engage in cumulative political and social radicalization to ensure that a national rebirth took place, even as they sought to preserve private property and an stratified social order.[20] The present work stresses the

powerful affinities that existed between both the Croix de Feu and the
PSF, on the one hand, and movements such as the Italian Fascists and
the Nazis on the other, but it argues that their goals were distinct in
some ways. La Rocque and his supporters shared with Hitler and Mussolini a virulent hostility to Marxism and liberalism, and they emphasized ultra-nationalism, the leadership principle, and a rhetorical desire
to end social conflict. The political strategies they developed to
advance their agendas were also very similar to the leading exemplars
of European fascism. Moreover, all these movements were founded by
veterans and inspired by what has been called "the myth of the war
experience." But the Croix de Feu and the PSF lacked the desire for
ongoing radicalization that proved so important to Mussolini and
especially Hitler. These movements wanted to break with the Third
Republic, but they envisioned a new polity and society characterized by
authoritarian stability.[21]

Regarding the issue of continuity between the two organizations,
this study recognizes that they evolved significantly and that the dissolution of 1936 signalled important changes, but it concludes that there
were also fundamental continuities. I contend that the transformation
from Croix de Feu to PSF was less about accepting integration into the
democratic republican system than about sinking roots into French
society in order to transform it. While the threat of a second dissolution and a changing political environment led the PSF to emphasize
its acceptance of electoral politics and to downplay the role of political
violence, in ideological terms the commitment to authoritarianism
remained powerful. Indeed, compared to the Croix de Feu, the PSF
grew more concerned with promoting an essentialist conception of
French national identity. Increasingly, it defined France as a "Christian
civilization" in opposition to a variety of opponents whom it saw as
lying beyond the proper boundaries of the nation. The development of
this exclusionary vision points to a clarifying and hardening of the
PSF's stance on some issues in comparison to its predecessor, rather
than a growing moderation. Thus in asserting that these movements
were authoritarian rather than fascist, this study does not imply that
they were essentially benign in character.

This book also contends that while they were ultimately unsuccessful, La Rocque and his colleagues advanced their agenda with cunning
and ruthlessness, and to considerable effect. Thus it contests the view
advanced by Eugen Weber and other scholars who suggest that while
he was a capable organizer, La Rocque was "too much of a gentleman,

hopelessly legalistic and republican." It also departs from the interpretation of La Rocque's biographer, who emphasizes the intemperate rhetoric and repressive actions of his enemies in explaining his difficulties.[22] To be sure, La Rocque and his colleagues made serious mistakes and faced determined opposition. But they understood the potential of mass mobilization and the futility of trying to achieve power through brute force alone. They were also cognizant of the need to cultivate elites while preserving the image and substance of independence, and of the fact that a significant proportion of the public feared them and invoked democratic, republican values against them.

These circumstances required a continuing process of adaptation. In its early years the Croix de Feu faced the challenge of raising its profile without acting precipitously or coming under the control of other groups. This problem was particularly evident during the 6 February 1934 riots. Subsequently, as the movement experienced rapid growth, its agenda shifted to sustaining momentum, dealing adroitly with the multitude of other right-wing personalities and movements in France, and responding to an increasingly united left. Of course, the electoral victory of the Popular Front and the dissolution of 1936 represented severe blows to La Rocque's and his associates' ambitions. Nevertheless, the Croix de Feu showed considerable agility throughout this period, building mass support, positioning itself as a more credible force for national unity and stability than its right-wing competitors, and seeking to outmanoeuvre the Popular Front.

With the creation of the PSF, the rules of the game changed, and it took some time for the new party to adjust. Some of the problems it faced were of its own making. Its aggressive rhetoric and behaviour encouraged further polarization, and it soon faced a renewed threat of dissolution. Simultaneously, the knotty problem of intra-right relations – in short, the forging of a counter-revolutionary coalition – was intensified by the fact that La Rocque and his colleagues did little to hide their conviction that they were destined to lead the French right. This attitude, plus their resistance to efforts to manipulate them, led to severe infighting by 1937. The PSF weathered this storm, only to find itself confronted after 1938 with the erosion of its nemesis, the Popular Front, and the growth in conservative support for the new Daladier government. Still, the party proved adaptable throughout this period. It sought to turn the tables on the Popular Front by presenting the Blum government as the true enemy of republican liberties. In its dealings with other elements of the right and eventually the Daladier government, it worked to position itself favourably for the future through intensive electoral planning and expanding what one historian refers to as its "counter-society."[23]

To understand the latter process, this work highlights the associational life of the Croix de Feu and the PSF. Many historians have recognized that the development of ancillary organizations – such as unions, women's groups, youth groups, social initiatives, and a welter of extra-curricular activities – was integral to both the Croix de Feu and the PSF. Of the initiatives themselves, however, there are relatively few studies.[24] In discussing the flanking organizations developed by La Rocque and his colleagues, the present work recognizes the contributions of previous scholarship but also questions whether this counter-society, in the words of its most assiduous analyst, "fulfilled a more mundane and less sinister need in those who participated in it than has sometimes been suggested."[25] Influenced by an paternalist brand of Social Catholicism adapted to the ideology of national reconciliation, the Croix de Feu's and the PSF's counter-society was intended to prefigure a France guided by its authoritarian nationalist principles. In the long run, it was hoped that the anomie and materialism which La Rocque and many of his supporters perceived as afflicting their country would disappear. As it turned out, there were limits to the counter-society's success, but the militants of the Croix de Feu and the PSF displayed tenacity and ingenuity in developing it.

In the end, of course, for La Rocque and his supporters, power proved elusive. Scholars have pointed to various features of the Third Republic in the 1930s that hindered the rise of the far right and its accession to power. They note that France was a satiated power, and that the impact of the Great Depression was less severe there than in some other countries.[26] French elites, while hardly uniform in their responses, did not feel sufficiently threatened by the left to embrace the far right wholeheartedly, though the situation was certainly fluid.[27] One of the reasons for this response was that the state itself remained capable of preserving order in the face of political violence; the circumstances were quite different, for instance, in Italy between 1919 and 1922.[28] When the nationalist right did mobilize, the French left cooperated against its foes at least for a time, in contrast to the enduring split between Socialists and Communists in Weimar Germany.[29] By contrast, the French far right was never able to unite under one banner, despite the Croix de Feu's and the PSF's best efforts. When the Popular Front coalition did fragment, the Radical party under Daladier shifted to form a coalition with more right-wing parties, demonstrating that the French political system had not become deadlocked as those of Italy and Germany had.[30] Most generally, historians have emphasized the strength of democratic, republican political culture in allowing France to resist the temptation of fascism.[31]

This study endeavours to give these factors their due weight in explaining why La Rocque and his colleagues did not achieve power, but it also draws attention to the role of contingency and the significance of particular political tactics and strategies. While France's political system delimited the prospects for the Croix de Feu and the PSF, it was in turn partially refashioned by these organizations' discourse, actions, and social presence. Indeed, in terms of political dynamics, few movements did more to encourage the polarization of France in the 1930s. A good deal of the Socialists' and Communists' political strategy turned on the actions of the Croix de Feu and the PSF, just as La Rocque and his followers were obsessed with demonizing and undermining the left. As for the right, both conservative formations, as represented by the Alliance Démocratique and the Fédération Républicaine, and ultra-nationalist groups such as the Action Française, found their energies diverted by their rivalry with the Croix de Feu and the PSF in crucial ways. This internecine conflict ensured that France did not develop a united counter-revolutionary coalition during the 1930s.

More generally, the Croix de Feu and the PSF synthesized many of the ideological currents that proved inimical to republican democracy. While avoiding the temptation to see the defeat of 1940 and the ensuing National Revolution as inevitable, historians such as Philip Nord have shown how from the inception of the Third Republic, various elements of French political culture adumbrated the authoritarian and exclusionary outlook of Marshal Pétain's Vichy government. Nord notes that the regime was established in the 1870s on the basis of a compromise which left considerable scope for those elements of French society hostile or indifferent to democracy. The result was that its "political culture was streaked with authoritarian impulses" and that it retained powerful enemies.[32] Ultra-nationalists – some avowedly anti-republican, such as Charles Maurras, others, such as Maurice Barrès, less fastidious about the form of government than its ideological content – promoted a vision of France at odds with pluralist values. Menacing organizations ranging from the supporters of General Boulanger to the far-right squads of the interwar era arose in times of crisis, contesting the regime.

In comparison to earlier nationalist formations, the Croix de Feu and the PSF exceeded their forerunners in mass appeal and on the eve of the Second World War appeared to be more durable. They did so because they tapped into the leading preoccupations of interwar French society as well as the authoritarian currents of an evolving republican political culture. In a country scarred by the First World War, they identified themselves with the memory of a disciplined wartime France divorced from its liberal roots.[33] At a time when democratic mores were savaged by thinkers such as the "nonconformists" of the 1930s, who called for a revamping of the nation through embracing spiritualist and communitarian values, the Croix de Feu and the PSF popularized similar critiques for their own ends.[34] In the face of persistent class divisions and sometimes bitter contestation between labour and capital, La Rocque and his supporters held out promises of social reconciliation. They also responded to anxieties about a perceived blurring of gender roles by endorsing a paternalist social vision.[35] When concerns about preserving French national identity in the face of new cultural influences gave rise to growing xenophobia, La Rocque and his followers reflected and nurtured such views.[36] Above all, they benefited from a fierce backlash against the Popular Front. In spite of the relative moderation of the latter's reforms, many French citizens feared radical social and institutional change and regarded La Rocque as a potential saviour, or at least a barrier against the left.

In the end, of course, while the Croix de Feu and the PSF promoted their ultra-nationalist agenda with fierce determination, they did not profit greatly from their efforts. The sidelining of the PSF by the Vichy regime, despite their ideological affinities, makes this outcome clear. Gradually the movement fragmented, some supporters choosing collaboration and others resistance. Those who remained loyal to La Rocque became in effect dissident National Revolutionaries, seeking to demonstrate that it was the PSF which was best qualified to implement the agenda initiated by Pétain's government. But they were isolated by their rivals and eventually repressed by the Nazis. The party was banned in 1945 and had to reform yet again; but with many former supporters questioning the PSF's stance under Vichy and with La Rocque's death in 1946, it was perhaps not surprising that its successor, Réconciliation Française, was never able to attract mass support.

Before the war, however, the Croix de Feu and the Parti Social Français had been at the heart of many of the problems that beset the late Third Republic: bitter political divisions, a crisis of confidence in democracy among much of the population, and a growing rigidity in conceptions of social relations and national identity. To be sure, La Rocque and his followers were not the sole exemplars of these trends. But by examining their role in advancing an integral nationalist agenda, this study hopes to shed light not only upon these controversial movements but also upon broader political and social trends during the twilight years of France's most enduring democracy to date, trends that figured importantly during the National Revolution. It also looks ahead to the postwar era, for while the PSF has sometimes been cast as the precursor of Gaullism, there are also some grounds for comparing it to a movement of the far right that has had a baleful impact on contemporary French politics, Jean-Marie Le Pen's Front National.

.

I

Vers le six février,
1927–1934

The Croix de Feu emerged as a prominent force in French public life in the wake of the 6 February 1934 riots, and naturally it is the actions of the league in subsequent years that have garnered the most attention. It is instructive to analyze its formative period, however. While the movement's leaders balked at committing themselves to a detailed program, what became known as the *mystique Croix de Feu* took shape at this time. Appealing to the intense patriotic unity that it maintained had characterized the French nation between 1914 and 1918, the league's message was intended to resonate beyond its ultra-nationalist core membership. It thus sought to appropriate elements of mainstream patriotic culture to its own ends. The Croix de Feu also began to develop the potent mixture of activism, discipline, and growing organizational sophistication which soon allowed it to capitalize upon the troubles that beset the Third Republic. On the eve of *le six février*, a general strategy and range of tactics had been developed which conditioned the movement's activities during and after that event.

THE FAR-RIGHT TRADITION AND
THE INTERWAR CRISIS

The Croix de Feu can be situated within a tradition of authoritarian nationalist movements that had posed an intermittent, yet serious threat to the French Third Republic almost from its inception. Beginning in the 1880s and re-emerging during the Dreyfus Affair at the turn of the twentieth century, again in the mid–1920s, and yet again in the 1930s, right-wing pressure groups – often known as "leagues" – mobilized against internal "enemies" and the failings of the republican system to impose their own exclusionary and hierarchical social vision. Affecting to disdain conventional politics, they were often extreme critics of the parliamentary system, preferring authoritarian government. They promoted an integral nationalism with a xenophobic and often antisemitic cast. They resorted to demagogy and frequently to street violence, though when it suited them, some of these formations also participated in elections. They were most prominent in periods of crisis, often waning once stability returned.

Until the 1880s, much of the French right was characterized by rejection of the revolutionary tradition, commitment to Catholic values and monarchism, and an elitist approach to politics. The Bonapartist tradition, most recently incarnated by Napoleon III, proved influential in its blend of authoritarian leadership with an appeal to the masses through devices such as referenda, though the Bonapartist movement itself was waning by the end of the 1870s.[1] With the emergence of groups such as the Ligue des Patriotes, new trends grew discernible. The Ligue's dominant figure, Paul Déroulède, was notionally committed to the republican system, but his impatience with the parliamentary process and his strident patriotism pointed to the emergence of what has been termed "politics in a new key," whereby nationalism became more associated with the political right and the political right became more receptive to mass politics.[2]

The Ligue des Patriotes soon aligned itself with the Boulangist movement, which posed a major challenge to the republican system in the late 1880s. At a time when the Third Republic was beset by economic troubles and scandals, General Georges Boulanger, a former minister of war with a reputation for Germanophobic nationalism, launched a movement of protest against the regime, running in and repeatedly winning by-elections and demanding a revision of the constitution. His followers blended the nationalism, populism, and distaste for the bourgeois parliamentary system evinced by the older "Jacobin" left with strong support from the counter-revolutionary monarchist right. The government of the day responded ruthlessly, initiating legal proceedings against Boulanger's advisers for conspiring against the state and threatening him with arrest; the movement soon collapsed, and Boulanger himself committed suicide. But for a brief time Boulangist candidates had been able to garner hundreds of thousands of votes, indicating that a blend of authoritarian nationalism with populist attacks upon the establishment – but also a willingness to work with conservative elites – could generate impressive support.[3]

Prominent veterans of the Boulangist movement included the novelist Maurice Barrès, whose writings influenced the discourse of right-wing nationalism well into the twentieth century. His evocation of the term "national socialism" reflected how the new generation of nationalists stressed the need for social unity in opposition to the class warfare which, they argued, was promoted by the left. Both Barrès and Paul Déroulède were also active in the antisemitic agitation that surrounded the Dreyfus Affair; Déroulède even attempted a coup against the republic in 1899. New formations such as the Union Nationale, the Ligue Antisémitique Française, and the Ligue de la Patrie Française were also active during this period. While some of these groups cultivated a more respectable image than others, all promoted an intense and exclusionary nationalism. Their propagandists stressed the centrality of Catholicism to French national identity and promoted hatred of Jews, Freemasons, and other groups deemed inimical to "true" French values.[4]

The most influential far-right formation to emerge from the Dreyfus Affair was the Action Française. Whether it should be considered fascist remains a matter of debate, but its enduring significance cannot be gainsaid. Intellectually, it provided an influential critique of the Third Republic, even though it would cause much friction with other nationalist movements. Its leading thinker, Charles Maurras, formulated a doctrine of "integral nationalism" which blended support for a monarchy and the primacy of Catholic values with the demonization of Jews and other outsiders who constituted "the anti-France." After 1908 this noxious world view was promoted to considerable effect by the league's daily newspaper of the same name. Not all elements of the Action Française's doctrine were equally influential; in particular, its commitment to monarchism proved contentious. But its attacks upon supposed republican decadence influenced many young thinkers and activists. The movement's adaptability also helped to keep it in the public eye. Members of its "protection service," the Camelots du Roi, never hesitated to seek out brawls with opponents; yet from 1914 to 1918 the league firmly supported the war effort, and it ran candidates in the elections of 1919.[5] But while the Action Française could cooperate with other right-wing formations, Maurras and his colleagues also fiercely attacked nationalists whom they deemed traitors to the cause, including La Rocque and the Croix de Feu.

The dramatic changes wrought by the First World War led in some respects to an evolution of the far right. The experience of the trenches created a cadre of men radicalized in their nationalist commitment and willingness to resort to violence. Fierce hatred of the political left was fundamental to ultra-nationalist discourse, but the Russian Revolution had given birth to a Communist state and an international revolutionary movement that provided new targets for French authoritarians. Not only could a more concrete "red menace" be added to their political repertoire; they could link Bolshevism to Judaism and further assail the Third Republic for its inability to withstand the revolutionary threat.[6]

These features became especially apparent in the new wave of nationalist agitation that followed the election of the centre-left Cartel des Gauches coalition in 1924, which resulted in the formation of a Radical-led government with Socialist parliamentary support. The first of the new leagues to be formed was Antoine Rédier's Légion, which presented itself as a movement of patriotic war veterans uniquely suited to rejuvenating postwar France. Accusing the Cartel of being a prelude to bloody revolution, Rédier was heavily preoccupied with promoting traditional gender roles and thereby restoring the French family. But his movement was eclipsed by Pierre Taittinger's Jeunesses Patriotes, which, like the Légion, was established in 1924. Compared to the Légion, the Jeunesses Patriotes were more openly committed to paramilitarism, but in their appeal to a veteran mystique and proclaimed goal of uniting the various elements of the right, the two formations were quite similar. However, the Jeunesses Patriotes proved able to construct a broader support base, gaining perhaps 65,000 members by 1926 and absorbing the Légion that same year.[7]

By this time another far-right formation, the Faisceau, had been launched. Its leader, Georges Valois, had initially been drawn to anarchism but had then moved to the far right, joining the Action Française in 1906 and playing a leading role in its Cercle Proudhon initiative, which sought to win support from workers. After the war Valois became convinced that the Action Française was growing sterile, and he launched his own movement in 1925. Compared to the other leagues, the Faisceau was less inhibited in claiming foreign inspiration – notably from Fascist Italy – and emphasized its ability to appeal to leftists. But there were fundamental similarities. Like the Légion and the Jeunesses Patriotes, it emphasized that war veterans should form the basis of a new elite, presiding over a state in which the revolutionary threat had been extirpated and in which labour respected employers. All three formations stressed the benefits of class collaboration within a corporatist framework and called for the preservation of social hierarchies within an authoritarian political system.[8]

By the mid–1920s, then, a far-right tradition was well-established in French political culture. Its autonomy and efficacy, however, was conditioned by a complex relationship with the traditional right. Rédier, Taittinger, and Valois all received financial support from conservative businessmen; Taittinger had been a deputy for the right-wing Fédération Républicaine and preserved his connections with that party while leading the Jeunesses Patriotes. The Légion, the Jeunesses Patriotes, and the Faisceau were also connected by shared membership, joint meetings, and ideological affinities with the largest formation created in response to the Cartel des Gauches, General de Castelnau's Fédération Nationale Catholique, which mobilized traditionalist Catholic opposition to the government on a massive scale, claiming 1.8 million members in 1926.[9] Finally, the fact that after the return of the conservative republican Raymond Poincaré as premier in 1926, the leagues lost some of their potency is indicative of how they thrived when traditional conservatives felt threatened by the left and were tempted to go beyond conventional parliamentary means to combat it. Poincaré's displacement of the Cartel meant that the leagues lacked an immediate menace with which to galvanize support.

The leagues of the 1920s had also been weakened by competition for supporters. The creation of the Faisceau, for example, had led to bitter conflict with both the Action Française and the Jeunesses Patriotes. This was compounded by the fact that Antoine Rédier encouraged former supporters of the now-defunct Légion to join the Faisceau. The response by Taittinger, Maurras, and their supporters was ferocious. Enraged at Valois's defection from and criticisms of the Action Française, as well as the fact that he was attracting some of its most activist supporters, Maurras and his colleagues engaged in verbal and physical attacks upon the Faisceau leader. The Jeunesses Patriotes tried to isolate the Faisceau by cooperating more closely with the Action Française. Cumulatively, these efforts, along with the advent of Poincaré, sent the Faisceau into decline; Valois himself would eventually turn back to the political left. But the relationship between the Action Française and the Jeunesses Patriotes was also characterized by friction.[10] Such infighting – even as the various leaders involved stressed the need for nationalist unity – would persist into the years to come.

As for the Croix de Feu, it was established in November 1927, but Poincaré's return to power meant that the political climate was unpropitious for rapid growth. Moreover, it was not until La Rocque established his authority a few years later that the league truly began to make its mark. As it did so, its debt to other, earlier formations was clear. It emulated their nationalist ideology, their appeal to the mystique of the veteran, their contempt for parliamentary democracy, and their willingness to engage in violence. It also contributed to, and became ensnared in, the fractiousness that so often characterized the French right. But it would enjoy greater success than any of these formations as it rose to prominence during the multifaceted crisis that France experienced in the 1930s. To understand how it was able to do so, the main features of this crisis must be reviewed.

For one, while the leagues of the 1920s had already sought to capitalize upon the mystique of the veteran, the impact of the First World War was so profound that its memory could still be appropriated to great effect into the 1930s. Victory had further legitimized the Third Republic, but it had also enhanced the appeal of the far right in some ways. Maurice Barrès, for example, helped to construct an influential myth of the Battle of Verdun of 1916, which became perhaps the defining moment for the French nation at war. In doing so, he glorified an essentialist view of national identity. Barrès equated the peasant-soldier with the virtues of the French race and emphasized the overriding need for unity – and by implication the enervating impact of pluralism – in the face of the enemy. Marshal Philippe Pétain, though not seen as a partisan figure at the time, echoed these themes in a 1932 speech commemorating those who died at Verdun. In it he expressed dismay that the primacy of loyalty to the nation characteristic of the war years was giving way to internal divisions.[11]

Such appeals to the legacy of the *union sacrée*, which neglected the divisions that had existed between 1914 and 1918, were made by La Rocque and his supporters to great effect. They also promised to confront the anxieties about the status of the family and gender relations which gripped huge numbers of French men and women after 1918. The country's staggering casualties had greatly intensified concern about the low birth rate, leading to growing support for pro-natalist groups. While not all of these movements were of a conservative bent, often connected to the pro-natalist agenda was a backlash against a perceived blurring of gender boundaries which had taken place during and after the war. The growth of the female workforce during those years and the image of the liberated woman that accompanied it encouraged a belief that as far as the roles of men and women were concerned, the world had been turned upside down. Various groups promoted an ideology of familialism that reasserted sharply demarcated gender roles.[12] The Croix de Feu contributed to this trend significantly as it mobilized thousands of women in support of its cause.

The hugely detrimental impact of the war upon France's international status became painfully clear by the 1930s. Over the previous decade the French had seen their position as a key member of the Allied coalition in the First World War erode; failing to attain security guarantees from Britain and the United States, they had been compelled to abandon their hardline stance towards Germany. During the second half of the 1920s the Third Republic adopted a more conciliatory approach in dealing with Germany, as exemplified by the Locarno Agreements. But the situation soon deteriorated. Serious differences between the two nations persisted, and the onset of the Great Depression in Germany, accompanied by a nationalist backlash upon which the Nazis capitalized, greatly compounded them. Within months of Hitler's coming to power, Germany had withdrawn from disarmament talks. The French felt dangerously isolated; many leaders of the nationalist right, including La Rocque, evinced a mounting bitterness rooted in the belief that France had won the war but lost the peace, and that the sacrifices of the soldiers had been betrayed.[13]

To ordinary French citizens an even more painful manifestation of the crisis of the 1930s was economic. The dislocation and severe inflation of the immediate postwar years subsided in the second half of the 1920s, and following the onset of the Great Depression, the French initially believed that they might weather it better than most countries. In some respects they did; unemployment never reached the same level that it did in the United States or Germany, for example. But while the Depression came to France rather later than it did elsewhere, its impact was debilitating. The Third Republic had endured since 1871 because it had integrated the masses into democratic politics and met the needs of a range of social classes – in particular, urban and rural small property owners and producers. These groups were now seriously affected by the downturn.[14] Some sectors of the economy, notably agriculture, had been in poor shape since the 1920s, with prices declining sharply. By the 1930s the crisis included urban groups such as shopkeepers, who found they did not have the resources to cope with declining revenues and competition from large department stores. The industrial working class faced wage cuts and job losses as a result of attempts at mechanization. In sum, with both the lower middle and the working classes feeling threatened, conditions were ripe for maximum social polarization.[15]

At the same time France's political class was increasingly discredited. After Poincaré's final retirement, the leading figure on the political scene was André Tardieu, a conservative who served as prime minister three times between 1929 and 1932. Believing that the French right had to overcoming its heritage of fragmentation, Tardieu sought to unite it and thereby realign the political system, but he succeeded only in encouraging divisions. His desire to expand executive power and outlaw the Communist party led to accusations that he was subverting the regime. In 1932 a centre-left coalition dominated by France's Radical and Socialist parties won the national elections but was unable to deal with growing economic difficulties. The Radicals, in the centre of the political spectrum, were willing to campaign with left-wing support but believed that balancing the budget was necessary in order to restore confidence, while their Socialist partners argued doing so would only aggravate economic misery. These differences led to paralysis, with six short-lived ministries falling between June 1932 and February 1934.[16]

Disaffection grew, manifesting itself in a variety of ways. Intellectual disenchantment with the republican system intensified; long-standing opponents of democracy such as Charles Maurras were joined by a new generation of thinkers who did not share his monarchism but were unsparing in their attacks on the regime.[17] Figures such as Robert Aron and Arnaud Dandieu of the journal *Ordre nouveau*, Emmanuel Mounier of *Esprit*, and Jean-Pierre Maxence of the Jeune Droite group developed a profound critique of the liberal democratic state and modern French society. While aspects of their programs differed, there were key points of convergence, especially when it came to the rejection of current social mores. Deeming them to be corrupt and materialistic, these "nonconformists" called for radical change. Though not in agreement as to what precisely this would entail, most of them contended that it would stress "the primacy of the spiritual" and promote the ideas of personalism, which emphasized the value of the socially situated individual in opposition to a mechanistic, bourgeois modernity.[18] Despite the limited circulation of the journals for which many of these thinkers wrote, the concepts they developed echoed in various political programs during the 1930s.

Citizens also expressed anger in the streets. Various groups ranging from taxpayers' to veterans' associations held belligerent demonstrations.[19] The Action Française and the Jeunesses Patriotes resumed a more activist stance, and new far-right movements entered the fray. The Francistes, created in 1933, mimicked the Italian Fascists with blue shirts and salutes but attracted little support. The Solidarité Française, launched the same year, was more successful, claiming 180,000 members by the time of the February 1934 riots. These figures were greatly exaggerated, however, and the movement soon declined as the perfume and press magnate François Coty, who provided most of its funding, lost much of his fortune. Rather more effective was Henry Dorgères, who emerged as a fiery tribune for disgruntled farmers. His Comités de Defense Paysanne – often known as the Greenshirts – would eventually attract thousands at rallies, where Dorgères proclaimed he was willing to "step outside legality" and create a new regime.[20]

All these organizations, however, were ultimately eclipsed by the Croix de Feu. Luck and contingency were factors here, but it also seems this movement best articulated sentiments and adopted postures that could appeal to a wider range of public opinion during the 1930s. Though beginning as a small group of veterans, under La Rocque's leadership it soon extended its reach. It did so by expressing views prevalent at the time but within the context of its own distinct message. It also combined demands for deep-rooted change with promises to preserve order, and it nurtured high-level contacts while cultivating an image of independence from the "establishment."

LA ROCQUE AND THE ORIENTATION OF
THE CROIX DE FEU

As we have seen, the Croix de Feu formed at an inauspicious time, just when the political crisis that had spurred the latest ultra-nationalist frenzy was subsiding. Nor did its founder, Maurice d'Hartoy (originally Hanot), appear to be particularly effective. A quixotic figure, he was preoccupied with matters such as the symbolism of the movement; it was he who chose its infamous death's head emblem. While he intended the Croix de Feu to be a patriotic pressure group, he was elusive about its specific goals and soon found himself at odds with the movement's patron, the ever-active François Coty, who provided it with subsidies as well as a headquarters. D'Hartoy was also engaged in a rivalry with another of Coty's associates, Marcel Bucard, founder of the Francistes. Matters came to a head as a result of d'Hartoy's affair with Coty's secretary, and he was temporarily "banished" from the latter's enterprises. He was succeeded as Croix de Feu president by Maurice Genay, a former member of Taittinger's Jeunesses Patriotes.[21]

It was during Genay's tenure that the first Croix de Feu manifesto appeared. Published in the inaugural issue of its new monthly, *Le Flambeau*, in November 1929, the manifesto described the association as an elite group of veterans, 10,000 strong. Motivated by the *esprit Croix de Feu*, a solidarity forged in the trenches during the First World War, the association's members demanded the setting aside of class and political differences to serve the national interest. They sought to promote French greatness and act as "a great anti-revolutionary and anti-defeatist force of the most incomparable moral value." In contrast to the anti-militaristic outlook of some veterans' organizations of the time, the Croix de Feu endorsed military discipline and hierarchy, seeing them as sources of national regeneration.[22]

The movement also professed an interest in the material needs of veterans. *Le Flambeau* discussed pension laws, and the association developed a retirement fund. At the core of its program, however, was a combative political vision informed by a nostalgia for the trenches and Georges Clemenceau's wartime government.[23] Early issues of the paper also expressed deep concern over France's international position. There was dismay at American insistence on the repayment of French war debts and anxiety over concessions being made to Germany. *Le Flambeau* also linked foreign problems with domestic enemies, especially pacifists and Communists. The former, it argued, had nearly brought France to defeat in 1917. The latter were a virus to be eradicated; special tribunals should be created for them, as had been done in Mussolini's Italy. The job of the Croix de Feu was to encourage this process of ridding France of Communism through appealing to the authorities, since the movement claimed it would not oppose the forces of order. That said, its attitude towards professional politicians was extremely negative. Even though the 1928 elections had supposedly brought an anti-revolutionary majority into the Chamber of Deputies, for *Le Flambeau* too little had been done to deal with the Communist threat. The paper expressed intense frustration at the divisions in parliament, noting that, in contrast, the Croix de Feu only cared about France.[24]

The problem was that a stable leadership was still lacking. As an active officer on extended leave, Genay could only be a short-term president. But François de La Rocque soon settled this issue once and for all, imbuing the movement with his own world view as he consolidated his leadership. It has been argued that as he did so, the new leader took a group with proto-fascist inclinations and steered it towards more moderate goals.[25] The evidence suggests a more complex series of developments.

La Rocque's background and outlook points to the influence of the military and the church, both of which had tenuous relations with the Republic during his formative years. His father, General Jean-Pierre-Raymond de La Rocque, was a naval artillery officer who became embittered with republican politicians as a result of dealings with them late in his career, and after retiring in 1899, he was actively involved in an association known as Justice-Égalité. This group, initially associated with the Assumptionist newspaper *La Croix,* sought to mobilize nationalist Catholic voters against what was seen as an aggressively laic regime. While François de La Rocque's own political career would be less visibily linked to specifically Catholic interests and he gave little indication that his father was a major influence, in their belief in the centrality of spiritual matters and the need for political engagement, there were clear parallels between the two men.[26]

After graduation from Saint-Cyr as a cavalry officer, La Rocque *fils* soon left France to serve in North Africa. Here he showed intense piety, participating in a retreat in the company of the ascetic soldier-turned-missionary Charles de Foucauld and reading Catholic thinkers such as Frédéric Le Play and René de La Tour du Pin.[27] By the eve of the First World War La Rocque was convinced that disinterested elites pursuing harmony provided the key to France's future. In a 1912 article written for *La Revue hebdomadaire* he stressed the need for the military profession to embrace "the cult of duty." Evident here was La Rocque's conviction that competent elites could make the people see that the things which divided them amounted to little in comparison to the imperative of serving France.[28] Conversely, the compromises and divisions characteristic of Third Republic politics repulsed him. In the same article he asserted that "government by the people, whereby each citizen intercedes on their own part, with no responsibility, in the management of affairs, has always seemed very dangerous to me." While some contend that his attitude later mellowed, there is reason to think otherwise.[29]

In 1913 La Rocque began service in Morocco under the command of Marshal Louis-Hubert Lyautey, inaugurating a period of considerable achievement but also frustrated ambition. While he subsequently emphasized how Lyautey's outlook had a profound influence on his own, La Rocque conceded that at the time he had little direct contact with his superior.[30] Moreover, he angered Lyautey in 1916 when, convalescing after sustaining leg wounds that would plague him in subsequent years, he applied for transfer to the Western Front. La Rocque fought bravely there, winning six citations; he also saw plenty of action after 1918, serving as part of Marshal Foch's mission to Poland (1921–23) and then in Morocco during the Rif war (1925–26). But following his 1916 transfer, he had never secured a consistent patron, and he grew frustrated, believing that his career was not advancing fast enough. With the onset of demobilization, the postwar years were a difficult time for the officer corps. It was shrinking in size, and pay was inadequate. With health problems – recurring bouts of malaria were another legacy of North Africa – and a family to care for and saddened by the death of his father at the end of 1926, which was soon followed by that of his eldest son, Hugues, La Rocque decided to retire.

He subsequently made efforts to move into civilian life but remained interested in military affairs. He took a job with the Compagnie Générale d'Electricité but also wrote articles on defence issues for *Le Temps*, *La Revue hebdomadaire*, and *La Revue des vivants*. La Rocque was also active in several associations devoted to national security. The first of these was Servir, which was aimed at galvanizing elite opinion in favour of a stronger national defence. Another was the Ligue de la Défense Aérienne, which was devoted to raising public awareness about the need to develop France's anti-air defences; La Rocque became president of this group and remained so until the end of 1933.[31]

But the future Croix de Feu leader had also developed broader interests. By this time he was increasingly convinced that France required civic and moral renewal in the face of a corrupt parliamentary system. While retaining his belief in the central importance of elites, La Rocque also felt that such renewal would have to take place through popular mobilization; in this regard he saw the work of contemporary Catholic Action organizations as an inspiration. Since the late 1920s, groups such as the Jeunesse Ouvrière Chrétienne, Jeunesse Agricole Chrétienne, and Jeunesse Étudiante Chrétienne had tried to reach out to various social milieu so as to revitalize the faith on the basis of lay militancy.[32] La Rocque, it seems, hoped to achieve a comparable goal in the service of French nationalism by bringing together different generations and social classes. Writing to the secretary general of French Catholic Action, Canon Stanislas Courbe, in 1930, he proposed creating a Groupement de Défense Sociale et Civique. His goal, he declared, was to promote a renewal of belief in a common goal for the people, "which finds itself more and more obscured, in parliament as well as public opinion, by the game of intrigues played by parties and clubs." To counteract the latter, the Groupement would bring veterans and youth together to effect a revival of patriotic spirit; La Rocque sought Courbe's support and hoped to attract young Catholic Action leaders to his cause. At the same time he renewed his relationship with Marshal Lyautey, seeking the latter's support for the Groupement as well.[33] As it turned out, the Groupement proved to be ephemeral, but the vision of an enlightened leader mobilizing civil society in the cause of anti-parliamentarism and nationalism would guide La Rocque as leader of the Croix de Feu and later the PSF.

La Rocque's rise to the leadership of the Croix de Feu, which he had joined in the spring of 1929, was rapid. He became its vice-president in June 1930, a little over a year after he joined, and then president in August 1931 after Genay returned to the army. The precise dynamics of his ascent are still disputed. La Rocque himself later claimed that he practically took over the running of the organization as early as the spring of 1930, largely at a beleaguered Genay's request. Conversely, Paul Chopine, an important figure in the movement's early years who later quit and wrote a hostile account of the organization, depicts La Rocque as an unscrupulous power-monger who marginalized Genay.[34] Whatever the case, La Rocque's ambition was evident, and it seems that he was viewed by senior military officers as a potential leader before he joined: he came recommended, for instance, by Marshals Foch and Fayolle.[35]

Nor did it take him long to make his mark. While his initial contributions to *Le Flambeau* were on military issues, they soon ranged more widely. In April 1930 La Rocque argued that parliamentary decadence meant that the problems of Germany, Communism, and pacifism were not being addressed. It was up to the Croix de Feu to make the deputies hear the voice of patriotism. Indeed, if they were "to lose interest in this vital task, [the Croix de Feu] will take responsibility for it." By contrast, during this period Genay's articles in *Le Flambeau* tended to focus on pragmatic matters such as the impact of the Depression on veterans; when he did tackle broader issues, there were few signs of differences with La Rocque. Indeed, Genay identified the vice-president as "the active spirit of our association."[36] Even before becoming president, then, La Rocque had injected vitality into the movement.

Once he took over as president, there was a complete break with Coty, and the Croix de Feu's doctrine was elaborated upon, though it remained vacuous on key points. A "program of action" drawn up in the fall of 1931 demanded that the political system, with its unstable ministries and overly powerful Chamber of Deputies, be subjected to a "reclassification." This would include making the president responsible for choosing governments and establishing a system of representation for the different sectors of the economy. Social progress was needed, not through raising wages or a higher level of state intervention, but rather through an "energetic struggle" against the fomenters of disorder and the development of effective collaboration between labour and capital. Economic problems would be dealt with through the control of speculation and foreign interference, the protection of agriculture, the expansion of private enterprise, and the development of overseas territories. Colonial policy had to consider the needs of indigenous peoples but also had to counteract agitation directed by the Third International in Moscow. In foreign policy La Rocque acknowledged the League of Nations but stressed that the threats of Bolshevism and pacifism remained; an emphasis on national security was thus essential. How all these changes were to be enacted was not specified. It appeared as though propaganda and pressure on parliamentarians, despised though many of them were, would be the main route. But whatever its approach, La Rocque left no doubt that the Croix de Feu would be an integral part of a national revival. As its members had saved France in war, so they would now stop the politicians from losing the peace.[37]

La Rocque also sought to raise the Croix de Feu's public profile; indeed, he regarded this goal as far more important than articulating a detailed program. To that end he intensified the league's attacks upon politicians who were associated with conciliatory policies towards Germany, notably Foreign Minister Aristide Briand. He also set up the Comité Permanent de Vigilance et d'Action des Anciens Combattants to campaign against any diplomatic "capitulation." This coalition soon fizzled, but the Croix de Feu made clear its foreign policy preferences in other ways.[38] In November 1931, for example, five hundred of its members were instructed by La Rocque to welcome Prime Minister Pierre Laval upon his return from the United States, where he had secured a one-year moratorium on the payment of French debts. The league also mobilized against pacifists. In late 1931, for instance, 1,500 of its members disrupted a meeting of the Congrès International du Désarmement, chaired by Édouard Herriot, with La Rocque seizing centre stage and attempting to deliver a brief speech while his men scuffled with security before withdrawing. Denunciations of conscientious

objectors and disruptions of their activities by the Croix de Feu continued into 1932.[39]

Demonstrations of physical prowess were thus central to the league's
activities, and La Rocque made ominous statements about having to
intervene forcibly in the event of a national crisis. But he alternated
such rhetoric with invocations to his supporters to avoid being provoked. Thus in March 1931 the Croix de Feu participated in protests
against the showing of a play on the Dreyfus Affair but avoided clashes
with the left; by contrast, demonstrations by the Action Française held
the preceding month had involved violence. In sum, while shows of
force were essential to the Croix de Feu, La Rocque also sought to present it as a disciplined bulwark against disorder that would not get out
of hand. At an April 1932 meeting he introduced the Croix de Feu's
new "Sections Forces," which soon became known as the *dipsos*. Their
objective, he concluded, was to enable the league to "mobilize troops,
to make meetings sizable, in short, as Lyautey says, to show our force
in order to avoid having to use it."[40]

By this time La Rocque was making regular reference to Marshal
Lyautey's influence upon the movement. While this was partly an
attempt to benefit from the latter's immense prestige, La Rocque was
not simply talking for effect. Lyautey's vision of patriotic renewal and
paternalist social harmony, first outlined in his seminal 1891 article
"The Social Role of the Officer," clearly had an impact on the Croix de
Feu leader. In that article Lyautey had stressed that officers should consider command a "social duty" and argued that the army could unite a
nation badly divided by political differences. La Rocque was no longer
a regular officer, but his belief that competent and selfless elites could
resolve social conflict paralleled Lyautey's convictions. In an article
published in *Le Flambeau* shortly after Lyautey's death in 1934, La
Rocque claimed him not only as a personal mentor but as an inspiration
for the Croix de Feu itself. Praising his former commander's quest to
achieve unity in France, he noted how "all his intellectual and spiritual
power shone in [his] will, unflaggingly set towards the coordination of
the diverse and complementary energies of which the national organism
is made."[41] La Rocque also emphasized Lyautey's commitment to social
harmony and to the inculcation of patriotic morality in France's youth,
making it clear the Croix de Feu would emulate these qualities.

La Rocque was not alone in his invocation of Lyautey as a mentor.
The marshal's ideas enjoyed renewed influence among French officers
during the 1930s, for they believed that his vision would help to counter-

act a perceived decline in patriotism. Other professions also found Lyautey's ideas compelling. Georges Lamirand, a future state secretary for youth under the Vichy regime, published the influential work *Le Rôle social de l'ingénieur*, with a preface by Lyautey, in 1932. In it he argued that engineers and cadres should promote social peace between workers and management. Ernest Mercier and Raoul Dautry, prominent advocates of technocracy, also claimed Lyautey as a mentor. So did Robert Garric, the Social Catholic founder of the Équipes Sociales, who became the director of Secours National, a national charitable aid organization, during the Second World War. A friend of La Rocque's, Garric saw Lyautey as the inspiration behind his efforts to encourage harmony between "the people" and the bourgeoisie.[42]

But while La Rocque's participation in what historian Daniel Lindenberg terms the "Lyautey moment" of the 1930s illustrates how the Croix de Feu's doctrine was connected to the broader intellectual currents of the era, the distinctiveness of the movement's approach must also be appreciated. Like conservative Social Catholics and technocrats, La Rocque had a firm belief in the need for strong leadership characterized by enlightened paternalism. Akin to his former colleagues in the officer corps, he held that the French people, and especially the country's youth, needed to have their faith in France restored. But La Rocque would not be satisfied with simply trying to influence its elite. Through building a mass movement that combined the desire for social peace with integral nationalism, he intended to suffuse civil society with a yearning for national revival that would ultimately sweep away divisive class conflict and political differences.

In order to encourage broad-based support, La Rocque and his colleagues worked to associate the Croix de Feu with the victors of 1914–18 both symbolically and literally. *Le Flambeau* highlighted the league's role in commemorative ceremonies for heros such as Marshal Joffre. In keeping with its glorification of the war experience, the Croix de Feu also emphasized its connections with the Clemenceau family, noting that Madame Jacquemaire-Clemenceau, the former prime minister's daughter, had served as a nurse at Verdun and was a supporter of the movement, as was his grandson René, a veteran of that battle. *Le Flambeau* juxtaposed the family's achievements with the degeneration of the political system, all the while stressing its association with the Clemenceaus: "We the Croix de Feu ... salute with emotion and infinite respect this family whose name, deliberately stifled by base politicking, lives on more and more in the memories of true veterans and true Frenchmen."[43]

As this passage suggests, while seeking the endorsement of influential figures, the Croix de Feu also presented itself as being fiercely independent of narrow political interests. In reality, links of various sorts existed. Members – vice-presidents, in fact – of the conservative Fédération Républicaine such as Xavier Vallat and Jean Ybarnégaray joined the league, though the Croix de Feu maintained a greater public distance from the Fédération in comparison to rivals such as the Jeunesses Patriotes. In 1931, for instance, La Rocque rejected an invitation from the Fédération's leader, Louis Marin, to hold a joint meeting.[44]

The relationship between La Rocque and André Tardieu is particularly revealing of the way in which the league sought to ingratiate itself with members of the establishment while publicly disdaining them. In 1937 the former prime minister claimed he had given the Croix de Feu government funds during his time in office. His assertions rested upon a collection of over thirty letters from La Rocque, his secretary Antoinette de Préval, and his daughter Nadine written between 1930 and 1933. In the letters La Rocque offered Tardieu support in the form of demonstrations against the left at opportune moments. Indeed, it seems that he was so anxious to ingratiate himself that on one occasion a letter written by de Préval told Tardieu that "you are 'the best,' not only in France but certainly in all nations of the world. The League of Nations knows this; it fears and admires you." Even after Tardieu left office, La Rocque requested that the former prime minister arrange an introduction for him to Pierre-Étienne Flandin, leader of the centre-right Alliance Démocratique.[45]

Some scholars are skeptical about the letters as proof that money changed hands. The letter that later caused the most acute embarrassment to La Rocque, in which he stated, "I will telephone your home around 9 am tomorrow to receive your orders," was written after Tardieu had left office. There is also no mention of money in the letters, though perhaps this omission is to be expected. Finally, the fact that Tardieu made the allegations as a politically motivated attack upon La Rocque encouraged skepticism about his claims.[46] But in any case it is revealing to note the discrepancy between La Rocque's private enthusiasm for a professional politician and the more ambiguous coverage that Tardieu sometimes received in *Le Flambeau*. Here he was praised for dealing with the Communists firmly, but the paper also intimated that the league's support for Tardieu was by no means unconditional.[47]

Evidently, a pattern was established wherein La Rocque and his colleagues would publicly scorn politicians as a group while at the same time recognizing the utility of some of them. This tension between a supposedly principled anti-parliamentarism and a desire for political influence is also evident in the movement's approach to the 1932 national elections. At the outset of the campaign La Rocque described the event as being of "an exceptional importance" and stressed the importance of choosing a candidate who would support Croix de Feu principles. While aware of the movement's limited size, he insisted it could play a crucial role, noting that it would now have the opportunity to influence a deputy from the day of his election.[48]

To do so, the Croix de Feu sent out a letter outlining its views to various candidates. Of those who responded some, such as Georges Bonnefous of the Fédération Républicaine, were positive; others, such as Frederic Pic, expressed reservations about the league's demand that the executive be reinforced. Lists of candidates who were Croix de Feu members, sympathizers, and non-sympathizers were also drawn up. One list of recommended candidates included twenty-seven members and twenty-three sympathizers, most of them from Paris. Among the members were Jean Goy of the Union Nationale des Combattants (UNC), France's leading nationalist veterans' association, as well as Ybarnégaray and Vallat of the Fédération. Sympathizers included Tardieu and Henri de Kerillis; conversely, both Louis Marin and François de Wendel, leading members of the Fédération, were identified as non-sympathizers. Successful candidates received follow-up letters and a subscription to *Le Flambeau*.[49]

The elections of 1932 proved to be a disappointment, with the victory of the centre-left coalition of Radicals and Socialists causing much bitterness. But the Croix de Feu remained convinced that it could shape politics and that it needed to keep organizing. In his post-mortem editorial in *Le Flambeau* La Rocque proclaimed, "It is time once and for all to put paid to the idiotic legend that veterans are inept in 'public affairs.' What! Because we gave our blood, risked our lives for four years of misery, they would dare condemn us to silence! ... We will use all means available to us. We will criticize, we will keep a close watch, we will intervene ... and will extend our grip by creating sections outside the cities, in the countryside."[50]

CONSOLIDATION AND EXPANSION

Over the course of 1932 La Rocque faced internal challenges but ultimately strengthened his control over the movement, all the while working on broadening its support base. At the general assembly held in February of that year, his presidency was confirmed despite some rumblings of dissent; d'Hartoy actually showed up at the meeting to hand out tracts criticizing the new leader. Six months later La Rocque aroused the ire of some members when he accepted a government proposal to slash veterans' benefits in tandem with other deflationary measures being adopted. He responded by submitting his resignation to an internally divided executive committee, which refused to accept it. He quickly resumed his duties in triumph, but it was not the last time his leadership would be challenged.[51] Structural changes soon followed. The Croix de Feu had initially possessed a president and a vice-president as well as an administrative council, but La Rocque abolished the post of vice-president and established a directing committee, a smaller decision-making body whose members would be readily available.

In addition to this centralization of power, individuals loyal to La Rocque became more prominent. Joseph Pozzo di Borgo, a wealthy aristocrat who was regarded as energetic though not politically astute, held several positions in the organization and was even designated La Rocque's successor. He also provided financial support at several crucial junctures. Paul Chopine was nominated chief propagandist for the movement in 1931; he and his assistant, Charles Varin, also headed up the *dispos.* Eventually, first Chopine and then Pozzo abandoned the movement and turned on their former *patron.* But others who were rising within the organization at this time supported La Rocque throughout the 1930s and during the Second World War. Georges Riché served faithfully as treasurer. Noël Ottavi, who joined the movement in 1931, was nominated to the directing committee in 1933 and remained a leading figure in both the Croix de Feu and the PSF until his death in 1945.[52] Antoinette de Préval was another important adviser, acting as La Rocque's counsellor on social issues. Both she and Ottavi preferred to work behind the scenes, and so their precise influence is difficult to gauge. Embittered former militants depicted Ottavi as a shadowy, malevolent figure who engaged in endless backroom manoeuvring and was responsible for La Rocque's increasingly dictatorial leadership. As for de Préval, assessments varied; Chopine suggested that she was responsible for La Rocque's more noble sentiments, while others denounced her as his "evil genius." No one disputed her influence, though; it was claimed by some former militants that she revised La Rocque's articles for *Le Flambeau,* and that she had practically written his 1934 book

Service public.[53] While these reminiscences seem polemical, La Rocque himself acknowledged the importance of these individuals.

The leader of the Croix de Feu was looking for quantity as well as quality. Maurice Genay had boasted at the beginning of 1930 that success would be achieved by "narrow phalanges" rather than big formations.[54] Given that the membership was not even 9,000 at the time, he was making a virtue of a necessity. But La Rocque gradually abandoned arguments of this sort as he worked to develop a mass base. This was achieved partly through the creation of new ancillary groups. At first the movement was open only to decorated veterans, but in 1929 the Briscards were created, allowing those who had simply served on the front line for at least six months to join. In 1932, in a move indicative of the growing attention the league paid to youth, the Fils et Filles des Croix de Feu (FFCF) was established under Pozzo's leadership. In 1933 came the creation of the Comité pour le Regroupement National autour des Croix de Feu, with looser criteria for adult membership – essentially a subscription to *Le Flambeau*.

Some of the old guard criticized La Rocque for diluting the veteran core of the league with such initiatives. Undeterred, he confirmed his chosen direction in October 1933 with the formation of the Volontaires Nationaux (VN), which was composed of the older members of the Fils and those, usually younger, male members of the Regroupement who had not fought in the war.[55] Plans were also underway to organize members on a socio-economic basis. The Croix de Feu had always invoked the principle of mutual aid, but in September 1933 La Rocque went further by requesting a list of all members involved in unions or corporative organizations.[56] By this time the recruiting efforts had begun to bear fruit, as table 1 shows.

Different sources provide conflicting estimates at some points, but the balance of evidence points towards steady growth into the fall of 1933 and then a takeoff following the riots of 6 February 1934. The figure of 35,000 suggested for February 1934 is almost certainly too low. It contradicts other evidence and suggests stagnation at a time when both the Depression was taking hold and political deadlock was becoming ever more visible, trends that tended to encourage Croix de Feu recruitment. Conversely, the figure given by the Bonnevay Commission, formed to investigate the 6 February riots, as well as La Rocque's own claim, are probably too high. To accept them would be to posit explosive growth for the Croix de Feu before the riots; what is more, it would imply that the growth experienced by the movement

Table 1
Croix de Feu membership, 1930–34

Date	Number
January 1930	8,922
January 1931	16,240
March 1931	18,000
January 1932	22,644
January/February 1933	28,903
July 1933	49,000
December 1933/January 1934	58,000–62,000 (Chopine, Coston)
February 1934	35,000 (Weng)
February/March 1934	100,000+ (Howlett)
	125,000 (Bonnevay Commission)
	140,000 (La Rocque)

SOURCES: Le Flambeau; Weng, "L'Historique et la doctrine"; Howlett, "Croix de Feu"; Nobécourt, *Colonel de La Rocque.*

during 1934 was relatively slow, which contradicts the overwhelming majority of evidence for that period. The figures given by Henry Coston, an extreme right-wing publicist, and Paul Chopine seem more credible. Both suggest that the Croix de Feu had under 100,000 supporters on the eve of the riots. Though they are clearly partisan sources, their figures are more in keeping with the steady pace of growth that had previously been established and allow for the unquestionable surge in membership after the riots.[57]

Before 6 February 1934 the Croix de Feu's geographic base had also broadened. Initially its membership had been so concentrated in Paris – 61 per cent in 1928–29 – that expansion elsewhere was seen as particularly urgent.[58] Efforts to redress this imbalance soon paid off. By October 1932 the league already had local organizations, known as sections, in forty-four metropolitan departments as well as in Algeria, Morocco, Syria, and Cochin-China. Twenty-eight of the sections were located in the north, northeast, and northwest, areas with a tradition of conservative politics, but sections had also been formed in predominantly left-wing departments.[59] With respect to growth in the major cities, Paris remained at the heart of the movement, but it had established a presence in Marseilles, Bordeaux, Lyons, and Rouen. The Algerian sections were also quite large; there were some 7,000 members in Algiers, Constantine, and Oran by the end of 1933.[60]

The early members of the Croix de Feu were a fairly homogenous group, though upon examination one can see the potential for a broader appeal. In terms of social class, a 1929 sample of approximately 3,000

individuals consisted mainly of mid-rank commercial and financial officials, industrialists, professionals, and proprietors. Those described as
"manual professions" constituted only 6.9 per cent of the total.[61] The
early cadres of the league were thus members of France's *classes
moyennes* or of higher social standing. Some were self-made men, such
as Joseph Levet, who founded the Rouen section in September 1931. He
went on to become the Croix de Feu's regional delegate for all of Normandy and would occupy a similar post in the PSF; eventually he also
assumed control over the party's five Parisian federations. Born in 1896,
the son of a Marseilles tram-worker, Levet had studied privately to qual-
ify as an English interpreter and had worked for an insurance broker in
Le Havre before being called up in 1914. He lost a brother in the war
and was himself wounded three times, ending the conflict as a corporal.
He then returned to the insurance business.[62] Jacques Arnoult, who
founded the Marseilles Croix de Feu in 1930, became the regional magnate for Provence and later performed the same role for the PSF. He was
an industrialist with a factory in Marseilles and an estate in its environs.
Armand Causaert, who became president of the Lille Croix de Feu in
1931 and then president of the Nord organization, later assumed
responsibility for the Pas-de-Calais and the Somme as well. He came
from a family of Catholic industrialists and had fought with distinction
in 1914–18, receiving nine decorations.[63]

One can readily envision such men being attracted to a group such as
the Croix de Feu. Beyond their status as members of social classes that
perceived themselves as threatened during the interwar years, army
connections and recollections of solidarity provided the most compelling reasons for joining. Jean Malicet, the president of the Nancy section, exemplified this impulse in a letter of May 1930 to La Rocque in
which he expressed his joy at meeting the then vice-president of the
association, "one of my commanders from our dear Army of Africa,
truly the only army where leaders and common soldiers knew how to
speak the same language and where all hearts beat so well in unison."
Sometimes, as in Algiers and Tours, retired military officers actually
served as section presidents; in other instances, such as Corsica, they
held the title in an honorary capacity.[64]

Judging from such militaristic trappings and the presence of individuals such as Xavier Vallat at its gatherings, it would seem axiomatic
that the Croix de Feu's members were politically on the far right; in
fact, as early as 1930 there were prospective joiners who would have
liked to see it adopt a more radical posture. Revealingly, some members

of the Action Française saw no contradiction between joining the Croix de Feu and continuing their own anti-republican activism.[65] Yet the Croix de Feu constantly emphasized that it was open to all patriots, and it appears some individuals took this claim seriously. In Béziers and Sète the police noted the presence of some Action Française members but believed the local Croix de Feu leaders to be, for the most part, level-headed moderates devoted to the Republic who had joined because of veteran camaraderie. In the department of Constantine in Algeria the local section debated the extent to which it should actually get involved in politics. In the city of Montpellier prominent Croix de Feu members described themselves as loyal to the regime, though they quickly added that they were determined to reform the parliamentary system. Here the authorities concluded that while the league had right-wing origins, growing public discontent "has rallied to [its] doctrine people of diverse views."[66]

It had done so because the character of the Croix de Feu's associational life and rhetoric meant that its doctrine could appeal to a spectrum of opinion, though it was never as broad as the movement's propagandists implied. La Rocque and his colleagues tirelessly evoked the spirit of wartime unity, proclaiming that they were the embodiment of it. One contributor to *Le Flambeau* elaborated upon this point by arguing that instead of the "politics of parties," the Croix de Feu practised "national politics." This purportedly involved setting aside political and religious divisions, such as when the anti-clerical Clemenceau had called upon the Catholic Marshal Foch to lead France's armies. By encouraging such disinterested attitudes rather than fractious games, the Croix de Feu represented the "red talons of this new aristocracy created by the veterans, [with] letters of nobility which they awarded themselves and which will be confirmed by history!"[67]

Such themes were reiterated at various Croix de Feu parades, conducted on occasions such as the commemoration of the armistice of 11 November, the feast of Joan of Arc, and the anniversary of the Battle of the Marne. At such events the Croix de Feu sought to assert its potency as a unifying force, the singularity of its patriotism, and the need for vigilance against France's enemies. Speaking to eight thousand Croix de Feu members and Briscards parading on 11 November 1932, La Rocque declared that they would serve as a "foundation for the reconciliation of the French, three-quarters of whom think the same way, though too often they express themselves differently." France needed a new mystique, that of the Unknown Soldier, and the Croix de Feu would lead the way in promoting it, transmitting the values of "the aristocracy of service imbued with spilled blood" to the nation's youth.[68] To be sure, the Croix de Feu's rhetoric was also divisive and negative in many ways; the league was unsparing in its criticisms of the republican political class and the ethos of pre–1914 France. But for those who yearned for the triumphalism of 1918, for those who glorified the spirit of the trenches, in short, for those already predisposed to be receptive, it was a powerful message.

Given the nature of the movement, the Croix de Feu's members were overwhelmingly male, but there was a female presence from the league's inception. As one of its local papers pointed out, during the First World War eight hundred French women had died as a result of military action and fifteen hundred had been decorated for bravery. Individual heroines were thus singled out for praise. In June 1930 La Rocque devoted a column to Isabelle Carlier, a teacher at a Moscow *lycée* since 1900 who had volunteered as a nurse during the war only to be imprisoned because of her protests against the Bolsheviks. Noting that Carlier had tended to the sick in her prison before being repatriated in 1922, he reprinted a letter in which she invoked Joan of Arc as the paragon of French values, concluding that Carlier herself was a modern maid of Orléans. Two and a half years later *Le Flambeau* proudly displayed a photograph of Octavie Delacour on its front page. Delacour, then living on a small pension, had helped to prevent the disruption of France's mobilization in 1914 by alerting the army to a German patrol. In the July 1933 issue it was reported how Louise Thuliez, "Croix de Feu no.1003," had discussed her experiences of war and captivity with members of the 85th section.[69]

Notwithstanding such acclaim, the role that women were expected to play in the movement conformed to the Croix de Feu's views on their place in society. Female members were to assist in the organization of meetings and banquets and to make items for charity bazaars to help fund the movement's social activities. They also ran the organization's annual summer camps and coordinated many activities for the FFCF, including recruitment. In 1933, for instance, Mademoiselle Mialon was praised for bringing ten new people to the 81st section's youth group in one month. In theory, women could also be propagandists; at a meeting of the Filles des Croix de Feu in Paris, the girls present were told that as far as the movement was concerned, they should aspire to be "a propagandist, auxiliary, and educator." In practice, it was the latter two roles that predominated. Croix de Feu propaganda directed towards women appealed to their fear of what renewed war might mean for their children, their antipathy towards political scandals because of the harm these did to their households, and their "natural" desire to perform civic and social work, especially for those deprived of the joys of motherhood by the First World War.[70]

Predictably, the female symbol most often invoked by the Croix de Feu was Joan of Arc, though she was interpreted by the league in particular ways. La Rocque felt that Croix de Feu women should emulate her through being patriotic, but in a manner that conformed to conventional gender roles. The fact that Joan had led armies receded into the background in *Le Flambeau*; instead, she was celebrated as a symbol of national harmony. The Croix de Feu emphasized that commemorating her provided an occasion for the French to forget their differences. Such an assertion harmonized well with the prevailing mood during the First World War and its immediate aftermath; at that time Joan was a relatively consensual symbol, emblematic of the victory of 1918. By the 1930s, however, this interpretive harmony had faded, as groups ranging from the Action Française to the Communists sought to appropriate her legacy for their own ends. The Croix de Feu held to the image of Joan as a unifying symbol but argued that only it could continue her efforts to unite the French. During the 1935 Joan of Arc ceremonies *Le Flambeau* proudly announced that "Croix de Feu coming from the most diverse political horizons, Croix de Feu and Volontaires Nationaux of all religions, render unto Joan of Arc the dazzling tribute that is due to her."[71] Such language conformed to the league's self-identification as the pre-eminent source of nationalist solidarity and further illustrated how it sought to tap into mainstream patriotism to enhance its own appeal.

ENTERING THE NATIONAL ARENA

The Croix de Feu radicalized as conditions in France worsened over the course of 1933. La Rocque saw the country as threatened by the "end of reparations, the constant progress of vengeful nationalism in Germany, ... the haughty intransigence of the United States, and a treasury out of breath," weakened by "deficiencies in governments, parliamentarism and parties, condemned to impotence for never having renewed themselves since the war." He then juxtaposed this image with a growing Croix de Feu, which he maintained would be the source of national salvation. Its members had been "from the Marne to the Somme, from

Verdun to the Dardanelles and at Montdidier, the knights errant of the nation in danger." They remained France's "highest aristocracy," around whom its people could gather to surmount a looming disaster. As such, the league's members had to be prepared to "weigh into the balance our moral worth and the collective mass of our energy."[72]

In October 1933 the association published a new manifesto, of which half a million copies were distributed.[73] Compared to the one issued in 1931 its tone was more strident. La Rocque declared that France's problems were the result of moral failings, especially on the part of its leaders. The situation could be reversed only by the disinterested patriotism of a selfless elite. "[France] must have a 'head': some bosses. Behind a commanded, spirited, adjusted France the world will rediscover peace and harmony." Such leadership was needed more than ever in the worsening international climate, for "no country will respect a timid, passive, humble, divided France." To ensure order, effective government, and security, the state needed to be radically recast. The manifesto was vague about the specifics of reform but categorical about the need for the Croix de Feu to be central to public life. Free of external influences, the movement would fix attention on France's problems and provide solutions to them.[74]

The manifesto also contained a number of proposals relating to economic and social issues. The government was to stay out of the economy but should fight hard against speculators. "Moral and material hygiene" needed to be developed. As for social conflict, collaboration between capital and labour – which would apparently be achieved with little difficulty – was the solution. The term *la profession organisée* was used to encompass this idea, though it was not defined with precision. The ultimate goal was "the protection of legitimate profit, of savings and of the family." The emphasis on women and youth was accentuated. The latter were reminded of the importance of service to the nation, and it was argued that the state monopoly in education and anti-patriotic propaganda by some teachers had done them a great disservice. As for the women of France, they were promised a role in public life, though they were depicted first and foremost as sources of national regeneration through their influence as mothers and educators. They – and indeed, all French citizens – were promised patriotic bliss in the Croix de Feu: "You will find there happily revived the fraternal union born under fire during four years of war. You will find there the fusion of classes, religions, wealth, and poverty. You will find there the wholesome honesty of disinterestedness and frankness. You will find there the meeting point, the living synthesis, of all interests, individual and collective."

Tied to this image of a united nation, however, was a menacing stance. If the Croix de Feu's efforts to raise public awareness and press for desired reforms did not lead to change, or if needed reforms were resisted by the government, more drastic measures would be required: "Our moral ascendancy, exerting itself from one end of the country to the other, will arouse the regenerative order. If the weakness of the public powers fetters its advent, our vibrant, organized mass will know how to impose it." La Rocque affirmed this challenge in an open letter to Édouard Daladier, who was prime minister at the time, announcing that "with us, order in France will be re-established, or indeed we will re-establish it." He was evasive as to what would happen if the movement decided to act, but he did suggest there would be a transitional period during which authority would be reasserted and subversion would end. A definitive reform of the constitution would follow, thus fulfilling the league's mission.

The Croix de Feu made it clear that its supporters would resort to physical force to advance their goals. On 29 October 1933 a group of them disrupted a meeting of conscientious objectors in Laon. The league claimed that the whole thing was over before the meeting-hall doors were open and that only two Croix de Feu had been slightly injured. La Rocque remarked how this action, along with "numerous" others in the history of the association, showed how a prepared use of force, whether of a "preventative" or a "curative" nature, could with the advantage of surprise overwhelm a numerically superior enemy. But while approving displays of the league's potency, he also warned members not to allow themselves to be provoked. A month after the Laon incident, a notice was published declaring that the movement was not "some kind of blue-horizon militia for hire"; though it would participate in the meetings of other associations, it would need specific information about them beforehand.[75]

In sum, in 1933–34 the republican system was under strain and the Croix de Feu took advantage of this to promote its own agenda. The league's goals at the time, however, tended to be long-term. La Rocque was happy to galvanize his supporters by declaring that the moment of crisis was at hand and to combine some rough-and-tumble actions with other activities. But it appears he believed that the Croix de Feu still had to extend its influence further before it could achieve its objectives on its own terms. Paul Chopine, for instance, claimed that La Rocque was distressed at the rapidity of events leading to the February riots. He had hoped that the league would dictate when an action took place and feared that a successful coup led by a variety of right-wing organizations would result in the Croix de Feu being sidelined. On the other hand, he was under intense pressure from militants to act.[76] Chopine's account was written as an attack upon La Rocque and thus has to be used cautiously. But since he normally emphasizes La Rocque's bellicosity, his claim that the Croix de Feu leader behaved carefully during the run-up to the 6 February riots is noteworthy.

The anti-parliamentary fury that culminated in *le six février* was triggered on 8 January 1934 when it was announced that Alexandre Stavisky, a bon viveur and swindler who was sought by the police for involvement in a scheme selling junk bonds, had committed suicide. Stavisky had friends in the government, including prominent members of the Radical party. The labour ministry had endorsed the bonds, and the finance and commerce ministries had been lax in reviewing the Crédit Bayonne, against which they had been issued. The justice ministry had previously put off hearings for charges of extortion laid against Stavisky nineteen times. The Third Republic had known worse scandals; in the case of Stavisky, only six deputies were implicated. But the outrage on both the left and the right was intense; as one historian puts it, "rarely would *L'Humanité* [the newspaper of the Communists] and *Action Française* step as prettily together as they did during the months of the Stavisky scandal." Rumours spread that the magistrates themselves, anxious not to let further information out, had Stavisky's blood on their hands. The entire republican system was now seen by many citizens as irremediably corrupt.[77]

The nationalist leagues were quick to act. On 9 January Action Française demonstrators took to the streets, their actions were, in the opinion of the police, "of a violence rare in recent years." By the end of the month the royalists enjoyed the support of a number of groups, including some veterans' associations and the Fédération des Contribuables, which lobbied on behalf of taxpayers. In the Chamber of Deputies the rightist deputy Jean Ybarnégaray called for a parliamentary commission of inquiry to look into the scandal. The short-lived government of Camille Chautemps fell and another one was formed – yet again – by Édouard Daladier. This change did not put an end to the tension, however. Among supporters of the right, word spread that some of Daladier's colleagues, most notably Minister of the Interior Eugène Frot, wanted to establish a "dictatorship of the left." La Rocque himself later claimed that Frot tried to co-opt him in this enterprise. While these assertions are disputed, it certainly was the case that supporters of the left disliked Paris's current prefect of police, Jean Chiappe, a friend of the nationalists, who was accused of being as lenient towards rightist demonstrations as he was harsh in dealing with leftist ones. Under pressure to remove Chiappe, Daladier on 3 February appointed him resident-general to Morocco. When news of this move appeared in the press, a number of veterans' groups and leagues, including the UNC, the Jeunesses Patriotes, and the Solidarité Française, announced they would protest it on 6 February.[78]

Various elements of the right saw the scandal as an opportunity to reverse the 1932 electoral victory of the left. But their actions were not well coordinated. There was an effort by the Action Française to co-opt elements of the military, but the various leagues, associations, and individuals involved had their own distinct goals, and contacts between them were only intermittent. Some hard-liners may have hoped that by marching on the Chamber they could overthrow the government, but for others, such as the Fédération des Contribuables, this strategy was further than they wanted to go. For his part, former premier André Tardieu hoped to ride the wave of protest to return to power and effect constitutional reform, involving the creation of a stronger executive.[79]

As for the Croix de Feu, it cast its reaction to the scandal as one of unmitigated outrage. At a meeting held on 10 January in the Salle Wagram, La Rocque declared that the Stavisky affair was the ultimate sign of the decadence of the regime. Twelve days later he sent an open letter to the president of the Republic in which he proclaimed that "a single solution presents itself to you: forget the artificial barriers between the groups who fight over your mandate and attack one another for their common mistakes. Impose the tricolour flag as a rallying sign. Following these principles, hand over our destiny to a small number of resolute personalities, morally beyond reproach, loyal, free from all compromises, strangers to backroom scheming." La Rocque concluded by emphasizing that while the president could be assured of the association's support in such an endeavour, it was up to him whether or not the Croix de Feu's members would limit themselves to defending their homes and families. Fifty thousand copies of the letter in the form of a poster were then distributed to the sections, as were an identical number of broadsheets denouncing parliament as being "infiltrated by bandits."[80]

La Rocque's tone was menacing, but the letter also hints that the Croix de Feu considered some sort of government of national unity – led by "right-minded" individuals – an acceptable solution, at least in the short term. This is not to suggest that the league was disengaged. While initially not involved in as many incidents as the other nationalist associations, some of its members partook in demonstrations on 10 January at the homes of two cabinet ministers as well as at the Ministry of Justice. During these incidents a policeman was injured and a dozen Croix de Feu members were briefly arrested. But La Rocque's public statements at the time can be interpreted as implying that he was primarily concerned with furthering his movement's influence over the long term. While boasting that "the hour will finally come when the truth, as defined by our leagues to M. Albert Lebrun, will be inescapably established" and declaring that the Croix de Feu had to make a good showing in the protests, he added that its current role was to "develop our intellectual, spiritual, and material power, prepare public opinion [and] plan decisive acts ... From one end of France to the other, especially in Paris and its 'red' districts, from our associations must grow a sort of 'organized virulence.'" La Rocque's private correspondence, dated some six weeks after the riots, echoed these sentiments. In it he indicated that he did not believe an overthrow of the current regime to be feasible, though he also made clear his ambition to carry out far-reaching changes. "If our association had, since its formation, the ambition of toppling the regime, it would have given itself over to anarchy or been pulverized. We are loyalists and we can only be loyalists with respect to the institutions that France has given itself." But La Rocque also emphasized that between "the republic as it is understood by certain governments" and the vision of the Croix de Feu "there is a wide margin."[81]

While he was anxious to exploit the Stavisky scandal, there are grounds for thinking that La Roque believed it would take more time before the Croix de Feu could reshape France according to its own lights. In fact, according Charles Trochu, a far-right Parisian municipal councillor who later broke with the organization, La Rocque was subjected to considerable pressure from the other leagues to participate in the 6 February demonstrations. Croix de Feu treasurer Georges Riché later suggested he was also swayed by members of the directing committee, who insisted that the movement had to demonstrate lest it be ridiculed. To this argument La Rocque purportedly responded that it would be risky to associate too closely with groups such as the Action

Française and thereby sacrifice the Croix de Feu's image of drawing together people from all political traditions – though this view had not prevented joint meetings with both the royalists and the Jeunesses Patriotes from taking place in some cities. La Rocque finally gave way but insisted that the protests be carried out in orderly manner, which amounted to giving the Chamber a "warning shot." In a similar vein, following a conversation with La Rocque about the event ten years later, Édouard Daladier concluded that the Croix de Feu leader "was primarily concerned with keeping control of his movement ... He couldn't very well refuse to be a part of the February 6 events, but he participated without enthusiasm, as if he had resigned himself to it."[82]

Once committed, though, the movement acted decisively. On 3 February the Parisian sections were notified that they would be put on alert two days later. On that day, 5 February, a "dress rehearsal" was held; two groups of Croix de Feu, four thousand strong in total, converged on the Ministry of the Interior. One group reached the building, only to be charged by the *garde mobile*. It withdrew and linked up with the second formation; the two had reached the Place de la Concorde when La Rocque appeared and told them to go home. While the Croix de Feu demonstration was not especially violent, in terms of the numbers involved, it was the largest held by a single organization since mass protests had begun in January. That same day the league promulgated a circular in which it stated its aim as being "to put an end to the dictatorship of socialist influence [presumably as a result of the Socialists' 1932 electoral alliance with the Radicals] and to summon to power a clean team, rid of politicians whomever they might be, with the goal of reestablishing national order within [a context of] external security."[83] Again, the language was strong, but the Croix de Feu did not stake any specific claim to power for itself and kept its options open; a "clean team" shed of "politicians" could, after all, mean many things.

As was the case with the dress rehearsal, on 6 February itself La Rocque did not assume personal command of his troops. He instead set up a command post with telephone links to various locations, including friendly cafés and even the Chamber of Deputies itself, since Georges Riché's brother Étienne was a deputy who was sympathetic to the movement. The Croix de Feu demonstrators tried to keep separate from the other leagues, though there were instances of mingling. The main scene of action was around the Place de la Concorde, where the Action Française, the Solidarité Française, elements of the Jeunesses

Patriotes, and several nationalist deputies and councillors squared off against the authorities. But the Croix de Feu did not get involved in these particular clashes. Instead, some two thousand members marched on the Palais Bourbon from the rear. After breaking through one police road block on the Rue de Constantine, the column ran into the last police blockade at the Rue Bourgogne. Here they pushed and shoved with the police for a quarter of an hour before La Rocque ordered them to withdraw. A second group of about four thousand formed up at the Petit Palais and headed for the Gare des Invalides, but ran into a barrier on the Quai d'Orsay. It eventually withdrew and dispersed. A third column also formed at the Petit Palais, but it was mainly intended to shelter the second from infiltration and saw little action. By the time it was all over, two Croix de Feu members had received bullet wounds and 122 were injured, some of them seriously.[84]

La Rocque requested that the section leaders provide him with reports of their experiences that day. Their accounts suggest many were surprised at the rough way in which the authorities had dealt with them. There was also speculation that many police officers had been drinking, a claim the government denied.[85] In any case, if La Rocque had ever suspected that the authorities might waver in a confrontation, the experience of 6 February disabused him of such an idea.

In the provinces, developments varied. Croix de Feu sections were ordered to demonstrate in solidarity with the marchers in Paris but to avoid contact with "political groupings." Things did not always go according to plan, however. In Cherbourg Joseph Levet disobeyed orders to avoid "any personal engagement" and led a demonstration, while in Caen his brother Claude headed a march conducted in unison with the Jeunesses Patriotes and the Camelots du Roi. In Lyons, by contrast, none of the demonstrators made a real effort to invade government buildings and the role of the Croix de Feu was limited.[86]

Did the Croix de Feu achieve its aims on 6 February? Kevin Passmore suggests that the 6th February rioters can be seen as a right-wing alliance which, if it had broken into the Chamber, might have constructed some sort of coalition government. Nor should the radicalism of the Croix de Feu be underestimated, he contends. The league was, after all, involved in clashes that day. But before the riots La Rocque seemed to imply that a takeover at that stage would not have been favourable to the movement's vaunted independence; this was an argument he persisted in making long afterwards. Ten years (to the day) after the event, he told Daladier in their Austrian prison that while

Maurras, Taittinger, and others had planned to enter the Chamber and proclaim a provisional government, he had distanced himself from them, believing that his movement had not yet taken sufficient root across the country.[87] While such claims have to be considered with caution, they are broadly consistent with his earlier remarks. It is also worth noting that the Bonnevay Commission concluded that the Croix de Feu "had not indulged in any serious violence," though its members "exerted strong pressure on the barricade" in front of the Palais Bourbon. It was members of the Action Française who had sustained the most casualties.[88]

Le Flambeau adopted a swaggering tone in the wake of the riots. La Rocque claimed that the Croix de Feu had accomplished precisely what it intended. Like much of the right, it approved the appointment of the former president of the republic, Gaston Doumergue, as prime minister. Indeed, Doumergue's accession to power can be viewed as broadly corresponding to the Croix de Feu's demand for the replacement of the supposedly "socialist-dominated" Daladier government with a team of supposedly non-partisan – but in reality nationalist – "resolute personalities." Doumergue himself described his administration as amounting to a party truce. Tardieu, too, raised hopes in some quarters as he returned to office as a minister of state, hoping to further his plans for constitutional revision.[89]

While some of La Rocque's claims were sheer bravado, he was not wrong to conclude that the Croix de Feu had benefited greatly from the events of 6 February. True, given the vigilance of the police, his boasts that if they had wanted to, the Croix de Feu's members could have occupied the Ministry of the Interior on 5 February and the Chamber of Deputies on 6 February ring hollow. These claims were sharply at odds with La Rocque's earlier, more ambiguous pronouncements, to say nothing of his reported caution prior to the demonstrations. Yet the riots did mark a turning point. While the movement had been growing in the previous months, it was now definitively catapulted onto the national stage.[90] Its seeming ability to combine militancy in the quest for change with discipline in the use of force made it appealing to a growing number of disaffected French citizens. It would embark upon a period of frenetic growth over the next two years.

Yet for all the changes that the league was about to experience, it bore the imprint of its formative stage for years to come. On the foundation of a nationalist myth of the war experience, La Rocque and his colleagues had crafted the beginnings of a discourse which, while situated on the far right, had syncretic overtones that under the proper conditions could attract a mass base. A network of ancillary groups aimed at broadening the membership was in the making, and La Rocque had consolidated his authority. The league had also established some contacts with elite circles in France even as it promoted an image of intransigent autonomy. With respect to mass mobilizations, the Croix de Feu presented itself as a potent physical, as well as moral, force, but one characterized by self-mastery. In its confrontation with the Popular Front between 1934 and 1936, the strengths – but also the limitations – of these strategies and tactics would be revealed.

2

Against the Popular Front,
1934–1936

Following the 6 February riots, the political atmosphere in France grew ever more volatile. The supporters of the left worked their way towards a common plan of action. Initiatives such as the calling of a general strike by the Confédération Générale du Travail (CGT) on 12 February were followed by the creation of anti-fascist front organizations at the national and local levels. In July 1934 a pact between the Socialists and the Communists was signed. While the coalition first known as the Common Front and later the Popular Front gathered steam, various French governments sought with little success to combat the effects of the Great Depression, even as they presided over international crises and the sharpening of domestic political divisions. Simultaneously, right-wing parties such as the Fédération Républicaine adopted a harsh stance in opposition to the Popular Front, while the nationalist leagues grew increasingly restive.

Though still professing its distaste for politics, the Croix de Feu was at the heart of political developments during this period. While La Rocque's precise strategy was malleable, the movement's broader objective was forge itself into such a potent force that, one way or another, France would be regenerated according to its lights. In terms of its public posture, the Croix de Feu aimed to position itself as the leading force of national renewal. La Rocque and various supporters refined the message of national reconciliation into an all-encompassing program. The league also used mass mobilizations, frequently of a paramilitary character, to demonstrate its capacity to muster patriotic sentiment and defeat its enemies.

The results of these efforts ranged from imposing successes to humiliating defeats. In terms of attracting support, the Croix de Feu had at least half a million members by the spring of 1936.[1] It was thus transformed from one of several noisy ultra-nationalist groups into a movement whose actions weighed heavily in the calculations of other political formations. However, its tactics encouraged serious rivalries and bitter enmities. The other right-wing leagues and many traditional conservatives resented La Rocque's ambition to lead the nationalist cause. The Croix de Feu's paramilitary mobilizations were controversial and evoked legal sanctions against it. In the winter of 1935–36 La Rocque began to reconsider aspects of his approach, but he and his supporters failed to prevent the election of the Popular Front. This outcome, however, should not lead us to underestimate the challenge that they had posed to the Third Republic. They had often skilfully exploited the weaknesses of the regime and shown ingenuity in adapting to a rapidly changing political context. Though the dissolution of 1936 spelt the end of the Croix de Feu, impressive foundations had been laid for the PSF to build upon.

TRACING THE PATH TO POWER

By early 1934 La Rocque's overarching goal of having the Croix de Feu become the focal point for a nationalist revival was clear enough. He remained elusive, though, as to what precisely this would involve. At times he suggested that he simply wanted to expand the league's influence to the point where it would transform public opinion, following which a true process of renewal could begin. He claimed to be more concerned that the movement's values conquer the hearts and minds of the French people than with achieving political power. Claude Popelin, a leading member of the Volontaires Nationaux, recalled how during this period La Rocque stressed that "our objective is to take power through our ideas, even if this takes twenty years and we are no longer there to see it! Above all, we do not work for ourselves, but for France." Similarly, in a conversation with the archbishop of Paris in 1936 La Rocque claimed that "we only desire one thing: to stop being collectively necessary as soon as possible, so that we can return to being individually useful, with each person occupying the place which Providence normally assigns us."[2] If these statements are taken at face value, then, La Rocque saw his primary task as creating a climate of opinion favourable to the restoration of national unity – as he defined it. While the Croix de Feu was needed to bring this about, once the process was underway, it might no longer be required. In other words, the movement had no real long-term ambitions of its own.

However, La Rocque's rhetoric also frequently pointed towards the actual conquest of power by the league. Even the phrase "take power through our ideas," as Popelin recalled it, left open the possibility of controlling institutions. On various occasions La Rocque explicitly asserted that the current system in France could not endure and that the Croix de Feu itself would have to solve the nation's problems. From time to time he predicted that the regime would somehow become deadlocked and implode, leaving a vacuum for his supporters to occupy. At a meeting in Metz held in June 1935, for example, he predicted the end of the parliamentary regime was near, suggesting that it might collapse in October when the government found could not balance its budget. At that point, he declared, the hour of the Croix de Feu would arrive, when "our association, once its ideas are in power, will take action to reorganize the country according to its needs."[3]

But whether it would serve only as a catalyst or would implement change itself – and surely the latter scenario appealed to most of its supporters – the Croix de Feu would have to achieve a hegemonic position with respect to defining and guiding patriotic sentiment. To do so it would have to define its stance in relation to other movements so as to demonstrate its superior nationalist commitment. For the Croix de Feu, that meant identifying itself as the antithesis of the Popular Front. La Rocque demonized the coalition as un-French, branding its cadres "apaches" and suggesting that it was filled with Germans, Russians, and "Asiatics" seeking revolution. In keeping with the imperative of reconciliation, though, he claimed to differentiate between the leadership and the ordinary militants. While the former were "a handful of delinquent rich people and parasites," the latter could be won over to the Croix de Feu.[4]

Frequently, attacks upon the Popular Front were framed within a broader critique of republican institutions, politicians, and governments. Testifying before the Bonnevay Commission, Pozzo di Borgo argued that the regime needed change, declaring that while the Republic "is an old lady whom I respect greatly," she "could use a trip to the beauty salon without offending anyone."[5] Even conservative politicians were not immune from criticism. While La Rocque and his followers were anxious to be seen as supporters of order and friends of certain politicians, they would turn on them if those individuals were later deemed unable to rejuvenate France. Increasingly, the Croix de Feu presented itself as the only possible solution.

Relations between the Croix de Feu and the government of Gaston Doumergue, which took power after 6 February, illustrate this pattern. At the outset Doumergue's moves towards constitutional reforms involving a stronger executive met with the Croix de Feu's approval, as La Rocque indicated in an October 1934 interview with *Excelsior*.[6] But the new prime minister's plans soon caused unease among Communists, Socialists, and many Radicals, who argued they might be a prelude to dictatorship. The Radicals broke with the government and it fell on 8 November. Three days later the Croix de Feu paraded to Doumergue's residence in a show of support. Even before that display, however, it had already begun to demonstrate impatience with him. La Rocque had advised Doumergue to create an atmosphere in which a true "national reconciliation" could take place through the purging of inept ministers, spending cuts, the adoption of "energetic sanctions" against suspect public servants and teachers, and the dissolution of the Parti Communiste Français (PCF). Unless such actions were taken, he insisted, all reforms were doomed. After Doumergue's government fell, La Rocque lamented that the premier had lacked the resolve to hold on. Indeed, he soon suggested that the government had merely been "a poultice on a gangrenous leg."[7] Between an ineffective government and a menacing Popular Front, only one viable force had emerged, he contended, and that was the Croix de Feu.[8]

The league took an even dimmer view of Doumergue's successor, Pierre-Étienne Flandin, leader of the centre-right Alliance Démocratique and prime minister from November 1934 to May 1935. Flandin had previously shown some sympathy for the leagues, but after taking office he distanced himself from them, decrying them as a political alternative. Though in private La Rocque offered to share information on Communist "agitators" with the government, in public *Le Flambeau* accused Flandin of encouraging "subversive agitation" and of being a "Kerensky," reaffirming the Croix de Feu's view that traditional politicians were not up to the task of saving France.[9]

With the government of Pierre Laval (7 June 1935 – 22 January 1936), the relationship was more complex; initially it seemed to present opportunities for cooperation, but these never came to fruition. Early in Laval's administration La Rocque curtailed the Croix de Feu's paramilitary mobilizations and even accepted cuts to veterans' pensions in order to support the government.[10] Moreover, *Le Flambeau* was generally sympathetic to Laval's foreign policy goals. The paper defended his decision to limit cooperation with the Soviet Union and applauded the prime minister's efforts to resolve the Abyssinian crisis through making concessions to Italy – a policy that eventually led the government's Radical ministers to defect, causing its downfall.[11]

However, the Croix de Feu became a critic of Laval's deflationary economic policies. When the first-decree laws calling for spending cuts were enacted, La Rocque commented that while they allowed the treasury to meet its short-term commitments, the policy would hurt small property owners, a key element of the Croix de Feu's constituency. He concluded that as long as the current institutional configuration of the Republic persisted, no durable results could be achieved. Laval had only been able to tackle the budget with ad hoc measures; the government was hampered in its efficacy by "groups and factions." The whole experience, La Rocque concluded, demonstrated that unless a government rested upon firm foundations, it could not stand up to "international high finance and its allies in London and Moscow." After Laval's fall, La Rocque declared that he had never believed the ministry would ensure the triumph of "civic order."[12]

Laval's successor, the Radical caretaker government of Albert Sarraut, which lasted from January to June 1936, was fiercely criticized by the Croix de Feu from its inception. By this time the Radicals had aligned themselves with the Socialists and the Communists in the Popular Front; in response, the Croix de Feu maintained that while many of their supporters were patriots who properly belonged in its own ranks, the Radicals' leaders were pushing France towards ruin. Charles Vallin, a rising propagandist in the organization and a future PSF deputy, accused the Radicals of being "at the service of the lodges." This was a very serious charge in La Rocque's eyes, for he was on record as describing Freemasonry as a "quasi-diabolical cabal." His scorn for Sarraut's administration knew no limits; when Germany moved into the Rhineland in March 1936, La Rocque published an open letter to the prime minister, stressing how circumstances dictated a policy of determination in a climate of national unity. Sadly, he continued, this was something that the Sarraut cabinet, a combination of "divergent and mediocre ambitions," would never be able to deliver.[13] In sum, though variable in its attitudes towards successive governments, ultimately the Croix de Feu felt that none were up to the task of restoring French grandeur.

At the same time the league was selective in cultivating allies, shunning associations it believed might harm its image. Naturally, the Croix de Feu deeply appreciated the endorsement of military heroes. When Marshal Pétain – viewed at the time as the epitome of non-partisan patriotism – praised the Croix de Feu in the pages of *Le Journal*, the interview was quickly reproduced on the front page of *Le Flambeau*. But La Rocque was just as quick to insist that the Croix de Feu was not beholden to groups such as Henri de Kerillis's Centre de Propagande des Républicains Nationaux, stating that he had refused an offer of 50,000 francs from it. Similarly, when faced with left-wing accusations that he was subordinate to capitalist interests, La Rocque distanced himself from figures such as Ernest Mercier of the pro-modernization group Redressement Français, who was asked to resign from the movement.[14]

This desire to maintain an image of independence had a major impact upon the Croix de Feu's dealings with traditional conservative parties, particularly the Fédération Républicaine. Following the 6 February riots, Fédération notables such as Philippe Henriot had praised the leagues for "warning the state and reminding it of its duty"; they hoped that the Croix de Feu, the Jeunesses Patriotes, and other organizations would serve as useful adjuncts to the party in what the Fédération's newspaper termed "parallel, but different and autonomous tasks." At the local level, however, Croix de Feu militants protested that they would not serve as the shock troops of tired, corrupt political parties. In 1935 members of the La Bernerie (Loire-Inférieure) section actually ejected a local politician from a meeting, declaring they would not be used for narrow "electoral" purposes. La Rocque, aware of such sentiments, scorned those who sought to use his supporters for their own ends.[15] True, when the stakes were high – as in the national elections of 1936 – there was cooperation between the Croix de Feu and the Fédération, but the tension between the two organizations grew.

As for the Croix de Feu's dealings with its closest competitors – the Action Française, the Jeunesses Patriotes, and the other leagues – these took the form of an uneasy balancing act. La Rocque's insistence that the Croix de Feu appealed to a wider audience than its competitors and his desire to preserve its autonomy caused problems. In 1934 he rejected a proposal to join the Front National, a coalition of the leagues initiated by the Solidarité Française and adhered to by the Action Française and the Jeunesses Patriotes. La Rocque even dissuaded Lyautey, who had initially encouraged the project, from continuing to support it.[16] The other leagues were outraged. Even before the failure of the Front National initiative, Admiral Schwerer of the Action Française had attacked La Rocque for refusing to permit dual membership in their respective organizations, contemptuously asserting that the "Croix de Feu has become an organization which is no longer national, but instead republican."[17] The animosity proved to be enduring. Some Croix de Feu meetings were disrupted by royalists, and in June 1935 the American embassy reported that the monarchists had even considered kidnapping La Rocque so as to render his followers more "amenable, at least in great part, to Action Française influences."[18]

But the level of conflict between the Croix de Feu and the other leagues was not always so severe. In Lyons, Lille, and Algiers there were instances of cooperation with the Jeunesses Patriotes and the Solidarité Française. At a March 1935 meeting in Constantine a Croix de Feu speaker, while emphasizing that members must be loyal to the association and that its insignia must be worn at the meetings of other organizations, stated that other "national" groups should feel welcome at its gatherings.[19] Even when La Rocque instructed his section leaders to disregard rumours about an alliance between the Croix de Feu and the royalists, he emphasized that these directives should be interpreted as a precaution and not in a spirit of hostility.[20]

Such concessions to the notion of cooperation were in large measure a response to pressure from below. Members of the Tourcoing Croix de Feu, for instance, were upset when they learned of the refusal to join the Front National. La Rocque could not afford to alienate too many of his supporters who felt this way.[21] Yet even when the Croix de Feu sounded more conciliatory, there was no doubt that it ultimately intended to achieve a position of dominance. Colonel Alfred Debay, who represented the Algerian sections on the league's directing committee, was unequivocal on this point at a meeting in Nantes attended by members of the Action Française and the Solidarité Française. He assured the latter that while his movement would not join the Front National, "parties with national ideas are assured of the Croix de Feu's sympathy." Immediately after speaking these words, however, Debay encouraged non-Croix de Feu supporters to sign up, arguing that his association would by sheer force of numbers eventually overwhelm all the others.[22]

Thus the Croix de Feu depicted itself as sharing the concerns of patriotic governments, nationalist leagues, and right-wing parties, but it fought to preserve its freedom of manoeuvre and never hesitated to criticize them. While scarcely alone in their fierce hatred of the Popular

Front, its leaders were convinced that the Croix de Feu provided the only route to true national salvation and should thus dominate the nationalist cause. No doubt other leaders of the French right had similar ideas, but given its rapid growth by 1935, the Croix de Feu seemed closer to achieving its goal. Unlike the Jeunesses Patriotes, it was not too closely and visibly linked to a traditional party such as the Fédération. Its inclusive-sounding rhetoric resonated with more people than the monarchism of the Action Française, which also lacked the advantage of being new. By contrast, the Croix de Feu projected an image of being true to its principles and untainted by links with either the establishment or extremists.

DEFINING NATIONAL RECONCILIATION

The Croix de Feu further asserted its position as the champion of patriotic regeneration through elaborating its program. At its inception the league had, in essence, simply called for a nationalist revival spurred by elite veterans acting as a vanguard. Under some pressure to do so, La Rocque and his colleagues now elaborated their views, recasting the amorphous notion of uniting patriots of all stripes into the more articulate slogan of "national reconciliation," with the intention of winning more respectability and support. In the process the syncretic nature of the Croix de Feu's ideology – drawing upon Social Catholicism, integral nationalism, and echoing aspects of the nonconformist critique of the era – became more apparent. So did the range of opinions that existed within the movement. But while La Rocque found himself compelled to respond to various demands to inflect the Croix de Feu's message one way or another, he also thwarted challenges to his primacy in shaping the movement's ideology.

After 6 February some Croix de Feu militants were dissatisfied with the lack of a definitive program. In an attempt to mollify them, Henry Guerrin, a member of the 15th section, published a pamphlet entitled simply *Croix de Feu?* – apparently without prior approval. He was not disciplined for his actions, perhaps because he presented the association's goals accurately. Guerrin revisited familiar themes concerning the irremediable corruption of France's political class and the need for a new, disciplined elite, "the living synthesis of all greater France which had sacrificed itself in action."[23] But it was La Rocque himself who at the end of 1934 finally provided a detailed exposition of his ideas in *Service public*. The book highlighted how the Croix de Feu's quest for national solidarity was inclusive and, it should be noted, lacked much of the extreme rhetoric with which the league often attacked its opponents.

La Rocque began *Service public* by outlining what he saw as the reasons behind France's troubles. He argued that the nation's institutions were immobile, and no one – either of the left or of the right – had made the necessary changes. Instead the various parties allowed themselves to be guided by the drift of public opinion, which itself was irresponsible. The men of the pre-war generation were paralyzed by their "bourgeois" mentality. Those who had fought in 1914–18 had either withdrawn from public life or were ineffectively represented. The women and youth of France represented significant reserves of civic and patriotic potential, but they were neglected and, in the case of the latter, badly served by an insufficiently spiritualistic education.[24] These various failings manifested themselves, he concluded, in social backwardness, excessive numbers of foreigners, who threatened to defy France's tradition of assimilating immigrants, and formidable challenges in foreign policy.

La Rocque's solutions to these problems were not much different from the ones he had proposed in earlier years, but they were now explored in more depth. Compared to its 1933 formulation, *la profession organisée* was more clearly defined as "combining the different categories of labourers, from the manual worker to the employer, for the same branch of production at the local and regional level." Establishing such a system would take time, but the process would lead to the creation of an economic council with the express role of advising the state, which itself would retain a coordinating but not overweening role.[25] In foreign affairs La Rocque expressed an interest in European economic cooperation, but added that this was looking very far ahead, since the international system was currently in chaos. Responsibility for this state of affairs, he argued, lay with the peace treaties of 1919; La Rocque condemned Woodrow Wilson – identified only as "the high priest of the 14 points" – for creating an overly complex system and burdening the victors, especially France, with "gendarme" duties. The League of Nations had quickly been reduced to sterility, unable to resolve the nationalist passions and conflicts that plagued Europe. Under these circumstances, French diplomacy should be guided by a spirit of "sacred egoism," a ruthless commitment to defending the national interest.[26]

Given these conditions, allies had to be chosen with great care. Soviet Russia was a potential threat; any dealings with it must be conducted with the greatest caution. Great Britain was focused upon its empire and took a short-term view of its security needs. La Rocque saw greater potential for cooperation with Mussolini, arguing that Italy and France had complementary interests and cultural affinities, but he added that France would also have to defend vigorously its interests in Central and Eastern Europe as well as the Mediterranean. As for Germany, while La Rocque believed that the havoc its soldiers had wrought in the First World War must never be forgotten, he also professed admiration for their bravery and concluded that France would have to engage in dialogue with the Third Reich. Before doing so, however, authority would have to be re-established at home, "on the condition of first having control of ourselves, of having put an end to revolutionary enterprises [and] of possessing an army, air force, and navy that are both sound and well coordinated."[27]

As on previous occasions, La Rocque defined the root of France's troubles in terms of moral shortcomings, especially on the part of elites who had forgotten that hierarchies were only justified on the basis of leaders providing "a constant model of civic virtues."[28] It was in this context that the Croix de Feu provided a solution. As the "men of victory," its members were "apostles" of such virtues and would show the public that the divisions created by the "men of politics" were artificial. As the national crisis worsened, the people would turn to them and against a corrupted political system. By combining the patriotism of the right with the social conscience of the left, the Croix de Feu would achieve reconciliation, which in turn provided the basis for renewal: "the sign of the resurrection is the spontaneous conjunction of the fervent strength of the left with the renewed forces of the right, each rid of their bogus leaders." The nation that emerged from this process would be stable and prosperous. Class struggle would give way to cooperation between enlightened elites and prosperous workers. Equality would be spiritual rather than the result of materialist levelling, but social concerns would nevertheless be of central importance. Authority would be re-established, but there would be no cult of the state. Individual liberty would be preserved, and the family, the cornerstone of society, would be strengthened.[29]

Exploring the influences behind *Service public* opens up broader questions about La Rocque's ideological outlook. Jacques Nobécourt believes the book illustrates how La Rocque was influenced by the 1848 constitution and wanted a "Christian republic founded on the right to fraternal assistance." On this point, that document did invoke

"La Famille, le Travail, la Propriété, l'Ordre Public," a slogan similar to the Croix de Feu's "Travail, Famille, Patrie," which began to appear on the front page of *Le Flambeau* in 1934. But when it came to choosing constitutional forms, La Rocque ultimately believed that "the goal is the national existence. A regime is a means." By contrast, the enthusiasm of the 1848 revolutionaries for a republic was far more passionate. Moreover, they were concerned about striking a balance between the power of the legislature and that of the executive, while one of La Rocque's main concerns was to curb the power of the former vis-à-vis the latter. The number of representatives was to be reduced, as was their ability to initiate legislation. Finally, the 1848 constitution explicitly affirmed that the president would be elected by universal male suffrage. La Rocque remained vague as to how his enhanced executive would be chosen. While he stated that he was anxious to introduce female suffrage, he added that this would be presented in conjunction with the "family vote." Whether or not women would actually control their own vote rather than just enhance that of their husbands, which some proponents of the family vote advocated, was not specified, nor was any formula for democratic representation. Far clearer was La Rocque's animosity towards the Third Republic. Recalling one occasion when he had viewed a sitting of the Chamber of Deputies, he stated that "nothing would be able to capture my disgust faced with this ludicrous tragedy."[30]

A Social Catholic influence is discernable in *Service public*. The book said little about religion specifically, but given La Rocque's background, it is not surprising that a vision of a harmonious and paternal social order inspired by the church permeated it. While he did not think it was appropriate to delve into matters of faith in a book aimed at emphasizing the Croix de Feu's openness to all, under the right circumstances La Rocque was forthright about the role of Catholicism in shaping his views. In a December 1934 interview with the Dominican journal *Sept* he stated, "I am happy knowing that, in my public action, which is outside the religious plane, I have done nothing which is contrary to the orthodoxy of my personal religion." Indeed, he tried to harmonize his movement's actions with that of a church which abstained from engaging in politics per se by stressing that the Croix de Feu was a "civic," rather than a political, organization. Such a characterization of the movement was bound to appeal to the church, since Pope Pius xi himself had stressed that Catholic Action organizations should be non-political in character.[31]

Simultaneously, however, La Rocque sought to present the Croix de Feu as non-sectarian. Croix de Feu sections attended memorial services for Protestants and Jews as well as Catholics. Édouard Soulier, a Protestant pastor and member of the Fédération Républicaine, joined the league; La Rocque's dealings with Jacob Kaplan, the rabbi of Paris, were initially cordial. In Algeria the Croix de Feu also cultivated the Muslim community. There were even efforts to recruit the indigenous population, though the movement lacked a clear policy on this issue and seemed to waver between seeking alliances with Muslim organizations and trying to incorporate Algerians directly into its ranks. Nevertheless, it has been suggested that eventually Muslims accounted for 10 per cent of the Algerian membership.[32]

But the Algerian sections proved to be hostile to the idea of being open to Jews, and this antagonism soon had consequences for the entire movement. The right in Algeria had long promoted a visceral antisemitism, and the local Croix de Feu proved to be no exception. By 1935 militants were launching incursions into Jewish neighbourhoods, making fascist salutes, and shouting "Long live La Rocque" and even "Long live Hitler." The authorities also noted that some of the league's supporters sought to encourage those attitudes among Muslims. La Rocque reportedly discouraged expressions of antisemitism, but not forcefully enough to have any appreciable effect. The result was that the growing anger of the left-wing Ligue Internationale Contre l'Anti-sémitisme (LICA) about the situation in Algeria led to a deterioration in relations between the Croix de Feu and France's Jewish community. Indeed, the situation grew serious enough for there to be a scuffle, reportedly instigated by the LICA, with Croix de Feu members during a memorial service at a Paris synagogue in June 1936. After that, official relations between the movement and the Jewish community were sundered.[33]

Such antisemitic impulses, as well as other features of its outlook, suggest that the Croix de Feu's program reflected the teachings of a certain kind of French Social Catholicism. While some Social Catholics were mainly concerned with social reform and accepted republican institutions, the broader tradition itself was partly rooted in the anti-liberal attitudes of nineteenth-century integral Catholicism. Reactionary influences remained strong, even in the Christian Democratic movement of the 1890s.[34] Its supporters engaged in mass politics but were often anti-liberal in economic and political terms; they demanded a corporatist state and vehemently attacked foreigners, Jews, and the parliamentary system. It was this brand of Social Catholicism to which La Rocque and his followers were arguably most indebted.

La Rocque did not articulate the Croix de Feu's program in isolation; several prominent writers lent their support. Gaston Rageot, a novelist, drama critic, president of the Société des Gens de Lettres de France, and former pupil of Henri Bergson, contributed to *Le Flambeau* and addressed several Croix de Feu meetings.[35] In arguments paralleling those developed by various "nonconformist" periodicals, Rageot stressed the fragility of France since 1919, attributing this to a mechanistic focus on politics and economics since the French Revolution. While the latter had been liberating in some respects, it had produced a society that cared only for the rights of the citizen and not the rights of man, and had a materialist conception of life which led to class conflict. French democracy was false because it had come to mean only electoral contests and stale party conflict. Renovation was necessary. Rageot proposed bringing together all classes and generations and convincing them of the need for a moral revolution grounded in the family, the professions, and France's regions. He also hoped that just as the French people would unite around the Croix de Feu, so France would become a magnet for all Latin nations, especially Fascist Italy, allowing these countries to form a solid bloc against Germany.[36] Rageot lent some respectability and depth to the Croix de Feu's sometimes intemperate rhetoric, with his emphasis on anti-materialism and moral reform refining the league's core ideology.

Other established writers who contributed to *Le Flambeau* included current and future members of the Académie Française such as Henry Bordeaux, Jacques de Lacretelle, and Claude Farrère; Henri Pourrat, who propounded the benefits of rural life; the popular historian and biographer André Maurois; André Demaison, an advocate of the French empire; the feminist writer Marcelle Tinayre; and Colette Yver, a popular novelist.[37] Naturally, their views diverged on some issues, but it is plausible to suggest that this diversity suited varying outlooks within the Croix de Feu's growing membership. When it came to politics, for example, André Maurois and Claude Farrère advocated a more executive-oriented republic, a suggestion with which many moderates were bound to concur. Henry Bordeaux, on the other hand, maintained that democracy was unable to cope with French decay, reflecting the stance of hardened reactionaries. Concerning the status of women, there was also a spectrum of views, even if its broadness should not be exaggerated. Marcelle Tinayre advocated political emancipation for women; Colette Yver opposed feminism and supported the notion of arranged marriages, even though she made an independent living from her writing and had personally refused several of the latter.[38]

While these writers diverged on some issues, cumulatively they reinforced the Croix de Feu's overarching priorities. André Demaison, for instance, lamented the loss of "enthusiasm" in French society since the end of the Great War, arguing that it had to be unleashed to ensure national greatness. Tinayre, writing on women's suffrage, believed that before that issue could be resolved, "a total reform ... which will allow values of all kinds, masculine and feminine, to serve the country effectively, is necessary." She also maintained that while women should not be excluded from the workforce, motherhood was also an attractive option, which raising male wages would encourage. Yver, for her part, asserted that "women, gentlemen, don't like politics. They only want a government." She warmly praised La Rocque's professed goal of reaching out to all segments of society: "the Croix de Feu are not confined to any division. Freethinkers, Jews, Catholics, Protestants, they are bound to the heights of all noble convictions; whether they come from the left or the right they have a common goal, which is the interest of France." A powerful "civic" movement, the league was charged to "finally rescue the French from their egoism."[39]

Perhaps the most important of *Le Flambeau*'s contributors was Saint-Brice, who wrote a column on international affairs for the paper from February 1934 onward. He performed similar duties for *La Revue universelle*, which was edited by a leading member of the Action Française, Jacques Bainville.[40] Like most of his right-wing contemporaries, Saint-Brice criticized French foreign policy for being weak and thereby encouraging the resurgence of Germany under Hitler's leadership. Viewing the League of Nations as a chimera, he believed France should rely upon allies in order to contain the Reich. Only certain states were suitable for this task, however. While Saint-Brice believed that French security agreements with various East European states in the form of the Little Entente had to be preserved, dealings with the Soviets had to be avoided. When Foreign Minister Louis Barthou began treating with them in 1934, Saint-Brice criticized the policy at length in *Le Flambeau*. Bolshevik Russia, he argued, had cooperated with Germany in the past and could easily betray France by doing so again in the future. For the time being, Hitler's anti-Communism might preclude such a scenario, but Saint-Brice believed he would not last in power for very long; a future German-Soviet alignment could not be ruled out.[41]

Saint-Brice was far more enthusiastic about Fascist Italy as a partner. Certainly, he did not oppose its invasion of Ethiopia in 1935. When the League of Nations passed limited sanctions against Italy, hurting relations between Mussolini and the Western democracies, Saint-Brice was incensed. For this turn of events, he did not blame France's prime minister at the time, Laval, whom he correctly perceived as being friendly to Italy; instead, he directed his anger at the League of Nations and Britain. The League, he contended, was deliberately stirring up animosity against Fascist Italy and had made a grievous mistake in granting a non-white nation such as Ethiopia equal status within the international community.[42] As for British, they were hypocrites; they had initially accepted what Saint-Brice saw as Italy's right to expand, only to renege on this commitment and join in criticizing Italy even as they jealously guarded their own imperial interests. These attacks on the League and suspicions of the British were fully endorsed by La Rocque, who declared in October 1935, "The League of Nations is, like the Treaty of Versailles, a noxious product of Anglo-Saxon ideology. ... France will not struggle against Italy to preserve the sources of the Nile for Great Britain, to please the assassins of Moscow, to enrich the merchants of the City [of London], to inaugurate the world revolution, [or] to resuscitate Geneva's dubious enterprise."[43]

Saint-Brice and La Rocque were further disillusioned when the anti-Soviet and pro-Italian Laval was succeeded by the Radical Sarraut, who was prime minister when Germany reoccupied the Rhineland in March 1936. For Saint-Brice the inability of the Western democracies to contain Hitler proved that they were decrepit. The only solution was to reform France along authoritarian lines akin to what Léon Degrelle's Rexists were seeking for Belgium – a combination of dynamism with an appeal to tradition, informed by Christian ethics but "against the collusions of politics and religion." Thereafter discussions with Germany could proceed from a position of strength.[44] For his part, La Rocque believed that the League of Nations was worthless; France should quit the organization and look to traditional alliances to defend its interests and achieve "durable reconcilation" with its former enemies. But while he still evinced suspicion of Germany, he was now more insistent than ever that a war had to be avoided at all costs. He believed this was precisely what the Soviets, supported by the French Communists, wanted: a "European war, a direct profit for the USSR, with the indirect, eventual possibility of introducing world revolution." In adopting this position, La Rocque participated in a general

shift in outlook within the French right at the time, away from a belligerent stance regarding Germany towards a "neo-pacifist" position
based on the conviction that the Popular Front would lead France into
a war which in turn would lead to revolution.[45]

Between 1934 and 1936, then, La Rocque and Saint-Brice provided
a generally unified message to readers of *Le Flambeau* when it came to
international affairs, emphasizing anti-Communism, suspicion of the
British, and admiration for fascist and authoritarian values. But the
Croix de Feu leader's relations with some other contributors to the
paper proved less harmonious.[46] One of the disadvantages of having a
vague program was that others might try to shape it to their own ends;
beginning in 1934, a number of young thinkers had joined the Volontaires Nationaux as propaganda delegates with this goal in mind.
Among them were several *Ordre nouveau* nonconformists such as
Robert Loustau and Robert Gibrat; Claude Popelin, formerly associated with the Radicals; Pierre Pucheu, at the time the secretary general
of the Comptoir Sidéurgique; and Bertrand de Maud'huy, an employee
of the Worms bank. A sense of their general outlook can be gleaned
from an article de Maud'huy published in the American journal *Foreign Affairs*. In it he called for a non-parliamentary movement to unite
the various new tendencies that had developed in reaction to the degeneration of French politics. The Croix de Feu, he argued, could provide
the nucleus of a new political order characterized by authority, social
justice, and class collaboration. None of this implied a dictatorship, he
insisted; while lessons from other countries were valuable, "the Frenchmen's love for individual liberty" had to be respected.[47]

Upon first inspection, such conceptions could readily be harmonized
with the Croix de Feu's general doctrine. But it soon became apparent
that the "Maréchaux" (Marshals), as they became known, irritated La
Rocque. De Maud'huy and the others pressed for a more detailed program; indeed, it appears that it was partly in response to their demands
that *Service public* was written. But the Maréchaux were dissatisfied
with it and drew up an alternative document, which they presented to
La Rocque in the summer of 1935. Inspired by the "Plan of 9 July
1934," the work of a politically eclectic group of reformers which had
failed to cohere, the proposal called for extensive state planning to
ensure growing productivity and suggested the need for more heavy
industry. La Rocque responded that it was too technocratic and paid
insufficient attention to the crisis of spiritual values. His conception of

la profession organisée implied a less ambitious role for the state; it was primarily envisioned as a means of defusing class conflict, rather than encouraging American-style economic growth.[48] He rejected the proposal, and the Maréchaux quit. An attempt by Pierre Branellec of the Brest section to resolve the dispute was firmly rebuked by Ottavi, who declared to him that "we cannot contemplate retaining in our association any of the those who have resigned because of the attitude they have adopted."[49]

After the break, de Maud'huy assessed the differences between the Maréchaux and La Rocque. The former had been characterized by "the will for action," which, he suggested, had been constrained by the "sensible maturity" of the latter. But these remarks glossed over other issues at the heart of the dispute. According to the police, de Maud'huy and other Maréchaux were perturbed by La Rocque's ongoing contacts with politicians of various stripes. These included Darquier de Pellepoix, an antisemitic Parisian municipal councillor and former member of the Action Française, and some unnamed "leftists." More generally, control over the direction of the movement was at stake. Popelin had actually resigned before the others since he faced expulsion, having been accused of intriguing against La Rocque. In a private letter Popelin called for greater control by the directing committee, presumably as opposed to La Rocque and his coterie. In a similar vein, Pucheu had wanted more independence for the Volontaires Nationaux. In subsequent missives to the sections, La Rocque decried such ambitions as sheer egotism, betraying the Croix de Feu's ideal of service to a higher cause.[50]

The whole episode illustrates La Rocque's determination to control the orientation of the Croix de Feu. He did not hesitate to prompt the departure of the Maréchaux and to insist that the league retain an imprecise syncretic message which pointed towards a reconciled, orderly, and hierarchical society. The Croix de Feu would continue to stress how it incarnated the spirit of the *union sacrée* and to avoid overly "rational" arguments in favour of "appealing directly to the unconscious instincts of the average Frenchman."[51] As the movement attracted a growing number of supporters, this appeared to be compelling logic; the slogan of national reconciliation allowed it to continue doing so while laying claim to a degree of ideological cohesion. As for the leaders of the Popular Front and others who opposed its project, they had in effect rejected France altogether. They were to be defeated by exposing them for what they were, but also by displays of force.

THE PERILS OF
PARAMILITARISM

In 1934 and 1935 tightly disciplined mass mobilizations were essential to the Croix de Feu's efforts to intimidate enemies, influence politicians, and exhibit its power. Such displays were not simply defensive or intended to channel militant activism away from extremism, as scholars such as Rémond and Nobécourt suggest.[52] The rhetoric was frightening and there was real violence; the police believed that even when the Croix de Feu's militants were not the aggressors in the strict sense of the word, their behaviour was intentionally provocative and led to clashes.[53] Anxiety about the intentions of La Rocque and his followers was particularly intense among supporters of the Popular Front, but it soon spread. Governments were urged to take action, and soon threats were made to dissolve the league.[54] Though he came under considerable pressure from within the movement to maintain a belligerent stance, La Rocque's tactics were tempered by these considerations, as well as by a desire to prevent an organization that prided itself on its discipline from appearing disorderly. As a result, at the end of 1935 the Croix de Feu attempted to regain the initiative by offering to disarm for the sake of national harmony. It also tried to present the Popular Front as the real source of political unrest. While these measures did not entirely solve the Croix de Feu's problems, they showed political agility on the part of La Rocque and his colleagues.

Following the 6 February 1934 riots, the left sought to recapture the initiative in the streets, starting with the huge demonstrations that took place on 12 February. Early attempts by the leagues to respond by utilizing the commemoration of Joan of Arc in May and the funeral of Marshal Lyautey in August to build momentum met with only limited success. As their frustration grew, so did the potential for violence. On 8 July 1934, twelve thousand Croix de Feu and Jeunesses Patriotes members gathered at the Arc de Triomphe, while seventeen thousand Socialists and Communists met at the Bois de Vincennes; only the intervention of the authorities ensured that a clash was avoided. Later that summer the situation was calmed by the fact that many of the Croix de Feu's middle-class supporters were on vacation. But the movement fully intended to heat things up in the fall; the directing committee instructed section heads that the "campaign" planned for the closing months of 1934 would have to be very well-planned. Ominously, it told members, if asked by potential converts what their plan was, to reply that they sought to create a core of disciplined people who would be ready to restore order when the old parties crumbled.[55]

The Croix de Feu made good on its promises to ratchet up the tension. At the beginning of September 1934 *Le Flambeau* defiantly announced that because of excessive conditions imposed by the government, the Croix de Feu would not take part in the official commemorations of the Battle of the Marne scheduled for that month. Instead it would hold its own ceremony at a time of its choosing; this took place on 30 September at Chantilly, with a column of twelve thousand men forming up very rapidly. Observers such as the American ambassador speculated that the parade was a dry run for more dramatic measures; certainly, La Rocque's rhetoric seemed to hint at this when he declared, "The current parliamentarism is forfeit ... Nothing sound will be gained without a preliminary cleansing of committees, journalistic and other headquarters where anonymous powers exercise their absolutism over a blinded universal suffrage ... As for the Croix de Feu movement, its path is clear ... the bulk of our fellow citizens are waiting for us to organize, guide, and lead them in order to serve them better."[56]

But while La Rocque intimated that a wide-ranging purge of the current system inspired by the Croix de Feu was both necessary and imminent, he also sought to ensure that his followers appeared orderly and remained under his control. He warned them to avoid provocation, even as he kept them in a state of anticipation: "let us remain clear-headed, in full mastery of ourselves, above the decay of the parties; the time is coming when we will be the arbiters." Such caution reflected concerns about image but also an awareness that the government might take action. Indeed, in the closing days of Doumergue's administration La Rocque had been directly warned by Minister of the Interior Paul Marchandeau about disturbing public order. He even demanded the Croix de Feu leader wait to hold a demonstration in support of Doumergue until after the latter had resigned, insisting that to do so beforehand would inflame opinion dangerously. When Flandin succeeded Doumergue and bruited the idea of legislation to regulate public meetings, La Rocque surmised that the dissolution of the Croix de Feu was a possibility. Publicly he mocked the idea, boasting that the league would simply reform under another name, perhaps the "Pêcheurs à la Ligne." Tellingly, however, a January 1935 internal circular instructed that "if a government commits the folly of dissolving us, our comrades should remain calm. Every precaution has been taken [to ensure] that nothing checks our movement." During the winter of 1935 the league was less boisterous than it had been over the preceding months, with La Rocque stressing the need to minimize clashes.[57]

Yet demands within the ranks for an activist policy remained intense, and La Rocque could not ignore them. Fissures opened in some sections; in Senlis, in the northeastern department of the Oise, one faction of the local membership was convinced that they had to be cautious, but others were frustrated by inactivity. Talk within the movement of inertia on La Rocque's part grew; there were even rumours of replacing him with the former president Maurice Genay, who had recently returned from overseas military service.[58] In response, La Rocque continued to show caution while allowing paramilitary displays. Thus, after an attack upon an office of the Socialist newspaper *Le Populaire* in April 1935, he reminded members to avoid "provocations," but soon thereafter massive open-air meetings resumed.[59] La Rocque claimed that these would overawe potential opponents, thereby avoiding conflict with the left; but they also encouraged a mood of belligerence which could take on less disciplined forms once the occasion had ended.

Certainly, events in Algeria bore this pattern out. One of the first big Croix de Feu rallies of the year, held at Oued-Smar outside Algiers in June 1935, involved fifteen thousand supporters and was touted as an example of the orderly and harmonious nature of the movement; orators depicted the event as both "virile and gentle." However, while speakers emphasized that the movement's supporters were "neither conspirators nor fascists," they were clearly tantalized at the prospect that the movement could form "a sort of Committee of Public Safety to wrest France from the hands of politicians." The prefect regarded La Rocque's threats to unleash the Croix de Feu if he deemed it necessary as most disturbing.[60] Furthermore, although the Oued-Smar parade ended peacefully, many local militants did not take this outcome as indicating how to behave in other situations. In Algerian cities and towns Croix de Feu sections became increasingly aggressive. While there were certainly occasions where their opponents struck first, officials reported numerous instances of incitement on the league's part, such as when supporters in Affreville cajoled Muslims to cry "Down with the Jews!" in the town market and menaced the mechanic of a train arriving from Oran for responding to their cries of "Vive La Rocque" with a Communist salute.[61]

A framework was thus created in which violence was highly probable, notwithstanding assertions that it was not desired. This was the case in France itself as well as in Algeria; events such as the enormous commemoration held for the Battle of the Marne in September 1935, which involved tens of thousands of people and sixteen thousand cars, might themselves avoid violence but could galvanize militants for future, less restrained actions.[62] Fights were especially likely to occur when Croix de Feu members carried out motorized expeditions to working-class areas, which invariably aroused left-wing counter-demonstrations. This reaction occurred, for example, when the league held a meeting in Limoges on 16 November 1935. The local Popular Front contingent, viewing the Croix de Feu members as invading outsiders, organized a protest led by the Socialist mayor. The crowd broke through a police cordon and came face to face with the Croix de Feu security force. Shots were fired; La Rocque subsequently claimed that it was the demonstrators who began shooting and that his followers only acted in self-defence. Yet it appears members of the league did use firearms. No one died, but over a dozen Croix de Feu members were injured, with similar casualties on the opposing side.[63]

By this time a substantial element of French public opinion, extending beyond the Communists and the Socialists, saw the right-wing leagues as a threat to public order. The Radical party, shocked by attacks on some of its members – Pierre Cot had acid thrown in his face by an Action Française supporter – began urging Laval to dissolve them.[64] After the episode in Limoges, Laval came under additional pressure and was accused of colluding with the leagues. His response, according to the US embassy, was to concentrate large numbers of *gardes mobiles* and troops, many of them North African, around Paris in the fear that elements of the army sympathized with the leagues and the belief that such troops would be more obedient. Moreover, La Rocque was reportedly warned that "his arrest will be ordered immediately if there is any move on the part of the Croix de Feu."[65]

Publicly, La Rocque was furious at the suggestion that Laval might dissolve the movement. In an open letter on 22 October he had already boasted that such a measure was "morally impossible" in light of the strong support the Croix de Feu enjoyed across the country.[66] Yet according to an informer for the American embassy, he did not intend to resist arrest if the police acted, and he had taken measures to ensure his movement's survival. These included appointing a successor whose identity was secret, though the ambassador reported, "I am in a position to say that ... a very important part would certainly be played by General Weygand."[67] At the same time the Croix de Feu sought to bolster its image as a promoter of national harmony by trying to shift the blame for the violence onto the left. *Le Flambeau* emphasized how Croix de Feu and Volontaires Nationaux supporters had suffered assaults at the hands of Popular Front militants, prominently displaying their portraits. In December 1935 the movement published a special magazine entitled *La Dissolution des Croix de Feu?* which contrasted its "disciplined" supporters with their violent foes. The magazine also highlighted the organization's social work initiatives, accompanied by pictures of children in soup kitchens. La Rocque may have hoped that such an emphasis upon social action would encourage benevolence on the part of the authorities.[68]

Most strikingly, on 6 December the right-wing deputy Jean Ybarnégaray, with La Rocque's approval, offered a mutual disarmament pact to the left on behalf of the nationalists, though without admitting that the members of the right-wing leagues were actually armed. The supporters of the Popular Front accepted, and the Chamber of Deputies applauded the avoidance of further conflict. However, the legislation that was passed as a result of this agreement went further than Ybarnégaray had intended, since it empowered the government to ban organizations it deemed to be a threat to public order.[69] Though no dissolutions were carried out yet, a legal framework was now in place. For its part, the Croix de Feu had curtailed its mass mobilizations.

It is surely the case that the Croix de Feu dispensed with paramilitarism partly because the attendant violence threatened its image as force for order.[70] But La Rocque's options were also limited at this juncture by his awareness that the Croix de Feu might be dissolved. In response, he and his colleagues had been creative, trying to shift responsibility onto their foes and suggest that it was misguided to ban a movement which sought to encourage social harmony. There is evidence to suggest that Ybarnégaray's "gesture" was a part of this process. An American attaché reported a conversation with a retired French general in which the latter explained that the offer of mutual disarmament was made in the hope it "would enrage the left, place his [La Rocque's] party in the position of making a generous offer and being refused, and might even precipitate a crisis. In offering the olive branch to the left he felt he was making a master stroke. To his complete amazement and dismay, the left accepted his offer with enthusiasm, removed the immediate danger of a crisis, and placed the colonel in a ridiculous position."[71] While more evidence to corroborate this account would be helpful, it conforms with the Croix de Feu's efforts to depict its foes as sectarian and itself as the source of French reconciliation.

Various elements of the far right saw the offer of disarmament as a disastrous move; the Solidarité Française and Action Française denounced Ybarnégaray and La Rocque for assuming they could speak for all nationalists. There was unrest among Croix de Feu supporters as well. While some members such as the Abbé Ritz in the Moselle presented Ybarnégaray's act as magnanimous, in Saint-Quentin Croix de Feu members attended an Action Française meeting where they heard Maxim Real del Sarte, head of the Camelots du Roi, attack La Rocque's "futile" tactics. He argued that the Croix de Feu had crippled the only organizations which stood between France and the Popular Front.[72] Still, while some of the consequences of the disarmament offer were negative, given the fact that the Croix de Feu's image was tarnished and that it faced a possible dissolution, the pact seemed a plausible way out. If the supporters of the Popular Front had rejected Ybarnégaray's offer, the Croix de Feu's claims to be selfless patriots would have been enhanced at a critical point. Conservative newspapers such as *Le Temps*, for example, had praised Ybarnégaray for offering a constructive solution to a serious problem.[73]

THE ELECTIONS OF 1936

As the Croix de Feu came to grips with the pitfalls of its paramilitary strategy in the fall of 1935, La Rocque and his supporters considered other ways of asserting the league's presence in civil society. Realizing that the upcoming national elections were crucial, La Rocque pondered whether to transform the Croix de Feu into a political party. For the time being he decided not to, instead emphasizing the need to reorganize its ancillary organizations, use the election campaign to make its views more widely known, and encourage a united opposition to the Popular Front. In the short term this strategy was a failure; the league's impact on the elections was unclear and the Popular Front emerged victorious; the new government of Léon Blum quickly moved to dissolve the Croix de Feu. But in the interim the league had spread its message to an ever-larger audience, and La Rocque and his followers were ready for further confrontation.

In late 1935, as controversy over the Croix de Feu's paramilitarism raged, the movement's structure was revamped both to attract new supporters and to deflect criticisms and potential repression. That November the Mouvement Social Français des Croix de Feu (MSF) was established. As with the Regroupement of 1933, this formation was open to non-veterans, men and women alike; but unlike the Regroupement, it was to act as an umbrella for the various Croix de Feu organizations. As its title suggests, the MSF was created to demonstrate the "social" orientation of the league. La Rocque insisted it be established as quickly as possible and reprimanded section heads who, perhaps hoping for more dramatic operations, temporized.[74] No doubt he also hoped its creation might dissuade any government from dissolving the Croix de Feu. Outlawing a movement oriented towards social action would be more contentious than banning one conflated with avowed enemies of the regime such as the Action Française.[75]

Care was also taken to reassure the public that the league's intentions were not menacing. In an interview published in *Le Journal* in late November 1935, which was subsequently distributed as a broadsheet, La Rocque stressed that while the Croix de Feu rejected "the current degeneracy of parliamentarism," it did not wish to put an end to it. "It is necessary," he added, "that, *not wanting to change our country radically, but rather to reconcile it and reconstruct its framework*, we absolutely must not begin by introducing revolution, not even in terms of appearance." Other propaganda sheets firmly denied that the Croix de Feu had fascist goals, claiming, "LIBERTY IS TOO PRECIOUS for us not to defend it with all of our strength."[76] Public gatherings of the league now projected a softer, familial image; for the Joan of Arc parade of 1936, members were urged to bring their children.[77]

The MSF quickly moved to broaden its support. Leaflets and recruiting posters targeted specific groups while promising all a secure and patriotic future under the league's tutelage and making clear its intense hostility to the Popular Front and the current political system. Women were told that the MSF would protect their families and homes and provide them with the chance to contribute to national renewal through social service, since the war had deprived so many of them of the opportunity for motherhood. The message to those thrown out of work by the Depression was that "you will only win your just demands through order. Frenchmen, you will renounce the insolent tutelage of barbarous Asia." Shopkeepers were informed of how their innate good sense told them that the party system was not working and that the Croix de Feu's members were "the most qualified representatives of all classes and professions." Peasants were prompted to remember their wartime sacrifices and subsequent mistreatment by a "degenerate" parliamentarism.[78]

The Croix de Feu also took an increasing interest in elections, despite the objections of some militants. A precedent had already been set in 1932 for the movement to mobilize support for selected candidates. But its impact at the time had been unclear, and thereafter – for instance, in the cantonal elections of October 1934 – its involvement appears to have been limited. The situation began to change with the May 1935 municipal elections. These featured growing cooperation on the part of the left, and the Croix de Feu decided that it must respond. Section heads made the association's preferences known, and members were also permitted to run, though only as individuals who did not occupy leadership positions in the organization. The overall impact of the Croix de Feu upon these elections does not appear to have been dramatic, but there were signs of growing political engagement. This was particularly the case in Algeria, where some candidates were regarded by the authorities as Croix de Feu representatives in all but name.[79]

At the end of 1935 La Rocque went so far as to float the idea of running candidates in the 1936 national elections in *Le Flambeau*, denying that such a change of course would cause the movement to lose its cohesion, as some feared. He also weighed the pros and cons of electoral participation in a revealing internal circular.[80] Here La Rocque noted that the Italian Fascists and German Nazis had long realized that violence alone could not win them power; participation in elections was also necessary. "Hitlerism became a preponderant political force only on the day when, in 1929 [*sic*], it had 107 of its members enter the Reichstag." Fighting elections, he argued, would allow the Croix de Feu to extend the reach of its propaganda. It would also be able to intercede in "ministerial crises" and thus shape political life more directly. Finally, participation in elections and the presence of a Croix de Feu group in the Chamber would mollify the substantial segment of the French public that regarded the league as "seditious and violent" and attract new members by normalizing its presence in French political life.

But while La Rocque came close to adopting this strategy, suggesting that the creation of the MSF could facilitate a transition to party politics, for the time being he decided against it.[81] For one thing, he was concerned that if it did contest elections the Croix de Feu would lose its ability to present itself as being above narrow, sectional interests. Further, the fact that most of its representatives would come from the right would undermine its distinctiveness: "the difficulty would then consist in finding an original parliamentary position for the Croix de Feu group. It must not allow itself to be classified in the ranks of the old right. It must avoid a systematic opposition just as well as an exclusively conservative attitude. It must find a new parliamentary method of action and develop a sufficiently strong and appealing doctrine in order to withstand daily comparison with those of other parties." Turning to short-term issues, La Rocque added that there would not be enough time to secure a large number of good candidates; moreover, the fact that French elections were run on the principle of the *scrutin d'arrondissement*, involving two ballots and thus necessitating alliances, would make it all the more difficult to break through. Though running a small number of candidates in 1936 might be possible, such an approach would not befit a mass movement that claimed to embody the national mystique; "the Croix de Feu must only try their chance on the whole electoral chessboard when it is quasi-certain that they will elect at least 80 to 100 of their fellows."

Since current circumstances made this condition unlikely, La Rocque decided that the movement would instead support candidates "imbued with the Croix de Feu spirit, whether or not they are members of the association." While these men would run under their traditional political labels, after the elections they would hopefully create a Croix de Feu inter-group to support the league in the Chamber of Deputies. The movement, La Rocque declared, should also prepare a manifesto to be "circulated as widely as possible" during the campaign in which it proclaimed that it wished to rid universal suffrage of "the 'combinations' and sordid struggles which degrade and demean it." Finally, he concluded that during the campaign members must "intensify their propaganda, and reach the working-class milieu by accentuating the social character of their doctrine, as well as their animosity towards huge economic and financial feudalisms."

For some scholars, this document illustrates how La Rocque was inexorably placing the Croix de Feu on an electoral path and was determined to make it more palatable to mainstream opinion. This interpretation overlooks the fact that for the time being La Rocque opted *against* moving into electoral politics. Furthermore, as Passmore points out, his references to Hitler and Mussolini suggest that La Rocque's attitude towards electioneering was anything but orthodox. Instead, he envisioned a surge onto the parliamentary scene akin to one of the league's mass demonstrations.[82] The document also displays considerable cynicism. In it La Rocque stresses the need for the Croix de

Feu to avoid the appearance of being excessively right-wing or desirous of doing away with the parliamentary system. But at the same time he is aware that the movement was firmly on the right, notwithstanding its public proclamations. Finally, there is nothing to indicate that La Rocque believed that the Croix de Feu should modify the core of its anti-parliamentary, exclusionary, and socially paternalist doctrine in any meaningful way.

The course of action pursued by the Croix de Feu during the 1936 election campaign conformed substantially to the scenario outlined in La Rocque's memorandum. The league engaged in extensive propaganda, striving to stake out a distinct position on the political landscape. Three million copies of a manifesto entitled *Pour le peuple, Par le peuple*, published as a supplement to *Le Flambeau*, were eventually circulated. It forcefully affirmed that the Croix de Feu was open to every patriot: "Devoted solely to the general interest, uniting men of all tendencies and origins, the Croix de Feu are truly designated as guides, as arbiters." Unlike the right, which was afraid of any change, or the left, which conspired with the Soviet Union, it combined an intense nationalism with a genuine desire for social reform. Inspired by "the cult of tradition," concerned only for "the future of our children," the Croix de Feu sought to reconcile all good citizens and create a "new order," characterized by *la profession organisée*, the protection of the family, and spiritual values.[83]

As La Rocque desired, the manifesto differentiated the Croix de Feu from conventional right-wing parties by emphasizing its "social" character. It contained sharp criticisms of traditional conservatives and proposed reforms such as retirement provisions to reduce youth unemployment. Mischievously, the satirical *Le Canard enchaîné* quipped that if La Rocque was to follow his ideas to their logical conclusion, he would have the Croix de Feu join the Popular Front.[84] In political terms, too, the league emphasized that its goal was unique. For instance, while both it and the Fédération Républicaine opposed the left, the latter party accentuated the polarization of France into two "implacably opposed" sides. In contrast, the Croix de Feu claimed, however implausibly, to transcend this struggle. Other anti–Popular Front parties such as the Catholic Parti Démocrate Populaire (PDP) and the centre-right Alliance Démocratique also professed to reject the "two blocs" but did so by appealing to the Radicals, warning them that they were incompatible with the Marxist parties and urging them to adopt a policy of concentration, meaning cooperation with the centre-right parties.[84] However, to La Rocque and his supporters this argument smacked of old-style politics, rather than the Croix de Feu's call to submerge all differences for the sake of the nation.

For all its insistence upon eliding old divisions, the manifesto also made clear that the Croix de Feu's most intense hostility was directed towards the left and that it envisioned a far-reaching break with the institutions of the Third Republic. Attacking the Popular Front, it concluded that "the Marxist leaders, among whom the Socialists represent hypocrisy and the Communists cynicism, dare to speak to you of family and reconciliation ... [while] from their gatherings arise blasphemies against religions, obscenities, and clamours of death. Their masters in the USSR have legalized abortion, broken paternal and maternal authority, and killed or caused the death of a million *muzhiks*." The Croix de Feu held that for opponents of this ilk no quarter could be given. Its demand for the "severe punishment" of all groups who opposed "military or civic duty" or "loyalty with respect to the country or institutions" suggested that the France which La Rocque and his followers envisioned would be characterized by intolerance. Their "renovated" nation would also reject the legacy of the Third Republic, which the manifesto claimed was founded upon an sterile compromise of old-fashioned conservatives and Radicals.[86] And while *Pour le peuple* stated that, in contrast to Nazi Germany and Fascist Italy, France had an "individualist" tradition which precluded a servile copying of those countries' practices, its demand that all citizens surrender their "partisan" interests was disturbing.

In addition to the manifesto, La Rocque wrote a series of articles making recommendations to both voters and electoral candidates. The voters were called upon to rally against Bolshevism. As for the candidates, La Rocque believed most of them should be younger men, since the energy of the more youthful extreme left in comparison to their right-wing counterparts was glaring. He thus urged his followers to eliminate "with deference and firmness the coterie of old-timers from the gates of the Palais-Bourbon." He also bemoaned the corrupting use of money in the elections, especially from foreign sources. The only solution to such problems would be a "great purifying wind." Predictably, he concluded that his supporters' triumph was imminent but added that in the meantime, "if the Croix de Feu Movement's intervention in the electoral campaign is confined to giving it a little honesty, order, and conscientiousness, what a change that would already be in national life!"[87]

When the actual balloting began, Croix de Feu members were instructed to be restrained. They were ordered not to act as bodyguards for candidates whom they supported, and the wearing of insignia was banned during the elections for fear that elements of the press might exploit it. A substantial number of militants ostentatiously poured their efforts into social work at this time.[88] Nevertheless, when it came to the voting choices of the rank and file, there was some cause for concern. The leadership was worried that some traditional conservatives would be so unpalatable to local Croix de Feu militants that a Popular Front candidate might receive their votes instead. There was also an awareness that in some cases a candidate might be scuppered by being too closely associated with the league and thus rendered unpalatable to a wider range of voters. Balancing acts were thus necessary; while local cadres were constantly reminded that their duty was to stop the Popular Front, they were also informed that they "must at the same time work in a spirit of independence, sang-froid, self-sacrifice, and tact."[89]

It is difficult to determine precisely the extent to which members followed their voting instructions and how much of a difference the Croix de Feu's intervention made. In some areas the scenario unfolded as La Rocque and his colleagues had directed. In the northeastern departments of the Aisne and Oise, for instance, supporters rallied to their respective candidates. To the south, in the Gard, the police surmised that most militants voted as instructed, though they believed that many would have supported the same candidate anyway.[90] In some cases it seems the league held the balance of power. After his re-election Henri de Kerillis informed the Fédération Républicaine leader Louis Marin, "I am in large measure a candidate of the Croix de Feu."[91] In Paris's 6th arrondissement Weidemann-Goiron, the candidate endorsed by the league, beat the conservative incumbent Duval-Arnould. The latter was a member of the Croix de Feu but was deemed by the local section to have been in office too long; the decision to oppose him aroused the ire of Xavier Vallat and the Action Française. In the department of Constantine in Algeria the Croix de Feu was compelled to reverse course but still had a major impact upon the campaign. Here the league had initially supported a challenger against the conservative incumbent, Paul Morinaud. But after its candidate floundered, the Croix de Feu decided it had to block the left by supporting Morinaud, despite the fact that its members regarded him as the epitome of an opportunistic old-time parliamentarian. Tellingly, the movement's support was given on the condition that Morinaud campaign on a more intensely nationalist and antisemitic platform.[92]

But Croix de Feu supporters were not uniform in their views; nor were they always obedient. In Sète, in the southern department of the Hérault, the section was given a candidate to vote for, but the subprefect doubted this directive would be universally followed. In Senlis in the Oise twenty-five members were eventually brought before a disciplinary meeting for not voting as they had been instructed, and four were subsequently expelled.[93] Similarly, some Croix de Feu members were upset at being directed to vote for Paul Reynaud and were tempted to support his rival, Dailly, who also had the backing of the Action Française. There were even rumours – vehemently denied by La Rocque – that a few had voted for the Communist candidate instead.[94] Clearly, there was a volatility that the league's cadres could not always channel.

When it was all over, the Popular Front coalition reaped the rewards of superior electoral cooperation, even though its total share of the vote was only slightly higher than what the left had achieved four years earlier. While La Rocque tried to claim success by asserting that 121 deputies owed their seats to the support of the Croix de Feu, he soon found that if that had indeed been the case, most of them were not especially grateful. His hopes of a substantial Croix de Feu group in the Chamber were not realized; only 8 deputies elected in 1936 eventually joined what would become the PSF's parliamentary caucus. Another 47 joined the Comité de Sympathie pour le PSF et de Défense des Libertés Républicaines, but it met only once.[95]

SIGNIFICANCE

The Croix de Feu's members were embittered by the victory of the Popular Front. One report of a meeting held in Paris's 18th arrondissement noted that "after the results were proclaimed for a moment one could think that the Croix de Feu's members would be targeting Popular Front demonstrators but Pillot, the newly elected deputy, advised his supporters to go home, which they did." This episode was emblematic of the movement's response; while the authorities worried there would be violence, the majority of supporters were convinced this would not work. For his part, La Rocque oscillated between berating conservative politicians for handing victory to their opponents, accusing the Popular Front of appropriating the Croix de Feu's social agenda, and proclaiming imminent revolution while also promising that it would be defeated. But for the time being he counselled his followers to maintain their composure. Section heads were instructed that "the people want to try the Popular Front experiment." It was better to let disillusionment set in – which the movement insisted would happen soon – and capitalize upon it. Physical opposition would only produce revulsion against the Croix de Feu, especially on the part of the working class, and strengthen support for the new government.[96]

When Léon Blum assumed office in June 1936 as France's first Socialist prime minister and his government announced the dissolution of the leagues on the 18th of that month, worries about mass resistance resurfaced and the Croix de Feu's activities were carefully monitored. The league tried to argue that the decrees affected only the Mouvement Social, as opposed to the Croix de Feu's component organizations, but the government brushed these objections aside, asserting that its intentions were to dissolve the movement completely. At the local level there were some incidents: in Saint-Quentin a "Cercle Lyautey" was established as a cover for Croix de Feu members, while in Pontoise in the Seine-et-Oise several members defiantly continued to wear their insignia. But there was little in the way of mass upheaval; for the time being the streets belonged to the supporters of the Popular Front. The day after the dissolution was announced, La Rocque called upon supporters to show the tricolour in response to displays of the red flag. Yet in Paris, aside from the districts surrounding the Sorbonne, relatively few flags appeared.[97]

A number of La Roque's colleagues, believing he had been excessively cautious, now grew so frustrated that they broke with the movement. Pozzo di Borgo's resignation was the most theatrical. At the final meeting of the Croix de Feu's administrative council on 25 June, he accused La Rocque of ignoring his colleagues' input, which had led to the movement's lack of firmness in the current crisis. He then refused to endorse the proposed new course of action: namely, accepting the dissolution and establishing a political party to replace the Croix de Feu. A couple of those who were present meekly seconded Pozzo, but only he decided to quit then and there. One account suggests that Pozzo shook La Rocque's and Ottavi's hands, but then declared, "I wanted to do it [quit] months ago. It was only because of discipline that I did not leave earlier." Within days he was spreading rumours about divisions within the association.[98]

While some of La Rocque's associates charged him with betraying the ideals of the Croix de Feu, other observers concluded that he was simply inept. As early as the summer of 1935 the British ambassador, Sir George Clerk, had decided that the Croix de Feu leader, while a capable organizer, "has no great political or oratorical gifts. If he had, in fact, the driving force and powers of a Mussolini or a Hitler, he might long ago have seized the popular imagination and imposed himself upon the country." Historians such as Eugen Weber concur.[99] But there are grounds for arguing that La Rocque was far from incompetent. While it cannot be said that the movement's strategy in 1936 was a success, the context in which the Croix de Feu operated must be fully considered. As Robert Paxton has pointed out, the interwar crisis of French democracy was attenuated by a number of factors. In comparative terms France's democratic political culture was more deeply rooted than that of, for example, Weimar Germany. The state apparatus also remained generally robust and capable of maintaining order. And while the economic troubles and political deadlock of the 1930s were severe and the response of some of France's elites alarmist and reactionary, the situation was not as dire as that in Germany between 1929 and 1933 or Italy between 1917 and 1922, where extreme nationalist movements took power. Finally, the French left had the experiences of its German and Italian counterparts to draw upon, rendering effective cooperation against the far right more likely.[100]

Under these circumstances the strategy of the Croix de Feu between 1934 and 1936 made considerable sense. With respect to the obstacle of a democratic political culture, the league did not present itself simply as a stalwart foe of a long-established system. Instead, it appealed to those aspects of the evolving republican heritage – such as the *union sacrée*, with its calls to suppress political variations to ensure national survival – which could be dissociated from democracy. As for confronting the state apparatus, La Rocque was constantly reminded of the risks inherent in violence. He thus tried to avoid it as circumstances required, arguing in 1936 that by standing aside rather than being reckless, the Croix de Feu would let the Popular Front discredit itself; popular sympathy would then turn towards the league.[101] While such an approach was decried as timid by other right-wing groups and by some of La Rocque's own followers, the rapid growth of the PSF in subsequent months suggests that it was perceptive. Finally, the Croix de Feu had begun to surmount another obstacle that Paxton has identified as a barrier to the success of the French far right at this time, namely, the lack of a "synthesizer" to unite various strands of protest. The league sought to be all things to all people, claiming that it could represent the interests of workers as well as employers, peasants, and urban shopkeepers.

Yet even as it worked to unite all "true" patriots under its banner, the Croix de Feu angered other elements of the right. It claimed to challenge France's elites; hence the growing emphasis on its social conscience and La Rocque's verbal attacks on "financial interests" and conservative parliamentarians. The significance of all this can be overstated; after all, the Croix de Feu also provided elements of the elite with support, notably in the electoral arena. But established conservatives such as Louis Marin did not forget the ridicule, and the lingering resentment had major consequences after 1936. As for its dealings with the other nationalist leagues, the Croix de Feu did not wish to appear uncooperative, but its members were guided by the firm conviction that they were destined to lead the right, an attitude that naturally furthered the potential for conflict with other movements. The problem would intensify after the creation of the PSF, culminating in a bitter internecine feud.

Despite these problems, the Croix de Feu's political strategy as a whole represented a concerted effort to prevail against the obstructions that the social and political characteristics of interwar France presented to any ultra-nationalist opponent of democracy. And the league was, denials notwithstanding, indisputably anti-democratic. Its abiding hostility to the parliamentary system and its belief that political pluralism should give way to a rigid conception of national solidarity make it highly probable that La Rocque and his colleagues, given the opportunity, would have established an authoritarian regime. The supporters of the Popular Front were right to be worried.

On this point, it is true that the Croix de Feu provided an important target which helped to ensure the unity and dynamism of the Popular Front coalition. Noting an occasion when La Rocque failed to show up at a meeting where leftist activists had intended to demonstrate, one former Popular Front supporter likened the experience to "a football team whose adversary has scratched."[102] It is also true that the highly charged political atmosphere led to false accusations. Left-wing papers such as *L'Oeuvre* and *L'Humanité* raised charges about the storing of weapons by Croix de Feu militants, though subsequent police investigations would conclude that these were groundless.[103] But the Croix de Feu was not above such actions either; in 1936 La Rocque circulated "plans" documenting a purported Communist insurrection.[104]

Caution must also be exercised in assessing the Popular Front's dissolution of the Croix de Feu after Léon Blum took power. Nobécourt has criticized the dissolution as an arbitrary action not in keeping with Blum's characteristic respect for legality.[105] But it must be remembered that the new government did accept the creation of the PSF and other parties descended from the leagues, even though it was intensely suspicious of them. Would La Rocque, had he held power, have permitted the Communists or the Socialists such leeway? The severe punishments for groups deemed subversive of public order promised in the Croix de Feu's 1936 manifesto suggest otherwise.[106]

Yet although the Popular Front was correct in its belief that the Croix de Feu posed a serious threat to French democracy, its characterization of the movement as "fascist" was – and remains – contentious. Before we take up this problem, however, it is first necessary to explore the league's evolving social base and its efforts to articulate a coherent institutional, social, and cultural network for its supporters. Only by having a fuller appreciation of the outlook and aspirations of the Croix de Feu's militants as well as its leaders and by undertaking a more detailed comparative analysis can the issue of classification be properly addressed.

3

La Famille Croix de Feu

On the eve of its dissolution in 1936, the Croix de Feu had perhaps 500,000 members. Around its core membership of veterans had gathered thousands of new supporters. In crucial respects the movement's growth was reminiscent of those of other ultra-nationalist movements that arose in Europe between the wars. Like the Nazis and the Italian Fascists, the Croix de Feu thrived in a time of crisis, attracting support on the basis of promises that it would counter a revolutionary threat and replace a deadlocked political system. Sociologically, the result was a movement that drew upon a wide range of groups for support but especially from those of lower-middle-class or higher social standing.

But while the Croix de Feu can be understood as a vehicle of social defence or even reaction, its appeal was not solely negative. It articulated a "positive" vision of an all-encompassing nationalism that would reinvigorate the country with the virtues that had ensured the triumph of 1918. A France governed by its principles would be bereft of social conflict and wasteful political bickering, and instead would feature rule by the competent and the selfless, who would oversee the re-emergence of a harmonious, patriotic country. As we have seen, the league professed to transcend political, religious, and class divisions, and while the realities of its support base belie these claims to an extent, the range of its appeal was still impressive. It united many adherents of various right-wing leagues under its banner, who were joined by disaffected conservatives and people who were new to politics or had previously inclined towards more moderate options.

One particular feature of the Croix de Feu that was attractive to many supporters was the intense associational life it offered. Within a variety of ancillary groups, militants could find practical support but also a more general sense of camaraderie. And while men of various ages dominated the movement, it steadily developed a more familial image. It sought both to mobilize French women and also to assert the importance of distinct gender roles and devoted considerable energies to imbuing youth with its values. More generally, for men, women, and children alike, the Croix de Feu tried to encourage a specific loyalty to its principles by associating these with mainstream patriotic symbols and values. In ideological terms the result was to promote a vision of national renewal which was comparable to, but also distinct in some ways from, what either Hitler or Mussolini sought. That said, in light of the fact that La Rocque and his supporters viewed themselves as prefiguring the ideal France, the scope of their ambitions should not be minimized.

THE SOCIAL BASES OF THE CROIX DE FEU

Gauging the growth of the Croix de Feu is challenging. Evidence is fragmentary and sometimes suspect. The movement itself was inclined to exaggerate the size of its following, and the provenance of official information is sometimes unclear. Estimates are contradictory for some regions and lacking for others. Determining sociological composition is complicated by the fact that the Croix de Feu was eager to demonstrate that it enjoyed support from the less-well-off. Police and prefectoral reports often provide information on the background of the leadership, but are more impressionistic when it comes to ordinary militants.[1] Nevertheless, table 2 provides a partial listing drawn from a variety of sources.

Assessing the total membership for the period 1934–36 remains contentious. La Rocque claimed that the movement had 300,000 members in January 1935, that a year later it had 700,000, and that by the time of the April 1936 elections the total stood at 1 million. Nobécourt suggests that these figures cannot be dismissed and notes that La Rocque claimed only 600,000 out of the 1 million members were voters.[2] Most sources are considerably more cautious, yet even when they revise figures downwards, it is clear the Croix de Feu experienced tremendous growth, outstripping all of its rivals. In February 1935 the police estimated the total membership (excluding those under sixteen) at 132,500, with another 80,000 applications being processed. That this information was derived from another of La Rocque's own pronouncements – even though he had previously suggested the total was much

Table 2
Estimated Croix de Feu membership by department, 1934–36

Department	Date of source	Estimated membership
Algiers	December 1933	2,500
	July 1935	8,440
	June 1936	15,000
Aube	June 1936	3,000
Aisne	April 1935	1,000
	April 1936	3,350
Bouches-du-Rhône	1932	700
	December 1934	3,000
	December 1935	12,000
	April 1936	15–20,000
Constantine	December 1933	2,000
	July 1935	3,000
	June 1936	7,000
Côte d'Or	June 1935	1,250
	April 1936	4,000
Finistère	June 1934	400
	May 1935	1,000
	April 1936	2,650
Gard	May 1934	350
	June/July 1935	1,200
	April 1936	1,500
Gironde	Summer 1934	1,200
Hérault	March 1934	400
	April/May 1936	4,000
Nord	December 1935	15–20,000
Oran	December 1933	1,500
	July 1935	2,520
	June 1936	6,000
Rhône	1932	300
	June 1936	6,000
Seine-et-Oise	December 1935	11,450
	April 1936	21,750

SOURCES: Ferragu, "Croix de Feu et le PSF en Indre-et-Loire"; Florin, "Des Croix de Feu au PSF"; Howlett, "Croix de Feu"; Jankowksi, *Communism and Collaboration*; Lefebvre, ed., *Laon 1936*; Nobécourt, *Colonel de La Rocque*; Passmore, *From Liberalism to Fascism*; Prévosto, "La Fédération du Nord"; APP "Ligues/Croix de Feu," dossier, April 1936; AN F7 13241; AN F7 13033; AD Aube 110J 10; AD Gard 1M 715; AD Hérault 1M 1118; AD Loire-Atlantique 1M 470; AD Yvelines 4M2 66; *Les Croix de Feu de Rouen et de Normandie*, 15 June 1935.

greater – demonstrates the extent to which contradictory information was being promulgated. Still, it does seem that by the summer of 1935 membership had passed the 200,000 mark. In June the American embassy reported estimates of 200–230,000, based on Croix de Feu and Action Française sources.[3] Judging from the rate of growth in 1935–36 – in many departments membership doubled – a figure of 500,000 by the spring of 1936 seems plausible.[4]

The data also show that the geographical distribution of the Croix de Feu was uneven. It was primarily an urban movement. Paris was a bastion, with possibly over 100,000 members by June 1936. The league also established a substantial presence in other major cities such as Lille, Lyons, and Marseilles. In general, growth was more robust in northern areas, where Catholic observance and right-wing voting was stronger. By the summer of 1935 over 10 per cent of the league's membership came from Normandy, while in departments such as the Nord and the Eure, expansion was steady.[5] Algeria, too, provided a substantial number of recruits, with roughly 14,000 members in the summer of 1935 and double that number a year later. In fact, the movement's executive committee was restructured to take the increased Algerian membership into account.[6] On the other hand, with their left-wing traditions, parts of the south tended to be less hospitable. In Alès (Gard) the Croix de Feu's bulletin attributed the slow development of the local section to the fact that the city was predominantly "red." By contrast, in the Alpes-Maritimes, a department with a tradition of more conservative politics, there were fewer difficulties.[7]

If we remain at the level of broad generalizations, in terms of age and gender, the typical Croix de Feu supporter was male and fairly young. While the proportion of women in the movement increased substantially after the creation of the Section Féminine in 1934, they continued to be distinctly in the minority. When the police estimated that the league had 132,500 members in February 1935, the Regroupement, the umbrella organization for supporters other than Croix de Feu or Volontaires Nationaux, accounted for only 30,000 people in that total, not all of whom were women.[8] With respect to age, data provided on Croix de Feu supporters by several prefectures suggests most were born after 1890. This profile was altered somewhat by the rapid growth of the Volontaires Nationaux, which attracted younger men and had some 33,000 supporters in the Paris region by early 1935, compared to 65,900 Croix de Feu members.[9]

Evidence concerning the social status of Croix de Feu members is limited, but for 1934–36 the trends that emerge indicate substantial support from a spectrum ranging from the well-off to the lower middle classes, with an under-representation of the working class and peasantry. The movement's cadres – section presidents and delegates charged with various tasks – often consisted of professionals and businessmen of various sorts. In the Aisne the occupations of eight section presidents are known: one tax inspector, one industrialist, one butcher, two architects, two entrepreneurs, and a commandant in the army reserve (two others were also reserve officers). Two were eventually replaced, one by a farmer and former military aviator and another by a funeral monuments dealer. In the Hérault the section leaders in the cities of Montpellier, Sète, and Béziers were a restaurateur, a doctor, and a dealer in enclosures and hedges. The first two were later replaced, one by a professor at Montpellier's medical faculty and the other by a business employee.[10] In the Drôme and the Aube, industrialists took the initiative in starting up sections, though in both cases they initially found it difficult to develop a mass base.[11]

The composition of the general membership, as far as it can be discerned, was similar. In the spring of 1934, for example, the majority of the 350 members in Nîmes were "bankers, merchants, industrialists, and urban property-owners, most of them [former] front-line officers and non-commissioned officers." By July 1935 recruitment was still taking place among those "of a middling or above social station," although there were efforts directed towards the "'worker' milieu, whose members are currently very small in number."[12] There were exceptions; in Algeria, artisans and workers were more prominent, comprising 40 out of a sample of 116 in Djidjelli. But in Algeria the non-European population was employed in the most menial tasks, and the social status of all Europeans was relatively higher. Moreover, the largest single group in the Djidjelli sample was still white-collar workers, with a total of 37 individuals.[13] Other evidence from France itself affirms the prevalence of the lower middle and middle classes. Milza states that in mid–1934, 41 per cent of Croix de Feu membership was from the middle classes, with 25 per cent from the bourgeoisie and high-level cadres and 28 per cent from technicians, office employees, and other workers in the tertiary sector.[14] These figures suggest that emergent social groups – technicians, white-collar workers, office managers – had a substantial role to play in the league.[15] But they coexisted with more traditional elements, whether landowners in the Loire-Inférieure or hat-making industrialists in the Aube.

The Croix de Feu worked ceaselessly to widen its support. As early as 1934 its propaganda targeted the peasantry; the following year La Rocque and his colleagues intensified their efforts, publishing pamphlets and articles in *Le Flambeau* in response to the Depression, which was ravaging the countryside.[16] This push achieved only limited results. In June 1935 La Rocque claimed that 40 per cent of those who had joined since November 1934 belonged to the rural population. But it has been estimated that by June 1936 no more than 10 per cent of the membership was rural, and the scene at the local level suggests that even this figure is optimistic.[17] In the Hérault the Croix de Feu remained overwhelmingly urban into 1936, though the prefect believed that "small groups of five to twenty [persons] in the small communes must be taken into account."[18] In the Aisne the league focused its propaganda on the rural population in 1935 and 1936, but the results were steady rather than spectacular. One possible reason is that peasants were instead rallying to Henry Dorgères's Greenshirts, whose membership in northern and western France peaked at this time.[19]

Even when the Croix de Feu did achieve some success in the countryside, new members were not, it seems, always acting on their own volition. In Senlis (Oise) Jean Wattebled, a twenty-four-year-old farmer-proprietor, encouraged landowners to enrol their agricultural labourers in the movement; about 40 were signed up in such a manner in May and June 1935. Many of these individuals likely joined out of fear of losing their jobs and were unenthusiastic. In Algeria, too, Croix de Feu landowners mobilized those who worked for them for their own political ends. In Maadid this action extended to Muslim farmhands, who were "invited" to disrupt the activities of the Popular Front and whip up antisemitism.[20]

The story was much the same with the league's appeals to urban workers. Its efforts at reaching out to this group peaked in the winter of 1935–36 through initiatives such as soup kitchens. Meetings increasingly featured a working-class orator who would tell the story of how he had been betrayed by politicians but had found solidarity in the Croix de Feu.[21] These measures achieved some results. The prefect of the Aisne observed that in Saint-Quentin the population, suffering under the burden of high unemployment, "is not unappreciative of the material aid the Croix de Feu provides it," though he believed that the organization could still not be described as "popular." Officials in the

Seine-et-Oise concurred, noting in the spring of 1936 that among the movement's newest supporters "can be found numerous left-wing extremists." But these had signed up only "to find work" and could not be regarded as sincere adherents.[22] Similarly, in the Gard, members of the Section Féminine used their contacts with the wives and families of working-class men to bring pressure to bear on them. In several factories in Compiègne, workers who refused to join the league were dismissed under specious pretexts.[23] No doubt there were workers who were sincerely devoted to the Croix de Feu, but there is no evidence of any other group whose loyalties had to be bought or coerced to such an extent.

At one level, then, the Croix de Feu was a movement of social defence for France's property-owning classes. The efforts made by the organization to enrol agricultural labourers and urban workers indicate a desire to appear as a force for class conciliation and to defuse potential threats from people who might support the Popular Front. But there were other dynamics at work as well; local variations were critical in determining the aggregate profile of the movement. Passmore's study of the Rhône organization, for example, suggests that activists there "must also be placed within the context of the mobilisation of subordinate sections of the right." Small- to medium-scale businessmen who felt marginalized by big firms and managers who yearned for influence played an important role in the local Croix de Feu. So did disaffected peasant proprietors, who were reacting to a breakdown of elite influence.[24]

Thus support for the Croix de Feu can be explained partly in terms of a right-wing mass base frustrated by the preponderance but also the failings of conservative notables. Related to this phenomenon is the correlation, first noticed by Jean-Noël Jeanneney, between high levels of right-wing electoral support, lack of a strong local organization on the part of the Fédération Républicaine, and extensive Croix de Feu implantation in a given department.[25] For instance, in the Eure the Fédération lacked a permanent organization and thirteen Croix de Feu sections had been created by 1936; in the Bas-Rhin the situation was similar, with eleven sections being established before the dissolution. Conversely, the league had less than half a dozen sections in departments where the Fédération was solidly implanted, such as the Loiret-Cher, the Charente, and the Maine-et-Loire.[26] The trend was not universal, though. In the Gironde, the Bouches-du-Rhône, and the Rhône, local Fédération organizers took their job seriously, but the

Croix de Feu still enjoyed considerable support, though as Passmore's study demonstrates, this can also be interpreted as reflecting rank-and-file resentment towards members of the political establishment.

Suggestive as these trends are, however, the Croix de Feu's hostility to traditional elites should not be overstated. The league frequently denounced failures by right-wing governments and parliamentarians, but under the right circumstances – such as the 1936 elections – it would support many of these same figures, even at the risk of alienating some activists. Furthermore, if one adopts a more expansive definition of elites to include local notables who were not necessarily politicians but were in a position to shape opinion, it is clear that such people could be crucial to the fortunes of a particular section. The Croix de Feu often relied upon the support of provincial newspapers to publicize its activities, at least before it could develop its own local press. In Alsace, for example, its anti-Marxism and emphasis on respect for regional traditions won support from Catholic, conservative, and even mainstream papers.[27] The stance adopted by religious authorities could also be very important. In Luçon (Vendée) the Croix de Feu did not enjoy much success, with only 30 members by March 1936. Here the frigid attitude of the local bishop was seen by the authorities as a key reason for its weakness.[28] Militants also had to be careful about whose support they relied upon. In the Saumur, a region of small wine growers, the Croix de Feu's failure to expand was the result of its association with the unpopular Baron de Saivre in the Segréen region.[29]

Finally, more idiosyncratic factors such as the capabilities of the local leadership have to be considered. In the Haute-Vienne the assumption of the section presidency in January 1935 by Pierre Le Tanneur, an engineer, contributed greatly to the growth of the organization there. In the Loire-Inférieure the movement did not strike a chord with public opinion until early 1935, when the president of the Nantes section was replaced. The assumption of the Gard leadership in August 1935 by Dr Marcel Rocher, a veteran of 1914–18 and of France's intervention in the Russian Civil War, associate of the Maison Maternelle du Gard and the Maison de Santé Protestante, and according to one source, "very combative, an enemy of the democratic regime and its institutions," breathed new life into the local Croix de Feu.[30]

Militants reached the movement through a variety of pathways. Affinities with the military were often crucial, though gauging the exact level of support is difficult since many military men who actually joined the league had quit or were retired, and it is hard to assess the role of sympathizers who did not sign up because they were still on active duty. Still, at least twenty general officers, including two admirals, were active in the Croix de Feu by 1935. Prominent active officers such as General Weygand and Marshal Pétain did not hesitate to make clear their public approval of the organization on occasion. Weygand was photographed at a 1935 Croix de Feu tombola with La Rocque, and as we have seen, Pétain praised the league in an interview held a year later. Other, lesser-known senior officers could be found at many local commemorations. The Croix de Feu always recognized the vital importance of these military networks; even when it attempted to widen its popular base, it continued to bolster its veteran core. In 1935, for example, the league actively propagandized among regimental associations. That October La Rocque stressed the continuing need to recruit from the Union Nationale des Combattants, though he cautioned that some of its members found the Croix de Feu too "turbulent."[31]

Other associational networks provided additional sources of recruitment. Many of the Croix de Feu's early cadres evinced a strong commitment to Catholicism. Perhaps the most famous individual whose Catholic background helped to orient him towards the Croix de Feu for a time was future president François Mitterrand. Coming from a religious provincial background, he had moved to Paris to study at the École Libre des Sciences Politiques and joined the Volontaires Nationaux in 1934. In a lecture he gave on the Croix de Feu in 1935 he explained his attraction to the movement in terms of its social concerns as well as its patriotism.[32]

Membership in other ultra-nationalist leagues provided yet another route. Adherents of the Action Française, the Jeunesses Patriotes, and other groups had been joining the Croix de Feu for years, but after 1934 the process intensified. By July 1935, for example, nearly all the roughly 100 members of the Action Française in Constantine had also joined the Croix de Feu, while in Alsace there was substantial overlap between the latter and the Jeunesses Patriotes.[33] Nobécourt argues that this pattern represented an effort at infiltration by the other leagues, who hoped to pressure La Rocque into a more radical course of action. There is some truth in this view; police reports attest to it, and frustrated Croix de Feu section leaders sometimes demanded that their members choose between one association or another.[34] But the situation remained fluid, for many right-wing activists did not see their loyalty as resting with one particular group. One leading Croix de Feu propagandist in the Loire-Inférieure, who was also the director of Saint- Nazaire's Collège Aristide Briand, considered himself a royalist. Yet he told the father of one of his students that France would benefit from having La Rocque as a dictator. Such a lack of regard for doctrinal niceties may help to explain why the overall trend at this time was for the Croix de Feu to pick up support at the expense of its rivals. As the Popular Front expanded and it became clear that the Croix de Feu was its largest opponent, the temptation to merge into one big movement became stronger. In Montpellier in January 1936, for instance, the Croix de Feu absorbed the local Solidarité Française; it is hard to see this as a successful infiltration by the latter.[35]

Not all Croix de Feu supporters came from the far right. Militants endlessly insisted upon the league's ecumenism, to some effect.[36] In the department of the Finistère by the summer of 1934, the league had attracted men "of diverse political tendencies," and the police were convinced that the local cadres should not necessarily be considered "leaders of truly dangerous men." In the Seine-et-Oise the authorities surmised that those individuals who balked at joining the Action Française or the Solidarité Française because they were too extreme would readily do so in the case of the Croix de Feu because it seemed "more democratic."[37]

But while people did join the Croix de Feu for a variety of reasons, an explicit attachment to democratic institutions was not often one of them. The sense of belonging that the group provided was no doubt a strong motivation for many. A commitment to social reform and harmony was likely important for others. And if the league's propaganda – such as a 1935 tract aimed at civil servants – is any indication, then a belief that it would restore a lost sense of status to the lower middle classes also counted for something.[38] But it is noteworthy that a 1967 survey of former militants in the Haute-Vienne suggests the primary motivations for people to join were fear of Communism, disgust with the inefficacy of parliamentary institutions, and the belief that France's decay could only be reversed through unity, firmness, and nationalism. Similarly, in the Seine-et-Oise, where growth was very rapid in 1935-36, one official was convinced that a combination of economic crisis, external dangers, and political paralysis at home had resulted in "a distinct psychological state which has greatly favoured the efforts of the Mouvement Social's militants." Thousands of people in the department were drawn to the Croix de Feu out of fear of the Popular Front, especially the Communists. "For many of the new members of the

Croix de Feu, it is the instinct for social and national preservation which has led them to a party that they consider, under the circumstances, a veritable lifeline."[39]

The need for a profound transformation of France's institutions was also a recurring theme in the speeches of local Croix de Feu orators. While intended to convert audiences, these declamations could also reflect the latter's sentiments as well. A speaker at a meeting in Aix-en-Provence presented his listeners with a stark choice between "Socialo-Communist tyranny" or the establishment of a "fourth republic" founded on the ideals of the Croix de Feu. In the Aisne, prospective members were told about "the intense life of the movement" but also about its aim "to reconstruct the French state by installing an authoritarian republic." In Nantes a speaker called for "a true France, armed, militarized, disciplined." Clearly, while some new members may have been moderates, they were not joining under circumstances that made for moderation.[40] The argument that by seeking wider public support, La Rocque was intent upon moving the Croix de Feu away from extremism is thus problematic.[41] Instead, the league was forging a coalition ranging from veterans of the ultra-nationalist leagues to people who may have voted for traditional conservatives or perhaps even the Radicals in the past, but were now inclined towards harsher political solutions.

It was predictable that a movement with such a diverse support base would experience internal tensions, especially in 1935–36, when paramilitarism was downplayed in favour of propaganda and social work, and later when the Croix de Feu accepted the victory of the Popular Front. In response there was considerable malaise, and a significant number of people quit. On 29 May 1936 the directing committee conceded that it had received about 15,000 letters of resignation, though it quickly added that during the same period 31,584 applications had been received.[42] It has been suggested that impatient extremists were the ones who left at this time, leaving moderates behind. On this point it is clear that some of those who broke with the Croix de Feu, notably Pozzo di Borgo, believed that La Rocque was too passive. But the league certainly did not wish to drive hard-liners away, as developments in the department of the Hérault following Ybarnégaray's December 1935 offer of a truce with the left indicate. In Montpellier, La Rocque publicly appealed to the alienated section president to stick with the movement, though apparently without success.[43] In Sète a split developed between the Croix de Feu and the Volontaires

Nationaux, with the latter wishing to continue paramilitary mobilizations and the former wanting to obey La Rocque's orders that these be curtailed. The response of headquarters in Paris was not to encourage either group in particular; instead, it tried to maintain control over both by placing them under a single executive.[44]

There were also local leaders with a reputation for belligerence who nevertheless stuck with the organization despite the criticisms of La Rocque. In Marseilles, Jacques Arnoult's threats about a coming seizure of power by the Croix de Feu were so inflammatory that on one occasion La Rocque felt obliged to explain them away. When Arnoult instructed his section members how to vote in the 1936 elections, he stated that they would never need to engage in such an act again. Yet his obvious contempt for parliamentary institutions did not prevent him from continuing into the PSF. In the Gard, too, while Dr Rocher was seen by the authorities as a committed foe of the regime, he urged members to follow orders, despite ongoing controversy.[45]

AN EMERGING FAMILIALISM

As the Croix de Feu expanded, its structures took on an increasingly "familial" character. Integral to the league's message was the assertion of the patriarchal family as the societal model for France, in reaction to the undermining of gender and generational hierarchies that much of the public believed had taken place since the First World War.[46] The Croix de Feu manifesto for the 1936 elections forcefully emphasized that "no national reorganization can be undertaken unless it is based upon the family, the elementary unit of the country." Of course, many organizations in interwar France, some on the far right but including other groups, held similar objectives.[47] Yet the Croix de Feu's effort to develop familialism in a concrete form, intended to prefigure a France under its leadership, was more ambitious in scale than that of many other movements, even though the project experienced internal tensions.

Encouraging familialism involved drawing women into the public sphere, something that elements of the French right had already attempted. In previous decades Catholic and nationalist groups had attracted female supporters, sometimes in huge numbers. The most important was the Ligue Patriotique des Françaises (LPF), created in 1902 originally to lobby against republican anti-clerical legislation in the wake of the Dreyfus Affair. It claimed 1.5 million members by

1932, when it was transformed into an adjunct of Catholic Action.[48] Yet while the LPF was concerned in the first instance with Catholic issues, it had eventually embraced the cause of female suffrage even as it insisted upon women's distinct moral and spiritual qualities. Moreover, while the organization highlighted the role of women as mothers in the private sphere, it also hoped its supporters would act to ameliorate class conflict, thereby ensuring social peace.[49]

The parallels with the Croix de Feu were considerable, though not total. La Rocque believed women had a role to play in public life; they were the source of "splendid initiatives" in hygiene and other works aimed at building solidarity. But he was quick to add that "new conditions must not deprive [women] of their essential, traditional attributes." Though a few Croix de Feu cadres called for female suffrage during the 1936 election campaign, La Rocque remained vague on the subject, only supporting the measure within the context of the familial vote, which could involve women simply augmenting their husband's vote rather than making independent political choices.[50] He thus saw women primarily as agents of social peace rather than autonomous citizens.

As we have seen, women had joined the Croix de Feu from its inception, but with the creation of the Section Féminine in March 1934 a sustained organizational effort truly got underway. Antoinette de Préval was the driving force behind its establishment, but she did not have a formal title and preferred to keep a low profile, claiming that poor health and a desire to prevent La Rocque from being swamped with admirers trying to use her to contact him dictated this role. Leadership of the Section Féminine was instead entrusted to two lieutenants, Marie-Claire de Gerus and Germaine Féraud.[51] They spent the spring and summer of 1934 speaking to groups of women, mostly in Paris, and sections were soon established in most of the city.

Activity also spread to the provinces. In the Nord 60 women joined within the first two weeks after the creation of the local Section Féminine in March 1934. Other groups were soon established in the Eure, the Gironde, and Alsace. Elsewhere success was slower in coming; in Tours a women's group was not created until December 1935 because the local cadres were not anxious to secure female participation. In the Gard the Section Féminine attracted only 76 new members in January 1936, compared to 108 Croix de Feu and 135 Volontaires Nationaux during the same month.[52] All the same, the Section Féminine's first congress, held in October 1935, saw 525 delegates attend. Three months later 1,200 individuals attended the first general meeting of the women's section in Marseilles, while the police noted very rapid growth in the Parisian groups after the April 1936 elections. A very partial sampling of membership figures suggests a female-to-male ratio of no less than 1:10, meaning that by 1936 the Section Féminine may have had 50,000 members, a figure that compares favourably with the women's groups of other parties.[53]

One of the major roles intended for the Section Féminine was to carry out social work in the interest of class conciliation. In November 1934 sections were instructed to designate a delegate for social action who would coordinate youth groups, the distribution of clothing, and social work. Most of these efforts were to be directed at families within the association, but two days a week were set aside for non-members.[54] Those undertaking social work were quick to claim success; according to an October 1935 report, half a million meals had been served in Paris, Rouen, Bordeaux, Strasbourg, and Nancy, and tens of thousands of clothing items distributed. On occasion, these efforts were carried out in cooperation with private businesses. In Nantes, for example, the Citroën company helped the local Section Féminine to acquire a château to use as a canteen. In general, the organization prided itself on its ability to coordinate diverse efforts and stressed its desire to avoid duplicating services.[55]

Theoretically, non-members who received assistance were not to be subjected to immediate proselytizing on behalf of the Croix de Feu: "memberships are only received later, when they do not correspond to a service that has been directly provided."[56] It does not appear that this directive was always observed; certainly, the political objectives of women's social action were clear. In the Algerian commune of Hussein-Day the authorities observed that the distribution of food and the job-placement efforts of the local Section Féminine "has attracted public sympathy and fortunate results with respect to new members." During the 1936 election campaign the prefect of the Seine-et-Oise reported how Croix de Feu women were very effective in spreading propaganda through the distribution of aid.[57] To be sure, there were challenges; a report on the league's family social centre at Saint-Ouen indicated that while, "little by little," mothers developed the habit of coming regularly, fathers were more hesitant. As for the children, in the beginning most were "very undisciplined ... real little wild beasts," and were thus "treated as such." The female monitors responded by initially giving them some leeway but worked at "gaining the upper hand." When families – or mothers and children abandoned by "Communist" husbands or lovers – were won over, Croix de Feu women did not conceal their pride.[58]

It has been argued that Croix de Feu social work provided scope for female activism beyond "an extension of the familial role" and encouraged autonomy for a range of women, including married ones. Many of the senior women activists had extensive experience or formal training in the field of social work, and a significant minority of them – at least 49 out of a sample of 174 – were married. For those who lacked such qualifications, courses were developed to train them as social work assistants or summer camp monitors. The latter were paid employees of the movement, and some other volunteers received compensation. In other words, despite the movement's glorification of the traditional maternal role for some women, membership in the Croix de Feu involved paid employment. Moreover, the qualifications and experience of the senior female cadres gave them a degree of authority. For instance, in April 1936 Madame Gouin, a professional social worker associated with the movement, asserted that the social services were qualified to comment upon the morality and suitability of prospective members of the Volontaires Nationaux. Gouin's assertion of such a role shows how professional credentials and utility could give individual women power within a male-dominated organization.[59]

But while some female Croix de Feu cadres had considerable influence, the assertion of traditional gender roles remained of paramount importance, even if it involved contradictions. The fact that many prominent members of the Section Féminine were unmarried would seem to reinforce the notion that for La Rocque and his colleagues, mothers had only a limited role to play in the public sphere. De Préval was single, as were a number of her colleagues. So was a young woman who for a time held a major symbolic role in the organization: La Rocque's daughter Nadine. For two years before her death from typhoid in August 1934 at the age of twenty, she was a dedicated social activist for the movement, sacrificing her university education to work with her father. Thereafter she was compared, as earlier female Croix de Feu idols had been, to Joan of Arc. The popular 1930s series of *Bouboule* novels, which recounted the adventures of a female supporter of the far right who ultimately joined the Croix de Feu, told a similar story. The title character was able to engage fully in the movement only after one of her daughters had entered a convent and the other had married.[60]

The women's organization also encountered obstacles in acquiring a stable leadership and gaining support within the broader movement. A year after the Section Féminine's creation, de Préval requested that a secretary general be appointed. Mademoiselle Marcajour, a trained nurse and former factory superintendent, was selected. But several months later she married and had to be replaced by Simone Marochetti.[61] A report on the social services for the first four months of 1936 emphasized the difficulties in getting underway, noting that only seven people had been designated as social action delegates during that time and two of them could no longer continue in that function. The report added that male cadres "do not always show a full understanding of the role of the social delegate and thus greatly complicate her work." Some meddled in social action, distributing clothing and other items on a whim. There were senior leaders who urged Croix de Feu members to endorse the Section Féminine, but some section presidents were, it seems, unsupportive.[62]

It also appears that the expectations of the cadres for the average female militant had initially been too high, in terms both of the level of commitment and of aptitude. In Montpellier, for example, only about 20 out of 200 female supporters came regularly to help with the distribution of clothing.[63] The 1936 report on social services concluded that "it is difficult to find persons possessing tact and orderliness who have some technical experience and enough time for a job which quickly becomes very demanding." Such comments indicate the degree to which Croix de Feu social activists were committed to professionalism. But they also suggest that some of the women involved had difficulty relating to the people they were working with. Thus in November 1935 the Croix de Feu leadership decided that only a minority of their female members possessed sufficient time and professionalism for social work. They now emphasized that this segment of the female membership, at their own request and with the agreement of their delegate, would engage in such activities. The rest would be confined to paying dues, attending meetings, and acting in auxiliary roles as members of the Mouvement Social Français.[64]

To meet the demands of those women who were approved for social work, professional training courses were held under the direction of Suzanne Fouché. The initial results were disappointing, however; most of the first group of students were unaware that they had to prepare for a final exam. Revealingly, when Fouché wrote an upbeat column on the courses for *Le Flambeau*, emphasizing the competency with which the students were being imparted, she closed by quoting La Rocque's reaction to the first set of exam results: "You are the sowers of peace, and we are but your servants. It is up to you, social workers, to bring our natural tenderness to those whom we love." While emphasizing the importance of these women to the movement, La Rocque's words also evoked classic notions of maternity, implying that traditionalist impulses were at work in the Croix de Feu's mobilization of women, even if it did entail public engagement.[65]

In short, the Croix de Feu was able to attract women in considerable numbers, but its efforts to make use of them could be problematic. At the outset there was a hope that they could serve directly as agents of social pacification and thus national reconciliation. These efforts bore some fruit, with a minority playing a central role in enhancing the social dimension of the league's activities. But the indifference of male leaders and the realities of life for most female supporters meant that by 1936 the majority of Croix de Feu women were still playing a vaguely defined and clearly auxiliary role. It was a contradiction from which the PSF also found it hard to escape.

Inculcating youth with the *esprit Croix de Feu* was no less important a task for the league, though it has received less attention from scholars. Youth movements flourished in France during the 1930s, and La Rocque himself came from an officer corps committed to regenerating the country through the education of the young. Prominent military figures such as Lyautey, Pétain, and Weygand believed that schooling should foster elites through physical and moral training rather than a narrow focus on intellectual development.[66] Like many of his erstwhile superiors, La Rocque was critical of the Third Republic's education system, suggesting that it was overly rationalistic and failed to produce leaders: "[France] makes holders of licences, diplomas, and certificates. She centralizes and rationalizes her teaching rather than decentralizing it and stimulating it through the direct intervention of spiritual forces and professional bodies." In the pages of *Le Flambeau* he expressed concerns about the teachers who, while a minority within their profession, nevertheless spread dangerous revolutionary doctrines. Other contributors, such as the novelist Auguste Bailly, seconded his views.[67]

Therefore providing the right kind of education – one that was patriotic, allowed for "spiritual" (namely, religious) intervention, and reproduced elites and hierarchies – soon became a central task for the movement. La Rocque and his colleagues were especially preoccupied with males over the age of sixteen who would, they believed, play an vital role as propagandists and provide the movement with further dynamism. In an early issue of *Le Flambeau* these young supporters were characterized as "a sort of body of scouts, a reconnaissance cavalry at the disposal of the Croix de Feu's leaders."[68]

But while these young men received priority, other youth were not ignored. In symbolic terms, children grew in importance as they were given increasing prominence at events such as the commemorative parades for Joan of Arc.[69] At large meetings they were dressed in appropriate regional costume and presented La Rocque with flowers. The Croix de Feu leader also became the godfather of dozens – and under the PSF, scores – of members' offspring. Reflecting this growing attention, the Fils et Filles des Croix de Feu (FFCF) was reorganized in 1932 under the leadership of Pozzo di Borgo to provide activities for four categories of youth: boys over sixteen, boys between thirteen and sixteen, girls over thirteen, and boys and girls under thirteen. *Le Flambeau* regularly carried a page devoted to the "postwar generation"; parents were encouraged to enrol their children, and parties were held for the different cohorts. The gala for the under-sixteen groups held in June 1934, which featured live entertainment and a speech by La Rocque, was typical in this regard. A year before that particular event the FFCF had already claimed 10,000 members.[70]

Most Croix de Feu activities, even for the very young, had a didactic goal. One of the earliest encounters that many children had with the movement took place at Christmas parties, sometimes referred to as *arbres de Noël*. The local Section Féminine arranged these parties, while the *dispos* would help to decorate. The parties began with singing and sometimes clowns. Then gifts and candy were distributed, often by Père Noël. But at some point the children would have to listen to a brief talk about the movement. In December 1935, for instance, Pozzo reminded an audience of three hundred boys and girls that the motto of the Croix de Feu was "neither white nor red" but rather "blue, white, red." In terms simple enough for his listeners to understand, "he entreated the children to always love their country [and] their tricolour flag, and to defend these as much as would be necessary, following the example given by their elders." For another such party held that same year in the department of Algiers, one speaker reportedly advised his young listeners about their toy guns that "with these revolvers you will not kill anyone; but kill those wicked people who are against the Croix de Feu and who write against them, in order to permit France to restore her national unity."[71]

Older children continued their patriotic education in a variety of ways. Croix de Feu monitors organized trips to museums, factories, airports, and other places. The goal, as Pozzo put it, was to have the children visit "all which is liable to develop, in their mind, the notion that France is a marvellous country." Sporting events were held to attract and sustain interest. In all this activity FFCF organizers and monitors sought to achieve several potentially competing objectives. Obviously they wished to encourage a specific loyalty to the organization; at a meeting of children of the 18th section, for instance, young listeners were urged to consider the movement itself as a family, "where the Croix de Feu are grandfathers, the Volontaires Nationaux fathers, and the members of the Section Féminine mothers." At the same time the league tried to encourage strong family ties, emphasizing that it posed no threat in this regard. Thus a gathering at the Brasserie de l'Univers in Vannes in May 1933 allowed an audience of Croix de Feu supporters – men, women, and children together – to hear local section leaders lecture about the Chinese army and criticize conscientious objectors.[72] Finally, while there were some common activities for both sexes, especially among the younger children, the movement sought to encourage what its leaders saw as proper gender roles. Both Fils and Filles were encouraged to propagandize on behalf of the movement, but only the older boys received practical instruction in this subject and only Fils over sixteen could attend propaganda meetings with the Volontaires Nationaux. Girls of the same age were enrolled in hygiene classes.[73]

For those past school-leaving age, females continued on until age twenty-one in monitored groups. Males joined the Volontaires Nationaux, but in keeping with its concern about the formation of elites, the Croix de Feu also developed particular initiatives for university students. The Groupe Universitaire for Paris was set up in embryonic form in early 1934 with the aim of building connections between Volontaires Nationaux engaged in all kinds of post-secondary study, though it was another year before its first official meeting was held. In November 1935 its permanent office opened, while a month earlier a Foyer Universitaire for female students had been established. The Croix de Feu launched similar initiatives at provincial universities as well, though specific information and membership totals are elusive. It is important to note, however, that while the association stressed its intention to shape France's future leaders, it also reaffirmed its ongoing commitment to class conciliation. The Foyer and especially the Groupe were not intended to be self-contained entities; students had to remain active in their local sections. Addressing a meeting of the Groupe held in May 1936, La Rocque himself emphasized the importance of cooperation between workers and employers. Indeed, some students who were attracted to the Croix de Feu never actually joined the Groupe; such was the case with François Mitterrand, for instance.[74]

The PSF would build upon these efforts, and compared to its predecessor, documentation on the outlook of its university students is richer. By contrast, perhaps the best way of grasping the atmosphere of the Croix de Feu's youth culture is through an examination of its annual summer camps, or *colonies de vacances*, which offered a more intense experience than school-year activities and were a centrepiece of its youth initiatives. Inspired by Madame Saulnier, who went on to become a member of the executive committee of the FFCF, the *colonies* began in the summer of 1931. The league set up a facility at Plainfaing (Vosges) for members' children which was inspected by Pozzo di Borgo and run by several monitors with the cooperation of the local mayor. The following year a second camp was held at this location, with some of the funding coming from a spring charity bazaar. In light of national legislation concerning children's summer camps, control was entrusted to Mademoiselle Morin, who had been a nurse during the war. An additional camp organized by the Bouches-du-Rhône section was set up at Saint-Martin-de-Marseilles, using the farmhouse of a local landowner.[75]

Over the next two years attempts were made to improve conditions and accessibility. In 1935 enrolments increased substantially, necessitating the establishment of a total of thirteen *colonies*. Among the new locations were Houlgate (Calvados), Guéthary (Basses-Pyrénées), and the Auvergne; the latter was established in honour of Nadine de La Rocque. That summer the camps ran at staggered intervals, with separate ones for boys and girls of different age cohorts. In November 1935 *Le Flambeau* claimed that five thousand children were involved, though earlier reports suggested a total of three thousand. Plans were made for 1936, but the dissolution of the movement disrupted these activities.[76]

Colonies de vacances were not unique to the Croix de Feu. By the 1930s they were a well-established activity for various religious and political groups. Republican educators and Protestant evangelicals had organized them in the late nineteenth century; Catholic parishes and organizations had followed suit shortly thereafter and were later emulated by the Socialists and the Communists. Croix de Feu practices bore considerable resemblance to Catholic ones. The latter were characterized by predominantly single-sex organizations structured by age, a relatively informal but intense pedagogical approach on the part of the monitors, an extremely full schedule for each day, and the inculcation of an appreciation for rural life, as opposed to the troubling effects of the urban environment.[77] Croix de Feu summer camps sought to imbue children with camaraderie in a similar fashion. The children would get up at 7:30 a.m.; their day included breathing exercises, gymnastics, and walks. Girls would take lessons in cooking and sewing; time for letter-writing was allotted once a week; naps were taken after lunch. Monitors held and distributed all pocket money given to the children, and those who broke the rules were sent home immediately. In addition to a medical certificate, parents had to provide details on a child's physical and religious needs and were not permitted to interfere with the camp regimen, though visits were allowed. The *colonies* stressed cleanliness and tidiness; *Le Flambeau* featured descriptions of spotless rooms and neatly made beds.[78]

Behind such apparent banalities, most *colonies de vacances*, of whatever type, strove to inculcate a particular world view in their charges. For Catholic groups the goal was re-Christianizing a predominantly secular society as well as encouraging bourgeois norms, especially with respect to proletarian children. The Communists adapted some Catholic techniques to a very different end, namely, the constitution of a "children's republic" where members could envision and work to build a socialist society. Both initiatives involved forging "alternative child societies," whose members would later militate for their preferred utopia.[79]

In the case of the Croix de Feu's *colonies de vacances*, the central goal was the development of a nationalist ethos, though the league certainly did not seek to displace the children's religious beliefs. For young children the ideas were cast in very general terms. In 1931, for instance, the children of Plainfaing made a "pilgrimage" to the battlefields of the Vosges. The aim, as Jacques Arnoult described it, was "to raise them in the tradition that was theirs: the cult of memory and of the nation." But a distinctive loyalty to the league was also instilled. Visiting a *colonie* in 1935, La Rocque recounted to a young audience how his own mother had "raised nine children in modesty and love for the country." He then instructed his listeners that "all classes are represented here, [for] they form but one fraternity ... that of the Croix de

Feu … Young or old, we all owe allegiance to our 'mother,' France; she gives us the imperious order to reunite the national family in the folds of her tricolour robe." The newspaper account of his visit to the camp also highlighted the natural surroundings, implying that the presence of local "courteous and smiling peasants" encouraged appreciation for rural values.[80]

Quite succinctly, La Rocque had conveyed to that group of children both their task as part of the Croix de Feu "family" and a sense of the league's wider vision for France. Their role was to forge a familial movement that would provide a model for and help to realize a disciplined, ascetic France, free from social strife and fiercely nationalistic. The new national family would be harmonious; what should happen if members disagreed was rarely commented upon. It was hard for the Croix de Feu to claim a monopoly on such patriotic values, but clearly its young supporters were taught that it was the central purveyor of them.

FORGING SOLIDARITY

Alongside its familial structures, the movement developed a range of initiatives aimed at encouraging cohesion among its members. These included mutual aid and organizing on an occupational basis. Entr'aide, an ancillary group within the league, provided support and found jobs for needy members. By 1935 the fact that the Croix de Feu was apparently recruiting some individuals on the basis of material aid meant that Entr'aide delegates had to assure prospective employers they could provide "all guarantees from a moral point of view." But La Rocque wanted to go further. As early as September 1933 he requested from the section presidents lists of members who were involved in corporative or union organizations.[81] While this effort did not receive a great deal of fanfare, by the spring of 1936 a variety of "professional groups" had been established, including ones for insurance agents, taxi drivers, and store employees. By this time special propaganda meetings targeting various occupations were being planned. Just before being dissolved in 1936 the Croix de Feu also established a syndicalist office as a preliminary step to forming "apolitical" unions. As for the professional groups, they formed the basis of what would become the PSF-inspired Syndicats Professionnels Français (SPF).[82]

More generally, La Rocque and his colleagues sought to ensure that their followers could enjoy their leisure activities in an atmosphere conducive to camaraderie. They encouraged local sections to develop foyers to support conferences and sporting and cultural activities. The Centre Guynemer, named after the famous First World War aviator Georges Guynemer, was set up in Paris's 10th arrondissement. There were also the Centre Social Français located in the 18th arrondissement, the Foyer Driant in the 19th arrondissement, and the Centre Perronnet in Neuilly-sur-Seine. Information on the provinces is sketchier, but there were groups such as the Cercle Lyautey in Laon. Perhaps in the hope of heading off a dissolution, many of these centres had their own particular statutes to give them a separate legal identity, but there was no doubt in the minds of the authorities that they emanated from the Croix de Feu.[83] Equally obvious was the fact that leisure could be suffused with politics. During an artistic soiree held in Neuilly in February 1936, Charles Vallin took the opportunity to discuss the Croix de Feu's electoral strategy to an audience of some fifteen hundred people and to comment upon the recent assault on the Socialist leader Léon Blum by members of the Camelots du Roi. While declaring that his association condemned violence, Vallin was quick to add that "really, we cannot pity M. Léon Blum, whom we hate. He and his friends did not pity us after [the 1935 incident at] Limoges."[84]

The Croix de Feu's institutional network thus promised patriotic harmony to those who embraced it, provided a congenial site for the articulation of its ideology, and served to remind observers and enemies of its power. Occasions such as the movement's annual charity sale, held to garner support for its various social initiatives, highlighted its softer side but played a similar role. Describing the May 1935 sale in an interview for *Le Flambeau*, La Rocque stressed that it would "create an atmosphere of healthy and genuine gaiety ... The sale [also] represents a dignified and enthusiastic homage to the blessed wine ration of the war, a wine that has reverted to the carefully prepared, cultivated great vineyards of peacetime." The decorations for the fair represented the vibrant culture of the provinces as well as that of Paris, allowing visitors to complete a "tour de France." In this way both regional identity and national unity were simultaneously affirmed. Class solidarities were also encouraged. The Salle de Vins, La Rocque explained, afforded the Parisian worker the opportunity to "welcome and thank" the winemaker as well as the farmer.[85]

The 1936 sale, held after the national elections, was again showcased as embodying the peaceful, joyous atmosphere of the Croix de Feu, but this time in starker contrast to the supposed divisiveness of the

Popular Front: "Our fair has provided an image of the France we want; happy, proud because she is sure of herself, enlightened by understanding of social problems." Organizing the event also demonstrated the league's capacity for action on a national scale; in 1936, given its ostentatious abandonment of paramilitarism, the gathering provided an alternative outlet for the *dispos*. *Le Flambeau* thanked them profusely for their efforts in moving provisions, cleaning, and ensuring order over four arduous days. Special credit was also given to the Section Féminine for its work. In short, *Le Flambeau* concluded, "the Croix de Feu Movement, a model of the future France, has shown that it knows how to realize it – with discipline and orderliness."[86]

Given the rapid expansion of the Croix de Feu, creating a ethos of solidarity among its increasingly diverse membership posed a considerable challenge. La Rocque and his colleagues made a constant effort to convince their supporters that spiritual, generational, and familial bonds existed within the movement and to imbue members with a common moral code. The veterans of the Great War remained central to defining this code. In a speech given to commemorate the Battle of the Marne in 1935, La Rocque identified his movement as composed of the comrades and heirs of those who had given their lives: "You who fell on the battlefields of the Marne for the safety and honour of the country, for world peace, today I bring you the salutes of your companions, brothers, and your youngest." In their memory, Croix de Feu militants were enjoined to reunite France, eliminate petty political divisions, and create an enduring national solidarity. This task was a sacred trust: "we will betray our mission if, from the greatest to the humblest of responsibilities that we have taken on within our associations, any one of us for a single moment loses sight of our higher objectives." Nevertheless, Croix de Feu propaganda implicitly acknowledged internal tensions, such as those between the older Croix de Feu and the younger Volontaires Nationaux, even as it sought to deny they existed.[87]

Like the fallen of 1914–18, the men of the Croix de Feu were characterized as being inspired by the cult of public service. The noble quality of the militants' task necessarily entailed "a spiritual, moral, and even physical asceticism." Members were assured of their eventual victory. The league represented moral enlightenment and purity and embodied the nation's virtues; no opponent could prevail against it. "The triumph of the Croix de Feu movement in achieving the peace of a reconciled country is not in doubt. It will emerge luminously from the fog in which we are still living. The ardent force that it possesses will brush

aside, perhaps without struggle, the powers of destruction and dark-
ness. France awaits the truth, she requires leaders ... France expects
that we return to her the cult of the family, the right to work, and the
means to raise children."[88]

La Rocque left open the possibility that the Croix de Feu would triumph peacefully, but members always had to be willing to combat a
revolutionary threat. Intervention against the authorities also remained
a possibility if they failed to ensure order. The movement's claims of
possessing a distinctive, disciplined virility and moral purity were in
fact hardly unique to the Croix de Feu; invocations of them can even be
found in the counsels of early Third Republic politicians concerning
manly conduct.[89] But the fact that the association's proscriptions were
inspired by its belief that the First World War had united the French as
never before heightened the premium placed upon solidarity and
loyalty to the cause.

Moral guidance for the militants was also provided by heroic examples. Joan of Arc continued to be a prominent figure for the Croix de
Feu, even though by the mid–1930s her image as an embodiment of
national unity during the Great War had become strained. The Communists, for example, now sought to employ her as a symbol in order
to appeal to Catholics. In 1936 the Parti Communiste Français (PCF)
emphasized that Joan was one of the common people oppressed by the
upper classes, the daughter of a peasant family who saved the nation
only to be betrayed by the king. Croix de Feu orators ridiculed such
notions, while La Rocque continued to draw parallels, as he had done
in the past, between the achievements of Joan of Arc and those of the
Croix de Feu. Though claiming that the movement did not seek to
monopolize her, he proceeded to note that, like Joan, the Croix de Feu
sought the abandonment of internal divisions so as to serve the nation,
that both she and the league were deeply concerned about the poor,
and that both were horrified at the sight of French blood being spilled.
La Rocque ended by emphasizing the Croix de Feu's willingness to
act, but only in the interests of long-term harmony, as "the virgin of
Lorraine" would have wanted: "Violence can never make us fearful;
we would know how to crush internal or external enemies if they
intended to reduce our children to slavery, misery, and decadence. But
reconciliation is our goal. Joan of Arc taught us that."[90]

Despite the significance accorded to Joan of Arc, La Rocque was the
Croix de Feu's leading hero. Though he was certainly criticized – sometimes very harshly – within the association, his public image was the

epitome of the veteran who had given enormously of himself in war and continued to make tremendous sacrifices for France. Though by some accounts he was not a magnetic orator, in the eyes of his supporters this limitation was more than compensated for by his bravery, purity, capacities as a man of action, and qualities an exemplary leader and organizer. Their enthusiasm could be very intense. The Joan of Arc parade for 1934, at least according to *Le Flambeau*, "was an ardent and compact whole that received communion in the forms of affection and recognition, which went in a reasoned fervour towards Colonel de La Rocque." At a 1935 rally in Algiers La Rocque's speech reportedly aroused "the highly moving sentiment of a total communion of thought and will between the leader and the admirable troops whom he guides." Militant exuberance thereby melded self-discipline with a fervent belief in the cause. Similarly, while La Rocque was depicted as being fully in control of himself, his own remarks could take on a messianic cast: "It is in the order of things that the spirit of purity, self-sacrifice, friendship, and vigour launched by the Croix de Feu Movement will soon dominate the fate of France. Nothing can break it; the cries for death made against me, indeed, death itself, will not prevent the growth of the seed of national renovation passed on by our martyrs of 1914–1918, which has been sown by our labour."[91]

In 1935 the aviator Jean Mermoz joined the Croix de Feu pantheon. Born in Aubenton, in the department of the Aisne, Mermoz had had a difficult childhood in the shadow of a tumultuous relationship between his parents, who eventually divorced. He volunteered for the air force at the age of nineteen in 1920 and served chiefly in the Levant, but returned to civilian life four years later, having earned the Croix de Guerre. Mermoz then joined the Compagnie Générale Aéropostale, winning fame as one of the pilots to develop a South Atlantic air route linking France with Latin America via West Africa and breaking the world record for an Atlantic crossing in 1930. Within a few years he was the most famous flier in France and an immensely popular figure. In 1935 he joined the Volontaires Nationaux and soon became a member of the Croix de Feu's administrative council. La Rocque also gave him control over the league's aviation activities.[92]

It is not surprising that the Croix de Feu regarded Mermoz highly, for the movement had a long-standing interest in aviation. La Rocque had been active in civil air defence lobbying since the early 1930s, and *Le Flambeau* had often demanded more support for the French air force and anti-aircraft defences, insisting that the French people, especially the country's youth, had to develop a "taste" for the air. In 1934 the league formed an Amicale de l'Aéronautique, eventually attracting some 1,800 military and commercial pilots. By the following year aircraft were prominently featured at some of the larger Croix de Feu parades. Fears on the part of the Popular Front that these aircraft would be employed against their supporters led to a suspension of fly-bys in late 1935. But the cultivation of "air-mindedness" remained important to the league; its orators liked to stress how its determination was inspired by the heroism of the First World War ace Guynemer.[93]

Mermoz was attracted to the Croix de Feu through his military background, a sense of nationalism, and dissatisfaction with the parliamentary system, which he saw as largely responsible for crippling efforts to enhance French grandeur in the skies. He was not very interested in the details of politics and reportedly disliked giving speeches.[94] But his value to the league in terms of enhancing its public appeal was enormous. This was especially the case at the particular time he joined, for at that point La Rocque had fallen out with leading members of the Volontaires Nationaux such as Popelin, Pucheu, and de Maud'huy. By contrast, Mermoz provided an example of a young hero who loyally served his chief. By the spring of 1936 his prominence was second only to La Rocque's; pictures of both men were sold at that year's charity sale.[95]

Mermoz's appeal went beyond his apparent willingness to follow La Rocque's directives. He was one of a generation of pioneering aviators who flew long distances at great personal risk; they and their crews formed close-knit units, sharing an outlook that in many cases carried over from wartime experiences. The potential parallels between this ethos of solidarity and the Croix de Feu's message of national reconciliation were considerable. Like many pilots of his day, Mermoz believed that flight had an ennobling, spiritual quality. But as he emphasized to Croix de Feu members, it also required discipline and an ability to submerge personal and political differences for the sake of the team. In the long run, such sacrifices could pay off in the form of enhanced national prosperity and prestige, but there were major domestic obstacles, in the form of short-sighted politicians, to be overcome. Mermoz summarized his views in a talk given at the end of March 1936: "At the present time, personality must abstract itself into a common action, and if I take up my perpetual subject of the France–South America line, this is because it is a marvellous example of common action, the result of a great many pooled initiatives, of efforts too often obscured and spurned by despicable internal or external policies." Reiterating the point, La Rocque closed the conference by describing Mermoz as the embodiment of Croix de Feu values; not only did he possess courage and determination, but he also wished to serve the higher interests of his nation even if it meant offending certain capitalists or the government. "Mermoz," he concluded, "couldn't care less about any influences, [or] any political forces!"[96]

Mermoz combined a spiritual outlook with physical courage, but alongside these age-old virtues, he was also a thoroughly modern hero, a champion of one of the most technologically demanding professions of his time. The same qualities that had, in the eyes of the Croix de Feu, ensured the triumph of 1914–18 were carried on by Mermoz in a new, thrilling endeavour. As a symbol, he perfectly complemented La Rocque, the two providing exemplars for Croix de Feu and Volontaires Nationaux militants respectively. They, and the women and children affiliated to the movement, were called upon to achieve class harmony, to render France's enemies harmless, and to work towards a new kind of society. Where, then, does that leave the Croix de Feu in relation to the political landscape of interwar Europe?

THE QUESTION OF FASCISM

La Rocque viewed the Croix de Feu as part of a broader trend for national renewal within Europe. When considering whether or not the movement should contest the 1936 elections, he drew upon the Nazi and Fascist experiences: "to scorn universal suffrage, to resort solely to a romantic *coup de force* in order to seize power, that is a conception which, in a large Western country, will not withstand scrutiny. Neither Mussolini nor Hitler – despite the extreme nature of their doctrines – fell into this error. Hitlerism, in particular, hurled itself to total power through elections." But there were also occasions when La Rocque stressed the differences between France and those two countries. In a lecture given at the Royal Institute of International Affairs in February 1935, he noted that Italy had been geographically fragmented for centuries, and in the wake of the First World War it was threatened by a similar dislocation. Perhaps, he suggested, a totalitarian state was the only remedy. As for Germany, it was "convalescent from an unprecedented defeat, animated by a spirit of revolt," and thus it "sought in Nazi violence the use of its excess of energy." France's problems were also rooted in the aftermath of the First World War, but these were engendered by a failure to win the peace rather than bitterness over defeat. La Rocque implied that the country required less radical change, arguing that it needed "to be reworked, reordered. It needs harmonious, purely French solutions." Some members of the audience, it must be noted, were unconvinced. One suggested that the Croix de Feu's willingness to oppose an attempted Communist takeover with force and perhaps seize power echoed what had happened in Germany; his comments visibly frustrated La Rocque.[97]

This evidence is suggestive of the problems inherent in situating the Croix de Feu on the interwar European political landscape. Are public statements implying moderate aims to be credited, or should more confidential analyses and unguarded speeches to the converted be considered the surest guides? Furthermore, what is the value of parsing rhetoric for understanding the Croix de Feu in comparison to assessing the movement's actual behaviour? Finally, analyzing whether or not the movement was "fascist" is further complicated by the fact that there are different views as to what the most salient features of generic fascism are. For some scholars, fascism should be assessed primarily as an ideology demanding nationalist radicalization which had revolutionary implications. For others, it is more important to focus on how fascist movements and regimes evolved and to understand the functions they performed not only for their leaders but for the various sectors of society that supported them.[98]

In functional terms the Croix de Feu shared many features with the Fascists and the Nazis. It emerged within the context of an economic, social, and political crisis. In a fashion reminiscent of Hitler and Mussolini, the solutions it proposed to the failures of liberal democracy were informed by a mythical understanding of the experiences of the First World War. The national community had to be recast and energized. Social conflicts were to be "transcended" rather than managed; those who caused strife were to be repressed and tamed within the context of a corporatist-style economic system.[99] The impediments to this process came most immediately from the left, but La Rocque extended his criticisms to include liberal democrats and traditional conservatives (though the latter were also potential allies), blaming them for abetting political and social divisions.

Sociologically, the three movements were comparable, if we bear in mind that the National Socialists and the Croix de Feu existed much longer – and in the latter case only – as movements, while for the Italian Fascists the transition to a regime occurred more rapidly. Drawing on a membership whose outlook was decisively shaped by the First World War, all three professed to surpass traditional class and partisan divisions in their quest for mass appeal. In reality, the situation proved more complicated; support for these groups resulted from various social and political dynamics. Elites saw them as useful allies in defeating threats from the left, but they also attracted some dissident leftists and a conservative rank and file who in a time of crisis decided that more conventional right-wing politics had to be abandoned.[100]

In organizational and behavioural terms, too, striking parallels exist. Each movement developed dense associational tissues to enhance its appeal, ensure continuing solidarity, and prefigure the rejuvenated nation that it hoped to forge. Again, Italian Fascism's more rapid seizure of power meant that most of its initiatives in this regard took place after it gained control of the state apparatus. Nevertheless, all three movements were strongly devoted to inculcating their values in youth and sought to mobilize women while at the same time encouraging them to embrace traditional familial roles.[101] Moreover, all three resorted to paramilitarism in their quest for power, though the differing intensity of the national crises and the varying capacities of the respective states meant that, in comparison to Germany and especially Italy, the Croix de Feu's forays tended to be more circumscribed, though still menacing and disruptive.[102]

When it comes to ideological goals, the situation becomes more complicated. The thrust of much recent scholarship has been to highlight both Hitler's and Mussolini's objective of a right-wing revolution involving a radical reshaping of national culture and values, though not class structures.[103] Both, it has been argued, sought to use mass support to achieve power and then effect change through a process of ongoing nationalist mobilization. A core myth behind this process involved the recreation of the "spirit of the trenches" informed by notions of an integral nationalist "third way." This provided a dynamic alternative to the perceived threat of Marxism but also to the depredations of liberal democracy and international capitalism. Central to the fascist utopia was the creation of a "new fascist man." This ideal combined traditional virtues of self-discipline and sacrifice with an appeal to activist dynamism. Variation according to national context was considerable, however. Compared to National Socialism, Italian Fascism was less systematic in its drive; racial ideology gave the Nazis more scope for radicalism, and the greater power of the German state also worked in Hitler's favour.[104]

It is crucial to bear in mind that Mussolini and Hitler were often willing to dispense, at least temporarily, with their most radical demands in order to reassure more conservative right-wing allies. Especially in the case of the Nazis before 1933, a concern with broadening voter support tempered some activists. Moreover, after arriving in power, Hitler and Mussolini had to contend not only with the wishes of their supporters but also with the agendas of the state bureaucracy and the professional, business, and military elites.[105] This factor constrained their actions, leading to disillusionment on the part of some of their supporters. Hitler with the passage of time increasingly broke free of such restrictions, but his Italian counterpart had less success in this regard.

The Croix de Feu clearly exhibited some analogous features, though it never made the transition from movement to regime. Its ideology was a variant of the interwar "third way," calling for a rejection of the traditional left and right and a fusion of nationalist and social concerns. According to circumstances, La Rocque and his colleagues attenuated their demands, insisting that they posed no threat to the Third Republic. This was especially the case when the league's paramilitarism was increasingly criticized. But during the 1930s the nature of French far-right discourse was such that what was at stake was the ideological content of the regime, rather than a formalistic debate about the merits of a monarchy over a republic.[106] Emphasizing that La Rocque simply wanted to reform the Third Republic obscures the far-reaching changes he and his followers sought.[107]

That said, the movement exhibited some differences from the Fascists and the Nazis which must be considered. For one thing, while the Croix de Feu, like each of them, drew on a mythical understanding of the experiences of the First World War, the nature of that myth varied according to the national context. The image of wartime France which pervaded the *esprit Croix de Feu* was that of a nation which had recognized the primacy of a common goal – to endure – and had set aside internal divisions to achieve it.[108] In the case of the Italian Fascists, memories of the war were tied up with the campaign for intervention and the belief that the war experience could be revolutionary, leading to the forging of a new Italian state and citizens. For the Nazis, the conflict had unleashed powerful sentiments of *völkisch* unity, stirring the belief in the creation of a distinctive national and racial existence. Both Mussolini and Hitler also believed that renewed policies of militaristic expansion – new "revolutionary" wars – would allow them to break free from the restrictions imposed by traditional elites and enable them to remake their respective societies. The differences in program and degree of implementation were great – Hitler progressed much further towards his horrific vision than Mussolini did – but the parallel still existed.[109]

For the Croix de Feu, national reconciliation was of course intended to enhance French grandeur, and the preservation of France's empire was crucial to La Rocque and his supporters. But the evidence suggests that a Croix de Feu–dominated France would not have engaged in expansionist adventures which encouraged a nationalist revolution at home. Rather, the emphasis would have been on an enduring national-familial solidarity. This focus is suggested in the development of the movement's ancillary organizations and on occasions such as La Rocque's 1935 New Year's address:

Croix de Feu and Briscards, my brothers, I wish for you the triumph of this reconciliation, this French order of which you are both the apostles and protectors.

Volontaires Nationaux, Fils de Croix de Feu, my children, I wish for you the coming vision of a victorious country rising from our battlefields, resuscitated by your efforts so that an honourable peace is established and endures.

Ardent propagandists of the Section Féminine, I wish for you the dearest, most beautiful reward: the triumph of the union of classes for which you have worked with such courage, intelligence, and self-sacrifice.

Members of the Regroupement, I wish for you the rapid advent of a national mystique which you have hastened to help us realize, leading in your villages an innumerable crowd of good servants of the country.[110]

In fairness, Nazi party orators on the campaign trail made similar claims, promising the German people a "peace of the fortress" rather than a second Armageddon within a generation.[111] Moreover, some movements that are often labelled fascist were not expansionist. Fascism was more likely to take on an expansionist dimension when a given nationalist tradition had previously identified the quest for territorial acquisition as integral to the country's grandeur, as was the case with both Germany and Italy from the late nineteenth century onward.[112] In nations such as Great Britain and Spain, which either had an established empire or could not aspire to imperial renewal, indigenous far-right movements such as Oswald Mosley's British Union of Fascists and José Antonio Primo de Rivera's Falange Española sought an endogenous national revolution.[113] But even for these groups, the desire for renewal included the forging of a new fascist man, comparable in some ways to the Nazi and Fascist aim of remaking their respective societies, though without resorting to imperialist war.[114]

Such impulses for ongoing radicalization and the creation of a new man were often lacking in the rhetoric of Croix de Feu members and in La Rocque's writings. There were exceptions: one orator in Algiers, for instance, declared in 1935 that the Croix de Feu were "neither conspirators nor fascists, but simply 'new men,' uniting themselves into a kind of Committee of Public Safety to wrest France from the hands of the politicians."[115] In general, though, while the Croix de Feu espoused the patriarchal family as a model and wanted robust militants, its members rarely portrayed themselves as harbingers of a revolutionary culture. Even during the 1920s, when Mussolini was more inclined to be accommodate Italy's elites, he declared that Fascist youth organizations would imbue the future new men with "a virile warrior education" and a "sense of virility, of power, of conquest," enabling them to overcome the "traditional weaknesses" of the Italian character. La Rocque wanted the Fils des Croix de Feu to be guarantors of French grandeur, but he rarely endorsed violence in these terms, even though he sometimes resorted to it or threatened to use it to further his goals.[116]

There is an analogous contrast in sensibility between the Croix de Feu and the fascist intellectual milieu in France. A few links existed between the league and the coterie of thinkers that Zeev Sternhell and others have seen as central to the development of French fascism in the 1930s, but not many.[117] *Le Flambeau* published a discussion of the Belgian politician Henri de Man, who is an often-cited example of the transition effected by some socialists towards fascism. Pierre Drieu La Rochelle, one of France's leading fascist intellectuals, wrote an article for the paper in June 1936.[118] But fascist thinkers such as Maurice Bardèche and Robert Brasillach, like self-proclaimed fascists elsewhere, also invoked the need to create the new fascist man, a goal that the Croix de Feu did not emphasize. Moreover, against Drieu's contribution to *Le Flambeau* and the favourable reference to de Man, writers such as Brasillach and soon Drieu himself developed a contemptuous attitude towards the Croix de Feu, regarding it as staid and overly cautious.[119] Authors such as Henry Bordeaux and Saint-Brice, who contributed regularly to *Le Flambeau*, certainly promoted the integral nationalism of the extreme right, but they have not been classified as fascists.

Do such distinctions mean that the Croix de Feu is better viewed as "authoritarian" rather than fascist? The notion of authoritarianism as a phenomenon in its own right, distinct from a watered-down version of totalitarianism, has received limited scholarly attention. Much of the writing that does exist focuses upon authoritarian regimes rather than movements. Nevertheless, in important ways the Croix de Feu fits the authoritarian mould. In contrast to fascists, who seek ongoing radicalization, authoritarians are more oriented towards stability, ensured by an organic conception of the national community directed by elites. A common feature of such systems is a degree of institutional pluralism, though of a non-democratic kind. Such systems should not necessarily be seen as purely traditionalist, for they can embrace modernity, with its criteria of efficiency and rationality.[120]

The Croix de Feu's vision of a future France suggests that it was an enforced, patriotic harmony along such lines which was being sought. La Rocque emphasized the failings of the old elite and the necessity to establish a new, superior one. But stability was to be paramount. And while he certainly looked to the Fascists and the Nazis as models when it came to assessing how the Croix de Feu might come to power, it is less clear that he felt a regime such as that of Nazi Germany or Fascist Italy could be transposed onto France. As the Croix de Feu's 1936 manifesto put it, "Fascist or Nazi imitation, by imposing upon France a regime contrary to her aspirations and genius, contrary to a respect for [her] personality, would inevitably drive her to the horrors of red revolution."[121] To be sure, the Croix de Feu was seeking to reassure the public at the time, but the proclamation does not contradict the general thrust of its propaganda. And given La Rocque's simultaneous insistence that the league would respect individual "personalities," it can be argued that, in line with general authoritarian precepts, the movement envisioned a regime which allowed for a degree of pluralism, though hardly of a democratic nature.

The authoritarian model has its limits. In adopting it, there is the danger of presenting the Croix de Feu as a monolith, obscuring the fact that the membership was diverse in outlook. In Algeria, for example, a number of militants readily adopted the fascist salute, and some section heads did not hesitate to extol "the benefits of fascism which has done great good for Italy [and] which is more honourable than the fascism of Blum."[122] There is also a risk of implying that there was a rigid distinction between authoritarian nationalists and fascists when in fact the line between the two was blurred.[123] Furthermore, authoritarian

regimes tend to eschew mass mobilization in favour of passive acceptance of authority. Political parties in such systems are often adjuncts
to a government that relies heavily upon the army, the civil service,
sympathetic intellectuals, and the churches – "natural elites." La
Rocque's organizations, by contrast, aimed to mobilize mass support.
Nevertheless, when the Croix de Feu leader's endless admonitions
regarding the necessity for social peace, respect for spiritual values, and
the need for elites to recognize their duties are considered, one can
envisage a regime dominated by him and his colleagues as being
authoritarian in terms of political valence. The fact that the Croix de
Feu sought to further its goals through paramilitary mobilizations can
still be reconciled with the fact that the utopia the movement endeav-
oured to realize differed from those of Nazism or Italian Fascism.[124]

Arguing that the Croix de Feu is better understood as authoritarian
than as fascist should not be equated with implying that it was somehow moderate. While in ideological terms it differed somewhat from
the Fascists and the Nazis, it was situated within the field of right-wing
movements ranging from authoritarian conservatives to fascists, all of
whom "believed moral order was to be imposed on the world by some
degree of fusion of nation and state" and who profoundly destabilized
Europe in their quest to do so.[125] Paul Preston's work on the nationalist
alliance in Spain during the 1930s reminds us that broad counter-revolutionary coalitions could unite fascists, authoritarian conservatives,
militarists, and traditionalists, with different elements predominating
in different contexts.[126] Such a lesson is particularly instructive for considering the fortunes of the Croix de Feu's successor, the PSF. For while
it shared the goals of other elements of the French far right, it was soon
after its creation at the heart of a bitter conflict within France's counter-
revolutionary movement.

4

A Turbulent Transition, 1936–1937

On 22 September 1936 the PSF section of Moulins, in the department of the Allier, held a meeting at which a M. Parouty was elected president by acclamation. Reflecting upon the new party's situation, Parouty combined bravado, fear, and hatred in equal measure as he addressed an audience of roughly one hundred people, most of whom had been members of the Croix de Feu. Conceding that the dissolution had been a terrible blow, he nevertheless assured his listeners that the Popular Front government would soon be finished; already elements of the Radical party were deserting it. What the PSF really had to concern itself with now was "the red wave of Communism" which threatened "soon to submerge France."[1]

Yet in spite of the urgency of the situation, Parouty declared that criticisms of La Rocque for not seizing power before the Popular Front assumed power were unwarranted. While the Croix de Feu could have launched a coup, it had lacked the support of politicians such as Doumergue, Flandin, Laval, and Tardieu. Above all, Marshal Pétain had told La Rocque that "no, the moment has not arrived: let us be patient." But now change was imminent; already, Parouty asserted, a working alliance with the Action Française, the Francistes, the Jeunesses Patriotes, and Jacques Doriot's new "national Communist" organization had been established. As in Spain, where Franco was near victory, in France "J-Day and H-Hour are close; let us be vigilant, so that each man is at his post for the National Revolution."

Though his claims and language were bombastic, Parouty succinctly identified many of the issues confronting the nascent PSF. The situation was turbulent as the new party established itself in the wake of the dissolution. Rumours of left-wing conspiracies abounded and were furthered by PSF militants even as they themselves intimated at violence. Decisions about how to combat the left, informed by hatred as well as political calculation, could not be taken in isolation since relations with the other elements of the French right – far more problematic than Parouty let on – also had to be managed. His address also captured the atmosphere prevalent within PSF circles at the time, for in conjunction with an intense loathing for their left-wing enemies, La Rocque and his colleagues exuded confidence that the French would soon reject the Popular Front experiment and accept their leadership.

By the end of 1937 their mood was rather less exuberant. Like its predecessor, the PSF confronted a fairly robust state apparatus which Blum's government did not hesitate to use. But even as La Rocque and his colleagues came under pressure from the police and the courts, their response to the Popular Front proved to be both cynical and to some extent effective. Seeking to provoke its opponents while at the same time decrying the government for undermining the republican values it proclaimed to uphold, the PSF worked to demoralize the Popular Front. Simultaneously, though, tensions with various conservative and nationalist movements intensified. La Rocque's new party provided a concrete electoral challenge to established formations, and the confidence of PSF orators in their pre-eminence annoyed rivals. The result was protracted legal, electoral, and even physical infighting.

Thus by the time the Popular Front entered its terminal decline in the winter of 1937–38, the PSF had altered its strategy and tactics in some respects. It was more cautious in resorting to paramilitarism, and of necessity it had to concern itself with elections to a greater extent. It also began to try to manage relations with other nationalist organizations more deftly. But these shifts had not made the PSF more conciliatory towards republican democracy. It still promoted a vision of a hierarchical society overseen by an integral nationalist state.

THE PSF AND THE BLUM GOVERNMENT

Since La Rocque and his colleagues had long been aware that a dissolution was possible and had already considered the possibility of creating a political party, the PSF took shape rapidly. In the Chamber of Deputies only eight deputies officially adhered to the new formation, but the potential for a mass movement was quickly created. Organizationally, the section remained the basic unit, but the party added local committees to do electoral work. Each section executive would now have a delegate for purely political tasks as well as a president, vice-president, secretary, and treasurer. At the departmental level the PSF was organized into federations; soon regional federations, consisting of two or more adjacent departmental federations, were also established. The *dispos* were replaced by the Équipes Volontes de Propagande (EVP), whose name carried fewer paramilitary connotations but who were initially instructed to display the "Croix de Feu spirit" of their predecessors. In many departments these structures were in place within a matter of weeks, and by the fall of 1936 the PSF appeared to be experiencing rapid growth. Though a substantial number of former Croix de Feu supporters were disillusioned with La Rocque, far more flocked to his new party, and they were joined by many newcomers. By the end of 1936 the PSF claimed that it already had 700,000 new members, despite competition from movements such as Jacques Doriot's Parti Populaire Français (PPF).[2]

From the start the PSF also made clear its virulent opposition to the new Popular Front government. It was far from alone, of course; the enemies of the Blum administration were numerous. The extreme right-wing press – *Gringoire, Candide, Je suis partout* – engaged in vicious antisemitism and slanderous attacks that eventually led to the suicide of Minister of the Interior Roger Salengro. In the Chamber the Fédération Républicaine's tone was frantic, with its deputies arguing that if France managed to avoid revolution, it would still be ruined by the Popular Front. In contrast the Alliance Démocratique and the Parti Démocrate Populaire proclaimed themselves the responsible opposition, supporting some legislative initiatives and exercising caution when it came to inflammatory rhetoric. They called upon the Radicals to quit the Popular Front and form a coalition with them.[3]

Along this spectrum La Rocque and his colleagues must be counted among the most intransigent opponents of the Popular Front. The PSF leader berated the Blum government's reforms and accused it of the most sinister ambitions. "Draconian" measures, he claimed, were strangling industries, excepting those that had connections with the new government. The consequences of the nationalization of the defence industry would be especially calamitous. The creation of a wheat board presaged the transformation of French peasants into "simple *muzhiks*," since the Popular Front was a stalking horse for Communist revolution.[4] On 8 August La Rocque declared that "the work of the Comintern in Western Europe is reaching its decisive phase. Its headquarters are in Paris. The Blum ministry has created a favourable atmosphere and cleared many obstacles. The preliminary conditions for the Bolshevization of our country and North Africa have already been met. *There has already been notification* of Moscow's instructions." In this apocalyptic situation only the PSF could save the country: "it alone possesses the numbers, training, homogeneity, territorial breadth, and confidence from all classes and quarters."[5] Such rhetoric served to further the polarization of French society and the PSF's quest for mass support and leadership of the right.

To be sure, the parties of the left had their own demons; they had long argued that the Croix de Feu had sought to overthrow the Republic and they accused the PSF of doing the same.[6] With his aristocratic name and rumours of his connections to powerful capitalists, La Rocque was a frequent target of the Communist and Socialist press. A disturbing incident arose in August 1936 when Hugues de Barbuat, the former deputy head of the *dispos*, committed suicide at the Château de Villars near Clermont-Ferrand, where La Rocque's family was staying for the summer. The PSF leader and his colleagues concealed the cause of death to the authorities, reportedly because of the Catholic sensibilities of Barbuat's mother. But the police found out, and their suspicions about the provenance of the firearm used led them to investigate. Ultimately they concluded that Barbuat's death was a suicide and that La Rocque was apparently unaware of the circumstances under which the gun had been purchased. But in the meantime leftist papers such as *L'Humanité* speculated as to why Barbuat had been driven to suicide and why La Rocque had misled the authorities.[7]

Yet the PSF was not above personal attacks itself, especially when it came to France's new Socialist prime minister. Antisemitic slurs against Blum, both coded and overt, became increasingly prevalent within the party. In a speech delivered in Lyons in September 1936, Charles Vallin, a former member of the Volontaires Nationaux and now head of propaganda for the new party, responded to inaccurate charges that La Rocque's ancestors had been émigrés during the revolution by wondering where Blum's grandfather had been at the time, suggesting that "perhaps he wasn't very far from Coblenz. He was going to sell some little souvenirs to the soldiers of the emigration."[8] Other PSF militants were even less subtle, especially in Algeria. At a rally of nationalist groups held in Constantine in August 1936, Stanislas Devaud, one of the PSF's new deputies, announced that as "Frenchmen of true stock, or *indigénes* who are French by adoption, we must unite against Jewry, against the Jew Blum, to ensure finally the triumph in this country of our ideals of justice, liberty, and fraternity."[9]

As a strike wave enveloped France in the summer and fall of 1936, the PSF did not shrink from threats – and worse. La Rocque regularly claimed that force would only be used in the event of an attempted revolution, and then added that the PSF would decide when such an attempt was being made. In party communiqués where he first stressed the PSF's defensive orientation, he would go on to whip up alarm about the intentions of the left, claiming that the Communists were planning for a civil war. On occasion, his remarks came close to inciting violence; speaking in Algiers in September 1936, he reminded the audience of the need to obey orders but then distinguished the PSF from the Croix de Feu by noting that "certain directives given to the Croix de Feu, notably those which prescribe not to respond to provocations, are no longer valid."[10]

With such rhetoric emanating from the party leadership, it is not surprising that many PSF members felt they could take matters into their own hands. At a meeting held in Mûr on 17 October 1936, attended by some three hundred people, Dr André Jude, a local militant, claimed that within a month the PSF would launch an assault on the Palais Bourbon. He urged his listeners to arm themselves, proclaiming that "we will dislodge from the government the scum who cling to power."[11] Many of La Rocque's supporters went beyond words. In Constantine there were repeated clashes between former Croix de Feu supporters and members of the city's Jewish community in the days following the dissolution. In Paris about ten thousand people, many of them former Croix de Feu members as well as supporters of other dissolved leagues, fought with the police at the Place d'Étoile on 5 July, injuring over one hundred officers. That same month Croix de Feu/PSF supporters briefly took over the prefecture of the Puy-de-Dôme, while in November militants "pre-emptively" occupied factories in Troyes and Dijon.[12]

The evidence suggests that such actions were not explicitly ordered by the PSF leadership. It is also true that false accusations that the PSF was storing weapons and planning an insurrection were made on more than one occasion.[13] But fears of how far La Rocque's followers might go were not entirely misplaced. In Oran, a department characterized by severe political tensions and several days of violence following the victory of the Popular Front, a number of PSF members and sympathizers were caught and charged with procuring and distributing arms. While the authorities ultimately concluded that the connection between the party itself and this particular incident was unclear, individual party members had certainly been involved. In at least two cases firearms had been picked up at PSF headquarters, and two party members were jailed for their actions.[14]

Thus while La Rocque and his lieutenants may have decided that armed subversion would not get the PSF into power, their followers nevertheless exacerbated a polarized atmosphere. Many party members believed civil war was likely and some seem to have relished the prospect. A police search of documents held by one party organizer, Robert Désobliaux, turned up instructions regarding "rapid liaison" between party militants, notably "in the eventuality of an attack as well as the execution of a plan of defence." Such plans highlight the conspiratorial outlook that characterized many PSF supporters at the time. The comments of two investigators in the Côtes-du-Nord aptly describe the demeanour of the PSF in the fall of 1936. While their own searches for weapons caches had produced nothing definitive, they concluded that the party's rhetoric was so apocalyptic that rumours of armed conspiracy on its part seemed credible.[15]

La Rocque and his colleagues did try to avoid entanglement in conspiracies such as the Cagoule plot, which had begun to take shape in the spring of 1936 and aimed to launch a *coup d'état* to overthrow the regime. They also kept their distance from the Corvignolles, a secret organization formed later that same year, which sought to root out purported Communist subversion in the army.[16] During their captivity in Austria in 1944, La Rocque told Daladier that he had knowledge of both groups at the time but avoided them. Though a few PSF supporters were individually involved, no alignment developed.[17] This restraint needs to be situated in context, however. La Rocque had long believed that an armed uprising simply would not work, and PSF officials who heard rumours of such organizing feared that it would prove to be a trap.[18] Genuine commitment to the preservation of democratic institutions, it seems, was not a major motivation for the PSF to avoid colluding in subversive activities.

As early as the fall of 1936, PSF strategists had envisioned undermining the Blum government in a more subtle way. Edmond Barrachin, the head of the new party's *bureau politique*, was convinced that the PSF had to present itself as a defender of democracy and strive to avoid accusations of fascism lest such charges encourage left-wing cohesion.

To this end he suggested that it organize a massive public demonstration "in the style employed with so much success by our adversaries" – namely, a rally in defence of the republican regime. This action would both enrage the PSF's opponents and "have an effect on the average voter, who believes only what is said and repeated to him firmly."[19] Barrachin did not elaborate further upon this cynical scenario, but his general strategy was discernable in the PSF's subsequent confrontations with the Popular Front.

On 2 October 1936 Paris's prefect of police banned a PSF rally at the Vélodrome d'Hiver which was scheduled to take place that day on the grounds that the PCF had threatened to disrupt it. La Rocque's anger increased when he learned that the prefect had decided not to ban a proposed Communist meeting at the Parc des Princes on 4 October, even though the PSF had made it clear that it would protest that meeting. Claiming that the Communists would use the opportunity to march through Paris's affluent 16th arrondissement after the meeting, the PSF planned a counter-demonstration. On 4 October between fifteen and twenty thousand militants – the PSF claimed forty thousand – turned out to disrupt the Communist rally. But they were confronted by a sizable force of police and *gardes mobiles*. La Rocque's supporters threw stones at buses taking PCF supporters into the stadium, but the only clashes that resulted were between the PSF and the police. Thirty of the latter and an unspecified number of the former were injured; 1,149 arrests were made and eleven PSF members charged, two for carrying firearms and one for having an offensive weapon – a dog leash, something the party later used to ridicule the Blum government.[20] Then on 8 October police raided the PSF's Parisian offices as well as La Rocque's residence and those of several other leading members; a total of fifty searches were conducted. La Rocque and other PSF leaders were accused of illegally reconstituting the Croix de Feu and "provoking an illegal assembly ... with felonious intent," a violation of an 1848 law.[21]

The PSF's response was defiant. La Rocque depicted the party's action as a "massive, spontaneous levy of 40,000 Parisians" which had stopped "the ascension to power of the Communist plot," and he compared the actions of the Blum government to those of the Soviet Cheka. He declared that "it is not the trial of the PSF which has begun, it is the trial of republican liberties." In Toulon Jacques Arnoult denounced the government at a party rally, instructing his audience that "all PSF members must abstain from responding to the investigating magistrates."[22]

Arnoult's advice might have originated from a central directive; in the weeks that followed, police who interrogated PSF members were frequently confronted with terse denials or glowering silence.[23]

The charges and police investigations gave rise to concerns about a second dissolution, but a number of PSF sections remained combative nevertheless. Only days after the Parc des Princes incident, party militants in Béziers met opposing demonstrators with phials of sulphurous gas. Two months later the prefect of the Seine-et-Oise observed that "the repetition of PSF meetings, organized with demonstrations by 'protection' forces and an air of quasi-military preparations, has caused a growing nervousness among the population of the Paris suburbs, which consider them provocations." French authorities in Algeria reported that local PSF militants were very belligerent, carrying out motorized expeditions and rallies.[24]

In conjunction with actions likely to exacerbate the cycle of political violence, the PSF continued to accuse the Popular Front of abusing governmental power and inequitable treatment. This approach had begun to be traced out by the Croix de Feu in 1935–36 and it fit with Barrachin's strategy of seizing the moral high ground by depicting the PSF as a defender of the Republic. In the winter of 1936–37, when the Blum government banned its meetings in public places on the grounds that a confrontation could result, the PSF responded by using the private properties of supporters and emphasizing that the Communists did not receive the same treatment.[25] Members of the EVP were given specific instructions about what to do after being involved in a clash. This included providing detailed information to the authorities, maintaining a medical record of all injuries sustained, and having themselves photographed, either in bed or with their bandages.[26]

In the wake of attacks on four party members – Édouard Formysin, Charles Moreau, Charles Müntz, and Jean Creton, in the latter two cases fatal – by leftists between July 1936 and March 1937, *Le Flambeau* asserted that the ministers of the Popular Front government were doing their best to ensure that the culprits went unpunished and that the "assassins" were being officially encouraged: "the cult of Marat has borne its fruits." In May 1937 it reported that the nine-year-old son of a PSF member had been killed by students from a laic school in a working-class area while he was selling tombola tickets for a Catholic charity. While *Le Flambeau* noted the father's desire that the affair not be used for polemics, it commented that the incident was not the fault of the "wretched" children, but rather of the adults who implanted hatred in their minds and the propaganda of the Popular Front, which encouraged it.[27]

Not even this tragic occurrence, however, had the impact of the violence that took place at Clichy on 16 March 1937. Reacting to rumours that the PSF was holding a family film showing at a local cinema for its members and that La Rocque might turn up, local Popular Front militants planned a demonstration. The way the Clichy PCF and SFIO organizers went about this was problematic. Calls for a rally were printed and posted on official paper and signed by the Socialist mayor, the PCF deputy for Clichy, and a Communist councillor. On the other hand, the authorities did exercise some caution by trying to arrange the march so that the demonstrators would carry out a procession but avoid the cinema and by having 400 police officers on hand to ensure order. Things did not go well, however. At 8 p.m., after the PSF members – of whom there were anywhere between three and five hundred – had entered the cinema, the demonstrators moved on the police barricades set up there. Clichy's elected representatives tried to defuse the situation by encouraging the procession to follow another route, but only some of the demonstrators, perhaps two thousand people, followed this suggestion. Meanwhile, a larger crowd continued to assail the police barricades outside the cinema.

To make matters worse, the smaller procession eventually returned to the demonstration. Pressure on the barricades increased, with about nine thousand people facing the police. Shortly thereafter the latter ordered the PSF supporters out through the emergency exit, and the building was evacuated without any injuries to them. Ironically, after that the violence escalated. Police reinforcements – 238 in all – arrived in vans and were accompanied by the prefect of police and Minister of the Interior Marx Dormoy. The crowd attacked the vans with stones, and at around 9:45 there was gunfire. The situation was confused; while it appears that the police opened fire, there were also claims of various extremists being responsible for the use of firearms. When the gunfire subsided, no police were dead, but 257 had been injured, 5 by bullets. As for the demonstrators, 5 had been killed and 107 wounded, 48 of them by firearms.[28]

The PSF stressed the responsibility of the government and, more widely, the left for what had happened. *Le Flambeau* emphasized the familial nature of the meeting, juxtaposing this with the provocative acts of the Communists and Socialists. While the paper described the police at Clichy as "the admirable defenders of order," in the Chamber

Ybarnégaray compared Blum to the German Social Democrat Gustav Noske, who had ordered the repression of the far left in Germany in 1919. For good measure, Ybarnégaray reiterated that while the Popular Front government was supposedly democratic, it persecuted the PSF while letting the Communists carry out violent and subversive activities.[29]

Outside the PSF, reactions to Clichy varied. On the right, criticism of the government was intense. Even centrists still formally associated with the Popular Front such as Daladier and Ludovic Frossard voiced concerns about a threat being posed to the freedom of assembly. Some elements of the right privately admitted that the PSF's behaviour was provocative but insisted larger principles were at stake. In a discussion with an official at the American embassy, Bertrand de Maud'huy, formerly of the Volontaires Nationaux and now a member of Doriot's PPF, asserted that even though the Clichy meeting "might not have been necessary," it was justified on the grounds that if the PSF or the PPF could not hold meetings in Communist districts, then Communist influence would spread.[30] American officials themselves were more equivocal, observing that "Clichy ... is in the heart of the Communist quarters and, though the Parti Social Français were well within their rights in holding a meeting, duly authorized, anywhere that suited their purpose, the whole affair savoured of 'bearding the lion in his den.'"[31] As for the general public, it seems that elements of it felt that *both* the PSF and the PCF now posed serious threats to public order.[32]

Ultimately, however, the Clichy affair primarily served to further undermine the unity and morale of the Popular Front. The Radicals, frightened by the strike wave and the Communists, grew more critical of the Blum government's handling of the PSF, while the Communists excoriated the Socialists for repressing the working class. The CGT called a strike on 18 March; Blum, having already been forced to curtail the Popular Front's reforms and adopt more conservative financial policies, now seriously considered resigning. For the time being he decided not to, and in the meantime legal proceedings against the PSF for its actions at the Parc des Princes moved forward. On 5 April the *juge d'instruction* responsible for the inquiry ordered a trial of La Rocque and his senior colleagues for the events at the Parc des Princes and for reconstituting a dissolved league. Charges were also drawn up for the incident at the Place d'Étoile in July 1936, but it was deemed that there were insufficient grounds to pursue them.[33]

The court proceedings did not actually commence until after Blum resigned in June 1937, following unsuccessful attempts to gain decree powers to halt capital flight. In the meantime, the PSF reiterated well-worn attacks on his government in its death throes. In the Chamber of Deputies Fernand Robbe denounced Blum's attempts to gain decree powers as a violation of parliamentary rights.[34] By this time the PSF's claims that it was the defender of the republican system against the dictatorial Popular Front had become quite familiar. However misleading these claims were, the party's strategy of provocation and accusing its opponents of being the true enemies of democracy must have had a demoralizing impact upon many Popular Front supporters. La Rocque and his colleagues were not in a position to rejoice, however, for even as they excoriated the Popular Front, they had to confront growing problems with ostensibly kindred spirits.

"PRENEZ LEUR TÊTE": THE PSF AND THE RIGHT

As tensions mounted in 1936–37, it seemed to many opponents of the Popular Front that the PSF provided the most imposing vehicle for combatting it. This was the case even for some who had previously considered the Croix de Feu distasteful. For instance, in Senlis (Oise) the local UNC section considered fusing with the PSF, even though "numerous veterans have until now refused to join." Former members of the other dissolved leagues also signed up. In Béziers the PSF section was founded by former Croix de Feu and Solidarité Française supporters. Previous adherents of the Jeunesses Patriotes, rather than the Croix de Feu, took the lead in creating the PSF section in Châteaubriant (Loire-Inférieure). In Hirson two former members of the Faisceau played a leading role in establishing a PSF presence there. In Philippeville (Constantine) the authorities believed the PSF had rallied members of all the dissolved leagues; its members met in former locales of both the Croix de Feu and the Jeunesses Patriotes.[35]

Such a degree of success meant that La Rocque and his followers were regarded with suspicion and often hostility in various right-wing quarters. *L'Action française* was among the fiercest critics of the PSF, accusing it of integrating fine patriots into a political system that the paper despised. For its part, the Fédération Républicaine feared the new party as an electoral rival.[36] But under the circumstances, right-wing groups initially decided they could not afford to appear too sectarian and made a number of efforts to cooperate in the summer and fall of 1936. In Algeria, for example, the Abbé Lambert launched the Rassemblement National d'Action Sociale (RNAS) as an umbrella for various right-wing groups. It drew an audience of ten thousand to Algiers on 10 August. They listened to a variety of orators, including the PSF's Fernand Robbe, who expressed his hopes for "a great national reconciliation which, however, can only happen when we have extirpated the Popular Front and the anti-national cell it contains, and when we have driven out all the wogs [*métèques*] who are leading the country to ruin."[37] A similar effort at coalition-building was made the following month in La Roche-sur-Yon, where ten thousand people attended a meeting of the "Rassemblement National du Vendée." They heard speakers from the Fédération, Pierre Taittinger, a delegate from the UNC, and Léon Pierrat, a columnist for *Le Flambeau*. All of the orators stressed the need for unity against Communism, but Pierrat added that while all "men of good will" were working together, they were also waiting for La Rocque to take power.[38]

Pierrat's remarks were provocative but completely in accord with PSF policy. From the party's inception it had issued directives regarding cooperation with other groups to ensure that the PSF would eventually predominate. Gaston Rouillon, head of the PSF's directorate for the provinces, urged liaisons with non-party groups such as workers' and employers' associations as a means of ensuring cooperation and extending PSF influence. But when it came to other political parties, members had to exercise due caution; alliances were permissible only with the approval of the central leadership. Above all, "political under-standings, if they are concluded, must operate under the leadership of the strongest party, *which means our leadership*." La Rocque forcefully reiterated this directive in *Le Flambeau*, instructing section leaders to "accept the anti-revolutionary alliance of all men of goodwill. BUT TAKE THE LEAD."[39]

The PSF's emphasis upon preserving its autonomy and claiming a lead-ership role complicated its dealings with other groups. Its relations with the UNC are a case in point. The UNC leader Jean Goy was particularly vocal about the need for an anti-revolutionary alliance, and during the fall contacts between the two groups were developed. Privately La Rocque expressed some enthusiasm about an accord, surmising that it might eventually extend to include other formations. But he was careful to ensure that the PSF's freedom of manoeuvre was preserved. An agree-ment was eventually signed, but it was restricted to ententes at the local level and sought to preserve the independence of the respective organiza-tions. La Rocque was perturbed by rumours that he had instructed PSF supporters to join the UNC; so to ensure his supporters got the message, he sent out a circular reminding them that since the PSF was the most powerful "force for order and French rebirth," they must not allow it to be absorbed or marginalized. It soon became apparent that PSF-UNC relations were not going to be very close. During the fall some speakers stressed the unity of spirit that existed between these formations, but by March 1937 differences had emerged. The UNC, for instance, was less hostile than the PSF towards Blum's attempts to float a large loan for national defence.[40]

With the Fédération Républicaine the situation was even more tenuous, since it feared the usurpation of its voters by the new party. These fears did not immediately preclude attempts at cooperation; some Fédération members, including Xavier Vallat, soon to be one of the PSF's harshest critics, addressed joint meetings at first. But it did not take long for problems to surface. At their national council meeting in November 1936, members of the Fédération accepted that the PSF might prove to be a valuable ally, but they also devoted a good deal of time to discussing the threat it posed as a rival. Thus when the PSF tried to encourage links between its deputies and those of other right-wing parties through the creation of the Comité Parlementaire de Défense des Libertés et de Sympathie pour le PSF, the Fédération was deeply suspicious. A number of its deputies refused to sign up, citing their belief that the PSF would not fully cooperate with other nationalist parties in an election. As we have seen, the Comité itself amounted to little; the forty-seven deputies who joined met only once. Before long the strain between the Fédération and the PSF was such that even perfunctory endorsements of cooperation were controversial. After the PSF deputy Paul Creyssel made some complimentary remarks about the Fédération at its Rhône organization congress in January 1937, the PSF press felt compelled to emphasize that his remarks in no way meant that the PSF was subservient to the Fédération.[41]

Elections during this period were often the occasion for friction between the two parties. Again, there was some cooperation at the outset; in November 1936 Le Flambeau acknowledged that the Fédération had stood down on the second ballot of a cantonal election which allowed the PSF's Robert Poiget to be elected as a conseiller d'arrondissement in Lyons. The paper also pointed out that PSF votes had helped the Fédération win a senatorial election in the Eure that same month.[42] But the PSF could not dispel the Fédération's concerns about losing its parliamentary dominance of the nationalist cause. This problem became painfully apparent during the Mortain by-election in the spring of 1937.

That constituency fell vacant when its representative, Gustave Guerin, was elected to the Senate. The PSF candidate, Dr Gautier, received the endorsement of Guerin, who was a member of the Fédération and had also been a supporter of the Croix de Feu. Unbeknownst to Guerin, however, the Fédération had its own candidate, Georges Normand, and its press attacked Gautier and criticized Guerin for supporting the PSF. The situation was further complicated when the Fédération backed yet another candidate, Jacques Legrand.[43]

All throughout the campaign there were verbal assaults on the PSF; according to its regional paper, its rivals even spread rumours that La Rocque had been condemned by the pope, an especially damaging charge in a heavily Catholic district such as Mortain. But in the first round of voting Gautier emerged so far ahead of Legrand and Normand that for the sake of unity in the nationalist camp the Fédération's candidates withdrew for the second round. But the previous attacks on the PSF had made their mark; at least three hundred of the Fédération's voters refused to support Gautier, which meant that the Alliance Démocratique won the seat instead. Adding insult to injury, Pierre Taittinger rebuked the PSF, citing the incident as proof that no party, no matter how strong it was, could stand alone. The PSF was indignant; *Le Flambeau* insinuated that the Fédération was engaged in some kind of unholy alliance with the Popular Front to damage the PSF. In its internal *Bulletin* the party depicted itself as the true partisan of unity, noting that it had recently supported Jean Goy's successful candidacy in a by-election in Falaise.[44]

To a degree, this increasingly bitter intra-right conflict was predictable. The Fédération had little to gain from the growth of a new right-wing party. The UNC was not in quite the same position, but it still had reason to fear losing its support base to the PSF since the latter continued aggressively to recruit veterans. It also seems that beyond competition for supporters and pre-eminence, differences of approach were a factor in stimulating tensions between the PSF and other right-wing parties. The Abbé Desgranges, a deputy for the PDP, believed that by conducting provocative rallies, La Rocque had strengthened the Popular Front, giving it a menacing foe to unite against. He also feared that the PSF would cause electoral defeats for the right because it would displace conservative rivals, but also mobilize left-wing votes against itself. In private conversation one of the PSF's own deputies, Devaud, admitted Desgranges had a point.[45] A PSF record of a fall 1936 meeting between one of its cadres and a right-wing notable, both unnamed, fur-

ther underscores the divisions that were emerging. The PSF supporter
stressed the need to build a mass support base gradually. His interlocutor, by contrast, emphasized the urgent need for right-wing cooperation in the face of a looming Communist threat. In his view, the PSF's
"isolation" and "arrogance" were major obstacles in this regard. The
PSF representative retorted that most of the other movements were
guided by "false leaders" who were unwilling to appreciate the significance of a mass movement with a constructive program.[46] Such
remarks reaffirm that the goal of the PSF leadership was to unite nationalists under its banner, rather than join a coalition of organizations.

But while La Rocque and his colleagues hoped to displace the
Fédération and other such formations, they also had to fend off poach-
ing by a new competitor, the PPF. Doriot launched his party in the summer of 1936 and initially recruited former Croix de Feu supporters at a
rate that worried PSF cadres. In Vence (Alpes-Maritimes), for example,
the local PSF section simply dissolved itself and joined the PPF.[47] The situation was especially serious in North Africa. In Algiers the former
head of the Croix de Feu, Georges Faucon, defected to the PPF, hamper-
ing the development of the local PSF organization. There were similar
problems in Constantine, and in Oran the growth of the PPF initially
outpaced that of the local PSF.[48] In November 1936 the PPF claimed
that almost one-quarter of the delegates to its first national congress
who had previously belonged to a political organization had been supporters of La Rocque. Not surprisingly, both some domestic and some
foreign observers of French politics, including the British and American
embassies, believed Doriot was poised to overtake La Rocque. Within
months they were proven wrong; as early as March 1937, PPF officials
privately admitted that the PSF's membership was ten times their own.
But in the fall of 1936 competition was fierce and the outcome was far
from clear.[49]

The affinities between the two movements helps to explain their
intense rivalry but also why there was pressure upon them to cooperate.
Both called for the unity of "patriotic" elements and political reform
along authoritarian lines, and both promised greater camaraderie and
social engagement than the traditional right-wing parties. There were
differences in doctrine and style; at its inception the PPF was more
explicit and enthusiastic about forging a "new man," and its initial
promises of more radical activism won the support of intellectuals such
as Bertrand de Jouvenel and Drieu La Rochelle.[50] For certain right-wing
militants these distinctions were meaningful. In Sète (Hérault) it was

reported that "among the middle classes ... the general tendency is to regard Colonel de La Rocque as the sole, eventual heir of the political situation in France if the Popular Front collapses," while if "Doriot was victorious, French blood would flow."[51] But while some supporters of the right distinguished between the two movements, there was also a significant, if inchoately expressed, desire for cooperation at the grassroots level. Perhaps too much can be read into the efforts of a young soldier and his companion who were discovered daubing "France for the French," "Long live Doriot," *and* "Long live La Rocque" on various buildings and public urinals in Nîmes. But elsewhere, such as the Algerian port of Bône, PSF supporters were permitted, even encouraged, by their section leader to attend PPF meetings on the grounds that "Doriot's party is a nationalist party."[52] In short, the various right-wing movements had to avoid appearing too sectarian and emphasize their commitment to a common nationalist cause, even as they jockeyed for position and tried to stake out a distinctive platform.

While efforts were initially made to coordinate the activities of the PSF and the PPF, as with other nationalist organizations, their relations soon deteriorated. Agreements to cooperate were made in some departments, such as the Alpes-Maritimes in the fall of 1936.[53] At the national level Doriot was an outspoken defender of the PSF following the violence at Clichy several months later. But intense competition for members remained a preoccupation for both parties, and tempers readily flared. In December 1936 many PSF cadres were upset when Doriot hinted that the PSF's aviator-hero Jean Mermoz, who had just disappeared over the South Atlantic, had expressed an interest in joining the PPF.[54]

Not surprisingly, when Doriot launched his appeal in March 1937 for the creation of a "Liberty Front" to coordinate the activities of all genuinely "patriotic" parties against Marxist subversion, La Rocque and his supporters were suspicious, seeing it as an attempt to gain control over the PSF's membership. But they had to respond carefully, as Doriot exercised an appeal over some party members and the PSF did not want to be seen as divisive.[55] La Rocque and his colleagues therefore indicated their willingness to entertain Doriot's invitation but at the same time continued to differentiate themselves from their prospective partners. La Rocque publicly approved Doriot's proposals that republican institutions and the social reforms of the Popular Front be preserved; by doing so, he underscored the PSF's own "moderate" credentials at a time when it was threatened with dissolution and he reaffirmed the party's commitment to addressing social problems. But as far as Doriot's desire to forge a coalition was concerned, he expressed doubts, explicitly requesting that the Liberty Front not be used to seduce PSF members away from their own party. Indeed, La Rocque went so far as to suggest that the Liberty Front, while raising hope, seemed to promise little in the way of substance.[56]

Reflecting this general skepticism, when the Liberty Front was officially formed on 8 May 1937, Robbe and Barrachin were sent as PSF emissaries but with little fanfare. Two weeks later, in an interview with *Gringoire*, La Rocque questioned the sincerity of Doriot's commitment to unity. He claimed that at the time of the PSF's agreement with the UNC he and Jean Goy had urged Doriot to associate himself with their efforts, but the PPF leader had demurred, implying that Doriot was not interested in cooperative agreements that he could not control. And while insisting he favoured a "tangible union," La Rocque added that "the idea of placing this effort at coordination under a 'hat' of any sort appears to me to be of only secondary importance."[57]

A *conseil national extraordinaire* held by the PSF on 9 June decided the issue once and for all. The party leadership asserted that the Liberty Front would not achieve anything durable and noted that the Fédération Républicaine's wish that all sitting deputies belonging to the Front should keep their seats worked only to its benefit, since its parliamentarians constituted the majority of the potential adherents concerned. The PSF also claimed that the creation of the Liberty Front would only encourage a revival of the now weakening Popular Front. In rejecting Doriot's proposal, the PSF leaders did not wish to appear overly truculent, of course; they added that cooperation over specific issues and electoral alliances were desirable.[58] But subsequent efforts in this regard often came to grief because of continuing friction between the PSF and the PPF. True, when Doriot was removed from office as mayor of Saint-Denis because of accusations of corruption, a PSF speaker in Amiens classified the action as "unjust and arbitrary" and promised his party's support. However, when new elections to the city's municipal council took place on 20 June, Doriot was defeated and there were soon accusations that the PSF's support had been lacklustre, even non-existent.[59]

The PSF's refusal to join the Liberty Front denied that coalition its largest potential member and seriously weakened the initiative, though the Fédération, Taittinger's PRNS, and the PPF did sign up. It has been argued that the episode should be seen as the thwarting of an attempt to separate the membership of the PSF from its leader in the service of a fascist-style formation. In this view La Rocque's rejection of the "extremist" Liberty Front is evidence of how he wished to discourage further polarization that might have resulted in civil war, and thus of his essential moderation. This is certainly how La Rocque and other PSF luminaries later characterized their intentions.[60] But the PSF's immense ambition throughout this period suggests that its leaders' desire to achieve hegemony over the French right and avoid subordination to other groups was their overriding concern. Attacking the Liberty Front on the grounds that it encouraged political polarization allowed the PSF to differentiate itself from other right-wing formations.[61]

Yet in order to project an image of being fully devoted to nationalist unity, as well as for practical reasons, the PSF had to be more cooperative when it came to matters such as elections. While rejecting the binding coalition of the Liberty Front, it sought collaboration with the other right-wing parties during the cantonal elections of October 1937. In part, this strategy was a response to pressure from below; for instance, veterans' groups in the department of Oran threatened to have their supporters resign from both the PSF and the PPF if the two parties did not cooperate. Under such circumstances, La Rocque ordered that PSF members were not to seek revenge for what had happened during the Mortain by-election. Subsequently arrangements resulting in an anti-Marxist single candidature were reached in over eighty departments. The PSF claimed that it had 689 candidates out of a total of 3,390 seats being contested. There was still some sniping on the eve of the election; Doriot accused the PSF of boasting that it would dominate the right, while Barrachin responded by accusing the PPF leader of being petty.[62] But compared to the debacle at Mortain, the right seemed rather more unified.

Yet the results proved disappointing as far as the PSF was concerned. The party claimed that it had elected 306 *conseillers généraux* and *conseillers d'arrondisement*. But one contemporary observer contended that it had elected only 43, while *Le Temps* did not even report the PSF as a separate category when it gave election results. These discrepancies resulted partly from the vague etiquettes adopted by the candidates in order to achieve unity. Indeed, of the 689 candidates claimed by the party, only 250 actually presented themselves as representing the PSF specifically; others ran under such labels as "Union Anti-Marxiste" or "Union Républicaine."[63] Moreover, PSF militants were sometimes upset by the concessions they had to make in order to reach local agreements. For instance, cooperation between the various movements in Oran was impressive, but the PSF itself had little to show for its efforts. There, as in the Rhône, its members were chosen to run as the single candidate of the right in mostly left-leaning constituencies. Indeed, in the latter department one Fédération candidate ran against the PSF anyway and was only "vaguely disowned" by his local organization for doing so. In the Nord there were no instances of such infighting, but here again "the *modérés* only abandon[ed] to the PSF cantons they consider[ed] lost to them." Thus, even though the makeup of the *conseils généraux* – often dominated by incumbent local notables – meant that cooperation with other movements was the only practical policy, the PSF felt that the single candidature disadvantaged it. After the elections it announced it would now seek anti–Popular Front unity only on the second ballot.[64]

Serious as the tensions over cooperation were, by the fall of 1937 they were overshadowed by a coordinated effort made by La Rocque's leading opponents to discredit him in the eyes of his supporters. The range of interests involved in this venture was considerable, for in addition to long-standing foes such as *L'Action française* and rivals such as the Fédération and the PPF, the PSF had also aroused the ire of influential conservatives such as André Tardieu, who supported the Liberty Front initiative. Furthermore, by late 1936 La Rocque was moving towards acquiring a daily newspaper for the party, a step greeted with hostility by conservative press barons, most notably Léon Bailby of *Le Jour*. In the era of the Croix de Feu, right-wing dailies had given valuable coverage to the movement while militants read the monthly and then weekly *Le Flambeau*, which had posed little commercial threat. But with the creation of the PSF, this symbiosis was less operative, for the party deemed it essential to have a daily in order to reach an ever-broader audience. The PSF leadership was also motivated by the fact that growing conflict within the right could mean less sympathetic coverage. During the Mortain affair, for example, the PSF had accused *Le Jour* of misleading its readers about party policy. La Rocque believed that since he faced potential isolation in the mass press, he needed to acquire his own paper.[65]

Henri de Kerillis, editor of the conservative *L'Echo de Paris* and one of the PSF's few consistent allies throughout this period, tried to soothe tensions and warn La Rocque against alienating Bailby and others by acquiring a daily, but to no avail. The PSF decided to purchase *Le Petit*

Journal from Raymond Patenôtre, who ironically had been a supporter of the Popular Front. On 25 May 1937 it announced its acquisition of the paper. By that time plans for a sustained public relations offensive against La Rocque and his party were underway. Tardieu, still harbouring his own ambitions and resentful of La Rocque's success in building mass support, was one key player. Xavier Vallat of the Fédération, by now a confirmed hater of the PSF, was eager to cooperate. They were joined by Pozzo di Borgo, embittered with La Rocque and desirous of steering former Croix de Feu supporters away from him. Bailby facilitated contacts between them, especially with respect to Pozzo and Tardieu. Believing that their own ambitions were being subverted by La Rocque's foiling of initiatives such as the Liberty Front, they sought to disgrace him totally. Pozzo summed up their views as follows: "we have business with an adventurer who is a danger to the country, if only because of his unfathomable ignorance – it is imperative we settle with him, without any word games."[66]

What ensued was thus premeditated. Writing in the ultra-nationalist newspaper *Choc* on 15 July 1937, Pozzo made familiar accusations that La Rocque had sacrificed the national cause to personal ambition, but in addition, he claimed that André Tardieu had confided to him that he had secretly paid La Rocque 20,000 francs a month in exchange for support from the Croix de Feu.[67] Pozzo's revelation was devious, for had Tardieu himself made the allegations, he could have been challenged directly; but under these circumstances he could instead appear as a witness for Pozzo if the latter became involved in a lawsuit. This strategy would also make it easier to drag things out in court, enhancing the chances of damaging La Rocque's reputation. It had been agreed in advance that Vallat would serve as Tardieu's attorney.[68]

Pozzo's article was soon accompanied by a bevy of denunciations from predictable quarters. *L'Action française* attacked La Rocque's military record, suggesting he was an insubordinate coward. It also accused the PSF of secretly working with the new Popular Front government of Camille Chautemps. This was a charge that Léon Bailby was only too happy to second in the pages of *Le Jour*. Jacques Doriot proclaimed disingenuously that the PPF was not taking sides but added that it would do nothing to stop "the admirable soldiers of the PSF from uniting with the other fighters for the Liberty Front."[69] Hope that a recalcitrant leader might be separated from his appealingly large base was growing among various ultra-nationalists.

La Rocque flatly denied all allegations and contended that by attacking him, his accusers were undermining the PSF and thus the entire nationalist cause. "In these days full of peril for France's very existence, they are doing their utmost to destroy the only force capable of defending her."[70] In *Le Petit Journal* the PSF tried to minimize the conflict by focusing on the Popular Front and the worrisome international situation, but the problem would not go away. When several PSF members assaulted Colonel Guillaume, the editor of *Choc*, not only the party's right-wing opponents but also left-wing papers such as *L'Oeuvre* seized upon the issue, implying that the PSF leadership had ordered the attack.[71]

La Rocque soon came under pressure from his supporters to respond to the charges. At first he did so by undertaking an inspection tour of the departments, travelling to seventy-six of them in slightly over three weeks and constantly denying Tardieu's accusations. At this stage he believed this approach was preferable to going to court. But that course of action became inevitable when Pozzo advanced a defamation charge against La Rocque after one of the latter's verbal counterattacks, characterizing Pozzo as a "disqualified" patriot for having his false accusations reproduced in the left-wing press, inadvertently wound up in a PSF communiqué. In response, La Rocque decided that counter-lawsuits were necessary. On 3 September seventeen writs were issued against various newspapers for defamation, including *Choc*, *L'Action française*, *Le Jour*, *Le Populaire*, and *L'Humanité*. Twenty-eight writs against journalists were added to the list in October, followed in December by a further twenty-five in connection with other defamations; nine of these alone were directed against *L'Action française*.[72] Alongside charges of reconstituting the Croix de Feu and disrupting public order, the PSF now faced additional litigation.

TRIALS

From the fall of 1937 through the winter of 1938 La Rocque and his colleagues devoted a considerable amount of time and energy to court battles. In the end the PSF received little satisfaction, and it was the target of fierce invective from many of its foes. The party was more than willing to respond in kind, though, and it emerged from the various trials bruised but intact. Yet even as the court cases highlighted a resiliency within the PSF, they also help to illustrate why power eluded the French far right during the 1930s.

Opening in Lyons on 26 October 1937, the trial against La Rocque for defaming Pozzo di Borgo occasioned many attacks on the PSF leader in the right-wing press. The fact that the party was also under investigation by the authorities at the time aroused little sympathy from other ultra-nationalists. *L'Action française* criticized the effort to charge La Rocque with reconstituting the Croix de Feu, but only on the grounds that it was the work of a "crypto-Communist" government. The paper made clear its disdain for La Rocque himself by endorsing his claims that he was no threat to the regime, sneering, "He has a neophyte's faith in and attachment to republican institutions."[73] For *L'Action française* at least, this was why La Rocque had to be punished; he had betrayed the nationalist cause.

André Tardieu testified at the proceedings, and what he said proved to be damaging for the PSF leader. He affirmed Pozzo's accusations about funding the Croix de Feu, though he claimed to be annoyed that his views were published without his consent. Tardieu produced letters from La Rocque during his time in government in which the latter made clear his eagerness to impress him, employing expressions such as "At your orders!" Not deigning to conceal his political motives, he concluded that La Rocque was unworthy of his supporters: "I say to these masses of brave men from his party who still believe in him and do not want to stop believing that by telling the truth about an unworthy leader, I wish to do them a service." In his testimony La Rocque responded by emphasizing his general deference to authority at that time in his life. "If I am not mistaken, I had quit the army three years previously. For me, a *président du conseil* [prime minister] ... had more of an impact on me than he does now, I must admit." The court did not find this explanation convincing. It decided that Pozzo's claims of defamation were plausible and on 9 November found against La Rocque, fining him 200 francs but granting Pozzo only 3,000 francs in damages, a fraction of the 150,000 he had demanded.[74]

As for the charges made by La Rocque against various newspapers and journalists, these resulted in ten trials, which began in Paris on 15 November and also had disappointing results from his perspective. The bitterness between the claimants resulted in a turbulent courtroom atmosphere. At one point Léon Daudet of the Action Française was so belligerent that proceedings were temporarily suspended. Despite the obvious acrimony, La Rocque's opponents contended that their remarks were intended merely to shed light on matters of public import, and to an extent the court seemed to agree when it rendered its judgment on 3 January 1938. *L'Action française* was found guilty of three counts of defamation, but other defendants such as Philippe Henriot and the Communist *L'Humanité* received relatively light penalties. A couple of journalists were acquitted altogether. La Rocque later appealed some of these judgments but decided not to pursue any of the additional charges he had drawn up in December.[75]

Aside from the fact that La Rocque had few courtroom successes, it also appears that the smear campaign against him was damaging, though not decisively so. Initially the accusations that he had taken money from Tardieu led to desertions; to some La Rocque now appeared to be part of a corrupt political system which he had long denounced. There were reports of mass resignations in the Calvados, the Manche, and the city of Limoges. The Nord's federation president, Armand Causaert, was profoundly alarmed by the number of members who quit. He met with La Rocque and demanded that the latter swear he had not taken money, and then at a large meeting in Lille, he himself swore on the head of his children that La Rocque was innocent. This strategy appears to have halted the defections, though not all who left returned.[76]

It seems that elsewhere the allegations did not produce results on this scale, though some supporters were clearly shaken. In Chantilly an orator asked his audience to swear that since the PSF were La Rocque's "children," they would not separate from him. Some listeners responded "yes," but most were content simply to applaud. In Châlons-sur-Marne the authorities observed that "the colonel's supporters retain ... or pretend to retain their faith in their president."[77] Yet in spite of the doubts sown by the attacks on La Rocque, the PSF itself continued to attract new members, and in some departments the allegations had little effect. In the Alpes-Maritimes only 20 out of 8,000 members quit. In the Rhône Victor Perret, head of the Fédération Républicaine in that department and an ally of Tardieu, commented about the loyalty of the local PSF members to La Rocque, "These are impossible people; the colonel has truly succeeded in his efforts at division."[78]

Yet while La Rocque enjoyed considerable if not unshakable support within his own party, the feuding that accompanied the trial made clear he had few allies outside the PSF. The party emphasized the purity of its nationalist credentials, accusing papers such as *L'Action française* and *Le Jour* of forging an unnatural alliance with the left-wing press in criticizing it, thus blaming them for the divisions within the nationalist movement. One of the PSF's local papers even saw fit to attack Pozzo for visiting the home of a Jew. But in this war of words the PSF had only limited support. Henri de Kerillis, now editor of the daily *L'Époque*, supported La Rocque, but influential far-right papers such as *Candide* at best limited themselves to lamenting the "fratricidal" conflict within the nationalist cause.[79]

Furthermore, La Rocque was made painfully aware of the limited support he now had in the upper echelons of the army. While some of his former commanders testified on his behalf, neither Weygand nor Pétain would do so. In fact both downplayed their previous endorsements of him. La Rocque was embarrassed and angered by this about-face. He published an open letter to Pétain in the pages of *Le Petit Journal* in October 1937, and nearly seven years later he bitterly remarked to Daladier in prison about how Weygand used to lunch at Pozzo's residence.[80]

Tensions with other right-wing parties, already high because of the controversy surrounding the Liberty Front, were exacerbated by the trials. When La Rocque's colleagues requested that the Fédération Républicaine dissociate itself from Xavier Vallat's and Philippe Henriot's savage attacks on their leader in connection with the Tardieu controversy, Louis Marin responded that the PSF was simply looking for an excuse to enter into open conflict with the Fédération. He also accused La Rocque of cultivating the Radicals and other elements in the government – to the point of attacking the Fédération – in order to please them and avoid having the PSF dissolved. Such tactics, Marin added, only weakened the patriotic cause.[81] His criticism mirrored La Rocque's chastisement of his rivals for failing to cooperate with the PSF in opposing the Popular Front; ultra-nationalists sought a vehicle to coordinate their forces in 1937, but the different factions sought unity on their own respective terms. While formations such as the PPF and the Fédération saw a coalition – preferably without La Rocque but with his followers – as the solution, the PSF was motivated by a strong desire for independence and, the evidence suggests, the dream of attaining a hegemonic position.

That the imperative to unite, even in the short term, did not prove overwhelming might have been tied to the fact that, notwithstanding fevered accusations of revolutionary intent by its enemies, the Popular Front ultimately did not radically threaten the social order.[82] After the upheavals of 1936 the Blum government strove to reassure France's elites of its desire for stability, even though the PSF and others scoffed at such claims. Moreover, the Popular Front's own increasingly obvious internal divisions suggested to many opponents that it would not last very long. While many opponents of the Blum government were frightened and decried the weaknesses of republican democracy, they still felt secure enough to adopt a wait-and-see approach. Under such circumstances, the leaders of the far right had the latitude to indulge their individual ambitions and rivalries.

The trial of the PSF leaders for reconstituting the Croix de Feu opened on 11 December 1937, soon after the defamation case against La Rocque was concluded. While La Rocque's leadership of the PSF had been at stake in the defamation trial, in this case it was the existence of the PSF itself that was on the line. The party leadership realized this fact, and in the period between when the charges were first laid in October 1936 and the onset of the trial, they made a variety of efforts to differentiate the PSF from its predecessor. Charles Vallin, writing for the journal *Sciences politiques* in the winter of 1937, suggested that the dissolution of 1936 had allowed the PSF to break with a contentious past. Similarly, La Rocque contended, "Le Parti Social Français was not born from the [Croix de Feu's] ashes, but from the very principle of the dissolution. Nothing has been reconstituted. Nothing has been maintained." By the spring PSF propagandists were being advised specifically about how to argue that the movement was different from the Croix de Feu.[83] Throughout 1937 the PSF was also more cautious about provocative mass mobilizations, though there were some incidents involving right-wing rivals as well as ideological foes. This shift was part of a general decline in political violence. To encourage this process, the Chautemps government passed an amnesty law in July 1937 which dropped many of the charges laid in connection with incidents over the preceding year. For the PSF this legislation meant it would not be prosecuted for its October 1936 demonstration at the Parc des Princes.[84]

But the charge of reconstituting the Croix de Feu stood. These proceedings proved controversial since competing principles were at stake; the need for security and order had to be weighed in relation to the principle of freedom of association in a bitterly polarized atmosphere. But in contrast to accusations from the PSF of sustained persecution, the evidence suggests that the Popular Front took some care in deciding whether or not the party was a continuation of its predecessor. For instance, following the violent incidents during the summer of 1936, the Blum government had ordered that the PSF be monitored in order to discern whether it was essentially a revamped Croix de Feu. Furthermore, in the August 1936 memorandum in which he directed the prefects to assess how the new organization compared to the league, Minister of the Interior Salengro specified particular criteria. Officials had to judge whether a PSF section's activities were of a public or clandestine and paramilitary nature, under whose auspices its meetings were being held, and where they were held – whether at a new location or at a former Croix de Feu headquarters.[85]

Responses to the minister's directives varied. The report from Paris's prefect of police in January 1937 suggested that many former Croix de Feu members had not joined the PSF and that there was little proof the new party had violent intentions. But in other cases the outlook was different. A director of the *police judiciaire* for the Seine was utterly convinced that the PSF was a dangerous movement, maintaining that during an incident at Choisy-Le-Roi, members of the EVP had been caught with truncheons. In Oran the authorities concluded that continuities in personnel, along with the procurement of firearms by several of them, meant that "the [Croix de Feu] association ... has reconstituted itself, or rather, its leaders never dissolved it."[86]

Given the variation among different jurisdictions and the potentially large number of individual cases involved, the authorities centralized the trials, focusing upon the leadership in Paris.[87] In the courtroom La Rocque's early pronouncements to the effect that the new party was guided by the *esprit Croix de Feu* were used against him. So were internal directives seized at party headquarters following the Parc des Princes incident. An examination of the confiscated documents reveals a complex situation. While some indicate a clear concern that the new party had to avoid dissolution by changing some of its local leaders, in other cases PSF members entertained potentially menacing scenarios. For example, prosecutors pointed out that one PSF supporter wished to establish a "departmental information service" to monitor "the principal leaders of leftist organizations, including Freemasons, as well as [collecting] information of general interest concerning the department." Finally, the PSF leadership was also held to account for the storing of arms and the belligerence of party militants during incidents such as the aforementioned episode at Choisy-le-Roi. The PSF's militarized organization and avowed links to its predecessor, the prosecution concluded, showed that party was the heir of the Croix de Feu.[88]

Attempts by La Rocque to downplay the significance of some of his directives, to deny responsibility for what he characterized as the overheated enthusiasm of some supporters, and to suggest that in some cases evidence had been planted proved unconvincing. On 22 December, eight days after the trial had begun, he, Georges Riché, Noël Ottavi, Charles Vallin, Philippe Verdier, and Jean Ybarnégaray were found guilty of reconstituting the Croix de Feu. The court concluded that because of its structure, specifically intended to ensure rapid mobilization, the party bore a fundamental similarity to its predecessor. The EVP were deemed to be a party militia akin to the *dispos*. But while the court deemed that the law of 11 January 1936 had been violated, it did not order that the PSF should be dissolved. In monetary terms the penalties were not overly severe: 3,000 francs for La Rocque and 1,000 each for the others, though the PSF's assets dating from the last six months of 1936 were to be confiscated. La Rocque subsequently appealed the verdict, and in June 1938 the fines were reduced to 2,000 and 600 francs respectively. At that time the court also declared that the PSF was now no longer comparable to the Croix de Feu, though the previous conviction was upheld.[89]

The proceedings against the PSF aroused strong criticism. Predictably, the party itself decried the trial as an example of political justice. Foreign observers such as the American ambassador, William Bullitt, felt that a risky precedent was being set: "if a National Union government were ever to succeed the present Popular Front government, there would probably be pressure brought to bear to dissolve the Communist Party and perhaps even the Socialist Party."[90] La Rocque's biographer has criticized the Popular Front's handling of the issue, arguing that when one considers the small fines which resulted from a massive effort to prosecute the PSF, it appears that the charges had little basis in reality. They were, he maintains, part of a concerted effort to ban a party that was singled out by the Blum government while other more dangerous formations were ignored.[91]

Bullitt's point about a precedent being set for later dissolutions was prescient – the Communist party was banned in the wake of the Nazi-Soviet pact in 1939 – but Nobécourt ignores other actions by the Popular Front government and downplays the threatening demeanour of the PSF at the time. La Rocque and his supporters certainly loomed very large in left-wing consciousness, but they were not alone. Charles Maurras of the Action Française was jailed in the fall of 1936 after being charged with incitement to violence the previous spring. Jacques Doriot was removed from his post as mayor of Saint-Denis while the Blum government had him investigated for fraud, though he was later able to have the charge set aside by the Conseil d'État on the grounds that the minister of the interior had not allowed him an opportunity to respond to the accusations. Henry Dorgères, founder of the Greenshirts, was prosecuted by governments of various stripes six times between 1933 and 1939 and was jailed twice. It is true that his movement was never dissolved, but the prefect of the Seine had suggested doing so at one point.[92] Above all, it bears reiterating that large numbers of PSF militants engaged in violence during the summer and fall of 1936 and that they received encouragement from their leaders on several occasions. Given more latitude, the party might have persisted on an even more combative course. Prosecuting the PSF was controversial and politically divisive. But the overall picture that emerges is less one of a Machiavellian effort by Blum's cabinet to quash a hapless movement than of a government confronted with a vast array of enemies who, had they held the reins of power instead, would have been, one suspects, less restrained.

In a wider perspective, the actions of the Blum government in 1936–37 provide a specific example of how the durability of the republican state was a major reason why the French far right was frustrated in its quest for power. The cycle of events in the 1930s was not a pattern new to the Third Republic. During the 1880s the Boulangist movement had been thwarted partly by resorting to threats of arrest.[93] Fifty years later the French authorities had again remained essentially in control. This situation was in sharp contrast to that in Italy between 1919 and 1922, where the Fascists partially substituted themselves for the forces of order.[94] True, the PSF did not conceive of winning power through a coup. But it would certainly have benefited from being able to present itself as the sole force capable of ensuring order, even as it whipped up anxiety about revolutionary threats. To a considerable degree, this option was foreclosed to it.

A CENTRIST TURN?

As we have seen, accusations of subversion led the party to emphasize its republican credentials repeatedly. Furthermore, during this time La Rocque and his colleagues worked to split the Popular Front coalition by reaching out to members of the Radical party. These initiatives, as well as the PSF's growing isolation from much of the right, have led some scholars to emphasize that the party was moving towards the moderate centre of the French political spectrum.[95] But it seems more likely that these transitions were the products of calculation and circumstance rather than a genuine change of heart. The PSF continued to evince an authoritarian outlook; indeed, its views seemed to become more exclusionary in some respects. Its position on foreign affairs also located it firmly within the spectrum of far-right opinion.

The PSF's new chief political strategist, Edmond Barrachin, urged the party to present itself as a defender of the Third Republic at this time, but for tactical reasons. While Barrachin had previously been associated with the Alliance Démocratique and various centre-right initiatives aimed at reforming republican institutions, it does not appear that during his time in the PSF he had much faith in democracy. According to Xavier Vallat, Barrachin believed that many French voters would shy away from overtly extremist movements and that the PSF should thus cultivate a moderate image.[96] But there is no sign that he felt its ideology needed to change as well. As he put it in a 1936 memorandum, "it would be advisable, in order to seduce the masses, to give the party a more democratic and republican appearance" – nothing more.[97] The PSF's chief propagandist, Charles Vallin, charted a similar path. In a 1936 directive to party orators he reiterated that the PSF had to present itself as a defender of republican liberties, especially against Communism. He immediately added that only new methods, not new ideas, were to be adopted: "PSF propaganda must remain completely *Croix de Feu in spirit*, and become political in form. The mystique remains the same, and orators have nothing to change in this part of their exposé."[98]

The PSF's conduct in the fall of 1936 initially belied these calls for a softening of its image. But the subsequent threat of dissolution led to a redoubling of efforts in this regard. At the end of the year the novelist Jacques de Lacretelle published a pamphlet, *Qui est La Rocque?* which aimed to reassure the public that the PSF leader's "weapon is persuasion, [his] goal is to rouse the national conscience, not to tear it to pieces ... He wants to win over men through their good instincts, not the bad ones." Several months later Barrachin proclaimed in a public lecture that the PSF would only go into the streets with the army and police to prevent a revolution and that it was opposed to fascism and dictatorship. If any political force now presented a threat to public order, it was the left: "Our supporters never wear uniforms: they leave that to the Young Socialists."[99]

As the reconstitution trial got underway in late 1937, efforts to play up the peaceful intentions of the PSF were again intensified. In Paris militants were warned to avoid any actions that could be seen as provocative.[100] Barrachin used the arrest of a number of Cagoule supporters in February 1938 as an occasion to praise La Rocque for his foresight in following a "legalist path" and disciplining some militants who had carried arms. For the Joan of Arc commemorations held in May, *Le Petit Journal* strained mightily to explain how different the PSF's parades were from those of the Croix de Feu: "[They are] no longer the geometric formations of a while ago, marking time in a cadenced, military spirit which is not ours. No. These are men, women, and children, who go past as a crowd, gathering behind their placards. It is a familial, simple, and popular procession."[101]

Thus by design and under duress the PSF was seeking to distance itself from elements of the Croix de Feu legacy. But this effort did not extend to abandoning the league's "mystique." The 1936 pamphlet *Parti Social Français: Une mystique, une programme* was unequivocal that the PSF would continue the work of its predecessor in recreating the solidarity of 1914–18, which had re-established unity within a divided country. "The victors wanted to preserve, transmit and perpetuate this *revelation* throughout the country." Similarly, in January 1937 La Rocque was categorical: "As for the spirit, ... it is named, and will never cease to be named, despite all possible and imaginable dissolutions, the Croix de Feu spirit."[102] The PSF might retain the republican form of the regime, but it would be invested with dramatically new content. Stanislas Devaud summarized the party's outlook in this regard in a speech at the Vélodrome d'Hiver in January 1938. He explained how the PSF would infuse words such as "republic" and "politics" with "the meaning of nobility and disinterestedness which they have too often lost. In particular, the word 'party,' for the PSF, designates a bringing together, in a familial manner, of the French, rather than an instrument of division between fellow citizens."[103] In place of a fractious democracy, the PSF envisaged an authoritarian nationalist state under its paternal guidance.

It is in this context that the PSF's efforts to court elements of the anticlerical Radical party, the linchpin of the Third Republic's party system, must be understood. During the La Rocque–Tardieu affair the PSF was accused by the Fédération's Louis Marin of seeking alliances with "centrist" movements, notably the Alliance Démocratique, the Catholic Parti Démocrate Populaire, and the governing Radicals. In most respects such accusations were overblown. Relations between the PSF and the Alliance were strained; the latter was derided by Barrachin and others for not being a mass party.[104] As for the PDP, some of its members saw worthy qualities in the PSF, but others were suspicious of its past and questioned the depth of its new found commitment to democracy.[105]

With respect to the Radicals, however, Marin's claims had some validity. Reporting on the Radical congress held at Biarritz in October 1936, where strong signs of opposition to the Popular Front within that party appeared, the PSF's *Bulletin d'informations* distinguished between the "pseudo-rationalism" of the Radical leaders, who, it claimed, were opposed to all spiritual forces, and the outlook of their troops, many of whom were "fundamentally attached to the country, order, and liberty." In January 1937 the PSF further encouraged anti–Popular Front Radicals by supporting Lucien Lamoureux, a Radical critic of the Blum government, in a by-election at Lapalisse, which Lamoureux won.[106] Soon thereafter the PSF's Bulletin instructed militants, "Our propaganda must ... endeavour to convince the Radical voters attached to the country as they are to the Republic [that] against Communist dictatorship, the only salvation for the Republic and for the Country lies in the PSF."[107]

While its growing alienation from other right-wing parties may have encouraged the PSF's overtures towards the Radicals on tactical grounds, these initiatives also appear to have been the result of a broader strategy, outlined in a memorandum probably written by Barrachin. It argued that the Popular Front had to be divided by encouraging the Radicals to break from it. At the same time the PSF had to strive to "reassure the Radical troops and make them fall under our influence" by dispensing with frightening mass mobilizations, affirming its "clearly republican views," and "show[ing] itself to be more democratic than the Radicals." The document also stressed the need to encourage splits between pro– and anti–Popular Front Radicals.[108]

Thus when the Radical Camille Chautemps succeeded Blum, the PSF's deputies voted against his first government, which included Socialist ministers, but abstained in the confirmation vote for his second administration in January 1938, from which the SFIO had been evicted.[109] This signal of approval for the Radicals' break with the Popular Front was accompanied, it seems, by efforts to sow division between left- and right-wing Radicals. While *Le Petit Journal* continually warned its readers that leftist Radicals remained influential, the PSF cultivated the Jeunesses Radicales, known for their authoritarian demeanour and strident anti-Communism. The activities of this group, such as a meeting at Carcassone in April 1937 where the Popular Front was strongly denounced, were heartily approved of by the PSF. At a meeting in Nîmes Dr Rocher, president of the Gard federation, announced that the Jeunesses Radicales' views "represented exactly the opinion of the PSF."[110]

The PSF's overtures to the Radicals were part of a wider effort to reorient the ideological bases of the Third Republic. The document outlining the party's strategy towards the Radicals declared that their "laic stoicism" had died out with Clemenceau; in its current form the party was "a syndicate of appetites" that was unable to withstand Marxist "parasites." Nevertheless, the Radicals ultimately posed the chief obstacle to the PSF's effort to remake France. While "Marxism and, more particularly, Communism constitute the most immediate danger ... nothing will change in France until the Radical party and its Masonic cadres are hurled to the ground." The PSF, the document concluded, in fact represented the culmination of opposition to Radicalism. Previously, resistance to that party had taken on three forms: "a mystical current, both Christian and social," inspired by Charles Péguy; "a nationalist movement," promoted by Maurice Barrès; and "the syndicalist movement." The First World War had allowed these traditions to synthesize, giving birth to the *mystique Croix de Feu*, which had opposed the Radicals in a confrontational fashion before 1936. For the PSF the goal would be the same, but the methods would have to be more subtle.[111] In short, the PSF's final aim was not to attract Radical supporters so as to assume a position of pre-eminence at the centre of the republican political spectrum, as some have suggested.[112] Rather, it viewed itself as the antithesis of the Radicals and aimed to extirpate their laic and parliamentary impulses.

While the PSF sought to permeate republican institutions with authoritarian and nationalist principles, it was also more explicit than its predecessor, the Croix de Feu, in identifying with Catholicism. In an interview with *Sept* in early 1937, La Rocque proclaimed that the PSF's program represented "the exact transposition of pontifical precepts into our laic domain."[113] It may be that the party reached out more explicitly to Catholics because while members of the clergy had been able to endorse the Croix de Feu openly since it was a "civic" rather than a political association, some may have hesitated to do so for the explicitly partisan PSF.[114] In any case, the PSF did not take clerical support for granted. Some priests had embraced the party, denouncing the Popular Front and recruiting actively on the PSF's behalf, but others had reservations. A hypothetical conversation printed in the PSF's Marne paper *Réalité* implies as much. In it a Catholic militant, "Lefranc," reassured his *curé* that "the PSF is too respectful of spiritual forces to cause you the slightest worry. It does not request from you a support that your role forbids you to give it, but I would be happy if you understood that, if there are unbelievers among us, very sincere unbelievers, we are all partisans of Christian civilization, and we do not want Communism or Hitlerism."[115]

The PSF's identification with Christian values was distinctive in some respects. The party continued to present itself as open to people of all convictions while at the same time defining the Christian values it cherished as the antithesis to those of the Popular Front. From the autumn of 1936 onwards La Rocque increasingly referred to France as a "Christian civilization"; in this respect it is telling that his earliest invocation of this term appeared in a comment on France's first Socialist and Jewish prime minister in *Le Flambeau*. Noting that "the Jewish 'team' installed by Monsieur Blum ... forms the theme of foreign propaganda campaigns," he concluded that "it is incumbent upon the countless patriotic Jews to demonstrate their aversion for Marxism." While La Rocque stressed that racism was alien to France, he believed that Jews would only truly fit in if they accepted France's dominant ethos. National renewal depended upon a recognition of the country's religious tradition; there would be "no national reconciliation if it does not fall within the scope of our traditional civilization," which was "specifically, historically Christian."[116]

La Rocque juxtaposed the PSF's Christian-derived norms with those of the Socialist leader on several occasions. On 11 November 1936 he expressed outrage that an "unpatriotic" government would commemorate the armistice and include children in the ceremonies. Referring to Blum's controversial book *Du Mariage* (1907), which advocated greater premarital sexual freedom for women as well as men, the PSF leader commented that "the French family, whatever its origins, its religion, its condition, merits another example of traditional virtues than that of M. Blum, the disciple of free love." Such accusations of sexual immorality were a staple of antisemitic discourse at the time. So were linkages between Jews and revolution, an equation that La Rocque's supporters and the PSF leader himself did not hesitate to draw. In the first stages of Blum's government La Rocque termed the premier a "Kerensky"; later he argued that the Socialist leader was more akin to Robespierre and that he acted on Stalin's orders.[117]

One can draw distinctions between La Rocque's attitudes and the visceral antisemitism of, for example, *L'Action française*'s Léon Daudet, who characterized Blum as a "circumcised hermaphrodite."

The PSF leader presented himself as being above such things; on the day that the Socialist leader's wife died, he declared that he would refrain from criticizing Blum personally.[118] But there was a powerful antisemitic current in the party which was particularly evident in its regional press. The May 1937 issue of the PSF's *La Flamme du Midi* carried a front-page image of Joan of Arc chasing Léon Blum – portrayed as a Hasidic Jew – out of France.[119] In Algeria anti-Jewish sentiment in the PSF was powerful. Militants in Algiers chanted "Down with the Jews!" and "France for the French!" on the tramcars after attending a meeting in 1936. In Oran numerous supporters called on the party to adopt an officially antisemitic platform.[120] At the time La Rocque was not prepared to go that far, insisting that the PSF remained open to people of all creeds. But the condition he set for the acceptance of Jews into the national community – total acceptance of Christian mores – was shot through with exclusionary implications.

The PSF's position on reforms in colonial Algeria further illustrates this mindset. Tensions there heightened further when the Popular Front government introduced the Blum-Violette reform project, which called for twenty thousand members of the Algerian elite to receive the right to vote without having to cede their personal statute and thus obedience to Quranic law, as had traditionally been the case. Many European settlers strenuously opposed these changes.[121] The PSF was among the leading foes of the reform, and its position hardened rapidly. At first, indigenous supporters of the party such as Iba Zizen, a lawyer and the section president in Tizi-Ouzou, suggested that the Muslim intellectual elite should have greater rights while of course affirming their profound attachment to France. But the European settlers who dominated the Algerian PSF insisted that the French authorities should focus on improving the material and moral lives of Muslims rather than incorporating them into a flawed political system. Indeed, some PSF members doubted whether integration on an appreciable scale would ever be feasible, let alone desirable.[122]

In sum, as the PSF increasingly identified its supporters as "the great defenders of this Christian civilization, the adoption of which is the actual mark of French acceptance," its foes and those unwilling to accept its frame of reference were cast outside the national community, notwithstanding the party's claim that it was open to people of all faiths and no faith.[123] By comparison, the Croix de Feu had certainly displayed xenophobic impulses, but its focus was upon leading all patriots in a national revival. The PSF retained the myth of wartime unity but became more concerned with delimiting the boundaries of nationhood.

The PSF's commentary on the increasingly turbulent international situation harmonized with its domestic concerns. Its reaction to the outbreak of the Spanish Civil War provided another occasion to savage the policies of the Popular Front and indicate its support for authoritarian nationalism. La Rocque condemned the few steps that the Blum government initially took to support the Second Spanish Republic, emphasizing that France had to remain aloof from the conflict. But he was hardly indifferent to its outcome, characterizing the Spanish Popular Front as "organized immorality," claiming that it was the tool of Soviet policy, and arguing that "Bolshevism has unleashed its assault forces across the Iberian peninsula." La Rocque hoped that Franco would win "not for himself, but for us; his failure would mark a fearsome defeat of Western civilization."[124] Some PSF supporters drew even more specific links between the Spanish and French Popular Fronts, despite the fact that the Blum government ultimately decided not to support its Spanish counterpart. In Saint-Brieuc the local canon implored his parishioners to join with La Rocque, an "ardent Catholic and good Frenchman," claiming that this was the only way to ensure the Communists did not destroy French churches, as they had done in Spain. In French North Africa, where the war was followed with particular interest, several Croix de Feu and PSF supporters volunteered to fight for Franco.[125]

The PSF thus intensified the bitter polarization between left and right which the onset of the Spanish Civil War had encouraged in France.[126] When it came to dealing with the growing threat of Nazi Germany and France's apparent inability to prevent it, the party's first inclination was to condemn the Popular Front for sowing partisan divisions and serving the interests of the Soviet Union. When the king of Belgium declared his country's neutrality in October 1936, La Rocque argued it was primarily the result of French weakness, "especially the hold of the Soviet government and the Muscovite conspiracy over our national affairs." Returning to this theme in the winter of 1937, he contended that a more mobile strategy and greater independence for its military leaders would be needed to improve France's national defence. Above all, however, the country needed to be "rid of traitors and cowards" and to rediscover "its unity through the reconciliation of its sons, working and living in accordance with the Croix de Feu spirit."[127]

In recommending which diplomatic course of action to follow, La Rocque was clearer about which nations France should avoid than which ones to court. He saw Germany as a serious threat, one made worse by the negligence of various French governments. But allying with the USSR to contain this threat was unthinkable, as were notions of going to war with the Reich. Given the state of France's defence forces, conflict had to be avoided; besides, a Franco-German war would only favour the interests of the USSR: "the Comintern would be served by a Franco-German war leading to a mortal weakening of the two belligerents, thus introducing world revolution." Suspicious of the Germans and hostile towards the Soviets, La Rocque was also unsure whether Britain could be trusted. While its leaders emphasized their desire to rebuild their military strength, La Rocque displayed a streak of anglophobia by claiming that London wanted to see the Popular Front stay in power so as to better influence French policy, and that it saw France's security only in terms of how it benefited Britain.[128]

La Rocque also noted bitterly that prospects of having Fascist Italy as an ally had been diminished by the dispute over Ethiopia. He was broadly supported on this point by Saint-Brice, who continued to write on foreign affairs for *Le Flambeau* during this period. Contemptuous of the Soviet Union, intensely suspicious that Britain was seeking a rapprochement with Germany, and distressed that Mussolini was moving closer to Hitler, Saint-Brice concluded that a revival of Franco-Italian cooperation was necessary. Jean Ybarnégaray, while not dismissing the Franco-British alliance completely, maintained that France must strengthen its alliances in Eastern Europe, except with the USSR, and build up its own strength to preserve peace.[129]

Notwithstanding such differences in emphasis by individual party commentators, the PSF as a whole clearly embraced a stance of "conditional nationalism" during this period. Like much of the French right, it lamented the growth of German power but was unwilling to make ideologically unpalatable choices, such as forging links with the Soviet Union, to contain Hitler. This outlook distinguished La Rocque and his followers from "traditional nationalists" such as Henri de Kerillis and Paul Reynaud, anti-Communists who were nevertheless willing to pursue closer cooperation with the Soviets on strategic grounds, and "resigned nationalists" such as Jacques Doriot, who were more hopeful about the possibility of Franco-German cooperation.[130] Professing firmness but in reality ambivalent in their outlook, conditional nationalists such as La Rocque would find it harder to sustain their position as the Nazi regime became more aggressively expansionist.

By the beginning of 1938 it was apparent that the PSF had undergone a baptism of fire. In the first eighteen months of its existence it was indelibly marked by its confrontation with the Popular Front as well as with its nationalist rivals. The recourse to paramilitarism had waned, to a considerable degree as a result of pressure from the authorities. The transition from league to party shifted the movement's strategy from the vague one of applying pressure to directly contesting parliamentary seats. But this had proven to be a road fraught with obstacles, from avowed opponents but also from supposed political kin. La Rocque and his colleagues had been too bold and open in their ambitions to dominate the historically fractious French right and had paid a price for their high-handedness.

But the PSF had also made some adroit responses to the challenges it faced. It adapted its discourse in order to deploy the rhetoric of republican liberty against its foes, and its various efforts to demoralize the Popular Front were not without results. With respect to the intra-right conflict, it found itself increasingly isolated, and the effort to defame La Rocque did some damage. But the movement survived and maintained its position as the largest right-wing party in France, with membership approaching the one-million mark by 1938.[131] Nor was the PSF simply reactive. Its leaders also adopted a strategy of undermining the Radical party, the formation they identified as indispensable to the survival of the Third Republic in its current form. Such policies serve as a reminder that, like other ultra-nationalist movements in interwar Europe, La Rocque and his followers responded to the political opportunities and spaces that were open to them.[132] But French politics were about to undergo another major reconfiguration, leading to an environment quite distinct from the one in which the PSF had been created.

5

Remaking the Republic?
1938–1939

By the spring of 1938, with the Popular Front in decline and a long period of litigation winding down, La Rocque and his supporters confronted new opportunities but also new challenges. The PSF now experienced less pressure from the authorities, and its opponents were less militant and unified than they had been during the heyday of the Popular Front. But the change in atmosphere did not work completely to the party's benefit. In 1938–39 Édouard Daladier effected a rightward shift in governmental policies, and while some of his measures were amenable to the PSF, he also threatened to steal its thunder. As for relations with the other right-wing parties, the internecine conflict abated only partially; insults and recriminations persisted.

Under these conditions some observers began to write the PSF off. Alexander Werth suggested that by the fall of 1938 La Rocque had "degenerated into a not very competent newspaper editor." [1] But there is reason to think that he underestimated the movement. The PSF certainly encountered reversals during this period; in particular, its effort to co-opt and undermine the Radicals failed. But it also made continuous efforts to adapt. While tensions within the right persisted, it devised an electoral strategy to reduce friction with its rivals even as it still aspired to dominate the nationalist cause. The PSF also sought to maintain a high level of activism and to continue to expand its support base. One way in which it tried to do so was through the further elaboration of its program. Detailed policy proposals were drawn up; while this process revealed some tensions within the movement, it also reaffirmed the PSF's desire to refashion French political culture dramatically through the creation of an État Social Français. In sum, on the eve of the Second World War the PSF remained an imposing political force, determined to endow France with an authoritarian nationalist state.

A POLITICAL SEA CHANGE

After the fall of Camille Chautemps in March 1938, Léon Blum tried to construct a government of national unity comprising a variety of parties. When that effort failed, he then headed an all-socialist government, but this survived for only a few weeks. Throughout this period the PSF continued to lambaste the Socialist leader. Jean Ybarnégaray was indignant at Blum's national unity initiative, stating that such a government could be formed only by right-leaning politicians such as Poincaré and Doumergue because they were truly "Frenchmen and patriots." In Algiers a PSF orator predicted that the new socialist "government of Jews" would lead the country to ruin.[2]

Despite Blum's efforts, it was soon apparent that the Popular Front was in its death throes; the SFIO and the PCF were at odds over many issues, and the Radicals adopted a progressively more anti-Communist outlook. In response the PSF sought to maintain an atmosphere of polarization, with some section presidents aching for confrontation with the Popular Front. In January 1938, for instance, Dr Marcel Rocher led the Nîmes section in a disruption of a left-wing peace rally; only the intervention of the *gardes mobiles* prevented the incident from turning violent. Other sections continued the practice of organizing gatherings in Popular Front strongholds. In the Somme the PSF tried to hold a bazaar in a Communist-dominated area (Corbie) in July 1938; even after the authorities had forbade it, police had to be used to guard the site and turn people away.[3] Gradually, however, as the Popular Front fragmented, clashes between the PSF and supporters of the left declined. PSF organizers instead held *réunions contradictoires*, to which Socialist and Communist speakers would be invited to debate party orators.[4]

This changing climate was associated with the evolution of France's government under Édouard Daladier, who assumed office in April 1938. The new prime minister confronted an intensifying debate over how to deal with Nazi Germany, conducted in the wake of the *Anschluss* with Austria and in the face of Nazi demands for the cession of the Sudetenland from Czechoslovakia. On the left the Communists decried capitulation and called for cooperation with the Soviet Union. The SFIO was increasingly divided between a faction that emphasized the need for peace, led by Paul Faure, and one that stressed the need to oppose fascism, represented by Blum, who nevertheless sounded ambiguous because of his desire to keep the party united. Divisions were also apparent on the nationalist right. While a few individuals such as Henri de Kerillis called for a policy of firmness in dealing with Germany even if it required cooperation with the Soviets, "neo-pacifist" sentiment, informed by concerns about France's military prospects but also the fear that war would abet a Marxist revolution, remained widespread. As for the Radical party, it hosted an array of opinions on the international situation.[5]

Judging that France's military prospects were inadequate, Daladier decided both to appease Germany and at the same time to strengthen national defence. His actions would have profound domestic political consequences. When he took office, Daladier still relied upon support from Popular Front deputies, and his predominantly Radical cabinet included two independent socialists. But over the summer of 1938 his government moved sharply to the right, invoking the dictates of national security. On 21 August Daladier announced that for the sake of armaments production, "France must be put back to work." Shortly thereafter, the independent socialists resigned and the conservative Paul Reynaud took over as finance minister, cutting spending and abrogating the forty-hour workweek in some industries. In September the French government, along with its British counterpart, effectively abandoned Czechoslovakia at the Munich Conference. In doing so, Daladier had the approval of the majority of the Chamber of Deputies except the Communists, the Socialist Jules Moch, and the conservative de Kerillis.

But this support was not a sign of growing national unity. The divisions within the Popular Front were now more glaring than ever as the Radical party moved rightward and grew increasingly hostile towards its erstwhile partners, especially the Communists. At the Radicals' annual congress, held at Marseilles in October, the left wing of the party was effectively marginalized as various delegates made fierce anti-Communist speeches. On 10 November the break with the Socialists and Communists was formalized. Twenty days later the government moved harshly against a general strike by the CGT protesting Reynaud's economic policies. Up to 800,000 workers were temporarily fired, and the union's capacity to mobilize was broken.[6]

In December 1938 France went so far as to make a joint declaration with Germany guaranteeing their mutual frontier and endorsing future consultations between the two states. However, as Fascist Italy clamoured about rights to France's Mediterranean possessions and Nazi Germany tore up the Munich Agreement by annexing Bohemia and Moravia in March 1939, Daladier felt obliged to adopt a tougher stance. He joined with the British in guaranteeing Poland and blustered that France's colonial empire made the country more than a match for Germany. But French domestic politics continued along an increasingly autocratic course. More and more, Daladier governed through the use of decree powers voted by parliament. In July 1939 he prorogued the Chamber and the Senate and delayed the elections scheduled for 1940 until 1942. In support of this and other measures, the government invoked the need for national unity and regeneration, language familiar to its erstwhile opponents on the right. Even traditional Radical hostility towards the Catholic Church subsided. The enactment of a pro-natalist Family Code, more restrictions upon foreigners, and the bringing of ostensibly non-political experts into the government all testified to the growing prevalence of technocracy, conservatism in gender relations, and an exclusionary nationalism.[7] The fact that Daladier's growing popularity increasingly derived from conservative opinion highlights the profundity of the shift.

For the PSF, dealing with this new government proved to be tricky. Daladier carried out some policies that it endorsed, but it wanted to displace him. The result was an uneasy combination of qualified support, backroom politicking, and efforts to outflank the government through sharp public criticism. In April 1938 the PSF's coterie of 8 deputies were among the 508 members of the Chamber who voted decree powers to the new cabinet until the end of July. Writing in *Le Petit Journal*, La Rocque praised aspects of the new government but at the same time argued that in the long run it could not develop a coherent policy of national regeneration; only his supporters could. "The resurrection of the country remains far off. It is only possible if the moral climate is modified rapidly thanks to the innermost evolution known as reconciliation; the PSF has the task of pointing the way." Some regional PSF papers were more blatantly hostile, asserting that the new ministry was still a lackey of "un-French" interests. *Samedi*, the PSF weekly based in Poitiers, attacked two of Daladier's ministers with an antisemitic snide against the minister of the interior, "Jéroboam de Rothschild known as Mandel," and a reference to "M. Reynaud, who perhaps represents the bazaars of Mexico," an allusion to the finance minister's business connections with that country.[8]

The PSF's manoeuvring continued into the fall of 1938. The party supported some of the government's initiatives but also called for new elections to give the PSF the parliamentary weight it claimed it deserved. These demands intensified during the Czechoslovak crisis. The PSF endorsed the government's decision to appease Hitler, though adding that France would have to redouble its efforts to prepare militarily. It then reacted to rumours that Daladier was considering calling an election by forcefully demanding one. The PSF argued that the current Chamber, which had given rise to the Popular Front, no longer reflected public opinion. Moreover, since it claimed that it was now the PSF's program which was setting the agenda for France, the party concluded that it deserved a leading position. Summarizing the movement's outlook in September 1938, La Rocque conceded that the PSF supported some of Daladier's actions but insisted that "as for our permanent policy, that is another matter. In proportion to our importance in the electoral districts, we demand our rightful place in the legislative and departmental assemblies." He used the term "proportion" advisedly, for the PSF also wanted proportional representation introduced, as this would help it overcome its problems with making electoral alliances.⁹

For a time the PSF sounded as if it was gearing up for an election campaign. Writing in *Le Petit Journal* on 14 October 1938, one of its deputies, Eugène Pébellier, asserted that while the party had supported Daladier, it much preferred to carry out "its mandate" itself, since Daladier's government was still unreliable because of its past association with the Popular Front. Perhaps concerned that PSF supporters were becoming too enthusiastic about the prime minister, the party's internal *Bulletin* claimed that it was only at their October 1938 congress that the Radicals had "take[n] note of Communist duplicity."¹⁰ PSF orators raised the hopes of militants by suggesting that an election featuring proportional representation would give the party 130 to 140 deputies.¹¹

When by early November it was clear that elections would not take place, the PSF was infuriated. Barrachin argued that Daladier had sold out by deciding instead to cooperate with the old-style conservatives of the Alliance Démocratique and the Fédération Républicaine. He characterized Daladier's actions as "a definitive discrediting" of the parliamentary regime. Then on 19 November the PSF attacked Paul Reynaud's new package of decree-law economic reforms by arguing that they did not meet the needs of the less well off, families, or small business. Its deputies abstained in the vote on the decrees on 22 December, helping to reduce Daladier's overall majority to 7.[12]

The PSF's varying relations with the Daladier government, as documented in the press and parliament, were paralleled by more low-key communications between PSF leaders and some conservative Radicals. The details of these contacts are murky, but it is known that one of Barrachin's protégés, Pierre de Léotard, was in touch with Lucien Lamoureux and other Radical opponents of the Popular Front. The PSF lent its backing to Daladier only after Ybarnégaray conversed with Georges Bonnet, the pro-appeasement Radical foreign minister. PSF militants turned up at some Radical meetings, heckling supporters of the Popular Front such as Pierre Cot. For their part, left-leaning Radicals accused Édouard Pfeiffer, the party's former secretary general, of acting as an interlocutor between conservative Radicals, notably supporters of Bonnet, and the PSF.[13]

The PSF likely intended these contacts to be part of a longer-term strategy whereby it would undermine the Radical party by encouraging divisions within it and winning over at least part of its support base. But the overtures to the Radicals attracted attention and generated tensions within the PSF itself. This result was made evident by an "inquiry" carried out by the far-right weekly *Je suis partout* into the attitudes of PSF supporters towards a potential understanding with the Radicals. To be sure, the newspaper had its own agenda in soliciting these views; perhaps it hoped to discourage such an alignment. But its editors did not hesitate to publish a wide range of reactions from people who identified themselves as PSF supporters. Some of them expressed enthusiasm about cooperating with the Radicals, stressing that the PSF needed allies until proportional representation was adopted and defensively pointing out that seeking allies did not mean that the party had lost its desire to defeat Marxism. Others, however, were intensely hostile to the idea, seeing the Radicals as the PSF's greatest enemy.[14] Police reports provide further evidence of such divisions. In Reims, for example, some PSF members openly criticized their party's deputies for abstaining in the vote on Reynaud's financial decree laws, while others believed the PSF was too accommodating towards Daladier.[15]

These contradictory pressures led the PSF to persevere in a convoluted balancing act, praising Daladier's patriotism while continuing to suggest that the Radicals could not be counted upon. Thus in December 1938, when Daladier visited Tunisia in response to threats of Italian expansionism, he was greeted with such acclaim that the local PSF federation recommended its members join in. La Rocque himself then decided to pay a visit, hoping that the patriotism aroused by the premier would encourage greater enthusiasm within the Tunisian PSF.[16] Two months later, however, La Rocque attacked Daladier for his past support of the Popular Front, suggesting that his attitude towards the left remained ambivalent. Subsequently Edmond Barrachin argued that the Radical party was in decline, notwithstanding the current popularity of the government. He predicted it would soon disintegrate, with anti-Marxist Radicals shifting to the PSF and the left wing of the party defecting to the SFIO.[17]

Alongside these polemics the PSF continued, however, to make quiet overtures to leading figures in the Radical party. Indeed, in April 1939 La Rocque sent two letters to Daladier himself, requesting a meeting to discuss the threat of aerial bombardments as well as more general issues. He also publicly hinted at the possibility of greater cooperation. At a meeting in Amiens that same month, he praised Daladier's patriotism; a few weeks before, PSF members in that same city were informed that the party wished for a "national union above parties." During the PSF's *conseil national* held later that spring, La Rocque even conceded that France's military prospects were improving.[18]

These efforts were in vain. While there is no evidence that Daladier rebuked anti–Popular Front Radicals for whatever contacts they had made with the PSF, it appears he ignored La Rocque's letters. If the PSF's frequent criticisms were not enough to poison him against some kind of alignment, his memories of 6 February 1934 probably were.[19] His government had, after all, been the principal political casualty of that day. In addition, the PSF's efforts to align with anti–Popular Front Radicals were not having the desired effect. The Radicals of the department of the Var, known for their conservatism, refused an offer of electoral cooperation made by a delegation of right-wing politicians, including representatives from the PSF. Contacts between the PSF and members of the right-wing Jeunesses Radicales ultimately amounted to little.[20] By the summer of 1939, relations between the two parties had deteriorated sharply. The last straw was the government's decision to extend the mandate of the Chamber until 1942. Incensed, La Rocque accused Daladier of seeking "to slow the success of the PSF" and of plotting a return to a leftist coalition: "By prolonging the Chamber, is not Monsieur Daladier preparing to become the leader of a Popular Front government under Marxist influence, either in wartime or, if war is avoided, in three years?"[21]

The PSF's provincial press seconded La Rocque's bitterness. *Le PSF montcellin* criticized what it saw as complacent party members who were willing to tolerate the Radicals. "The Popular Front is dead, you say? Maybe, but it will revive! It must be reborn from its ashes! It is the will of STALIN, as one of the Communist leaders from Montceau told us. It must and will be reborn, *for the Radicals are accomplices and you are asleep.*"[22] In addition to illustrating the extent to which PSF mobilization relied upon anti–Popular Front sentiment, the paper had identified a waning of militancy that was evident in other regions as well. Sometimes the local press merely admonished PSF members to get more involved, but in other cases the rhetoric bordered on despondency. The bulletin of the Loire federation went so far as to claim that of the PSF's 3 million members, only 200,000 were committed militants; the rest felt that paying their dues sufficed. In April La Rocque toured various federations "to motivate the local leaders who, according to him, no longer offer proof of sufficient activism."[23]

But it would be wrong to present the PSF as a spent force by 1939. It was no longer inspiring the same levels of combativeness as it had at the height of the Popular Front in 1936–37, but its opponents, notably the Socialists and the Communists, faced the same problems and in fact saw their memberships shrink. The PSF registered a slight fall-off in its Parisian membership in 1939, but in other regions such as the Nord it was steady or even rising.[24] As for its right-wing rivals, the PPF, once regarded as a major threat, was now in sharp decline, Doriot having alienated many backers with his excessively pro-appeasement stance on foreign policy and dissolute lifestyle. Even the British ambassador, who had never thought much of La Rocque's political abilities, conceded that while Doriot was fading from view, the PSF was looking to increase its support. Thus when *Agir*, the PSF paper for the Indre, asserted that, in comparison to the anemic activities of other parties in the department, the PSF "has enjoyed real success," the claim was probably not entirely bombastic.[25]

As for the PSF's political strategy, there can be no doubt that it had been stymied in its efforts to undermine the Radical party. It had underestimated the ability of Daladier and his colleagues to shift to the right, and its effort to attack the Radicals while reaching out to the conservative elements of that party proved contradictory. But given the PSF's alienation from the other nationalist parties in 1936–37 and its need for allies, tactically the opening to the anti–Popular Front Radicals had made some sense. At the same time, party strategists genuinely believed they could win over some Radical supporters. The PSF press noted that in instances such as a by-election in Paris's 19th arrondissement and an election to the *conseil général* at Louviers (Eure), there were signs that disaffected Radicals were turning towards it.[26] In light of such evidence, the PSF's strategy of trying to win over Radical voters while forging contacts with right-wing elements of that party is comprehensible, even though it was ultimately unsuccessful.

In retrospect, what was most significant about the PSF's designs for the Radicals is what they reveal about the party's own outlook and goals. PSF strategists believed that while they were strategically powerful by virtue of their ability to oscillate between left and right, the Radicals were irremediably corrupt. In the PSF's quest to regenerate France through the *esprit Croix de Feu*, the "principle obstacle on its path" was "the sated party, the party with influence, the rotten party: the Radical party." Therefore the goal of La Rocque and his colleagues had been to demolish one of the mainstays of the Third Republic.[27] Although they had failed to do so, the PSF's options were not yet exhausted. It still sought to dominate the nationalist cause and in 1938–39 made considerable efforts in this regard.

ALLIANCES AND ELECTIONS

For the PSF, managing relations with the other right-wing movements was never an easy task and in some instances it proved impossible. *L'Action Française* was never reconciled to La Rocque and those who remained loyal to him. It tirelessly attacked the PSF's doctrine, accusing it of conniving with the government and ruining cooperation between nationalists. In the wake of the trial against La Rocque for defamation, it accused the PSF leader of deserting his post while serving in North Africa, claimed that Noël Ottavi was a Freemason, and made remarks about La Rocque's "Jewish" personal secretary, Édouard Carvallo.[28] With respect to the right-wing political parties, while the Fédération Républicaine, Pierre Taittinger's PRNS, and the PPF were now coordinating their activities, La Rocque still asserted the PSF's independence, refusing a renewed offer of cooperation from Jacques Doriot in March 1938. The PSF was now far larger than the PPF, but in a few departments such as Oran and the Alpes-Maritimes Doriot's followers were firmly implanted and the rivalry between the two continued. The PPF repeatedly accused the PSF of being sectarian; Barrachin shot back by calling Doriot a reactionary for aligning himself with the Fédération and the Action Française, though he would not rule out the possibility of limited electoral alliances.[29]

It was the Fédération Républicaine, with some sixty seats in the Chamber of Deputies, which was the most important competitor for the PSF, and the relationship between the two parties was predictably strained. Some of the Fédération's deputies were simply anathema to La Rocque's supporters; Philippe Henriot and Xavier Vallat had some of their meetings broken up by PSF militants, as did Pierre Taittinger.[30] In 1938 the PSF angered another two Fédération deputies, Pierre Burgeot from the Rhône and André Daher of Marseilles, by ordering them to either join its parliamentary group or face electoral opposition in 1940. Even when the PSF leadership urged tact in dealing with the Fédération, to the point of agreeing upon a single right-wing electoral candidate, local militants did not always comply. In a 1938 by-election in La Roche-sur-Yon, the local PSF cadres expressed their displeasure with the selection of the Fédération's candidate – presumably because their advice was ignored – by asking PSF members to leave their ballots blank; 2,250 did so. Barrachin was dismayed, disavowing the Vendean organization's actions.[31]

Yet cooperation was not impossible even though it was at best grudging, as the victory of Charles Vallin in a by-election in Paris's 9th arrondissement in October 1938 attests. The seat had belonged to a Fédération deputy (and former Croix de Feu supporter), Pastor Édouard Soulier. It was widely predicted that the right would retake the seat, but rivalries complicated the situation. Three weeks after Vallin announced his candidacy, the Fédération selected General Niessel, a former commander and friend of La Rocque's, as its candidate. Since he had initially agreed to serve on Vallin's electoral committee, Niessel was likely subjected to considerable pressure to abandon the PSF candidate and run himself. Moreover, once Niessel declared, General Weygand contacted La Rocque to convince him to let Niessel run unopposed. But the leader of the PSF would not give way; he told supporters in Nice that "the interest of the party comes before that of friendships." Vallin eventually triumphed, after Niessel withdrew on the second round. The PSF vice-president won 54 per cent of the total vote, as compared to Soulier's 53 per cent in 1936, though voter turnout in 1938 was down by 17.7 per cent.[32] The event demonstrated both the PSF's desire for primacy and the Fédération's efforts to block this; but it also suggested that in the final analysis, right-wing cooperation was possible.

In other cases, agreements proved easier to conclude, such as during a by-election held in Remiremont (Vosges) in the spring of 1939. Here the deputy elected in 1936, Dr Gaillemin of the Fédération, had vacated his seat after moving to the Senate. According to Barrachin, the various anti–Popular Front parties were able to agree upon the single candidacy of Marcel Deschaseaux, a PSF member, a *conseiller général*, and the mayor of Plombières. He also enjoyed the full support of the former Fédération deputy.[33] Revealingly, though, Deschaseaux's victory in 1939 was far narrower than the Fédération's had been in 1936 – less than 1,000 votes, as compared to a 4,000-vote margin four years before – suggesting that many conservative voters in the district were still uncomfortable with the PSF. This was the case even though Deschaseaux had run a "moderate" campaign.

Nevertheless, the PSF seized upon Deschaseaux's victory as a sign of its mass appeal within the context of growing right-wing harmony, and it was able to point to other instances of cooperation to bolster its case. In another by-election, held in the spring of 1939 in Angoulême (Charente), the leading candidate was the neo-Socialist Marcel Déat, who considered himself a man of the left but nevertheless campaigned on an anti-Communist platform. The PSF was not fond of Déat – Barrachin hoped that he would be forced to a second round, which he was – but the party withdrew its candidate on the second round, and right-wing voters gave him his winning votes.[34]

La Rocque's supporters scored another by-election victory that same spring in Nice, but through the use of different tactics, namely, the co-opting of right-wing candidates through understandings with local notables. According to the authorities, the local section had initially chosen an electrician named Canavese as its candidate. The police believed that the PSF central leadership had overridden this choice for fear of offending the Radical candidate, Marcel Sableau, a former leader of the Jeunesses Radicales who had ties with Barrachin. The police also believed that at most the PSF would present a candidate on the first round, merely to make a running; Sableau would be supported on the second round. But they had overestimated the extent to which the PSF was cooperating with the Radicals and were mistaken about the party's final choice for candidate. That turned out to be Jacques Bounin, a protégé of Nice's conservative mayor, Jacques Médecin, whose elevation to the Senate was the occasion for the by-election. Bounin was elected on the second round and joined the PSF parliamentary group.[35]

In short, increasing, albeit hesitant, cooperation with other nationalist parties and efforts to secure well-placed candidates had led to three
PSF victories in the eighteen by-elections held in 1938–39 – a respectable, if not spectacular, success.[36] Had the legislative elections originally scheduled for 1940 actually been held, would the PSF had
continued in this vein? A detailed, though only partial, planning document drafted in 1939 by Barrachin suggests that the party faced major
obstacles to achieving a sweeping victory, but it also outlines the measures he and other PSF strategists were developing to surmount them.[37]

In the document Barrachin analyzed 208 seats, taking into account
the margin of victory by which each had been won in 1936 and frequently providing notations on the political dynamics of a given district and the prospects of the suggested PSF candidate. Of the districts
Barrachin analyzed, 173 were held by deputies connected to the Popular Front, though this total included conservative Radicals. He planned
to run PSF candidates against 61 SFIO and 41 PCF deputies.[38] These particular seats had been selected, it seems, partly because the PSF could
mobilize an anti-leftist vote. In an analysis of twenty-eight by-elections
between November 1936 and January 1939 in which the PSF found
itself up against a single candidate from one of the three main Popular
Front parties on the second round, Howlett found that its score
increased from the first round. The average increase against the eight
SFIO candidates during this period was 8 per cent, and against the
twelve Communists it was 9.4 per cent, though against eight Radicals it
was only 1.1 per cent. Under these circumstances there could be a few
successes; for instance, in February 1938 a PSF candidate narrowly
defeated a Socialist in an election for Lille's *conseil d'arrondissement*.[39]
Barrachin, it seems, hoped that in at least some instances the PSF would
be able to rally the anti-leftist vote and pick up a seat.

Frequently, though, in these situations a first-round lead would turn
into a second-round defeat at the hands of the left, even if the PSF managed to increase its total vote. In fact, in parts of the Midi and the Paris
"Red Belt" the left was so well implanted that it appears the PSF's goal
was simply to show the flag and give candidates experience. The rea-
soning at work here can be gleaned from Barrachin's comments about
the candidate he wanted to oppose the leader of the SFIO: "Breton is 25
years old. A remarkable orator, and member of the party since November [1938]. He was the former secretary general of the Parti Démocrate
Populaire's youth organization for the Seine. While he is too much of a
newcomer to be elected, he is the man who must run against Léon

Blum." Similarly, the PSF made much of the fact that of all the "anti-Marxist" parties, it alone, "despite all obstacles, courageously carries on the fight THROUGHOUT FRANCE and INCLUDING THE MOST DIFFI-CULT DISTRICTS against the parties that have frittered away [France's] victory, sabotaged the peace, ruined commerce, and undermined savings."[40] But while such an approach had propaganda value, it was unlikely to win a large number of seats.

Further towards the political centre there were also challenges. Included among the 173 targeted Popular Front deputies were 46 Radicals and 11 members of the centre-left Union Socialiste Républicaine (USR). Since the USR only had 26 deputies, the PSF was making considerable inroads upon it. The reasons for this effort seem clear; the USR was in decline by 1939, and in 5 of the 11 constituencies involved, the PSF reckoned that it needed only a few hundred votes at most to displace the incumbent.[41] The stance towards the Radicals was more ambiguous; for 69 of them, including Daladier and Bonnet, Barrachin had not – at least yet – designated PSF candidates to run against them. Was this a legacy of the PSF's overtures to elements of the Radical party? If so, then its planning was not very systematic. When the 46 deputies who were being challenged are examined closely, it is difficult to detect a consistent pattern of support for conservative Radicals and opposition to their left-leaning peers.[42] Only about 20 of the 46 could be said to be unambiguously left-wing, and the PSF also planned to run against anti–Popular Front Radicals such as Gaston Riou, André Marie, and Camille Perfetti. While the plan dates from early 1939, at a time when the PSF was still trying to establish contacts, the party was clearly not placing all its hopes in this *démarche*. The narrow margin by which some of the aforementioned candidates had won their seats was no doubt a factor in deciding to contest them.

Finally, at the time the planning document was produced the PSF planned to contest the seats of approximately thirty-five right-wing deputies. Eighteen of them were members of, or had been linked to, the Fédération Républicaine; eleven were from the Alliance Démocratique; and there was also one Agrarian and several conservative independents with no clear party affiliation.[43] Motivations for running against these individuals varied. Among those targeted, Pierre Taittinger and Philippe Henriot were both strong critics of the PSF; Georges Mandel and Paul Reynaud were disliked because of their endorsement of a Soviet alliance. Yet it appears that more mundane considerations were also involved. Despite Xavier Vallat's bitter criticisms of the PSF, for instance, Barrachin seems to have been unable, at least at that time, to find a candidate to oppose him.

While Barrachin appears to have been quite selective when it came to choosing which right-wing deputies the PSF might challenge, his plan to recruit various newcomers as candidates reflects the the party's determined effort to unite the nationalist cause under its banner. While his planning document is not precise, it appears that a significant number – perhaps over thirty – of the individuals he had in mind were not, or at least not yet, PSF members. Barrachin may have hoped that some would run as candidates of a united right, as opposed to representing the PSF explicitly. Three of them had previously been deputies, and another twelve had run unsuccessfully in 1936. Two had been Agrarians, at least two were from the Alliance Démocratique, one was a member of the Radical Socialist Camille Pelletan group, and the rest had run as conservatives or independents. A half-dozen of them were currently or had been municipal or regional councillors. Among the most notable individuals selected as potential candidates were Henri du Moulin de Labarthète, an inspecteur de finances and later Pétain's chef de cabinet between 1940 and 1942, who Barrachin hoped would run against Pierre Mendès-France in the Eure. Barrachin also wanted to have Philippe Barrès, son of the ultra-nationalist writer Maurice Barrès and a former leader of the Faisceau, run in Paris's 1st arrondissement against Pierre Taittinger. Of course, it was not guaranteed that such individuals would run for the party. Barrachin believed that one of the PSF's selected candidates for Lille was "unbeatable" but feared that he would not run against the incumbent, Henri Becquart of the Fédération because he was a personal friend. Barrachin also worried that in departments such as the Doubs and the Hérault the attitude of local conservative politicians would be hostile and thus damaging.[44]

Clearly, achieving a sweeping electoral victory would be no easy matter for the PSF. In some cases right-wing parties might still not cooperate; the contradictions of the Radical party made a consistent strategy towards it difficult; and facing the left head-on might bring only limited results. Precisely how well La Rocque's supporters would have done in the elections scheduled for 1940 is, of course, ultimately a matter of speculation. While members and sympathizers proclaimed that it could have won over 100 seats, some recent scholarship has suggested that the party was losing steam by 1939 and that a total of 70 seats, or even less, was more likely.[45] Proportional representation, which the movement so desperately wanted, might have alleviated these problems. With the estimated support of between 12 and 15 per cent of the electorate, in a Chamber with 618 seats the PSF would have held 70 to 90 of them.[46]

Yet even with proportionality the PSF clearly had much work to do. Barrachin's document indicates that the party's planning was still getting underway; in a dozen departments there were as yet no candidates at all. Furthermore, in at least twenty cases the PSF's chief political strategist was dubious of local cadres' prospects. That said, Barrachin was impressed with the organization and dedication of a number of federations, notably those in Algeria, and believed that the party had many prospects. Joseph Levet, he surmised, had a good chance of being elected over a Communist in Sceaux (Seine), and Charles Goutry had a "clear place" at Provins (Seine-et-Marne). In Disne (Basses-Alpes), Dijon (Côte d'Or), and Tours (Indre-et-Loire), the SFIO had won by only a small margin; so here too there were opportunities.[47] Moreover, in some regions the party was setting down roots and winning favour with local notables; for instance, in the Calvados the PSF gained the support of the Duc d'Harcourt, the Catholic and pro-monarchist deputy for Bayeux, who shifted his allegiance from Dorgères's Greenshirts to La Rocque.[48] Thus, while it seems likely that the PSF's progress would have been steady rather than dazzling, it might well have established a presence in the Chamber after the 1940 elections comparable to what the Communists had achieved in 1936 – 72 seats – an outcome that had a major impact on French politics at the time.

The electoral potential that the PSF did demonstrate in the final months of peace was nullified by the prorogation and then the outbreak of war. It is therefore critical to remember that for all the energy expended into transforming what had been an anti-parliamentary movement into a vote-getting machine, the leadership was not only thinking in these terms. For his part, La Rocque was unequivocal that he would never run for a seat in the Chamber. In doing so, he continued to distinguish himself from other right-wing politicians such as Louis Marin, Pierre Taittinger, and Jacques Doriot. It could be implied that he was also signalling his ongoing rejection of the parliamentary system, even though of necessity his followers had to deal with the political establishment. La Rocque claimed that he preferred to concentrate upon the long-term work involved in preparing the transition to a new France under the PSF's guidance. In August 1939 he reminded readers of *Le Petit Journal* that "however urgent certain undertakings and tasks of popularization can be, preference has always been accorded to the nation and our social mission ... the PSF, the undertaking of today, and the État Social Français, the work of tomorrow, demand an inspiration of patriotic loyalism and humane solidarity."[49] We must now investigate the contours of the idealized polity meant to inspire PSF supporters at this time.

ENVISIONING THE ÉTAT SOCIAL FRANÇAIS

When it was founded, the PSF had declared that it would not be like other parties. It would avoid soulless programs and instead endow France with the Croix de Feu's mystique, the spirit of the *union sacrée*. "We cannot imagine how a program of reforms could be applied without the moral and psychological 'climate' to ensure their extension, effectiveness, and durability. Without an animating mystique, such a program will wither and remain sterile."[50] Unavoidably, however, the party found itself elaborating more specific proposals in its quest for electoral appeal and differentiation from its competitors, and increasingly it couched its program in terms of instituting an "État Social Français." Though La Rocque first used the term in the fall of 1937 with reference to overseeing the corporatist economic system he declared the party would establish, the concept came to denote the overall framework within which the PSF's tripartite slogan of "Travail, Famille, Patrie" would be realized.[51] As the content of the État Social Français was explicated, it became apparent that there were diverging approaches to a number of issues within the party. Yet as a whole, the portrait of a regenerated France which emerges from PSF discourse was that of a highly regulated national community modelled upon the patriarchal family, with its culture, values, and sense of nationhood defined in essentialist terms.

The working out of the PSF's program is most comprehensible if its overarching elements – Work, Family, and Nation – are considered in succession. With respect to the economy, the party held to the Croix de Feu's notion of la profession organisée, analyzed in more depth. The first detailed statement of the PSF's program, the pamphlet *Le Parti Social Français: Une mystique, une programme*, described it as the organization of production along regional and sectoral lines. The unions that would form its building blocks would stress employer-labour cooperation and "professional" concerns rather than the "political" ones of revolutionary organizations. A *conseil national économique* would coordinate the whole system and be consulted by the government, though it would have no legislative power.[52]

The movement denied that this program was actually corporatist, claiming that unlike the state-directed corporatism of "certain foreign countries," that is, Fascist Italy, its program was "based upon the principle of cooperation, through agreement and for the common good." But the PSF in fact foresaw an important role for the state in coordinating professional bodies and envisaged stringent regulations for financial speculation and capital transfers across frontiers. In more general terms, like the Croix de Feu, the PSF's debt to the paternalist corporatism of thinkers such as Albert de Mun and Frédéric Le Play was sizable.[53] This was apparent in its relations with a range of socioeconomic groups.

The party was soon encouraging employer-inspired initiatives aimed at building *la profession organisée* from the bottom up. As early as 1936, a number of Parisian employers involved in public works and construction who were sympathetic to the PSF had proposed the formation of professional groupings within their industries. Their ultimate goal was the creation of tripartite committees of employers, white-collar employees, and workers. The initiative lay with the bosses, who were to organize PSF supporters quietly. The authors of a report on the initiative, Louis Escande and Pierre Kula, described the objective as being to undo the destructive impact of "extremist syndicalism" and to re-establish "the confidence of our workers, inspiring them with the spirit of order and duty, and thus allowing syndicalism to regain its true nature."[54]

Over the long term, the PSF sought "to put an end to the proletariat" living in rundown cities lacking proper amenities. It hoped that new leisure facilities and transport between factories and homes in the countryside would allow for a blending of urban and rural lifestyles, free of the pernicious influences typically associated with cities.[55] In the meantime, the party tried to spread its paternalist message to workers. Its newspaper for workers in the Parisian region, *L'Ouvrier libre*, vociferously denied being a tool of employers as it condemned Marxism. The paper even floated a heavy-handed slogan coined by Pierre Forest, a leading PSF columnist on labour issues – "Neither for Marx, nor finance, but for France!" While this motto did not catch on, it did encapsulate the PSF's desire to appear as a "third force" between capital and labour, ensuring class collaboration in the national interest. Such rhetoric coexisted, though, with admonitions to workers that they had to be mindful of their obligations to other social groups. Similarly, in *Le Flambeau* and *Le Petit Journal*, Forest advised working-class leaders to be more "responsible" and not give in to the demands of the masses.[56]

La profession organisée was also extolled as the panacea for France's peasants. In contrast to the working class, here the PSF was less concerned about transforming values; instead, measures aimed at upholding the rural family were developed. Professional representation would help to ensure that peasant interests received their proper due, in contrast to the current system, which neglected them. More educational and technical support had to be provided. Most immediately, France's civil code had to be revised to ensure that farm plots would not be subdivided excessively by those who inherited them; substantial family farms, the guarantors of rural life, had to be reinforced. To ensure that peasants would flock to its banner and not that of the left, the PSF warned that the "Marxist" parties sought to reduce the French peasant to serfdom "like Stalin's *muzhiks*."[57] Yet despite its professed identification with rural values, PSF leaders discerned a troublesome cultural gap between their urban organizers and the countryside. The party's agricultural expert, Joseph de Nadillac, a former deputy for the Alliance Démocratique, stressed the need for propagandists to avoid "talking down" to the peasantry about agriculture.[58]

Such concerns were less evident when it came to France's middle classes, who, PSF notables such as Barrachin argued, needed a new champion since they had been deserted by the Radicals. By the spring of 1937, party militants were being instructed that "at the current time, the defence of the *classes moyennes* must join the defence of the peasantry and the familial patrimony at the highest level of our propaganda."[59] The PSF's definition of the *classes moyennes* was pliable, encompassing a spectrum from the liberal professions to shopkeepers and artisans. The solutions it proposed for the problems of these groups were similarly vague. The PSF constantly stressed the value of organizing along sectoral lines, though it also called for exclusionary measures to be directed against "foreigners." To support this agenda, Émile Sergent, a member of the Academy of Medicine who had long argued for the exclusion of immigrants – particularly East European Jews – from French medical schools, now became a contributor to the PSF press. And in 1939 Charles Vallin proposed that newcomers who sought positions as small businessmen and artisans should have to pay a "special tax."[60]

The PSF's claims that all the sectoral interests in the French economy could be managed through a representative system and good-faith bargaining were quixotic. Within the movement itself, ideological harmony was sometimes lacking. Consensual definitions of groups such as the middle classes proved elusive; in Lyons, different contributors to *Le Volontaire '36* alternately characterized them as either small property-holders or technically skilled professionals such as engineers. Some party notables felt that the PSF was neglecting entire social groups, notably agricultural labourers.[61] Indeed, contrasting ideas about the basic orientation of France's economy coexisted uneasily within the movement. La Rocque himself excoriated the effects of large-scale capitalism and tended to idealize rural life and small family firms. The pamphlet *Le Parti Social Français: Une mystique, une programme* bemoaned "the never-ending development of machinism [which] engenders an odious serfdom, a barbarous crushing of the personality." Yet there was also a current of opinion within the party which was enthusiastic about the technocratic organization of large-scale capitalism. The engineer Luc Touron, a contributor to *Le Flambeau de Bourgogne*, paid obeisance to the principle of class collaboration but envisioned a France where the state and a managerial class oversaw the development of a dynamic economy while at the same time preserving social order.[62]

Internal differences regarding economic policy were common among the many ultra-nationalist movements of interwar Europe. In 1935 the Croix de Feu had suffered the defection of some leading members of the Volontaires Nationaux partly for those reasons. It does not appear that the PSF experienced these tensions with the same intensity, though it is interesting to speculate on how the differences that did exist would have played out had the movement come to power. What is certain is that the entire PSF, visions of class collaboration aside, desired a paternalist brand of labour relations. Similarly, the elaboration of the party's outlook on the French "family" revealed internal fault lines, but also underscored its desire to reorient national mores in fundamental ways.

From its inception the PSF had proclaimed that "the family is simultaneously the goal, the justification, and the reward for human effort." Symbolically, the party's commitment to the family was demonstrated through practices such as La Rocque's serving as the godfather for a large number of militants' children. This practice received a good deal of attention in the PSF press, and on at least one occasion a baptism was disrupted by Socialist and Communist demonstrators.[63] Patriarchal fatherhood was essential to male PSF militants and integral to the regeneration of France. Under the current system, fatherhood was neglected; there had to be a revision of "individualistic legislation which practically asphyxiates and enslaves the family." Under a PSF government, the "familial factor" would be figured into the calculation of salaries and social insurance benefits, and firms would reserve jobs for workers with families.[64]

When it came to developing familial policy, however, the party gave more explicit attention to women and youth than men. In doing so, it built upon the Croix de Feu's efforts to mobilize women. A striking article for *Le Flambeau du Sud-Ouest*, which discussed how the wives of some Soviet officers had accused their husbands of treason during Stalin's purges, not only furthered the party's anti-Communist vision but also encapsulated the PSF's ideal of womanhood. The author, Jacqueline Benoit, proudly asserted that, in contrast to her Soviet counterpart, the French "wife of a leader" would "do her duty to unite with her husband and never betray his deeds," adding that women's courage might even stimulate "the moral strength that men sometimes need!"[65]

Charles Vallin made clear how important the mobilization of women was to the PSF in a 1937 lecture, declaring that history had taught that "we will not save France without women," though he cautioned that this understanding did not mean the party embraced the "sectarian" doctrine of feminism. Since women were deemed essential to creating the moral climate for national renovation, the PSF attacked the current system for denying female influence through the vote. It also scoffed at left-wing support for women's suffrage, suggesting that its opponents voted for it only because their leaders knew the French Senate would overturn it; in reality, they feared that women voters would change the country's political orientation. Like the Croix de Feu, the PSF demanded that women receive the vote, but first at the local level and only in conjunction with the "familial" vote.[66]

The conflation of female with familial suffrage illustrates the extent to which the PSF identified women's activism with buttressing the family. The prospect of married women working outside the home therefore remained distasteful to the movement. *La Liberté du Maine* disapprovingly noted the prevalence of women in the Soviet industrial workforce: "the state of things in the red paradise and which some would like to see established in France gravely compromises the development of a normal family life, to say nothing of the dangers to the health of the family in these conditions."[67] For young or single women, work outside the home was permissible. But the overarching thrust of the party's rhetoric was directed towards, as one sample lecture intended for party militants put it, "the return of the mother to the household," which was deemed essential in order to improve France's worrisome birth rates. The PSF asserted that the introduction of a family wage would "allow for the normal functioning of the labour market by bringing about the withdrawal of all female labour that duplicates male labour."[68]

Nevertheless, there was a degree of ambivalence in PSF discourse regarding women. For instance, whether a familial wage system might drive unmarried women as well as married ones out of the workforce was unclear. So too were the implications of the familial vote; the PSF never specified whether wives would actually control their own votes or simply "transfer" them to their husbands. This ambivalence caused frustration for some female militants, notably Mademoiselle Casanova of Marseilles, a propagandist of some note who demanded clarification. Casanova asserted that while the family vote was perfectly acceptable regarding a father's control over the "extra" votes conferred by children, a mother must command her own vote.[69]

But for other female militants, such matters were far less important. Writing in *La Flamme des Deux-Sèvres*, Odette Bernard suggested that the events of 1936 had shown that elections rarely reflected the people's will, and while the exclusion of women from voting was wrong, "in reality, it is opinion which governs us; and there, ladies, no law prevents you from being active." The idea that it was more important for women to have influence upon French values than formal political rights was reaffirmed by *Le Petit Journal* in May 1939 when it called for a government which would "consider women's participation in public life as a social, rather than an electoral, problem and make feminism a national force that would usefully serve the country, rather than the instrument of some feminine ambitions."[70] On the whole, PSF cadres seemed far more concerned about ensuring that female activism served to promote familial mores than defining women's role in politics. Even Casanova's distinctiveness in this regard should not be overstated; she was adamant that women's place was in the home, not the workplace.[71]

As for the PSF's proposals regarding youth, they were intended to mould generations of patriots who would embrace the organic community inherent in the concept of the État Social Français. The party's view of education was utilitarian and scornful of what it called "intel-

lectualism." As La Rocque put it at the movement's first university student congress, the role of intellectuals was "to serve"; evidently,
detached criticism was not appreciated.[72] François de Polignac, the
party's deputy for the Maine-et-Loire, encapsulated the PSF's general
principles in his report to the party's 1938 annual congress. Education,
he declared, should take into account the requirements "of *work* or the
profession, the rights of the *family*, and the necessities of the *nation*,
under the two merging signs of true *social progress* and the surest *spiritual tradition of France.*"[73]

Efforts by PSF supporters to specify details of the party's educational
policies entailed some contradictions. For contributors to *Le Petit
Journal* such as Marcelle Tinayre and the publisher Bernard Grasset,
the problem with the education system in general and the reforms insti-
tuted by the Popular Front in particular was that they threatened to
create a large number of "unemployed intellectuals." The current system was too concentrated upon academics; workers and peasants were
intelligent, but the nation would be better off, Tinayre maintained, if
people were encouraged to fulfill their proper roles. By contrast, other
contributors such as the popularizer of French colonialism André
Demaison projected a hostility to elitism: "The greatest nation of the
future will be that in which intellectuals work with their hands and
manual labourers are intellectually cultivated."[74] Collectively, the party
also sounded unsure about the role of the state in education. Its student
organization criticized the current education ministry for stifling familial and individual initiative and for its lack of respect for "spiritual"
forces. To this end, the PSF's university student organization passed a
motion in 1938 calling for greater funding and more autonomy for
Catholic institutions. At the same time, it proposed the creation of
what amounted to a super-ministry of education, responsible for overseeing radio, the press, fine arts, scientific research, technical and physical education, child protection, health and hygiene, and the defence of
morality against "immoral propaganda."[75]

In the field of education, then, the PSF's rhetoric was an amalgam of
religious-paternalist impulses with an ambitious desire for modernist
social intervention. When it came to defining the national community,
the party propagated a vision of what historian Herman Lebovics has
called the "True France."[76] La Rocque continued to emphasize that the
nation's ethos was integrally Christian, even though some of its members were not. Only by reasserting these values through the PSF would
France be regenerated. "Nothing will check [our] effort until Christian

civilization has once again opened the French route to complete social progress in a strong and regenerated country." While the party repeatedly declared that it respected all faiths and that "the ethnic question does not arise in France, ... we consider as foreigners all those who, through their attitude, sentiments, and conduct stand apart from the nation, even if they were able to acquire French citizenship."[77] It was up to the PSF to judge who was truly French.

To an extent, the party allowed for different modes of belonging to the nation. La Rocque and his colleagues championed regionalism as imbuing the French with communitarian impulses, in contrast to the supposedly atomizing rationalism of the Third Republic. Greater recognition of France's historic diversity would coexist with – indeed, reinforce – a more fervent enthusiasm for the nation as a whole. As Paul Creyssel, the former Radical and now PSF deputy, put it when he addressed a meeting in Grenoble, "the regionalist spirit" would be "at the root of success for a party that must organize France according to regions, allowing each its individuality and its own qualities." The wearing of local costumes at PSF festivals was common; even the party's Breton community in Paris had its own banquet. In Alsace, where autonomy was an ongoing issue, the movement's concessions to regionalist sentiment garnered it considerable support.[78]

At the other end of the spectrum of national identification, the PSF also advanced pro-imperial sentiment, applying its familial model to France's possessions. André Demaison proclaimed that within the empire "there are, let us be clear about it, a leader, an attentive mother, children of different ages, and even servants who, in their turn, will rise to a higher rank."[79] This phrase suggests that the PSF promised gradual integration for colonial populations, but in practice the bar was set almost impossibly high. La Rocque insisted upon total commitment to France's Christian civilization, observing of Muslims that "those among them who believe themselves to be sufficiently advanced must come to us and incorporate themselves totally into the great French family." While certain Algerians such as veterans were deserving of citizenship, it was material amelioration, not political rights, that mattered to the majority of them. "Above all, what must be given to the natives is a better existence." This, the PSF press indicated, could only come through additional French settlement and further economic development.[80] In emphasizing paternalist social intervention over the promise of assimilation, the party's doctrine reflected shifts then underway in French imperialist ideology.[81] But at the same time the PSF's consideration of the colonial question dovetailed with its own distinct emphasis upon the "social question" and the working out of its conception of French identity.

For La Rocque and his supporters, the issue of national identity inevitably led to discussion of the status of Jews in the French national community, and here Algeria continued to figure centrally in the evolution of the party's doctrine. Ever since the PSF's creation, cadres such as Marcel Sarrochi, the propaganda delegate for Oran, had responded to demands from militants for an overtly anti-Jewish stance by insisting that this was contrary to party doctrine and warning them about playing into Hitler's hands. But Sarrochi was also quick to conclude that many Jews were involved in Marxist revolutions and that the "Jewish question" was a result not of prejudice but of "the Jewish mentality and spirit, since for Jews everything goes back to three points – idealism – arrogance – anxiety." By the fall of 1938 La Rocque himself was willing to endorse antisemitism of a "respectable" sort in the territory. At the PSF's federal congress held in Constantine in October of that year, he declared that during the recent municipal elections the Jewish community had voted as a bloc against the nationalist parties and had singled out the PSF in particular. When a member of the audience then shouted, "Down with the Jews!" La Rocque countered: "I find it idiotic to be content with shouting 'Down with the Jews,' and after having bellowed this to feel satisfied and quietly return home to have an aperitif or listen to the radio. What I propose to you is far more difficult; as long as the Jews of Constantine hold this attitude, you must maintain a calm, even smiling countenance but ignore them totally from a social and commercial point of view."[82] Thereafter the PSF boycotted Constantine's Jewish community.

Across the Mediterranean, antisemitism was also on the rise within the PSF. In Alsace-Lorraine such attacks were particularly frequent. *Le Flambeau de Lorraine* depicted Jews as a source of trouble wherever they went: "Christ condemned the 'chosen' people to unending dispersion and distraction. Is that why Israelites are never able to settle and live in peace, even on their original lands?" In the Oise, where reports of antisemitism were less common, one PSF orator warned his audience that if they did not subscribe to *Le Petit Journal*, it might fall into "the hands of Jews."[83]

Such remarks were made within the context of a general increase in xenophobia. Yet even as the Daladier government enacted various restrictions upon foreigners, the PSF pushed for more exclusionary measures. In October 1938 it proposed restrictions upon immigrants similar to those demanded by Charles Maurras, who called for the expulsion of all foreigners involved in criminal or political activities, the introduction of special taxes on them, and a revision of naturalizations granted since 1936. In 1939 the PSF's *conseil national* went even further, passing a motion that called for the revision of "the massive number of naturalizations imprudently granted over the last ten years." By this time, refugees from Republican Spain were also arousing its ire. Jean Ybarnégaray conducted a violent diatribe against the government for accepting "thousands" of "looters, arsonists, dynamiters, assassins, and torturers."[84] But Jews were still regarded as particularly troublesome. When PSF orators discussed unemployment, they were instructed to point out that foreign labour was only part of the problem, since Poles, Italians, and others came to France because workers for certain projects were in short supply. Tellingly, Jews were not mentioned in this context.[85]

Officially the PSF continued to reject racism and remained open to all, but the rhetoric and attitudes of many militants frequently belied such claims. Efforts at restraint were overshadowed by demands for exclusion. Following Kristallnacht in November 1938, the PSF's *Bulletin* reminded militants that Nazism's biological racism was antithetical to Christian civilization, but it quickly added that the movement was not "philo-semitic," insisting that the naturalization of the many "foreign Jews" entering France must be tightly restricted.[86]

On the eve of the Second World War, then, the PSF was in the midst of an ideological realignment that can fruitfully be explored in relation to the analysis of populist movements developed by Pierre-André Taguieff and Michel Winock.[87] Both scholars emphasize that movements claiming to speak for the people can have both "protest" and "identity-oriented" dimensions. Protest populism emphasizes disdain for a corrupt elite and claims to speak for the people, transcending traditional political divisions. Identity-oriented populists also focus upon incarnating the popular will, but the focus shifts to the "foreigner" as enemy, and the issue of preserving the community's purity comes to the forefront. Obviously, populism does not have to be authoritarian, though in the interwar French context this was often the case. Nor are the two strands mutually exclusive; they can coexist within a movement, with one or the other predominating at a given time.

In the case of the PSF, when compared to its predecessor, the identity-oriented facet of its populism came to the fore. In comparison to the

Croix de Feu, it now frequently stressed its affinities with France's dominant Christian tradition. By the end of the 1930s, high-profile Catholic thinkers such as Gabriel Marcel and François Veuillot were writing in support of the party, identifying its quest for national reconciliation with the church's goals.[88] Speaking to an audience in Nantes, Veuillot compared the PSF and the faithful: "these two entities ... have the same mystique: family, peace, liberty; the same love and respect for the one who represents their ideals, God for one and La Rocque for the other." La Rocque affirmed this stance following the election of Pope Pius XII in March 1939, declaring that "believers of all sorts, sincere unbelievers, all fervent with French loyalty, the men and women of the Croix de Feu freely and respectfully bow before the most illustrious apostle of our national vocation."[89]

This statement represented a shift in emphasis rather than a complete rupture with the propaganda of the Croix de Feu. After all, in its constant invective against the Popular Front, the league had frequently asserted the latter's subservience to foreign interests. And in its disdain for traditional "politics" and its calls for the transcendence of partisan differences, the PSF echoed the protest-oriented populism of its forerunner. Even Catholics such as Veuillot emphasized that the party still embodied the *esprit Croix de Feu*.[90] But the PSF was more explicit than its predecessor had been in its antisemitism, xenophobia, and commitment to European supremacy in France's colonies. These modifications emerged in the context of the partisan struggles of 1936–38 and the anti-refugee sentiment that swept over elements of French society. But they were not inevitable; they were the product of conscious decisions on the part of the PSF leadership and ordinary militants.

THE INTERNATIONAL SITUATION

The PSF articulated its program against the background of a growing international crisis. During the era of the Blum government, La Rocque and his colleagues had made clear their foreign policy preferences and the close links they drew between diplomacy and domestic politics. Above all, France had to be united and revive its military power; removing the Popular Front from power was the crucial precondition for doing so. Nazi Germany should be confronted but only with suitable allies, in the hope of achieving a durable equilibrium rather than going to war. In this task Great Britain was essential, even though elements of the PSF regarded it with suspicion. Fascist Italy was a highly desirable partner; the PSF was dismayed that French and British criticisms of Mussolini following the invasion of Ethiopia had led him to align with Hitler, and it hoped this affiliation could be undone. By contrast, an alliance with the USSR had to be avoided. Stalin, supported by the PCF, sought only to encourage a war that would shatter the European powers and leave the continent open to Communization.

As the threat of war loomed, the PSF attempted to hold to these positions, but the realities of Nazi and Fascist expansionism necessitated some reappraisals. Like much of the French right, La Rocque and his colleagues gradually adopted a firmer policy towards Germany, though there was always the hope that war would be avoided. To their enduring regret, Fascist Italy could not be won over and even came to be regarded as a threat. But while it became apparent that cooperation with Britain and a policy of firmness were necessary, the PSF remained heavily preoccupied with the threat of Communism. It continued to be wary of the Soviet Union and criticized "bellicists" who it believed were too eager to confront Hitler and thus risk total war and the threat of revolution. Throughout this period the PSF also used the international situation to reiterate its preference for authoritarian, nationalist, and "Christian" political systems.

The German annexation of Austria in March 1938 crystallized the problems that France faced. Nazi expansionism was gaining momentum, but the leaders of the Third Republic did not believe that they could risk war. For its part, the PSF used the occasion to reaffirm its views on foreign policy and criticize the government. As German pressure on Austria intensified in early 1938, some members, notably Paul Creyssel, seemed fatalistic, concluding that the Reich "had a certain need of expansion."[91] But most PSF orators adopted a tougher tone, even though when all was said and done, the party still counselled acquiescence. Speaking in the Chamber of Deputies on 25 February, Jean Ybarnégaray used strong words but closed on a conciliatory note: "I am for a policy of vigilance and firmness toward Germany, a policy of support for Austria and of the *status quo* in Central Europe, a policy of friendship towards Italy while we stay on the side of Great Britain and, under the conditions that I have defined, for an immense effort to lessen the antagonism between two groups of powers and to save peace."[92] Ybarnégaray thus continued to rule out the possibility of cooperation with the Soviets and called for a revival of the Stresa Front, constructed by Britain, France, and Italy in 1935 to contain Germany, even though Mussolini was now aligned with Hitler. La Rocque supported this approach, concluding that until French strength was restored, no durable arrangement with Germany was possible. In the wake of the annexation, he chastised Blum as a "worthy successor" to the many politicians who, he claimed, had mismanaged French diplomacy since 1919, and he reiterated the need to improve relations with Italy and be suspicious of the USSR.[93]

Soon after the *Anschluss*, Germany intensified pressure on Czechoslovakia to cede the Sudetenland. While neither Britain nor France would ultimately go to war to prevent Germany's seizure of this territory, over the summer and early fall of 1938 it appeared to be a distinct possibility. Throughout this period the PSF supported the Daladier government's policy of appeasement, and in doing so, it stuck to many of the arguments it had used in the past. La Rocque maintained that France still needed to build up its military capacity and moral unity, insisting that the damage done by the Popular Front still lingered. To be sure, the PSF at times adopted a defiant tone towards Hitler. Writing in *Le Petit Journal* on 11 September, La Rocque addressed the "valiant soldiers of Greater Germany," advising them to remember that French arms had stopped them at the Battle of the Marne. But in the same editorial he also invoked the spectre of Communism, warning Mussolini and Hitler that should war break out, only Stalin would benefit: "Will you open our old continent, devastated by battle, to Bolshevik riots?"[94] La Rocque also continued to accuse the PCF, which called for cooperation with the Soviets and resistance to Germany, of wanting a war to create the preconditions for revolution. In addition, he and his colleagues attacked the small number of right-wing politicians who opposed the Munich accords, which ceded the Sudetenland to Germany, as "warmongers." Once the agreement had been reached, the PSF contended that pressuring the Czechs to capitulate had been a "realist" policy given France's internal divisions.[95]

The PSF, like many of France's political parties, was hugely relieved that war had been avoided, but La Rocque also concluded that "it is inadvisable to remain dormant." The country needed to proceed with rearmament and achieve political unity.[96] It also needed to be sure of its allies, but on this point the PSF only haltingly realized that reassessments were in order. Over the course of 1938 it had come to affirm more strongly the need for cooperation with Britain. A powerful streak of anglophobia persisted within the party; the regional newspaper *Samedi*, for instance, accused the British of constantly meddling in French politics and even suggested that they and the Soviets had financed the election of the Popular Front. But La Rocque stressed the importance of Franco-British solidarity; during the royal visit of 1938 he had termed it "the cornerstone of European peace."[97] By contrast, most PSF members, enthusiastic about the idea of having Fascist Italy as an ally, were utterly dismayed at Mussolini's continuing alignment with Hitler. After the Duce rumbled about acquiring parts of the French colonial empire, it was abundantly clear that Italy could not be regarded as a potential friend, at least in the short term. Commenting on Mussolini's demands, La Rocque questioned whether he imagined "he can intimidate ... the direct descendants of Kellerman's soldiers at Valmy, of Bonaparte's troops at Montenotte?" Despite this bravado, however, the PSF leader was distressed at the prospect of Fascist Italy becoming an enemy. A month before the German attack on Poland, he affirmed that "hostility between Rome and Paris is contrary to the nature of things."[98]

After Munich, the PSF's attitude towards Nazi Germany also hardened, a shift strongly encouraged by the now-indisputable collapse of the Popular Front. As the French left lost influence and the right's fears of a "war-revolution nexus" faded, some PSF members began to sound more belligerent. When the German army occupied Bohemia and Moravia in March 1939, Marcel Gatuing, head of the PSF's Oran federation, boasted: "Ah! Let them come now, the fanatics of the swastika! After twenty years of lethargy, the Christian West is reawakening." La Rocque stressed the need to support Poland as it resisted German pressure to cede Danzig, and over the summer of 1939 he repeatedly stated that France and the PSF would be ready should war break out. On 15 July he assured the readers of *Le Petit Journal* that "our people ... are ready to spring to arms if the madness of certain men and certain states forces us to." On 2 August he claimed that France "still bears on her soil and on her flesh the scars of recent battles; she does not maintain illusions about the potential reality of carnage."[99]

But while the PSF adopted a more assertive tone in dealing with the nationalist dictatorships of Mussolini and Hitler, it also remained intensely concerned about the Soviet Union. In January 1939 La Rocque had warned that "Berlin and Moscow could work in parallel against order and France's prestige."[100] In the months that followed, France and Britain began to seek an alliance with the Soviets to deter Germany, but La Rocque altered his views very little. Though he eventually conceded that "useful accords" might be signed with the Soviets, it appears he was thinking in economic, rather than military, terms, and in July 1939 he reiterated that "Russia, an Asiatic empire in the hands of the avowed enemies of the Christian tradition, forms the antithesis of our civilization."[101] La Rocque sounded almost relieved when the Nazi-Soviet pact was announced in late August. Declaring that he had long foreseen this agreement, he concluded that the battle between Christian civilization, on the one hand, and the forces of barbarism, paganism, and materialism, on the other, had finally been joined. "Let us make clear to France each day that the salvation of peace, like that of the homeland, depends and will depend upon the triumph of Christianity over barbarism." Once France declared war on Germany, the PSF leader called for "audacity" in dealing with the "neo-pagan" Hitler, but he viewed the USSR as no less of a threat, declaring that the Führer's war would unwittingly serve the cause of world revolution.[102]

In its shift from a pro-appeasement outlook in 1938 to a willingness to challenge Germany in 1939, the PSF was hardly alone on the French right. It continued to differentiate itself from conservatives such as Paul Reynaud, Henri de Kerillis, and Georges Mandel, who opposed German expansion even if it necessitated cooperation with the Soviets; La Rocque accused individuals such as Mandel of espousing preventative war. But the PSF also adopted a firmer stance than the "resigned" nationalists who were more willing to countenance German domination over central Europe. For example, La Rocque dissociated himself from former prime minister Pierre-Étienne Flandin's decision to send Hitler a telegram of congratulations for preserving peace through the Munich accords.[103] The PSF thus remained, along with formations such as the Fédération Républicaine, in the camp of "conditional nationalism." During the ascendancy of the Popular Front, proponents of this outlook had sought to avoid a war that they believed might trigger revolution. But once the conditions of ongoing German aggression, an alliance with Britain, and above all the end of the Popular Front were met, resistance to German aggression became acceptable.[104] However, for the PSF the connection between international and domestic politics remained crucial; in 1939 La Rocque was still worried that if war broke out, it might encourage a revival of the Popular Front.[105] This outlook would shape the PSF's conduct during the "phoney war" of 1939–40.

The PSF sought to harmonize its domestic policies with its diagnosis of the international situation in other ways as well. Its characterizations of growing diplomatic tensions and of certain regimes were conditioned by its authoritarian, nationalist outlook. La Rocque was categorical that if war between Britain and France on the one side and Germany on the other came, it should not be characterized as a contest between democracies and dictatorships. "Let everyone keep the regime of their choice and refrain from imposing it on the rest of the world." These words hardly indicated satisfaction with the status quo in France, however; as the international situation worsened, La Rocque continued to call for fundamental political change. "Without attempting impossible restorations, without undertaking any foolish adventures, let us prepare the reform of the state through the practice of responsibility, the tireless formation of new elites, and the continuous testing of existing elites, in the service of the people."[106] While these words ruled out a coup or a monarchical restoration, they did imply a reoriented France, one potentially open to a Catholic-inspired authoritarianism.

Certainly, PSF notables found various regimes of that ilk appealing. Before it was annexed by Nazi Germany, Paul Creyssel had visited Austria and praised the "very supple discipline" of its clerical-authoritarian regime.[107] Octave Aubry, author of a number of popular works on the Napoleonic era and a contributor to *Le Petit Journal*, was an admirer of the Portuguese dictator Antonio Salazar. He described Salazar as carrying out a process of national renovation while remaining faithful to Christian and humane traditions of cooperation, thus avoiding the demagogy, paganism, and personal excesses of Mussolini and Hitler. La Rocque, too, was taken with the Portuguese example.[108] Not surprisingly, after supporting the Nationalists during the Spanish Civil War, the PSF also expressed enthusiasm about the new dictatorship established by Francisco Franco. Returning from a trip to Spain shortly after Franco's victory, Stanislas Devaud emphasized his hope for "the swift setting aright of nationalist Spain, which the Catholic faith again animates." La Rocque urged Daladier's government to come to a political and economic understanding with Franco as quickly as possible.[109]

The PSF's admiration for such regimes is suggestive of its long-term goals and illustrates the extent to which it shared the outlook of the Croix de Feu. When it suited them to do so, individuals such as Barrachin and La Rocque liked to emphasize that the PSF had integrated into the party system. They had even attacked the Daladier government for delaying the legislative elections until 1942, accusing it of betraying democracy and using "dictatorial methods irreconcilable with the French spirit."[110] But given the PSF's admiration for authoritarian systems outside France and the paternalist and hierarchical qualities of its utopian État Social Français, it is hard to see such protests as motivated by genuine democratic convictions. Rather, they suggest yet another appropriation of democratic ideals for tactical purposes, echoing the PSF's accusations in 1936–37 that Blum's government was dictatorial because of the legal measures it had taken against the party.

In some respects, the Daladier government had proven to be a more difficult target. In light of its efforts at clamping down on unions, passing anti-immigration measures, and invoking the need for national renewal, PSF figures such as Paul Creyssel could only complain that their views had been co-opted, observing bitterly that Daladier "is often inspired by our program," even though he could never be guided by the party's "spirit."[111] Not only had the PSF been foiled in its plan to undermine the Radicals; the latter had seemingly reasserted their dominant position in the Third Republic, though they had become increasingly anti-Communist, xenophobic, and fond of executive power in the process.[112]

But if in the short term La Rocque and his followers were thwarted, they were also looking ahead. Though relations with its prospective allies remained tense, the PSF was devising a variegated electoral strategy. It had developed its program for national reconciliation, forging a comprehensive vision of a country renewed by its principles, even if this process revealed some variation of opinions within the movement. Above all, the PSF had consolidated into a truly mass organization, with the capacity not only for electioneering but also for having a profound impact on the lives of the hundreds of thousands of people within its orbit. Through the expansion of its counter-society, it tried to promote, in an effort to prefigure a future France, an authoritarian, nationalist sensibility to an unprecedented number of people. Who they were and to what extent La Rocque and his supporters shaped their world view must now be considered.

6

Anticipating the État Social Français

In the summer of 1937 the PSF established a welcome centre in Paris for members coming from the provinces to see the International Exhibition held that year. Among the attractions was a map of France with thirteen thousand drawing pins, each representing a party section. The green pins denoted a section with 100 to 500 members; the red ones those with over 500 members. There was also a map of North Africa and even a world map showing PSF sections in locales such as Buenos Aires and Honduras.[1] These charts illustrate in a striking fashion how the PSF sought to emphasize its ubiquity. But could the party truly live up to such an image? Moreover, in addition to attracting members, could it sink roots into French society that had a chance of enduring?

In terms of attracting sheer numbers of supporters, La Rocque and his colleagues achieved considerable success; the PSF was the largest political party of the Third Republic. While retaining a strong middle- and lower-middle-class base as well as an appeal to veterans, the PSF strove to attract more workers and peasants, with some results, particularly in the countryside. La Rocque and his colleagues also made clear their desire to win over disaffected supporters of the left; on this score they achieved some much-touted successes, but the PSF benefited above all from a right-wing backlash against the Popular Front. In addition to tens of thousands of former Croix de Feu supporters, it attracted members of other dissolved nationalist leagues and conservatives and moderates radicalized by fear and hatred of the Popular Front. As with the Croix de Feu, the PSF's claims to transcend the traditional political divisions of France were overstated; the outlook of its supporters was strongly on the right, though in terms of its scale and social presence, it represented a new departure for nationalist movements in the country.

One of the main reasons for its success was the party's robust associational life, which it had inherited from the Croix de Feu but expanded and refined in many ways. Dedicated militants poured considerable energy and resources into its women's and youth movements, social services, and cultural initiatives. They also created new organizations which, while under the control of PSF officials, professed to operate at arm's length from the party without taking an interest in politics. New trade unions encouraged patriotism and class collaboration, in contrast to strikes and left-wing militancy; new organizations for employers sought to encourage social peace through paternalism. The defusion of conflict in the workplace would be complemented by the efforts of social centres working to strengthen patriotic French families, whose members could benefit from invigorating sporting and cultural activities. Many of these initiatives can be regarded as a response to the practices of the Popular Front coalition and the measures of the Blum government, but they also represented an effort to begin erecting the État Social Français from the ground up, within the structures of the Third Republic.

From the time of its formation in 1936 to the outbreak of war three years later, the PSF confronted the gap between its rhetoric of patriotic harmony and the fact that its membership was divided by generation, social class, gender, and to some extent political priorities. Veterans of the Croix de Feu sometimes found it hard to adjust to the new party; competition for material resources created tensions within the movement; a number of supporters, especially within the women's organization, felt their talents were being underutilized. Nor did the various initiatives launched by La Rocque and his colleagues meet with uniform success; internal contradictions and contestation by other groups and interests blunted some of them. In spite of the reversals it sometimes encountered, however, the PSF and its ancillary organizations proved inventive and persistent, even though in terms of basic principles there were relatively few changes. The PSF continued to insist upon the need for patriotic discipline and to present itself as the avatar of a reconciled and rejuvenated France. In doing so, it made huge claims on the men, women, and children associated with it.

PROFILING THE MEMBERSHIP

As with the Croix de Feu, charting the growth and determining the size, geographic variation, and social composition of the PSF's membership is a challenge. Few scholars accept the movement's most extravagant claims about its support base, and there are contradictory estimates for some regions. In the department of the Rhône, for instance, the PSF claimed 30,000 members in July 1937 and close to 40,000 a year later; the real maximum appears to have been closer to 20,000.[2] Problems similar to those encountered when assessing the social base of the Croix de Feu remain. Sources are frequently imprecise when it comes to categories such as the social class, age, or gender of supporters.

Nevertheless, the data allows for some conclusions. Scholars have judged some PSF estimates to be judicious, such as Charles Vallin's assertion in December 1938 that the average size of a departmental federation was 7,600 members, a figure far below the one of 20,000 advanced nearly two years before. Several collections of primary material exist. Membership cards for the Nord survive, and there are other extant files, registers, and membership lists from locations such as Pau and its environs, the canton of Vernon in the department of the Eure, and Montreuil in the Paris suburbs. There are also central documents from PSF headquarters which track the pace of membership growth during specific periods.[3] Figures derived from departmental archives and local studies, collated in table 3, give some indication of the PSF's growth.

The numbers in table 3 indicate that the PSF grew impressively, though the specific pace varied according to geography. Some departments were slow to get started in 1936, and competition from Doriot's PPF hampered PSF development in places such as Algeria.[4] Still, the takeoff was rapid in many regions. In departments such as the Aisne, the Nord, and the Pas-de-Calais, the year 1937 saw the most intense growth, with the figures almost doubling. Elsewhere the peak came later, with departments such as the Indre-et-Loire still making considerable headway into 1938, while other federations showed slower growth by that time. In some areas – notably the Seine – stagnation eventually set in. The April 1938 total of 172,120 for Paris and its environs did not represent a great improvement over the estimated 168,000 supporters the party had had at the end of 1936, and by 1939 the total had actually fallen off, though only slightly so. Against these trends, however, there is evidence of continued growth in 1939 in districts such as the Nord and the Parisian suburb of Montreuil, both of which, interestingly, had substantial working-class populations.[5] The fact that the PSF was still gaining ground in some regions on the eve of war testifies to its staying power.

Table 3
Estimated PSF membership by department/region, 1936–39

Department/region	Date of estimate	Estimated membership
DEPARTMENTS		
Aisne	July 1936	1,000
	December 1936	4,500
	January 1937	6,000
	June 1937	10–11,000
	January 1938	12,500
	June 1938	13,000+
Algiers	1937	10,000
	1938	11,000
	1939	13,000
Alpes-Maritimes	January 1937	6,000
	August 1937	8,000
	January 1938	8,000
	March 1938	8,500
Aube	September 1936	2,000
	September 1939	7,000
Cantal	October 1937	1,500
Charente	October 1937	5,000
Côte d'Or	1936	750
	1937	11,000
Constantine	July 1936	1,200+
	February 1937	6,000
	1938	7,000
	1939	8,000
Creuse	1939	500
Eure-et-Loire	October 1937	3,500
Gard	October 1936	2,500+
Gironde	October 1937	20,000
Haute-Saône	October 1937	7,000
Haute-Vienne	1939	3,000
Ille-et-Vilaine	October 1937	10,000
Indre-et-Loire	October 1937	7,500
	August 1939	12,000
Isère	October 1937	12–15,000
Jura	1937	6,000
Loire-Inférieure	January 1937	12,000
	October 1937	20,000
Loiret	October 1937	6,700

Table 3 (continued)

Department/region	Date of estimate	Estimated membership
Meurthe-et-Moselle	January 1937	15,000
Morbihan	October 1937	8,000
Nord	January 1937	26,000
	June/July 1937	37–40,000
	May 1938	50,000
	September 1939	50–55,000
Oran	1937	4,000
	1938	4,500
	1939	3,000
Pas-de-Calais	January 1937	11,000
	July 1937	18,000
	March 1938	24,000
	July 1938	24,000
Rhône	July/August 1937	13,000
	November 1938	15–20,000
Somme	July 1938	13,000
Tarn	October 1937	4,000
Vendée	December 1936	1,000
REGIONS/COLONIES		
Alsace	1939	27,000
Seine	April 1938	172,120
	January 1939	174,872
	March 1939	172,098
	May 1939	170,840
Tunisia	April 1938	5,000
	December 1938	5,000

SOURCES: Machefer, "Le Parti Social Français en 1936–1937"; Prévosto, "La Fédération du Nord"; Irvine, "Fascism in France"; Goodfellow, *Between the Swastika and the Cross of Lorraine*; Ferragu, "Croix de Feu et le PSF en Indre-et-Loire"; Chouvel, "Croix de Feu et le PSF en Haute-Vienne"; Howlett, "Croix de Feu"; Passmore, *From Liberalism to Fascism*; APP B/a 1952; AD Alpes-Maritimes 4M 542; AD Gard 1M 715; AD Vendée 4M 413; AD Aisne 1M 19; AD Aube 110J 10; CAOM B3 327 (Constantine); CAOM Oran 70; Cantier, *L'Algérie sous le régime de Vichy*; *Le Flambeau*; *Le Flambeau de l'Isère*, 29 October 1937; *Le Flambeau de Flandre-Artois-Picardie*, 27 March 1938; *Samedi du Poitou*, 18 June 1938; *La Flamme*, 2 December 1938; Lefebvre, ed., *Laon*.

So too does the sheer size of the movement, though a definitive figure remains elusive. Some party sources claimed it already had 1.5 million supporters by early 1937; the following year a total figure of 3 million was touted. Outside observers were far more cautious. The police claimed that the PSF had 700,000 supporters by 1937, "many of them women," while the US embassy contended that the PSF could not hope to match the militancy and commitment of the Communists, regardless of its numerical superiority.[6] That said, recent scholarship has made clear that La Rocque and his supporters forged the biggest political party of the Third Republic. Howlett, extrapolating from data on Parisian shareholders in *Le Petit Journal* and the number of members in the Seine in 1938–39, has suggested a low figure of 750,000. At the other end of the spectrum, by calculating the percentage of members in the Nord in 1939 as a proportion of that department's population as a whole (2.5 per cent) and applying that figure on the national level, he posits a maximum of 1 million. Thomas relies upon internal party documents and takes into account the varying pace of growth in different regions. Industrial departments such as the Nord saw slower growth after 1937, but Thomas discerns a catch-up effect in less populous, more rural departments in 1938–39. He concludes that a total figure of 1.2 million is plausible.[7] By any estimate, then, the PSF's membership was larger than that of the Socialist and Communist parties combined and much greater than that of any right-wing competitor.[8]

In geographic terms, the PSF broke some new ground compared to the Croix de Feu, though in a few cases it was unable to match the achievements of its predecessor. In western France the Croix de Feu had established only a moderate presence by June 1936, but both the Ille-et-Vilaine and the Loire-Inférieure furnished the PSF with strong federations, though its presence in the Vendée remained weak. Conversely, the PSF could not equal the appeal the Croix de Feu had enjoyed in Dunkirk, since many local militants came to disapprove of La Rocque's caution in 1935–36.[9]

On the whole, however, it is the continuities that stand out. Like the Croix de Feu, the PSF did particularly well in northern France, urbanized regions, and departments with a tradition of right-wing voting.[10] Results in Normandy were especially impressive; that region alone became one of the three administrative divisions within the party, the other two being the Île-de-France and the rest of the provinces respectively.[11] The Nord, the Pas-de-Calais, the Aisne, the Meurthe-et-Moselle, and Alsace all provided crucial support for the new party, as they had for the Croix de Feu.[12] This was also the case regarding the Seine, even though here membership growth stagnated relatively early.

There were also some PSF bastions further to the south, concentrated in departments with large cities. The Gironde, the Rhône, the Isère, and the Alpes-Maritimes were important, and by 1937 the PSF had 15,000 members in Marseilles alone. Nor, despite ongoing rivalry with the PPF, should the importance of Algeria for the movement be ignored. By 1939 the colony accounted for some 26,000 PSF supporters; figures such as Barrachin observed that the militancy of the local federations set an example for France itself.[13] It was in central and southwestern France, especially in rural areas, where the PSF encountered the most difficulties. But even here it could build upon previous Croix de Feu support; this was the case in the Haute-Vienne, where the party enjoyed more support than it did in the Lot, Corrèze, or Creuse, where the Croix de Feu had been weak.[14]

Despite the geographic variation in its appeal, the PSF liked to insist that it had support throughout France; it similarly emphasized that its selfless patriotism made it uniquely appealing to all social classes. PSF officials eagerly pointed out that the movement not only drew from the middle classes but also won support "in the world of labour and especially in factories and workshops."[15] The Croix de Feu had made comparable claims, but had not really lived up to them. While the league had reached out to a variety of social groups in its latter stages, it remained disproportionately a movement of the middle classes, with under-representation of the rural population and urban workers. In the case of the PSF, claims of a wider social base were more plausible – to an extent. Various officials had the impression that the party drew from "all classes, but in the majority from the middle classes."[16] For the department of the Nord, Vernon and its environs in the Eure, and the quarter of Prébendes in the city of Tours, more precise information on the socio-economic background of an appreciable number of PSF members is available, as table 4 indicates.

Collectively, the samples in table 4 point to the ongoing centrality of the middle classes – admittedly a diffuse category – to the PSF. The bourgeoisie and upper classes also remain significant. Yet the data also suggest a capacity to attract other socio-economic groups. In the Nord the proportion of the working class was impressive; it was also respectable for Vernon, but less so for Prébendes, a middle-class sector of Tours. Moreover, the figures suggest that compared to the Croix de Feu, the PSF had a greater rural presence.

Qualitative evidence from elsewhere in France supports these trends, while also hinting at some of the dynamics behind them. Like the Croix de Feu, a proportion of the PSF's working-class adherents were probably not committed supporters. Authorities in the Seine maintained in early 1937 that the unemployed joined in order to find work. In Reims

Table 4
Selected data on PSF membership by socio-economic group (percentages)

Category	Nord (1939) (n=6,884)	Vernon (1939) (n=3,185)	Prébendes (n.d.) (n=438)
AGRICULTURE	16.0	16.4	2.9
Farmers	12.2	8.8	–
Labourers	3.8	7.6	–
WORKERS	32.9	16.3	11.6
Manual labour	3.8	2.5	–
Workers	25.1	12.6	11.4
Domestics	2.3	1.0	0.2
Foremen	1.7	0.3	
CLASSES MOYENNES	41.0	59.8	63.2
Artisans	5.6	21.8	9.1
Shopkeepers	9.3	5.5	15.2
Employees	16.0	12.7	21.5
Business employees	3.1	2.1	9.5
Teachers	0.6	0.8	
Students	1.3	0.5	3.4
Retired	0.5	6.8	4.5
No profession	4.7	9.2	
BOURGEOIS/ UPPER CLASS	10.1	7.5	21.6
Liberal professions	1.0	2.4	10.9
Senior managers	2.1	1.0	4.1
Company manager/head	3.4	0.7	6.6
Merchant	2.7	1.6	
Rentier/Proprietor	1.0	1.9	

SOURCES: Prévosto, "Fédération du Nord," 48–50; Ferragu, "Croix de Feu," 18; CHEVS LR4 Vernon *fichier*. The number of each profession was calculated by M. Gilles de La Rocque; the percentages were calculated by the author.

NOTE: Totals do not add up because of rounding. The classification scheme follows that of Prévosto, "Fédération du Nord," but the category of *employé de commerce* is counted as lower-middle- rather than working-class. Also, Ferragu's categories are not quite the same as Prévosto's. They have been dealt with in the following manner: Ferragu combines the categories of retired and without profession (4.5 per cent); her percentages for *militaires* (1.1 per cent) and *fonctionnaires* (0.4 per cent) have been placed in the category of *employé*, and her category of représentant (9.5 per cent) has been included in that of *employé de commerce*.

officials predicted that the PSF's charitable activities could win over textile workers whose livelihoods were threatened by cuts to their hours. In Nice laid-off Communist militants and CGT supporters reportedly hoped that by joining the trade unions inspired by the party (the Syndicats Professionels Français) they would get jobs. Scholars have also suggested that while there was some support for the PSF among workers in large firms such as Renault, many of its working-class members came from smaller, family-oriented firms, rendering them more susceptible to employer pressure. For example, many of the metallurgical workers in the Nord who joined the PSF were employed in such establishments.[17] In sum, while the PSF had more success than its predecessor in attracting workers, they remained a challenge.

In the countryside, too, there were obstacles, but mobilizing efforts had begun to pay off. The PSF appealed to the peasantry on the basis of opposition to the Popular Front's agricultural policies; within months of its creation, it claimed that farmers in regions such as the Loire-Inférieure and the Ille-et-Vilaine were flocking to it in the thousands.[18] True, in 1936–37 the party had to contend with other movements. In the Alpes-Maritimes, for instance, the PPF seized the initiative in the countryside. Dorgères's Greenshirts also provided serious competition; indeed, in some departments such as the Creuse the PSF at first simply backed them rather than trying to challenge them.[19] Over time, however, La Rocque's supporters gained the upper hand. Paxton notes that after 1937 the PSF made serious inroads into Dorgères's constituency. Peasants eventually constituted 30 per cent of the membership of the Haute-Vienne federation; by 1939 farmers in the Nord were joining in numbers disproportionate to their share of the general population. Even in rural areas where the SFIO and PCF did well, such as the Beauce region in the Gard, PSF sections were formed.[20]

Nevertheless, the urban lower middle and middle classes were at the core of the PSF's membership, as had been the case for the Croix de Feu. Given the wide range of groups encompassed within these categories, is it possible to be more specific about which sectors found the party especially attractive? For the Rhône, Passmore concludes that within the Lyons business community medium-sized firms and more modern sectors such as engineering tended to back the PSF, while older and bigger firms were inclined to support its rival, the Fédération Républicaine. He also notes that engineers and managers were overrepresented in the PSF; so were white-collar workers.[21] Evidence at the national level further suggests that the PSF appealed to the commercial and technocratic middle class. For the 202 members of the 1938 directing committee, the professions of 130 are known. There were 38 industrialists and entrepreneurs, 20 shopkeepers and merchants, 9 sales representatives, 14 cadres (senior managers), 12 engineers, 17 lawyers and doctors, 15 writers and journalists, and 5 office employees. The remaining 72 people included an airline pilot and several retired officers. Interestingly, the latter group – and military networks in general – were rather less important to the PSF than they had been to the Croix de Feu. Among the highest ranks, fewer generals (15) joined the party than the league (20), and proportionally their weight was even further reduced. In symbolic terms, Vallin's campaign against General Niessel in 1938 was also telling, signifying that the party would not align itself with individual officers unconditionally, despite its championing of a strong national defence.[22]

But while these trends are undeniable, patterns redolent of the Croix de Feu can also be detected. Though it was less ostentatiously "military" in orientation than the Croix de Feu, the PSF continued to court retired officers. Such individuals could be influential in local communities, and many reserve officer associations retained PSF supporters.[23] Furthermore, just as the military ethos remained influential within the PSF, so did the "traditional" lower middle classes, as the data from Vernon shows. The proportion of artisans within this particular sample is very high (21.8 per cent) and includes 25 saddlers, 21 wheelwrights, 87 carpenters, and 134 masons. Suggestive too are the diverse backgrounds of the PSF's parliamentary group. Out of the eleven who entered the Chamber of Deputies, two were trained as engineers (Bounin and Robbe), and one ran the local Compagnie des Thermes (Deschaseaux). But others came from less-technical backgrounds; two had received legal training (Ybarnégaray and Fourcault de Pavant), one had been a municipal civil servant (Peter), and another taught at a lycée (Devaud). De Polignac was a landowner, and while Vallin had worked as a banker, he was also a graduate of the École Libre des Sciences Politiques.[24] In short, though the PSF was developing a technocratic profile, it retained an appeal to more "traditional" elements of French society as well.

Like its predecessor, the PSF sought to project an image of youth and vigour. While the age structure of the party varied according to region and was shaped partly by local political constellations, here again its claims had some validity. The federation president of the Haute-Vienne claimed that in the Limousin the average age of a member in 1938 was thirty, in a region where the general population was relatively old. The average age of party militants was similar in the working-class quarter of Montreuil.[25] In the Rhône, recruitment was complicated by intense competition, with the PPF vying with the PSF for younger members. Yet La Rocque's supporters remained comparatively youthful in this department, with over 50 per cent of the membership aged between thirty and fifty, though this was partly because the Fédération Républicaine retained the support of many older voters. In Vernon, by contrast, PSF support was more evenly distributed in terms of age; 19.2 per cent of members were in their twenties, 20.9 per cent in their thirties, 17.8 per cent in their forties, the same proportion in their fifties, and a substantial number – 23 per cent – were over sixty.[26]

La Rocque and his colleagues also prided themselves on having the support of French women. Here the available information is particularly fragmentary. Only in some cases do police reports give an indication of whether and how many women attended party meetings, let alone if they were actually members. PSF records themselves do not always distinguish between male and female supporters. But there is enough evidence to conclude that a substantial number of women were in the party's orbit. The Nantes PSF boasted an impressive number of 2,360 female members in June 1938, but what proportion of the total membership this figure constituted is unclear. At the national level, records of incoming members in July 1936 suggest that women comprised between 15 and 20 per cent of the total. By contrast, subsequent figures for the Nord suggest a total of only 11 per cent, while in Cannes it was even lower, estimated at only 8.5 per cent. On the other hand, in Prébendes (Tours) 22.1 per cent of the membership was female, while in Montreuil the proportion reached 31.5 per cent. Thomas has suggested that the higher figure is more typical, and that the PSF had at minimum 200,000 female supporters and possibly as many as 30,000.[27] Even if a lower ratio of 15 per cent is used and it is assumed that the PSF had 1 million members, the resulting total of 150,000 is impressive, larger than that of the other parties.

Social trends do not tell us everything that we need to know about the outlook of PSF members; the issue of political antecedents needs to be explored in its own right. Especially in the early stages of the movement, figures such as Vallin were eager to stress that the PSF was attracting a new clientele, declaring that "though numerous they might be, the members of the old [leagues] are but a small minority within the party." Another recurring theme was that the PSF had attracted substantial numbers of former Popular Front adherents. *Samedi* and other regional papers carried interviews with figures such as Jean Dufour, a former member of the Young Socialists who found that "each day" the results of the Blum experiment "became ... more catastrophic." Fortunately, positive experiences with his conscientious PSF employer and insights from new PSF friends in his Tours boarding house, plus the inability of his Socialist comrades to find him work after he recovered from illness, had led him to attend his first PSF meeting. Now Dufour claimed that he wanted to "redeem" his past.[28] On the basis of such evidence, several historians suggest that, compared to the Croix de Feu, the PSF gradually lost extremist supporters who were disillusioned with La Rocque's caution and gained former leftist and moderate ones who were impressed by the party's acceptance of the Republic.[29]

On this point, there is scattered evidence of disillusioned workers abandoning the Popular Front for La Rocque. It also appears that in departments such as the Rhône some Radical voters defected, though whether they had ever been very enthusiastic about the Popular Front is unclear.[30] There can also be no doubt that a number of alienated Croix de Feu supporters joined rival movements. In Reims, for example, the antisemite Darquier de Pellepoix established a "Club National," composed largely of dissident Croix de Feu and PSF supporters, which the authorities concluded was "clearly further to the right and more violent" than the PSF.[31] Former Croix de Feu members also defected to Doriot's PPF, an act that is often interpreted as a sign of radicalization.[32] But it must be noted that despite these trends, the PSF remained open to hard-liners during this period. La Rocque and his colleagues were eager to win back embittered members, including those who had joined the PPF; certainly, this was the case in the Hérault and the Alpes-Maritimes.[33]

Rather than a drift towards the moderate centre, the most salient trends that emerge from a consideration of the PSF membership's political background are the large numbers of former Croix de Feu supporters who joined, the rallying of members from other ultra-nationalist groups to the party, and the radicalized outlook of the many traditional conservatives who signed up. While the PSF lost some organizers to rivals such as the PPF, other notables such as Joseph Levet in Normandy, Jacques Arnoult in Marseilles, and Marcel Rocher in Nîmes – all considered by the authorities to be extremists – remained active. As for the ordinary membership, evidence from some of the largest PSF federations is suggestive. Armand Causaert, the federation president for the Nord, believed that anywhere between 60 per cent and 90 per cent of the Croix de Feu's supporters in the department joined the PSF, a considerable overlap. Paris's prefect of police reported in early 1937 that the PSF "had to this point recruited above all from the former members of the dissolved Croix de Feu, Volontaires Nationaux, and Mouvement Social Français des Croix de Feu."[34]

The PSF also attracted support from the Croix de Feu's ultra-nationalist rivals, as the bitter rivalries within the French far right during this period attested. The *sûreté* in Constantine reported that following the dissolution of the leagues, former members of the Jeunesses Patriotes and Action Française planned to join the PSF, "despite their instinctive repugnance for La Rocque." In the Oise, the Action Française was effectively dead by 1939; "most of its members or sympathizers have joined the PPF and above all the PSF." Throughout France the polarization that accompanied the election of the Popular Front encouraged a gathering of various right-wing activists under the PSF's banner, as the *commissaire de police* in Fontenay-le-Comte concluded: "it is quite evident that the grouping together of these elements from the dissolved leagues has no other goal than the rallying of their forces within the PSF."[35]

La Rocque and his colleagues also courted supporters from more established conservative formations. The police in Guise (Aisne) asserted that within "the most active and influential right-wing groups, the PDP and A[lliance]," there would be converts to the PSF. In Alsace the party made inroads against the Catholic Union Populaire Républicaine, while in the Seine-et-Oise the prefect reported that "the PSF is pursuing a continuous effort at propaganda and organization; it seeks to aggregate all conservative right-wing elements," even though it claimed to respect the autonomy of existing organizations.[36] The growing vehemence with which the Fédération Républicaine and other parties attacked the PSF indicates the extent to which these efforts were bearing fruit.

Why were some supporters of the traditional right defecting to the PSF? Because of the party's mystique and its message of national reconciliation? Because the PSF provided more robust networks of support and sociability than the older, elite-oriented formations? For some, these factors were undoubtedly critical. "At the time we were not politicized, but I remember the attraction that ideas of national reconciliation held for us," recalled a former militant in 1973.[37] But the fact that the PSF promised a more energetic response to the Popular Front was also of integral importance. The party seemed to have particular appeal in regions where a strong conservative trend coexisted with a perceived left-wing threat. For instance, in the rural district of Saint-Yriex in the Haute-Vienne, which remained firmly under the control of conservative landowners, the PSF had trouble making headway. But it did better in "red" Limoges, where the Popular Front was strong, and also in Bellac, a district with large landowners and a tradition of conservative voting, but one where the left had made gains in the 1936 elections. The PSF's regional president for the Charentes and Périgord was clear about how the backlash against the Popular Front stimulated the party's growth: "in this region, where Marxism has made a considerable effort over the last years, only the PSF can fight effectively against theories whose triumph would mean the ruin of French civilization."[38]

In political terms, then, the PSF was not as inclusive as its claims to be the harbinger of national reconciliation implied. It did gain adherents from social groups often deemed refractory to the traditional right and won over some disaffected supporters of the Popular Front. But the preponderance of former Croix de Feu supporters, militants from the other leagues, and radicalized conservatives within its ranks ensured it would remain anchored in a counter-revolutionary milieu. To be sure, this spectrum of support was still broad enough to make for a volatile movement. By early 1938 it was clear to the police that even the federation leaders "do not all have the same religious or political sympathies."[39] Some cadres grew frustrated. Alfred Debay, who had served as the regional organizer for the Algerian Croix de Feu and then the PSF, quit his post (though not the party) following criticism that he was inept. In explaining his decision, Debay expressed frustration that he could not adapt to the goals and requirements of a political party, as opposed to a nationalist league. In Saint-Nazaire (Loire-Inférieure) Dr Dubois, who had been the section president and run unsuccessfully in the 1937 cantonal elections, quit the following year, citing the lack of cooperation with other "movements of the right to which he remains, for his own part, faithfully attached."[40]

Such tensions and frustrations were hardly unique to the PSF. Disputes about the utility of "conventional" politics and relations with other parties were common to many far-right movements in France and – indeed, Europe as a whole – at the time. Interwar ultra-nationalists tended to be impatient in their quest for power and to quarrel vociferously about tactics. Across the Rhine, for example, serious divisions had emerged within the Nazi party in the fall of 1932, which might have led to its breakup had it not been saved by the decision of German conservatives to make Hitler chancellor in January 1933.[41] For their part, the PSF leadership were no doubt keenly aware of potentially divisive currents and sought to expand and strengthen the counter-society established by the Croix de Feu to ensure greater cohesion.

REFINING THE COUNTER-SOCIETY

The dissolution of 1936 had compelled La Rocque and his colleagues to develop a new set of structures to accommodate the vast number of people who flocked from the Croix de Feu to the PSF, as well as thousands of newcomers. Their efforts involved a constant reworking of the organization and its financial arrangements. They also involved attempts to restart and then strengthen the sizable organizations for women and youth that the league had established. In the case of the PSF's Section Féminine, the party's efforts at reorganization proved unable to resolve some of the difficulties that its predecessor had encountered. As for its efforts to mobilize French youth, the PSF had to tread carefully; it had to be seen as complementing rather than supplanting traditional loyalties. Real though these tensions were, however, it is the determination of the PSF leadership and committed militants that stands out.

By 1938 a number of changes had been made to emphasize how distinct the PSF was from the Croix de Feu; these were undertaken primarily as a response to the reconstitution trial. For instance, the prominence of the EVP was reduced compared to what it had been in 1936.[42] The leadership also implemented a formal decentralization of the movement to highlight further the contrast between the Croix de Feu and its successor. In 1938 the PSF formally transformed itself into the Union Interfédéral du Parti Social Français. The federations were now made autonomous bodies affiliated to the headquarters in Paris. This measure would complicate any future effort to define the party as a single legal entity, thus making it harder to dissolve it.[43]

In spite of this formal devolution, central direction within the PSF remained firm. Ten regional delegates oversaw operations in the provinces. There were also inter-federal delegates who inspected several federations. Barrachin's *bureau politique* issued directives about policy and strategy, while the federations themselves were generally limited to financial and administrative tasks. The central executive also streamlined its operations, enhancing the concentration of authority in the process. The directing committee was retained; it consisted of La Rocque, the deputies, the regional and departmental presidents, and 130 members chosen from the national congress serving two-year terms. But the PSF also established an executive committee of 25 members, while day-to-day operations were overseen by the Permanent Administrative Commission, consisting of La Rocque, the vice-presidents (Ybarnégaray,

Ottavi, and after December 1938 Vallin), the general secretary, and 5 commissioners chosen quarterly from the executive committee.[44]

In general, La Rocque controlled the agenda and set the times when decision-making bodies met. The local organizations could suggest motions for the national congress, but it was the directing committee that drafted them. It is true that La Rocque had rejected a resolution advanced at the PSF's first annual conference in 1936 to make him president for life. But the fact that such a motion was made in the first place, as well as La Rocque's subsequent acclamation as leader, is indicative of the new party's outlook.[45] At the local level, section presidents were to be elected annually, but this process seems to have been formalistic. The bulletin of the party's Versailles-Montreuil section summed up the official attitude towards internal differences succinctly. While insisting that the PSF was a party in which all opinions could be expressed, it urged members with dissenting views to voice their concerns to the section president alone and in private. The bulletin concluded that "the French people have the reputation of being intelligent and spiritual. That is all well and good, but they often lack what Cardinal Richelieu called the spirit of purpose, namely, a sense of discipline ... in the PSF, we must avoid such abuses of criticism."[46]

This emphasis upon hierarchy and unity did not preclude tensions, especially when money was involved. While the PSF did rely on some wealthy benefactors – though some of these gave to other parties as well – much of its financing came from membership dues and the proceeds from various sales and functions.[47] Problems with late or unpaid dues, plus considerable costs, meant the party was frequently short of money. After it was acquired in 1937, Le Petit Journal proved to be a huge drain, losing some old readers and failing to replace them entirely with new ones. By March 1938 it was running a deficit of 550,000 francs a month. The leadership in Paris also complained that some local PSF papers were in effect competing with it. They instructed the local press not to repeat coverage of national events, which gave rise to disputes in Algiers and elsewhere.[48] Soon the problem of funding became more generalized, as federations demanded a larger share of the party's revenues to carry on their activities. Some local organizers even requested a complete review of the central treasury. That did not happen, but in the spring of 1939 the head of the commission which ran the party's central financial office accepted the demands of "a large number of federations" to reduce their contribution to Paris from 40 per cent of the monies they collected to 25 per cent.[49]

While the PSF had reworked its central administrative structures partly in response to legal pressures, the restructuring of its Section Féminine reflected an attempt to learn from previous experience. In this respect the PSF was not entirely successful, even though its women's organization grew and some ways prospered. The Croix de Feu had regarded women in general as agents of social peace, but the experiences of the Section Féminine had led the movement to conclude that most women could not perform the job of social worker per se. Only suitably prepared female members could engage in such activity; the rest would have concentrate on other tasks. In the PSF this division was continued. Each section was to have a women's group composed of two subgroups: Action Sociale, which practised social work, and Action Civique, which supported the party's propaganda efforts.[50] The result was that some women played a prominent role in the PSF, but others found their duties less well-defined and felt that their abilities were not put to good use.

With a clearly specified goal, Action Sociale provided some scope for the assertion of female professional competence and autonomy. It was headed by the *deleguée première pour l'Action Sociale*, who was designated by La Rocque and attached to the head office. Characteristically, despite her influence, de Préval did not occupy this post, preferring to work behind the scenes; in October 1936 Madame Gouin, who had twenty five years of social work experience and who also sat on the PSF's directing committee, took over the position. The PSF also established a Bureau des Études Sociales, headed by Jeanne Garrigoux, which provided training and policy research.[51] The central leadership also vetted the appointment of Action Sociale delegates at the local, federation, and regional levels. In relation to the tens of thousands of women who joined the PSF, the number specifically tasked with social work appears to have been relatively small; in late 1937 Garrigoux reported that there were 523 social sections throughout France with 1,350 personnel.[52]

In carrying out its work, Action Sociale encountered obstacles but insisted it was making progress. Its members had to contend with the indifference or hostility of some male militants, the difficulties inherent in penetrating isolated areas, and competition from other organizations such as Michelin's social services in Clermont-Ferrand. In some areas, such as Algeria, there was also the challenge of a lack of enthusiasm.[53] But Action Sociale reported at the PSF's second annual congress that over 15,000 children attended its study groups and another 15,000 its *colonies de vacances*, and that it had also trained over 2,000 young women in household management, while hundreds of social auxiliaries also received instruction. The importance placed by cadres such as Gouin and Garrigoux on obtaining proper qualifications was clear. In facilities such as the Centre Guynemer in Billancourt, all of the permanent staff either held state diplomas or were in training. And while Garrigoux asserted that women were particularly suited to social work because of their "maternal sense," she also stressed the need to obtain formal diplomas in suitable fields. The leverage obtained from such qualifications was made evident when a Madame Cavalier-Besnard, having resigned after La Rocque himself criticized her for absenteeism, secured another position within the organization because the PSF badly needed people with her skills.[54]

The experiences of women in Action Sociale must be situated in context, however. Many of the PSF's female members were associated with Action Civique, the mandate of which was less clear. To be sure, PSF cadres were willing to use women as propagandists as their opponents did, so long as the proper image was projected: "our adversaries, particularly the Communists, have perfectly understood the benefit that their propaganda could derive from feminine speeches, which, *when they are simple, sincere, prepared, and controlled*, always touch the hearts of listeners and often bring about their adherence."[55] And there were some PSF women orators of note, notably Mademoiselle Casanova from Marseilles, a devoted militant whose unease about the PSF's lack of clarity regarding the "family vote" has already been noted. Casanova addressed meetings throughout the Midi, and her speeches were often greeted with thunderous applause. She venerated La Rocque, referring to him as "not only a chief, but a master, an idol, whose spirit hovers over us." She was also virulently anti-Communist, stressing that PCF youth groups subjected children to iron discipline and taught class hatred.[56]

But Casanova was atypical; most members of Action Civique worked for the party behind the scenes in subordinate roles or supported the work of Action Sociale. While a few women speakers were featured in the PSF press, it was events such as the awarding of Madame Dumas of the Épinal section with the *médaille d'or des familles nombreuses* for her ten children that tended to be emphasized. Furthermore, the organizational structure of Action Civique sometimes inhibited female activism. Each group had a general secretary who was elected by the section, but only with the approval of the local PSF president. The latter thus had a decisive role to play, and the potential to marginalize outspoken women was considerable. Many joined because their fathers or husbands enrolled them, and section presidents often chose delegates for Action Civique to do the work of a secretary rather than a propagandist. The frustration of at least some Action Civique members was directed at party headquarters, for in late 1937 unnamed section presidents were scolded for not always making the PSF's *Bulletin* available to female propagandists.[57]

In a lengthy report to de Préval written in July 1939, Casanova drew attention to these problems as she detailed the "deplorable" state of Action Civique in the Bouches-du-Rhône and made suggestions about how to revive the organization. In her own department, current methods had proven unsuccessful and morale was very poor. In general, Casanova's report concluded that the enthusiasm of Action Civique militants was not fully appreciated and thus tended to wane. The section presidents exercised "nearly dictatorial" authority over Action Civique, which itself lacked regional delegates and proper representation at PSF headquarters. Male cadres had a shoddy understanding of the organization and misused the energy of its delegates. "Almost everywhere, the [Action Civique] delegate is an office employee, busying herself with wrapping newspapers, papers of all sorts, and receipts; in short, she does everything except her real work, PROPAGANDA AMONGST WOMEN."[58]

For Casanova, Action Civique's primary role was to ensure that the PSF's message, through women, reached the entire nation. Though she was a proponent of votes for women, she also emphasized that they should not engage in traditional politics. "[L]eave women above and beyond political action. Make them act through influence and radiance." It was essential that this task of enlightenment take hold: "in order for the État Social Francais to complete its mission, our comprehension of the social must penetrate everywhere, into all households; without it the country cannot be saved." Otherwise, French women would simply become "advanced suffragettes" or "the possible rivals of men," rather than "the purifying element of PSF politics." Concentrating upon higher ideals rather than short-term goals would also permit Action Civique to be of the greatest use to other PSF auxiliary organizations, especially Action Sociale: "the social delegates will find in Action Civique more than a reserve of collaborators; [rather, it is] a true centre for moral, civic, and social formation, whose influence reaches beyond our members and ensures the penetration of our ideals into all French households."[59]

Casanova's frustrations illustrate the contradictions implicit in the PSF's attempts to mobilize women. They point to the continuing tension between its desire to engage them in public life and its affirmation of their avowedly complementary, but in practice often subordinate, role within the party. Nor does it seem likely her suggestions were enacted; several weeks before she submitted her memorandum, the PSF had affirmed that Action Civique's delegates would remain firmly under the authority of male propaganda delegates.[60] Yet as Casanova's memorandum indicates, there were many women who fervently embraced the party's ideals even as they developed their own views on how best to make them a reality. Moreover, in the eyes of male leaders, the efforts of various PSF *militantes* were encouraging. Barrachin proudly pointed to the accomplishments of Action Sociale, noting in 1939 that "we ... have very important foundations in supposedly inaccessible red cities, suburbs, and neighbourhoods. There thousands of children are cared for and pacified, no matter the political background of their parents ... thus French reconciliation is realized in depth."[61]

The role for which the PSF deemed women uniquely suited was intricately tied to the party's effort to mould future generations of ardent French patriots. In many respects the party picked up where the league had left off. There were some changes: while the Croix de Feu had organized youth into four categories, with younger boys and girls in the same group, in the PSF youth groups were divided into six categories, with males and females separated into three different age groups.[62] But the ideals promoted remained very much the same. The PSF continued practices initiated by the Croix de Feu, such as Christmas parties, while at the same time developing new ones. Action Sociale's bulletin, for instance, discussed how its members could organize parties with an imperial or other theme which would "endow [the children with] a moral lesson, or ... give concrete expression to the great teachings of history."[63]

However, while the PSF may have wished to educate children about French grandeur according to its own lights, it also had to consider the prerogatives of the family and religious institutions. Beginning in 1938, parents were encouraged to enrol their children in the party itself, at a cost of 5 francs. The measure was presented by the leadership as "giving these children, from a young age, an ideal," though its primary purpose may have been to buttress a cash-starved organization. Nevertheless, some parents were suspicious of requests to enrol their children. In Versailles-Montreuil, a recruiting meeting held in January

1939 secured the membership of only 70 out of 210 children under the age of eleven. The local PSF bulletin had to reassure the adults that the movement did not want "to dragoon the children in spite of their parents, to separate them from their families, or to disrupt their studies."[64] Care was also taken to respect religious observance; many PSF girls' groups, for instance, held their Sunday promenades after mass. But as the following account by the young women of Creusot implies, the groups also promoted a specifically PSF sense of discipline and fun:

18 June 1939! A memorable date in the feminine annals of Creusot's PSF.

Put otherwise: a promenade offered to the young women as a reward for their devotion and goodwill.

Departure from Creusot by car at 8 a.m. precisely.

Destination: Nolay. Visit the city. The Château de la Rochepôt.

Noon; the caves of La Tournée; we arrive in high spirits and with an appetite. Our provisions are taken out of the satchels; then we think of those who are not with us and those who are sick and send them postcards. Then comes the assault on the rocks; the climb is not without its difficulties.

Then a visit to the Château de Sully and a tasting at Digoine.

We began the day with singing, we must continue and we start singing in chorus the "Fils des Croix de Feu" song, Mermoz's "La vie est belle," and "Les colons de La Rocque."

The time to go home has arrived; we must be punctual or our families will worry.

An all-too-short day of relaxation, of pure air, of PSF concord, the kind of memory that we will keep.[65]

A similar balance was struck as the PSF resumed the *colonies de vacances* begun by the Croix de Feu on an impressive scale. The party claimed between 15 and 20,000 youths were involved every summer. The evolution of the *colonies* attests to the PSF's desire to show how its values complemented religious and familial devotion. At the Jean Mermoz camp held in 1939 at Thannenkirch in Alsace, for example, the children participated in the feast of St Anne, with pews reserved for them by the local *curé*. Similarly, organizers were urged not to undermine family vacations; children were encouraged to stay with their parents if they travelled during the summer months. Indeed, the PSF stressed that each child could only attend one camp, regretting that some parents simply wanted to send their children away for the whole summer.[66]

Yet although the PSF made room for church and family, it also sought to strengthen its own distinct bonds. The party provided financial aid to families who could not meet the cost, but also began to stipulate that children would only be accepted for the camps if their parents were members. Monitors were to be carefully trained, guided by appropriate specialists applying insights from the works of Lord Baden Powell and the models of leadership provided by Foch, Lyautey, and others. They were to become true leaders who would instill in their young charges the cult of honour, initiative, a sense of responsibility, and above all, discipline.[67] As the years progressed, it seems there was also an increasing emphasis on uniforms. In 1937 the Nord federation stipulated only a blue beret was obligatory; a year later children had to be dressed in marine blue and have a shirt and beret with PSF insignia. By 1939 the federation specified materials and brand names (Lacoste), as well as the colours of scarves for different age groups.[68]

For those passing into adulthood, the PSF sought to ensure a that potential cadres were waiting in the wings; university students were deemed especially important in this regard. The Croix de Feu's Groupe Universitaire was replaced by the PSF's Centre Universitaire in October 1936, while the women's Foyer Universitaire continued its operations. These facilities provided material support in the form of a subsidized restaurant, grants, and locating part-time work, as well as moral support in the form of counselling. Such measures help to explain why some fifteen hundred students joined the Centre Universitaire and the Foyer, though not all of them were equally active. Information on the provinces is sketchy, but organizing was underway. For example, *Le Flambeau de l'Isère* reported in 1939 that the recently formed Centre Universitaire in Grenoble had already attracted over a hundred students. At the first national congress of PSF students, held in February 1938, Charles Goutry claimed that about 12 per cent of all French students were PSF supporters, a total of roughly eight thousand people.[69]

As with the Croix de Feu, PSF students were discouraged from restricting themselves to the university environment. Both the Centre Universitaire's bulletin, *L'Étudiant social*, and the Foyer's periodical, *Pourquoi s'en faire* (which was eventually absorbed into *L'Étudiant social*), encouraged mixing with other classes, though with a decidedly paternalist tone. *L'Étudiant social* emphasized to its readers that even though they would become society's leaders, they had to behave responsibly: "you simply have the advantage of benefiting from a superior education. Your duty is to extract the best results from it and have your fellow man benefit from this." *Pourquoi s'en faire* entreated its readers to get to know and appreciate the industrious peasants they encountered on vacation.[70] The second national congress of PSF students, held in 1939, affirmed the party's anti-intellectualism, maintaining that an exclusive focus on theories produced "an unbalanced, unhappy, even dangerous individual." As for female students, *Pourquoi s'en faire* urged them to avoid mere "politics" and throw themselves into civic and social action. Simultaneously, however, the PSF's youth periodicals also encouraged a fierce partisan sensibility. As *Pourquoi s'en faire* put it, "since you, my friends, have chosen to profess your intelligence, you must be PSF and extend the party's influence with all your intelligence ... In the anti-fascist groups, there are always some women students and they are no less fanatical or active. It is entirely up to you whether or not young intellectuals understand our ideal and follow through. It is entirely up to you whether or not tomorrow the intellectuals of the left are reduced to nothing."[71]

Nor were left-wing intellectuals the only opponents upon whom PSF students fixed their sights. For some, the fact that foreigners were coming to France not only for their education but also for future employment was a cause for grave concern. Xenophobia was evident, and the fact that among the foreigners were Central and East European Jews spurred antisemitism. Before 1936 the Croix de Feu had called for restrictions on foreigners to ensure future positions for French doctors and other professionals; the PSF subsequently did so as well, with an eye to university students. It has been suggested that since one of the presidents of the Centre, Jacques Bernard, was a Jewish medical student, such sentiments were relatively weak. But during the 1930s some members of the French Jewish community also called for restrictions, and doctors were among the most prominent groups clamouring for the exclusion of refugee professionals during the 1930s. On this point it is worth noting that Professor Émile Sergent of the Faculty of Medicine in Paris, who was very active in calling for the government to adopt harsher anti-immigration policies, was a supporter of the Centre Universitaire. Moreover, the PSF itself commissioned a survey on Jewish medical students, with disturbing overtones. Among its conclusions were the following remarks: "the figures reproduced [in the report] have illustrated the proportion of Jewish students settling in France and displaying revolutionary tendencies. Our concern for objectivity compels us to hide nothing on this subject, in the interest of the profession as in the interest of the country."[72] There is reason to believe, then, that the exclusionary conception of French national identity which took hold elsewhere in the PSF also resonated among a proportion of its student supporters.

In some respects the PSF's youth organizations partook of broader trends. A great many youth movements of the era, for example, evinced a desire to reshape the existing order and called for the mixing of social classes. But this characteristic should not lead us to identify La Rocque's views too closely with those of, say, Lord Baden-Powell, even though the PSF made use of his writings. Admittedly, both men were concerned about encouraging patriotism and "self-mastery." They also shared a desire to innoculate working-class youth against socialism and professed a distaste for "rich shirkers" as well as over-intellectualized children. But Baden-Powell, at least in the opinion of one of his biographers, also believed that individuality was a character trait to be encouraged.[73] While the PSF asserted that individual "personalities" were to be respected, such claims appeared faint in relation to the movement's overriding emphasis on discipline. The ethos of the PSF's youth organizations clashed even more sharply with the notion of a "republic of youth" – a democratic, self-organizing community – promoted by their Popular Front opponents.[74] For while PSF youth organizers emphasized the importance of mutual respect between social classes, they also stressed the need to produce elites who could serenely manage a hierarchical social order.

REACHING OUT

In addition to the extensive network aimed at strengthening the PSF "family" itself, from 1936 onward La Rocque and his colleagues established several organizations intended to promote the movement's ideals to an audience beyond the party, both in the workplace and through the organization of cultural and leisure activities. Arguably the most ambitious of these was a new trade union federation. Before the dissolution of the Croix de Feu in 1936, La Rocque had already planned to create "apolitical" unions; later that same year they became a reality with the launching of the Syndicats Professionnels Français (SPF), which soon established secretariats in several departments. The Confédération des Syndicats Professionnels Français (CSPF) was formally established in January 1937, with Roger Vitrac as general secretary. The SPF proclaimed itself to be independent of the PSF and disinterested in party politics as such. Its organizers stressed that the movement was open to workers not affiliated with the PSF and that the new unions were "purely professional and will have to be free of any political affiliation."[75] In fact, the SPF's rhetoric, to say nothing of its name, immediately betrayed close affinities with its parent organization, which soon caused difficulties for the new formation.

Like the PSF, the SPF faced the challenge of defining a place for itself, and it sought to do so by attacking the left while simultaneously promising more harmonious labour relations. It excoriated the CGT for engaging in "civil war trade unionism" and condemned the Catholic Confédération Française des Travailleurs Chrétiens (CFTC) for its confessional and therefore exclusive approach. The SPF, by contrast, claimed to represent the true interests of all workers and to incarnate a "positive" syndicalism, characterized by mutual respect between employer and employee. Rather than have disputes settled by obligatory arbitration, as preferred by the Popular Front, the SPF wanted a labour charter that would codify "the quasi-totality of relations between producers and employers." While the principle of arbitration would be obtained, it was hoped that commissions of employers, workers, and state officials would resolve any conflicts not covered by the charter. In any case, strikes could never be "political" in nature. Another leading concern of the SPF was to "protect" the rights of French labour against foreign workers.[76]

SPF propaganda depicted the unions as experiencing explosive growth, claiming 500,000 members in 1936 and 1 million in 1939. The SPF also asserted that it was attracting a growing share of worker and employee delegates chosen for various firms. For the period between 15 February and 31 May 1937 it claimed to have elected 67.8 per cent of all such delegates.[77] In fact the SPF's regional implantation was uneven; as of December 1937, six times the number of propaganda meetings (720) had been organized in the Seine as in the rest of the country. Though there was activity in Lyons, Dijon, Châteauroux, and Clermont-Ferrand, results in cities such as Tours and departments such as the Haute-Vienne were mediocre. The SPF had more luck in organizing among white-collar workers, artisans, and employees of smaller firms, especially skilled craftsmen or foremen, than among classic proletarians, though there were exceptions such as the 1,000 dockers in Algiers who signed up. In the Seine the SPF was strongest in insurance companies, chemicals, the food trade, taxicab companies, and department stores such as Samaritaine, though some success was also achieved in the Renault factories. In the Marne the SPF was most active in the food trade; in Alsace, food and stationery. In Lyons there were concentrations in banking, building, public works, and metallurgical firms.[78]

The SPF's obvious connection to the PSF, its emphasis upon class conciliation, and the challenge it posed to existing unions aroused considerable hostility. The hostility of the CGT was, unsurprisingly, consistent and intense. The situation with the CFTC was more complex. While in the Meurthe-et-Moselle the two unions signed collective contracts together, such instances of cooperation took place within a general context of competition for supporters. The CFTC denounced the SPF as "yellow unions," while the SPF responded by accusing the CFTC of aligning itself with the "Marxist" CGT. Nor did members of the national employers' organization, the Confédération Générale du Patronat Français, always see the SPF as an attractive option; they considered creating their own movement, with Jacques Doriot as a potential leader. The Commission du Travail in the Chamber of Deputies also excluded the SPF from discussions, on the grounds that it was too much of a "newcomer."[79]

Supporters of the left were predictably suspicious of the SPF's repeated claims that while it endorsed class reconciliation, it was not a tool of the employers or the PSF. Conversely, at least some PSF members felt that the new unions were too independent-minded. In Lyons, for example, some local PSF supporters objected to the SPF's attacks upon company unions and international finance, with one party member accusing the union of lacking the proper "Croix de Feu spirit." This response may help to explain why the PSF also created Propagande Ouvrière et Commerciale (POC), another organization aimed at promoting the party's values in the workplace. Unlike the SPF, POC remained directly under the direction of the PSF. It did not get involved in union organizing, instead calling upon all employees to "work with all our might to recreate, among workers in general, a solid moral code created by the will to work and confidence in the future of a strong and reconciled France." By the spring of 1939 POC claimed between 1,300 and 1,500 groups, though most were in located in Paris and its suburbs; in the provinces organization had only begun.[80] However, the creation of POC should not be taken as a sign that the PSF had simply abandoned the SPF. Tensions between the two organizations were not always high; in the Oise and the Alpes-Maritimes, for example, the authorities perceived the SPF and the PSF to be closely linked.[81]

The PSF also sought to collaborate with and win over the *patronat*. Though its initiatives in this regard tended to be more low-key than those involving workers, they provide a powerful example of its desire to refashion French society. One example is the initiative launched by Louis Escande and Pierre Kula, employers in the Parisian building and public works industry. With the cooperation of the PSF, they established professional groups consisting of bosses, white-collar employees, and workers within their industry. While care was taken to ensure the involvement of the PSF remained discreet and thus dissociate these activities from "politics," it was hoped that such groups would form the basis of a system inspired by the concept of *la profession organisée*, encourage the creation of a "new social spirit," and suppress notions of "class struggle." Similar initiatives were launched in other departments, though in Lyons the "individualist" outlook of local employers proved to be an obstacle.[82] Concluding that more had to be done to mobilize French *patrons*, the PSF created the Centres d'Information et de Propagande PSF dans les Milieux Patronaux, Intellectuels et Bourgeois in 1938, with the goal of providing education about the party's social doctrine.[83] In May 1939 the PSF held its first national congress for employers, at which they were urged to organize themselves and forge good relations with their workers so as to establish the basis for a "new social order."[84]

Clearly, then, for the PSF, establishing a substantial – even hegemonic – presence in the workplace was of great importance. No less clear by 1939 was the fact that it had a long way to go. The PSF's efforts to organize the *patronat* were in their early stages, while the experience of the SPF points to some of the obstacles the party faced in projecting its values. By the same token, the launching of POC shows the PSF did not give up easily. Moreover, the SPF enjoyed some success, even though it did not live up to its propaganda. In Marseilles its numbers were reportedly second only to those of the CGT; in the Seine-et-Oise, where the police believed it was making inroads on the CGT's membership, it already had 1,700 members by the end of 1937.[85] The SPF also proved to be tactically flexible. In rural areas its cadres tried to take over existing agricultural associations when they deemed the creation of a new union would be counterproductive. In urban centres the SPF took advantage of the dislocation in the union movement following the defeat of the November 1938 general strike to expand its influence.[86] In sum, the PSF's efforts to inject its values into French labour relations remained vigorous on the eve of the war.

The PSF also tried to promote its vision of France to those outside its ranks through ongoing social, cultural, and sporting initiatives. Here again the precedent had been set by the Croix de Feu; in the summer of

1936 the league had established three centres in the Seine – the Centre Social Français, the Foyer Driant, and the Centre Perronnet – which sponsored mutual aid and welfare projects and hosted games and cultural events. In a few provincial cities, organizations such as the Foyer Jean Mermoz in Tourcoing performed similar functions.[87] The PSF's ambitions in this realm were more expansive and diversified. Travail et Loisirs, created in November 1936, established social centres in Paris's "red belt," including Saint-Ouen, Billancourt, Colombes, Viry-Châtillon, Nanterre, Aubervilliers, and Gif-sur-Yvette. Enjoying support from politically active businessmen such as Raoul Dautry, the association offered social assistance, health care, sporting activities, and after-school supervision. The focus was on children, but adults were also provided with activities, including sports, concerts, and art exhibitions; the long-term goal was the "social encirclement" of Paris.[88]

In addition to Travail et Loisirs, there was the Société de Préparation et d'Éducation Sportive (SPES). While La Rocque had encouraged French children to become involved in physical activity since the days of the Croix de Feu, the SPES provided a coordinating structure for various initiatives along these lines. Its leading figure, Jean de Mierry, believed there was too much emphasis on spectator sport in France. The aim of the SPES was thus "the physical betterment of the greatest mass of individuals possible." Open to non-members and organized along departmental lines, the Société established physical education classes, swimming lessons, team sports, and camping groups. It also arranged gymnastic and synchronized swimming exhibitions; while the focus was on youth, the SPES's mandate extended to adults. By 1939 it had four sections in the Seine and organizations in eighteen other departments. In June of that year Barrachin reported that the SPES had given over 400,000 evening classes in physical training and 70,000 swimming lessons since its creation.[89]

Like the SPF, the SPES and Travail et Loisirs were notionally apolitical, but both were guided by the movement's principles and cadres. Just as the SPF can be viewed as a response to the growing labour militancy of the Popular Front era, so the SPES can be regarded as an "antidote" to the left's sporting initiatives. The Popular Front government took recreation seriously, as the Blum government's creation of the new position of undersecretary for sport and leisure indicates. When the undersecretary, Léo Lagrange, granted the left-wing Fédération Sportive et Gymnique du Travail official recognition, the PSF press denounced the move, presenting the SPES as a patriotic alternative. The SPES president in Limoges made clear his group's ideological affinities when he declared that sport was "one of the most powerful elements of the reconciliation of the French, since it always renders the fusion of all classes more intimate."[90] As for Travail et Loisirs, it can be viewed as an outgrowth of the Croix de Feu's previous efforts to wean the French working classes away from Marxism. Antoinette de Préval provided the chief inspiration behind the organization and regarded its efforts as complementing the party's other social initiatives. Reflecting on the goals and methods of Travail et Loisir's Centres Sociaux in 1939, Jeanne Garrigoux commented that their cultural activities could instill values cherished by the PSF. Among the regulars at one of the centres, she noted, were young "male and female factory workers whose terrible family environments I knew well. 'We are in the PSF,' they tell me, simply – it's very moving, I assure you."[91]

Both the SPES and Travail et Loisirs illustrate how the PSF was part of a broader trend towards the organization of mass culture and leisure for various political ends in interwar France.[92] While it is difficult to gauge precisely how far they encouraged the spread of the *esprit Croix de Feu*, such organizations were potentially of great benefit to the party, allowing it to insert its prerogatives into mainstream public activities and discourse. But as the PSF's experiences in the field of aviation demonstrated, there were also pitfalls, though here too the party evinced an ability to adapt to changing times.

The Croix de Feu had capitalized upon the mass appeal of aviation by deploying aircraft in its mobilizations but also by cultivating Jean Mermoz as an embodiment of its values. The election of the Popular Front and the creation of the PSF compelled some changes in approach. Aircraft could no longer be used at paramilitary rallies; more generally, the PSF had to respond to Popular Front aviation initiatives. In addition to the sweeping reforms Air Minister Pierre Cot ordered for the aircraft industry and the Armée de l'Air, his ministry established Aviation Populaire. It strove to put flight within the reach of the masses by subsidizing air clubs and organizing training sessions for youth. The program was hampered by a lack of funding and Cot's increasing preoccupation with its potential for nurturing military pilots and technicians in the event of war.[93] Nevertheless, it represented an innovative effort by the Blum government to further its cultural agenda, and as such, it could only alarm the PSF.

La Rocque and his colleagues responded to Cot's reforms by accusing him of destroying the morale of the air force, "Sovietizing" the aviation industry, and seeking to install a dictatorship of the CGT in aircraft factories. It fell to Mermoz to spearhead the PSF's alternative to Aviation Populaire. He was made one of the party's vice-presidents and furnished invaluable support to La Rocque, declaring at the PSF's inaugural meeting that he would follow his *patron* to the end.[94] As for Aviation Populaire, he dismissed its claims of wanting to making aviation available to all, insisting that in reality the initiative served political goals. This focus was unacceptable for an undertaking which Mermoz maintained, had to be a site of genuine reconciliation between youth of different classes and political creeds. The final goal must be to "create a generation of the air, each youthful element of which will be united with the other by a sentiment of fraternity, free from all influences of divergent opinions and clarifying its aspirations in a common action under the sign of the social spirit of the squadron." The PSF, he assured readers of *Le Flambeau*, was the organization to take up such a project. Mermoz made good on this claim immediately, requesting information from section presidents on members with aviation-related skills as well as local flight clubs.[95]

But the PSF's nascent aviation initiatives – and indeed, the party itself – were soon struck a heavy blow when Mermoz disappeared in his plane, the *Croix-du-Sud*, over the South Atlantic in December 1936. His death evoked anguish within the party. *Gringoire* noted that at the PSF's first national congress, held only days after his loss, "the great figure of Mermoz did not cease to hold sway ... In his turn, Colonel de La Rocque, recalling the one whom he still wanted to speak of in the present, could not master his emotion. The room sobbed."[96]

Thereafter the PSF embarked upon a systematic campaign to identify the memory of Mermoz with its quest for national reconciliation. In January 1937 *Le Flambeau* carried excerpts about Mermoz from other newspapers, thus emphasizing its vice-president's national following. The paper also staked the PSF's claim to the flyer's legacy, with La Rocque's editorial underscoring Mermoz's "indestructible faith in our noble disciplines of work, family, and nation." In the spring of that same year the PSF published a volume of Mermoz's memoirs entitled *Mes Vols*, with the aim of honouring a man who had enhanced French prestige worldwide but also a party vice-president "whose name is forever tied to our work, and to our triumph of patriotic and social renovation." Mermoz's mother, Gabrielle Gillet, was made the honorary president of Travail et Loisirs, and in March 1938 the PSF dedicated a special illustrated issue of *Le Petit Journal* to the flyer. The following

December La Rocque commemorated the second anniversary of the "Archangel's" disappearance by promising the PSF would persevere in achieving the goals that Mermoz cherished. If he had lived, La Rocque assured his readers, the aviator would have been charged with maintaining *l'esprit Croix de Feu*.[97]

But the PSF was never alone in its grief and found it hard to lay sole claim to Mermoz's legacy. Scores of newspapers from across the political spectrum eulogized France's cherished pilot, and some regretted his association with the PSF. The writer Antoine de Saint-Exupéry was deeply saddened by the loss of a friend but deplored Mermoz's political allegiances. Elements of the Popular Front presented the flyer as an ecumenical hero. At an official memorial service Pierre Cot declared that while he and Mermoz differed in their politics, they were nevertheless united "in the vast family of French aviation." *L'Humanité* went even further, ridiculing La Rocque for holding a banquet in Mermoz's honour and suggesting that had he lived, the aviator would have made common cause with the Communists, with whom he shared "the hope for the union of the French nation."[98]

PSF advocates found the left's appropriation of the language of patriotic unity infuriating. But even when Mermoz was praised by those who were not political foes, trouble ensued. Jacques Mortane, a popular writer on aviation, published a biography of the flyer in 1936 which pre-empted *Mes Vols* and outsold it, 140,000 copies being purchased as opposed to 60,000 for Mermoz's PSF-sponsored memoir. Like the PSF, Mortane prized Mermoz as a patriotic, moral leader, but he did not link his achievements to the party's agenda. Small wonder that La Rocque was frustrated by the appearance of Mortane's book.[99] Even more problematic was the account of Mermoz's life published in 1938 by Joseph Kessel, a well-established adventure writer and friend of his subject. The book, which became an international bestseller, broadly partook of the PSF's view that Mermoz was a "glorious archangel" who scorned the destructive partisan politics which undermined French aviation. However, Kessel also depicted Mermoz as a man with a self-destructive streak, who indulged in extramarital affairs, separated from his wife, and was unable to make any sacrifices that detracted from his passion for flying. Such a full-blooded portrait made it harder to promote Mermoz as a moral exemplar for French youth.[100]

Yet another blow to the PSF's identification with Mermoz came when the flyer's father, long estranged from his wife but apparently not his son, went to court to obtain some of the profits for *Mes Vols*. The case soon produced accusations that the royalties were going to the PSF and not Madame Gillet, and further criticism of the party's usurpation of Mermoz. *Le Démocrate de l'Aisne* quipped: "Of this admirable hero of the air, the colonel wanted to make an exclusively PSF hero whose cult would have been reserved for party members ... And today, all of a sudden, we learn that the PSF has gone a little too far in its so-called devotion to the aviator Jean Mermoz, and that it would have made, it seems, a substantial profit from it."[101]

Faltering in its efforts to associate a figure of national prominence with its agenda, the PSF also struggled to realize Mermoz's project of a national aviation organization. The new flying federation that bore his name was launched in 1937, and like many PSF initiatives of this nature, it was theoretically autonomous; party insignia were not to be worn at its meetings. The stated goals of the Fédération Jean Mermoz were to educate youth about flight and provide a coordinating body with which pre-existing flight clubs could affiliate. The former endeavour proved more successful than the latter. By the summer of 1938 the Fédération claimed to have instructed 4,500 students in model-building, gliding, and powered flight, although it was intended that only male children would become pilots; in the rival Aviation Populaire girls could sign up.[102] But when it came to organizing flying clubs, the policy of allowing pre-existing groups to affiliate, though facilitating rapid expansion, also ran the risk of admitting less-than- committed members. Thus as early as June 1937, five clubs had affiliated with the federation, but in the case of the club for southern Paris the directors subsequently ignored its directives. They flew many hours without recording them and failed to provide lessons for students who had paid in advance. Moreover, by the summer of 1938 the Fédération Jean Mermoz had financial problems. Full records of expenditures were not kept, and the auditor described the federation's general secretary, de Mentcque, as incompetent.[103]

Troubled though it was, the Fédération Jean Mermoz's existence nevertheless testifies to the PSF's determination to fuse sporting culture with mass politics. The organization declared its aim simply to be "the propagation of the aerial spirit and the spreading of aeronautical sport throughout the French nation," but its directives were shot through with the imperative of national reconciliation. Aviation for the masses, it proclaimed, must not be corrupted by social or partisan conflicts; instead, it had to be imbued with a "national character." Even more revealing was the hope expressed in a report to the PSF's executive committee that the Fédération Jean Mermoz would serve as the basis for a national aviation organization. While the report maintained that this body would be non-partisan and that creating it would require the backing of different political groups, the assumption that the Fédération – and by association the PSF – would define the goals of French aviation hints at the scope of the party's ambitions.[104]

The PSF was able to rechannel its energies away from the ailing Fédération and into new initiatives that reflected changing conditions. By the end of 1938, as France seemed close to another major war, the threat of aerial bombardment became the subject of intensified public concern. The PSF responded by developing lists of its members who were able to help with civil defence. The intention was to have the party organize these individuals into a group which would then be placed at the disposal of the authorities as needed, giving it a "semi-official" character. La Rocque made his intentions public in April 1939, when he called on PSF members to join the new group, which in July was dubbed the Auxiliaires de la Défense Passive (ADP). By July there were 120 ADP offices, half of them in Paris and its environs.[105]

The organization quickly aroused controversy. Le Populaire, for example, argued that the ADP represented an endeavour to extend the PSF's power over the general population. If the Socialists or the Communists had tried such a thing, the paper continued, the PSF would have denounced the initiative and the Daladier government would have taken measures against it; yet the ADP had been allowed to proceed unhindered. The PSF's Bulletin quickly retorted that the ADP was a voluntary, apolitical group that allowed "the party's admirable reserve of volunteers to serve in the defence of the population against the risk of aerial bombardments." As such, it concluded, the group ought to be "applauded" by all "good citizens."[106]

In creating the ADP, the PSF had produced a new opportunity to present itself as the pre-eminent defender of France. La Rocque asserted that the police, the army, and the emergency aid organizations lacked the resources to carry out operations such as evacuations properly. The PSF, he claimed, could bridge the gap with its vast resources, which included shelters, soup kitchens, and trained personnel. In short, as the "only organization capable of such a contribution, the PSF has a duty to bring it to the country ... Thus, once more, under the sign of the Croix de Feu, the representatives of the victors of 1918 will have given the nation the best of themselves without asking for any other encouragement save that of their conscience."[107] Yet again the French people could only be

saved through the spirit of national reconciliation, which the PSF had
inherited from the generation of 1914–18 via the Croix de Feu.

THE PSF IN CONTEXT

In the summer of 1939 France commemorated the 150th anniversary
of the storming of the Bastille, and La Rocque took the opportunity to
reflect on the significance of the revolution for France and the PSF in
the pages of *Le Petit Journal*. Decrying the "massacres [and] sacri-
leges" that took place, he nevertheless conceded that the Committee of
Public Safety had generated a powerful national coalition and repelled
foreign invaders. He also recognized that the revolution had brought
about "the entry onto the stage of the Third Estate, the popular
classes," and that "it is upon the republican base that the edifice of
tomorrow will be built." But La Rocque added that inveterate foes of
the revolution such as Joseph de Maistre also approved of the combative spirit of self-sacrifice that nationalism had unleashed. The PSF
leader thus implied that a commitment to French nationalism could
unite both the left and the counter-revolutionary right. His preoccupation with preserving hierarchy also informed La Rocque's comments as
to what PSF should learn from the events of 1789. The *ancien régime*,
he concluded, had faltered because elites had forgotten their obligations: "The sense of tradition had disappeared; Joan of Arc was forgotten." Intellectuals such as Voltaire had introduced a pernicious
rationalism that enervated French society: "the so-called democratic
fervour encouraged intriguers and parvenus, and allowed for the eva-
sion of responsibilities." Citing Auguste Comte, La Rocque called
upon his supporters to "arouse the elites, leaders, and servants of the
people, who are nourished by the people, for the material and moral
benefit of the people, in a humane society composed of 'families and
not individuals.'"[108]

La Rocque's words capture the syncretic ideological heritage of the
PSF and render problematic assertions that it was distancing itself from
the Croix de Feu's legacy. On the one hand, the party fully acknowledged the entry of the masses into political life and did not seek to dis-
own the revolution. On the other, its embrace of 1789 was selective,
emphasizing the nationalist facets of the event over its liberal and democratic ones. La Rocque also made it clear that the French people
required firm, dedicated leadership; both in diagnosing his country's
historic problems and in describing the way to solve them, he invoked

the centrality of elites. Nor did acceptance of the Republic as the start-ing point for a renovated France obviate in any way its role as an "essential pillar of Christian civilization."[109] Thus in its ongoing emphasis on paternal direction of the masses within an organic "famil-ial" state, the PSF preserved crucial aspects of the Croix de Feu's mes-sage. While this ideology may have prized hierarchical stability over the desire for radicalization that characterized the Third Reich and at times Fascist Italy, it remained within the spectrum of right-wing authoritarian nationalism.

It can be argued that the previous comparison overstates the conti-nuities between the PSF and its predecessor. After all, the party had abandoned paramilitarism and affirmed repeatedly its commitment to the republican system. Perhaps if the defeat of 1940 and the teleologi-cal thinking that event can impose on historical writing about the 1930s are removed from the equation, one can envision the PSF becom-ing a more conventional conservative party. After all, the Third Repub-lic was evolving in the late 1930s, as the reformist but conflict-ridden years of the Popular Front gave way to an increasingly right-wing pre-miership under Daladier. If the PSF is situated in this comparative con-text, its differences from the Croix de Feu can seem more impressive.[110]

It is thus worth noting that on the eve of the Second World War the party tended to reaffirm rather than downplay its heritage. In 1937 PSF orators often emphasized the extent to which the party was distinct from its forerunner, but by 1939, with the threat of dissolution having faded, La Rocque constantly reminded readers of *Le Petit Journal* that the PSF had to carry on the work of the Croix de Feu.[111] Though elec-toral success was of great concern, the party continued to present itself as above all an agent of moral renewal, the "great Croix de Feu family, partisans of the mixing of classes, of the primacy of work under the power of the patriotic collectivity, and the influence of spiritual forces," as La Rocque described it scant days before the outbreak of war.[112] The movement's aspirations to remould the French polity into the État Social Français, the sharpening of its essentialist vision of national identity, and its open admiration for dictatorial regimes must also be weighed against its professions of faith in the democratic rules of the game.

As for France's altered political climate, it is true that liberal tradi-tions within the Third Republic were under attack at the end of the 1930s. Not only did avowedly reactionary thinkers such as Charles Maurras enjoy lasting influence; disenchanted republicans ranging from politicians such as André Tardieu to writers such as Daniel

Halévy also decried the failings of the system, hoping they might be reversed by greater deference to the country's "natural leaders."[113] Ideas along these lines could be found, to varying degrees, in the platforms of several political parties. The Fédération Républicaine's outlook had hardened, while Doriot's PPF called for the creation of an "État Populaire Français." The Alliance Démocratique, a formation of the moderate right, now advocated a stronger executive, military training in the schools, and class collaboration within "professional frameworks" – a variant of corporatism, it would seem. Within the Radical party, as we have seen, a fierce anti-Communism and a zest for executive power was increasingly apparent.[114]

To characterize the PSF simply as another participant in this wider drift towards xenophobia and authoritarianism during the 1930s, however, would be to underrate its importance in furthering such notions. The movement popularized integral nationalism amongst a massive support base. In the Chamber its deputies, though few in number, demanded stringent application of policies such as greater restrictions upon foreigners. At meetings and in the pages of *Le Petit Journal* and the provincial press, PSF supporters were beseeched to pursue a suffocating national unity at all costs. As for the counter-society, there was hardly a sphere of the members' everyday lives where it did not seek to establish a presence. Cumulatively, the PSF's ancillary organizations reinforced its message of national reconciliation, promoting values that figured importantly under the Vichy regime. The emphasis on discipline and familialism adumbrated the goals of the National Revolution. The xenophobia and antisemitism of some PSF members strengthened a current of opinion that reached its culmination after the defeat of 1940. The emphasis upon unqualified support for a heroic leader, be it La Rocque or Mermoz, encouraged an outlook that could be directed towards other individuals.

In the ongoing debate over the direction in which the Third Republic was headed in the late 1930s, scholars have detected contradictory impulses. Xenophobia was on the rise, for example, but the Daladier government did pass restrictions on libel against religious or racial groups by the press in 1939.[115] Within the PSF, as the events of the Second World War were to reveal, there were also different currents of opinion, most notably about how to deal with the Nazi occupation. But as war loomed, the party's role in advancing receptiveness towards authoritarian nationalism betrayed little in the way of ambivalence.

7

War and Dispersion, 1939–1945

Following the outbreak of war in September 1939, the PSF emphasized the depth of its commitment to the war effort, but continued to advance its own particular agenda and thereby contributed to a growing domestic political crisis at a crucial time. Though the party was weakened by the mobilization of many of its members, La Rocque and his colleagues, through the efforts of the ADP and in the pages of *Le Petit Journal*, sought to buttress morale and official efforts. But they did so through their own ideological lens. Thus as the "phoney war" dragged on, their criticisms of the country's wartime leadership and insistence upon a looming Communist threat contributed to the fragility of governments and confusion over France's strategic priorities. Despite its image as the leading proponent of national unity, the PSF could only conceive of a war effort consonant with its long-term goals.

In the wake of defeat in 1940, the movement was compelled to articulate its stance in relation to the new État Français of Marshal Pétain. The winding path the PSF chose and the varying fates of its members testify to the complex ruptures imposed by wartime conditions, but they also point to continuities with its goals during the 1930s. La Rocque and those who supported him had to react to Pétain's initially overwhelming popularity and the fact that elements of the new regime sought to marginalize the PSF and cultivate its supporters. Dealing with the German authorities and collaborationist movements was a constant challenge. So too was ensuring the cohesion of the movement, something that became increasingly difficult as individual members chose alternatively to accommodate, collaborate, or resist. Moreover, the turbulent international situation had to be constantly reassessed and the PSF's stance adjusted accordingly. Yet in their efforts to reaffirm the PSF's centrality in French public life and their long-term plans for France, La Rocque and his supporters remained guided by their pre-war convictions.

Historians of Vichy France have long noted that the regime hosted a variety of ideological traditions, ranging from reactionary nationalism to pro-Nazi collaborationism. Within this framework it can be argued that the PSF represented a strand identified by François Bédarida as the "Vichy of illusions."[1] Organizations and individuals of this bent were committed to an authentic National Revolution but became disabused of the notion that it could be realized under occupation. They differed from collaborationists because of their reservations about aligning with Nazi Germany, but also from conservative patriots who initially supported Vichy and later broke with it because of their commitment to French independence. In fairness, as the war progressed, La Rocque began to move down the latter road by supplying the Allies with information, an activity for which he and a number of his supporters paid dearly when the PSF was suppressed and they were imprisoned. But even after those activities commenced, the movement remained hopeful that it would attain power and enact reforms in keeping with the spirit of the National Revolution; indeed, often the PSF's chief objection to Vichy's policies was that they were not being carried out effectively. To the end, La Rocque directed his colleagues to support Marshal Pétain, and he remained hostile to democracy and admiring of foreign dictatorships, even respecting some features of the Nazi regime, which he had come to oppose.

THE PSF AND THE DRÔLE DE GUERRE

As we have seen, over the course of 1939 the PSF's stance towards Germany hardened; in that regard the party shared in a growing national consensus.[2] But this position did not submerge its disdain for the current parliamentary system; nor were all of its members of the same mind. In April 1939 the PSF's national council resolved that among the chief reasons for the threatening situation in Europe was "France's years of weakness in the face of similar [German] conduct, resulting from eighteen years of illusions and resignations, prolonged by two years of sabotage to national defence," a damning indictment of interwar politics in general and the Popular Front in particular.[3] And while the PSF's parliamentary group joined in the unanimous vote for war credits in the Chamber of Deputies on 3 September, Fourcault de Pavant and Pébellier were among those who had signed a request for a closed session of the Chamber the day before. This move had been initiated by the anti-Marxist and pro-appeasement deputy Gaston Bergery and was aimed at encouraging debate on whether or not France should go to war.[4] The uncertainties of these two PSF deputies foreshadowed the divisions that emerged within the movement after 1940.

Nevertheless, once war was the declared, PSF members did their patriotic duty, and the movement signalled its determination to make a prominent contribution to mobilizing France. Barrachin, Ottavi, Vallin, and Bounin were all mobilized, in addition to thousands of ordinary militants and their cadres. Fourcault de Pavant, while free from military obligations, joined the training staff of the air school at Rochefort. Initially, La Rocque was unsure what to do, thinking he might serve best in a military capacity. But in a meeting with Ottavi the latter argued that his place was at the head of the PSF; "in the terrible moments that await us the government will need a man; they will summon you." La Rocque decided that continuing to serve as the head of his party would be more effective than a "theatrical gesture," though he believed the time would come when "I will usefully risk my neck." In October 1939 he reconsidered, but in the face of strong arguments from Ottavi and Vallin – and the unwillingness of the military – he reaffirmed his original decision.[5] Throughout the *drôle de guerre* the PSF leader thus devoted himself to guiding his party's social action and influencing the climate of opinion.[6]

In terms of social action, the PSF – chiefly through the ADP, to which many of its resources were now devoted – achieved noteworthy results. During the first two weeks of the war the ADP assisted in the evacuation of Paris, winning praise from the prefect of the Seine. The organization also established some eighteen hundred emergency aid stations, along with *centres d'accueil et d'hébergement*, infirmaries, restaurants, and canteens. In many cases these posts had previously been PSF property put to other uses; now they provided shelter and sustenance. Before the German offensive began in 1940, the ADP also helped the authorities to facilitate the transportation and relocation of thousands of refugees from the eastern departments, especially Alsace-Lorraine, to safer districts such as the Dordogne, Gers, Landes, and the Haute-Vienne. After the German breakthrough, the ADP again provided aid on a massive scale to refugees; it claimed that 4.2 million people received shelter and 55 million meals were served. For these accomplishments the organization would receive official praise from Marshal Pétain in December 1940.[7]

In less concrete terms, La Rocque's editorials in *Le Petit Journal* tried to galvanize his supporters. In them he demanded vigour and discipline on the part of France's leaders and the general public, at the same time injecting his calls to action with the PSF's particular concerns. The war represented a much-wanted break with the sterile political system, but the defenders of Christian civilization had to do their utmost. "The full resources of the country are at the disposal of those who wish to win. But the enthusiastic sacrifices of individuals must be employed and organized with a view to maximum efficiency. The era of political alliances made in corridors is over. The era of salvation is one of candour, sacrifice, labour, willpower, and vigour. France wants to be led by men worthy of those who will die for her. This condition met, France will triumph against barbarism, for Christianity, with unshakable audacity." The PSF's deputies echoed their chief's sentiments. Stanislas Devaud, for example, declared that "money and material power alone are not enough. Above all, the morale of the nation is crucial; it must be maintained at the high level it has displayed since the beginning of the war."[8]

The PSF also expressed dissatisfaction with the Daladier government's handling of the war effort, though in a relatively muted way. While wartime censorship prevented *Le Petit Journal* from going beyond oblique comments about the government, in private correspondence La Rocque conveyed his misgivings to Daladier and other officials. On 8 November 1939 he noted that inactivity at the front was bad for the troops' morale, and he complained to the prime minister that the preparations made for civil defence were inadequate. A subsequent letter transmitted to President Lebrun, General Gamelin, Jules Jeanneney, and Édouard Herriot criticized, among other things, the poor quality of French propaganda efforts, noting that the Germans were far more effective in having an impact on countries such as Belgium. On both occasions La Rocque concluded that the nation had not properly adapted to wartime conditions, and he bemoaned "the total absence of spark and inspiration in the attitudes and speeches of the leadership."[9]

The PSF's impatience with the government intensified as the "phoney war" dragged on. To be sure, the process of disaffection was gradual; at the end of November the PSF parliamentary group was among the 318 deputies who still supported Daladier, voting to grant him further decree powers.[10] Furthermore, recent scholarship suggests that La Rocque's concerns about inactivity at the front and shortcomings in propaganda were not entirely unfounded.[11] But the PSF also encouraged an obsession with the threat of domestic Communism and suggested that the Soviet Union was just as much France's foe as was Nazi Germany. In the Chamber, for example, Ybarnégaray stressed that the Communist threat to the war effort was widespread, and he urged the government to be more energetic in taking action against it. For his part, La Rocque insisted that "if Germany is the eternal enemy, Soviet Russia has become its criminal vanguard."[12]

In making such arguments, the PSF lent its political weight to the notion, also promoted by parties such as the Fédération and the Alliance and other anti-Communist politicians, that the war should not be regarded solely or even primarily as an anti-fascist struggle.[13] Such a view might in the long run encourage social radicalization and work to the advantage of the left. Before the war the PSF had depicted European politics in terms of a struggle, not between democracy and dictatorship, but between Christian civilization and the pagan barbarisms of National Socialism and Soviet Communism. It now adapted this conceptualization to the wartime context. In fairness, the PSF did not focus on Communism to the complete exclusion of the Nazis, as did some newspapers of the extreme right such as *Gringoire*. In the same speech in which he had called for harsher measures against Communists, Ybarnégaray also noted the threat posed to morale by Ferdonnet, a French journalist who propagandized for the Nazis. Nevertheless, it remains that the PSF encouraged a preoccupation with anti-Communism which, in retrospect, hindered the formation of a durable *union sacrée* against the more immediate Nazi threat.[14]

The situation was further complicated by the Soviet Union's attack on Finland at the end of November, which soon led to a growing chorus in favour of French military support for the Finns. But the motives for such an action varied according to political outlook and did not encourage a consensus on how to deal with Nazi Germany, or how to conduct the war effort in general. The Socialist leader, Léon Blum, made the case for intervention primarily on moral grounds, though he also suggested that there were strategic benefits, such as potentially ending Soviet economic support for Germany. However, he and other members of the non-pacificist left refused to accept the notion that the Soviets were replacing the Nazis as France's primary enemy. By contrast, a growing proportion of the right, while also invoking strategic arguments, seemed to relish the notion of an anti-Soviet war more than an anti-Nazi one. Flandin, the leader of the Alliance, argued that a Finnish victory over the Soviet

Union was of critical importance to French war aims. Marcel Déat, a dissident socialist rather than a traditional conservative but very much part of the growing anti-Communist consensus, believed that if French arms were directed against Stalin rather than Hitler, Germany might even join the anti-Bolshevik crusade.[15]

The PSF joined in the call for an anti-Bolshevik crusade. Indeed, it tried to show that it had a uniquely important role to play in such a movement. Within the party there were some differences in opinion when it came to foreign affairs; Paul Creyssel, for instance, appears to have had more reservations about the war with Germany than La Rocque did. But when it came to calling for harsher measures against domestic Communism or striking a blow against the Soviet Union in support of Finland, the PSF could readily unite. On 16 January 1940 Robbe and Ybarnégaray were among the signatories of a proposition by Philippe Henriot calling for the government to break off diplomatic relations with the USSR. Soon afterwards *Le Petit Journal* launched an appeal for skis.[16] After Daladier, under enormous pressure, announced that a French expedition would be sent to Finland, La Rocque made a trip to that country. The PSF stressed that its leader was "the first major Allied personality who actually went to investigate the situation" and "the No. 1 enemy of Bolshevism."[17] This effort to showcase the PSF as the leading anti-Communist force in France was partly aimed at rejuvenating a movement affected by wartime mobilization; with many members at the front, activity had dwindled in some regions, and the publication of some local papers had been disrupted. La Rocque's visit to Finland was thus accompanied by a renewed funding drive, and the PSF subsequently claimed to be still vibrant.[18]

However, La Rocque's journey was cut short, and the French expedition itself rendered moot, by the signing of a Finnish-Soviet armistice on 12 March 1940. This blow to French plans signalled the end of Daladier's prime ministership, and the PSF had a role to play in his undoing. La Rocque wrote up a personal report on the government's failure to intervene, stating that its policy was indecisive and improvised. The PSF also made its mark in parliament. Before the Finns capitulated, Fernand Robbe had already initiated a storm of criticism against Daladier's government by bemoaning the state of French aviation during a closed sitting of the Chamber of Deputies on 22 February. Once the armistice was signed, Daladier's position became untenable; on 19 March he resigned after 300 deputies – including the PSF's – abstained in a vote of confidence.[19]

Daladier's rival, Paul Reynaud, now had his chance to direct the French war effort, but he was even less palatable to the PSF. A long-time proponent of firmness in dealing with Germany, Reynaud was regarded with growing suspicion by those who wished to focus on the Soviet Union instead. The fact that this conservative now relied on support from the Socialists to form his government only heightened the invective directed against him; Marcel Déat saw the new administration as "a revival of Popular Front Bolshevism."[20] When Reynaud presented his cabinet to the Chamber on 22 March, the PSF group were among the 156 deputies who voted against it. Nobécourt claims that in doing so, they were not concerned with partisan affiliations but rather the "spirit" which animated the new government, commenting that Reynaud had excluded the PSF because of Socialist pressure.[21] But in fact partisan issues were critical. La Rocque was unequivocal in his dissatisfaction with a government under "the malevolent influence" of Léon Blum. At a national council meeting held on 6 and 7 April 1940, the party passed a resolution attacking Reynaud for associating with the Socialists and refusing to consult with the PSF. At local meetings the "Reynaud-Blum" ministry was continually assailed as unviable, with orators envisioning a scenario whereby, after its collapse, "if an appeal is made to the PSF, Colonel de La Rocque will accept, for he has decided to participate actively in public affairs."[22] By choosing this course of action, the PSF contributed to the political fragmentation of wartime France and Reynaud's isolation, encouraging him to entertain desperate scenarios such as bombing Soviet oil fields in the Caucasus to mollify anti-Communist sentiment.[23]

Even when the German offensive began on 10 May, La Rocque seemed fixated upon the failings of the wartime governments. As the Battle of France opened, Reynaud asked the PSF leader to allow Ybarnégaray to enter his cabinet. La Rocque agreed but also sent a seventeen-page memorandum to Reynaud in which he expressed further dismay at the conduct of the war, notably the "competition or quarrels between the principal leaders." The situation could be turned around, but there was no time to waste. Whether the premier found such advice useful at this particular juncture seems doubtful. Similarly, when Reynaud's *directeur de cabinet*, Dominique Leca, requested that all the PSF's resources be put at the disposition of the government, La Rocque responded by suggesting improvements to the current arrangements and further criticized the government for its "improvisational" approach. This reaction only worsened relations between La Rocque and Reynaud; the latter soon denounced the PSF leader for exploiting the crisis to allow his party enter the cabinet, while La Rocque accused the prime minister of trying to appropriate his supporters.[24]

As the German breakthrough became a French rout, La Rocque faced personal tragedy and political turmoil. On 13 May his eldest son, Jean-François, was killed in aerial combat, while on 6 June his son Gilles was wounded and captured. After remaining in Paris until 13 June, La Rocque left for Clermont-Ferrand, where *Le Petit Journal* had relocated. But shortly after he arrived, La Rocque received a call from Ybarnégaray requesting his presence in Bordeaux, now the home of the French government. Before leaving Clermont-Ferrand on 15 June, La Rocque completed an editorial that counselled resistance to the end, arguing that the PSF should set an example to the citizenry. Upon reaching Bordeaux, however, he found that circumstances had changed dramatically. Reynaud had resigned and a new government had formed under the leadership of Marshal Pétain. Ybarnégaray had joined the cabinet, taking over the portfolios for public health, the family, and veterans, but he was not seen as representing the PSF. For much of the spring of 1940, "Ybar" was regarded as a proponent of prosecuting the war aggressively, but he had been shaken by the German offensive and now favoured the idea of an armistice, which the new government quickly sought.[25]

La Rocque and other PSF cadres now considered their options, some of them doing so in an increasingly independent manner. At first, Ybarnégaray offered La Rocque the post of *directeur général* for his ministries, which the latter hesitantly accepted, though on the condition that he not be paid. But when it was decided to move the offices to Perpignan a few days later, Ybarnégaray informed La Rocque there was no room for him. Unsure what to do, La Rocque considered leaving for North Africa, contacting Pétain by letter but receiving no advice. Deciding to remain in France, he headed for Pau on 20 June, there publishing several issues of *Le Petit Journal* in which he urged obedience to Pétain and Weygand.[26] In the meantime, the PSF's deputies were faced with the decision to vote the Third Republic out of existence and transfer power to Pétain. Three of them – Creyssel, Peter, and de Polignac – did not attend the session, but the rest voted in favour, along with a strong majority of the other deputies present. In addition, Bounin, Pébellier, and Robbe were among the 97 deputies who signed the Bergery declaration, presented to the assembly that same day; it called for an authoritarian new order at home and collaboration with the Third Reich.[27]

In contrast to the divisions that now emerged, the PSF's outlook had remained relatively consistent over the preceding months. Shortly before the Germans launched their attack on France, La Rocque, speaking at a meeting in Paris, had proclaimed his faith in an eventual French triumph. But he added that "an excessively easy victory would be dangerous, for we would quickly see the difficult times of these past years reappear, and witness the same incompetents whom we have known for the past twenty years return to power."[28] His words encapsulate the PSF's stance during the phoney war. While proclaiming its commitment to victory, the party also wanted to see France tested by the conflict and emerge from it more amenable to the PSF vision, lest what it saw as the decrepitude of the Third Republic persist. To ensure that outcome, the party sought to consolidate its public presence through useful work, but it also promoted an anti-Communist agenda and thereby deepened the fissures that beset French politics during the *drôle de guerre*. To be sure, the PSF was not alone in encouraging this process, and the courage in conflict of party members who had been mobilized, such as Charles Vallin, should be acknowledged.[29] Yet the fact remains that throughout this turbulent time La Rocque and his supporters, notwithstanding their calls for unity, continued to be powerfully inspired by partisan interests and ideological hatreds. That continued to be the case under Vichy.

CONFRONTING THE NATIONAL REVOLUTION

The PSF faced the advent of Marshal Pétain's new regime with some trepidation. Even before the 10 July vote, Christian Melchior-Bonnet, editor of *Le Petit Journal*, commented that the new administration "want[s] to use our ideas without the man [La Rocque]."[30] Melchior-Bonnet had succinctly identified the dilemma the PSF confronted; while operating in an ideologically congenial environment, La Rocque and his colleagues had to cope with the indifference and even hostility of some of Vichy's new masters, who hoped to usurp the PSF's ideas and support base. The movement responded carefully by presenting itself as a faithful supporter of the marshal but worked to maintain a distinct presence as it did so. In the meantime its cadres hoped they would eventually be able to implement their own variant of the National Revolution.

The PSF's apprehensions about the new government were not misplaced. While Vichy was ideologically heterogeneous, it appropriated the PSF's slogan, "Travail, Famille, Patrie" – to La Rocque's displeasure.

The intra-right discord of the 1930s also had troublesome implications. The legacy of the Tardieu affair, for instance, meant that there were potential problems with Weygand and perhaps even Marshal Pétain himself. Finally, the fact that some PSF members expressed reservations about cooperating with Germany raised concerns among the leadership that the organization would be branded as anglophile and therefore subversive.[31] Certainly, rival movements such as the PPF encouraged such notions in order to bring about the PSF's suppression.

The PSF confronted this situation in a vulnerable state. Several of its largest membership concentrations now fell under direct German occupation. The Nord, which had over 50,000 members in 1939, was now governed by the German authorities in Brussels, while Alsace, with some 27,000 members, had been annexed. While the party could count on substantial support in some parts of the Vichy-controlled unoccupied zone, including thousands of members in the Rhône and in Marseilles and its environs, it also had to deal with the loss of some of its leaders.[32] Some, such as Edmond Barrachin, became prisoners of war for a time, though Barrachin himself subsequently escaped. Others distanced themselves from the organization. Paul Creyssel, for example, dissociated himself from the PSF in the hope of securing a position in the Vichy regime.[33]

Under these circumstances and in light of Pétain's enormous popularity at the time, La Rocque presented the PSF as a pillar of the new regime and argued that support for it was coterminous with loyalty to the new head of state. In keeping with Vichy's denunciation of the republican party system, the movement promptly changed its name to the Progrès Social Français and declared that it would henceforth concentrate on social issues. It also stressed its dedication to the marshal with increasing fervour. La Rocque's first endorsements of the new government had been cautious, but before long he was "reiterating the strict, imperative order to observe absolute discipline behind Marshal Pétain" as "the sole guarantor of the country given the current situation." It may be that denunciations by the PPF to the effect that the PSF was engaged in "Gaullist activity," which resulted in searches by German officials, encouraged this increased emphasis on loyalty.[34] Conversely, directives issued by Pétain's cabinet against these denunciations, in response to a complaint from La Rocque, might have earned the latter's gratitude.[35] Whatever the case, insistence on the need to support Pétain without hesitation soon became a staple of PSF rhetoric.

In adopting this stance, the PSF was hardly alone, given that exaltation of the marshal was intrinsic to the regime. However, the movement also hoped that by presenting itself as a leading supporter of Pétain, it would remain prominent in the public eye, secure in its relations with the regime, and relevant to its own supporters. When Pétain toured the major cities of southern France in the fall of 1940, PSF members not only turned out to greet him en masse but aided the authorities in various ways, a fact La Rocque was not slow to impress upon them in private correspondence. In an attempt to galvanize their members, section presidents claimed that La Rocque was close to Pétain. They assured supporters that he exercised influence in the development of measures such as the dissolution of Masonic lodges. For example, the president of the PSF's Gard federation, Émile Teyssedre, informed members that the organization was alive and well and stressed that its counsels were welcome at Vichy.[36] Teyssedre exaggerated; while La Rocque eventually composed a number of reports for the government on his own initiative, the extent to which they influenced policy is uncertain. This lack of interest did not dissuade the PSF leadership, though; their rationale appears to have been that if Pétain enjoyed the respect of the public, they could only benefit by stressing the movement's connections to him.

Yet La Rocque and his associates did not intend simply to function as an adjunct to Vichy propaganda; they were also looking ahead. The police reported that at a meeting in Lyons La Rocque stated that the eighty-four-year-old Pétain would not live very long. Another reported him saying that the government was weak and divided, that the marshal would soon be "retired," and that his supporters must get ready to take power.[37] Denunciations of the PSF as subversive must be treated carefully, but there is reason to think that these reports reflect views within the movement at the time. Melchior-Bonnet, for one, was convinced that Pétain would not be around much longer. Moreover, at a February 1941 meeting the PSF executive affirmed they would continue their work "in all domains until the moment when the men of the Croix de Feu, having taken power, will carry out in full the program of the National Revolution, for which they have struggled for many years."[38]

In the interim, however, the PSF had to conduct a very difficult balancing act. Though it praised the marshal endlessly, it was distinctly more reserved about the officials of the Vichy government itself, who in turn were suspicious of the movement. As early as September 1940, La Rocque announced that while loyalty to the head of state was required, the PSF also had to exercise an "absolute reserve" with respect to the members of his government. Indeed, he added that "never has the ostracism directed against my person (considered not from a private point of view, but in terms of my function in the PSF) been more marked, total, or persistent." For their part, the authorities observed that while he preached support for Pétain as the new head of state, La Rocque was disdainful of the new head of government, Pierre Laval.[39]

A pattern quickly emerged whereby the PSF depicted itself as a watchdog of the National Revolution, asserting that it had to be implemented more vigorously, while at the same time protesting that the authorities were dismissive of the movement's contribution to national renewal. Writing in *Le Petit Journal* on 1 October, La Rocque warned that "it would be an insult to the Head of State, the Government, and France herself if the National Revolution is envisaged as a slogan, an illusory facade whose heroic sign masks a persistent torpor."[40] Though cryptic, his words seemed to imply that the current team was not up to the job. Certainly, he felt that his own organization was being snubbed. For instance, La Rocque was advised by Pétain's cabinet that the PSF would participate in a special winter aid committee in Paris, but he then found out that this invitation had been withdrawn. In February 1941 La Rocque complained to the marshal's *chef de cabinet* that in spite of his desire to keep Pétain up to date through reports collated from various PSF sources, he was being ignored.[41]

While La Rocque wished his supporters to be regarded as an integral part of the new order, he also wanted them to maintain their autonomy and to be ready when their chance to take power arose. He and those associates who remained loyal to him thus fended off what they regarded as various attempts to co-opt the PSF. When Marcel Déat and Gaston Bergery, having been officially charged with exploring the option of creating a single party, approached La Rocque, he quickly rejected the idea, seeing it as an attempt to siphon off his followers.[42] In January 1941 La Rocque was made a member of Vichy's Conseil National, a group of "notables" who were named to serve as the regime's body of public representatives. He did not last long in this role, however, as he resigned six months later. In a similar vein, the PSF sent five representatives, including La Rocque and Vallin, to the Comité de Rassemblement pour la Révolution Nationale (later the Comité de Propagande Sociale). This body was intended to act as an umbrella organization for various nationalist movements in support of a harmonized propaganda effort. But La Rocque and his colleagues soon found themselves in conflict with other committee members, most notably the representatives of the PPF, and quit.[43]

From the PSF's perspective, the Légion Française des Combattants posed an even greater threat. Inspired by a proposal from La Rocque's old rival Xavier Vallat, the Légion was an amalgam of veterans' groups intended to inculcate the values of the National Revolution in the population. It promoted the official ideology and enjoyed state sponsorship, attaining some 1.5 million members at its peak. Given the ideological similarities and the fact that many of the PSF's members were also veterans, a rivalry between the two organizations rapidly emerged. La Rocque reacted to the creation of the Légion contemptuously, noting that among its leadership there was not one friend of the PSF and "a number of men ... who ... have made their hatred for our work clear." He did not forbid his followers to join, but instructed them to remain "PSF first." Nevertheless, it appears that a significant number of his supporters joined the Légion; for instance, six of the latter's departmental presidents came from the PSF. While genuine enthusiasm for the National Revolution was likely a consideration for some in making this choice, the potential benefits that accrued from membership in Vichy's official movement were no doubt also a factor.[44] Some PSF members did not see any contradiction in belonging to both movements, but others turned on their former leader. One disillusioned PSF supporter who became a Légion section president denounced La Rocque to the police, claiming that he had slandered the Légion as "a bunch of men with no ideals." Such assertions, in addition to the opposition to the Légion that came from some PSF federation presidents such as Teyssedre in the Gard, confirmed the government's belief that the movement was a serious obstacle to its plans.[45]

The growing conflict between the PSF and the Légion suggests that La Rocque's troubled relationship with the Vichy regime was primarily the result of a power struggle, rather than major philosophical differences. It has been suggested that the latter were of some significance because La Rocque did not like the idea of carrying out a grandiose reform project while France was restricted by the conditions of the armistice. On this point, it is true that in his 1941 book *Disciplines d'action* La Rocque rejected the idea of immediately replacing the Third Republic's constitution. Moreover, the novelist Jacques de Lacretelle, who had written an adulatory pamphlet about La Rocque before the war, claimed in the *Journal de Génève* in March 1941 that the PSF leader was uncomfortable with the term "National Revolution," with its connotations of undue haste. Edmond Barrachin, while generally positive about de Lacretelle's writings, took issue with this point: "I am in agreement if by 'revolution' a change of regime or civil war is meant; I strongly disagree if 'revolution' means *putting the regime back in order* while effecting a complete transformation of mores ... La Rocque does not wish to *conserve* the republic; he wants to *remake* it."[46] Certainly, La Rocque himself insisted on total change: "the French organism must be entirely healed, the brain, the limbs, the muscles simultaneously playing their respective roles in the general harmony finally re-established."[47]

From the outset the PSF convincingly insisted that it shared the new regime's priorities. To be sure, the fact that the movement had an established tradition of mass mobilization gave it a distinct perspective compared to the top-down attitude of many of Vichy's officials who suddenly found themselves in power. Both, however, were characterized by an emphasis upon elitism; when it came to regenerating France, La Rocque believed that class collaboration under the auspices of strong leaders was crucial, asserting that "the rehabilitation of the elite is the key to social reconstruction."[48] The PSF also condemned the same groups that loomed large in Vichy's demonology. In one of his many attacks upon the Gaullist movement, for example, La Rocque linked it to other domestic and foreign foes in a vast conspiracy: "the French who have entered into England's service have in a way added to their initial mistake, voluntarily or involuntarily, the offence of colluding with our internal enemies ... [There are] seditious machinations that currently take on an anarchist form and are hatched, guided, and led by Communism." The influence of Freemasonry, a bugbear for the PSF and for Vichy, also had to be eradicated: "all those who are militants of the Lodges, even if they sincerely regret it, are disqualified from the planning for a resuscitated France."[49]

Nor did the PSF refrain from commenting on the status of the Jews in France. While a postwar investigation concluded that *Le Petit Journal* did not fixate upon antisemitism in the way that collaborationist papers such as *Je suis partout* had, it did endorse Vichy's first anti-Jewish laws, passed in October 1940. La Rocque reiterated his rejection of biological racism but also his concerns about the "undesirable multitude" of Jewish refugees and the fact that the Popular Front had given too many positions to radical and "ostentatious" Jews. Of course, he added, the problem had to be solved in a "humane" fashion, one that recognized the contributions of Jews who honourably participated in France's Christian civilization. Perhaps the adoption of "some measures" similar to those of Fascist Italy was in order, he suggested. In any event, many naturalizations needed to be revisited, especially in cases where Jews had contravened the laws of the state or the precepts of Christian civilization. Even those who were born in France should not be exempt from such measures. La Rocque thus approved both the cancellation of previous naturalizations – a move that left many Jewish residents terribly vulnerable – and the abrogation of the 1870 Crémieux decree, which had given North African Jews citizenship. In sum, the PSF leader shared the Vichy regime's initial aim of expelling foreign Jews as well as "the submergence of longer-established Jews ... into a newly homogenous French nation."[50]

It is true that behind the scenes La Rocque was sometimes less comfortable with aspects of the regime than his writings in *Le Petit Journal* let on. But this was because he felt that its program to remake France was not being implemented with sufficient rigour or integrity, and that the PSF was being thwarted in its efforts to further the process. In an April 1941 memorandum addressed to Pétain, La Rocque expressed dismay at his inability to secure an audience with the marshal as well as the failings of the regime in general. Many officials hindered the application of Vichy's new laws to the extent that "often the best [citizens]" were led to ask themselves whether "the local underlings do not seek to discredit the generous inspiration from which such texts derive." Pétain, he noted, had condemned the power of "the trusts," but the general perception was that these exerted an ever-greater influence, despite the material suffering of the population. Young men were flocking to the Gaullists, but no action was taken against those who failed to prevent this shift. The Riom trials, intended to prosecute those responsible for France's defeat, dragged on interminably, and the marshal had regrettably not made use of his prerogative to carry out "immediate punishments" and set some examples. La Rocque went so far as to warn Pétain that "not only does it seem that the National Revolution, wanted by you and desired by the country, has not begun; a revolution – in the subversive sense of the word – is readying itself, and is perhaps imminent." La Rocque closed by noting his own disinterested desire to serve and the fact that "the civic and social organizations under my presidency which work intensely every day, through homogenous and fraternal teams, *throughout the territory*, are at your disposal."[51]

Admittedly, when it came to the matter of collaboration with Germany, La Rocque could sound ambivalent. He would not rule out the idea; in August 1940 he told his supporters that Nazism involved an adaptation "to the necessities of world evolution since 1918" and that it and the PSF shared some concerns. Furthermore, after Pétain's infamous meeting with Hitler at Montoire in October, when he proclaimed that his government would pursue a policy of collaboration, La Rocque professed his loyalty to the head of state: "the country's total support must be given to the victor of 1918, the guarantor of national revival after the defeat of 1940."[52] He insisted, however, that French interests had to be respected in any cooperative undertaking. For instance, La Rocque decried the Anglo-Gaullist attempt to take Dakar in September 1940 and declared that France now had a "free hand" as far Britain was concerned, but he added that this situation should not lead to subservience to the Third Reich: "No collaboration with Germany will be possible if it is carried out between representatives of the victorious power and Frenchmen abdicating their dignity, converting themselves into slaves or valets." Such remarks, it seems, aroused German suspicion; in early 1941 La Rocque was briefly detained, ostensibly for crossing the demarcation line into the occupied zone without a permit.[53]

Even after this incident, the PSF did not publicly rule out Franco-German cooperation, though again there were signs of hesitation. La Rocque never concealed his distaste for Laval, who strongly favoured collaboration, but he was initially hopeful when Admiral Darlan became the head of government in February 1941. And when it turned out that Darlan intended to go quite far in accommodating the Germans, the PSF acquiesced. In May 1941, during Darlan's pursuit of a major Franco-German settlement, La Rocque reminded the readers of *Le Petit Journal* that the admiral was given this task by Pétain, to whom "France must give full support, precisely in those fields where the current drama sometimes compels us to accept, observe, [and] require an impenetrable discretion: the domains of diplomacy and imperial national defence."[54] But the PSF leader did remain circumspect about certain wartime developments. Following the German invasion of the Soviet Union in June 1941, he declared that the destruction of Bolshevik power was desirable but also cautioned that Russia was historically a formidable trap for invaders.[55]

By this time the PSF's frustration with the regime was palpable, even though it also saw itself as a vanguard of the National Revolution. In a

June 1941 memorandum La Rocque complained privately to Pétain about the way the movement was being treated. The marshal publicly commended the PSF, but its suggestions were not heeded, and the Légion remained a constant problem. The time had come, La Rocque concluded, for the PSF "to choose between confirmed support ... and the adoption of a more distant, reserved attitude."[56] At its annual congress, held in Lyons two weeks later, the PSF reiterated its commitment to Vichy's principles but also implied that it could outperform the current regime. La Rocque cautioned that collaboration with Germany must not become the plaything of "professional and particular interests," though he also condemned Gaullism, boasting that he had convinced "innumerable" patriots from being won over by this "emigré ex-general on foreign soil." As for Vichy's domestic policy, he conceded that implementing the National Revolution would take time, but he took heart in the fact that the PSF provided "an immense, homogenous, and well-forged team." He also sought to outflank, at least rhetorically, the current anti-Jewish policies of the government. Commenting on the second Jewish statute of June 1941, which expanded the regime's definition of Jewishness and further restricted the entry of Jews into the professions and universities, La Rocque continued to reject biological racism. But he also asserted that entire families should be deprived of their citizenship in cases of "evident lack of assimilation," and he urged that naturalizations be handled more stringently, asserting that "in [terms of] practical execution my suggestions surpass what the most severe ones have ever called for."[57]

MAKING CHOICES

The summer of 1941 marked a turning point for Vichy. In the face of growing public disillusionment and resistance – including the unequivocal hostility of the Communists since the USSR had been invaded – the regime toughened its stance. On 12 August Pétain proclaimed that an "evil wind" was blowing through France; thereafter Pierre Pucheu, the minister of the interior, moved to reinforce the state's authority and developed plans for the creation of a single party. In foreign policy, however, Darlan was repeatedly stymied in his quest for "fruitful" cooperation with the Third Reich. Disgruntled, he was eventually replaced by Pierre Laval in April 1942. Laval and many of his ministers were largely indifferent to the National Revolution but firmly committed to cooperation with the Nazis, despite the entry of the United States into the war and Germany's difficulties in the USSR. In the meantime, Pétain's own authority began to wane.[58]

The PSF's response to the situation was complex. At first – admittedly under pressure – it sought to come to terms with the changes being introduced, deepening its cooperation with the regime to an extent. But when it came to collaboration with Germany, there was eventually a parting of the ways, as La Rocque and some of his colleagues expressed growing discontent and supplied the British with intelligence. Nevertheless, the PSF was still committed to remaking France in ways strongly concordant with the principles of the National Revolution, and it lamented the "Vichy that might have been."[59]

In the fall of 1941 the PSF's standoff with the Légion abated somewhat, as each turned its attention to Pucheu's desire to incorporate both movements into a new single party for the regime. The PSF and the Légion now engaged in talks about closer cooperation, but for Pucheu this rapprochement did not suffice. Meeting with La Rocque and Vallin on 16 September, the minister of the interior elaborated upon his intentions and offered La Rocque the *résidence générale* in Morocco in return for his assent to the merging of the PSF into a single party. La Rocque refused, declaring that he would not abandon the movement, though he remained open to the possibility of further "coordination." Three days later he met again with Pucheu, this time in the company of Pétain and Darlan. It was now decided that a fusion of the PSF and the Légion would indeed take place, but only gradually. La Rocque would become a *chargé de mission* attached to Pétain's cabinet, responsible for coordinating the PSF's activities with the Légion's.[60]

By doing so, La Rocque had in effect bought some time for the PSF, during which he might secure greater influence for its members within the corridors of power at Vichy. After the compromise was reached and La Rocque assumed his post, he requested jobs for three of his associates, suggesting that Stanislas Devaud be named a prefect and that both Noël Ottavi – now in charge of the PSF's organization in the occupied zone – and Edmond Barrachin be made members of the Conseil National. While nothing came of these requests, the PSF's Charles Vallin was appointed to Vichy's Conseil de Justice Politique, established to advise on disciplinary action for those deemed responsible for France's defeat. After he defected to the Gaullists in 1942, Vallin told the British that he was an opponent of what he called this body's "anti-constitutional" work. The Foreign Office, however, noted that the Conseil had unanimously recommended that Blum, Daladier, and Gamelin be imprisoned because of their "responsibility" for the catastrophe of 1940.[61]

It appears that La Rocque believed working with the regime would allow the PSF not only to survive but perhaps even to expand its influence. In this respect the ongoing cooperation between the Vichy regime and the PSF-inspired ADP (now renamed the Artisans du Devoir Patriotique) may have served as a foundation upon which La Rocque hoped to build. During the war the ADP operated in conjunction with the Secours National, a regime-sanctioned charitable organization, in a wide range of relief activities. The close cooperation between the two is not very surprising given that Robert Garric, head of the Secours National, was a friend of La Rocque's. Even if the figures they provide are inflated, both groups evidently did much to help refugees, the sick, victims of bombardments, and others. The ADP alone reportedly sent 16,000 tons of parcels to POWs in Germany, and it claimed that by October 1942 a total of 4.6 million meals had been served in its canteens and restaurants, though at least in the Finistère the restaurants were reportedly accessible only to the relatively well-paid. Nevertheless, the scope of the ADP's contribution was impressive; one official declared that it accounted for three-quarters of the Secours National's efforts in the southern zone, though it has been suggested that this figure is somewhat exaggerated.[62]

Neither the Secours National nor the ADP was ideologically neutral; both helped to project Vichy's message, while the latter simultaneously tried to highlight the PSF's distinctive contribution. Antoinette de Préval, who played a leading role in the ADP's efforts, was careful to specify the inspiration behind it. Though she called upon its members to venerate the marshal and was recognized by the regime for her services, she explained the ADP's successes in terms of the guiding message provided by La Rocque – "serve and do not serve oneself" – and called upon members to "have the constant sentiment of the equality of souls" and "abolish all class struggle."[63] Though discussions of political matters per se did not take place at ADP meetings, the police never doubted that La Rocque's tours of the organization's facilities were aimed partly at keeping the PSF intact. Indeed, in the final stages of the war the authorities suspected the ADP of attempting to infiltrate organizations such as the Red Cross, and in 1944 it was suggested that the ADP might serve as a platform for a revival of the PSF itself.[64]

But while the ADP was a useful vehicle for the PSF in terms both of image and of facilitating connections with the authorities, in general the relationship between the PSF and the government remained precarious, especially as far as the Légion was concerned. La Rocque found that his new position as an aide to Pétain did not give him the influence he desired; the American ambassador observed that he was given very little to do.[65] He used his time to delay the PSF's fusion with the Légion by touring France and North Africa; ostensibly, his goal was to "psychologically prepare" his supporters for the transition, but during his visits he reiterated the PSF's concerns about the Légion. In the Haute-Garonne, La Rocque reported, PSF "patriots" were concerned that the Légion's departmental president had kept his job after it was revealed that he had failed to acknowledge his Masonic past. His counterpart in the Aveyron was viewed by the PSF as "very controversial in moral terms, even by his own family." Once the tour was finished, La Rocque praised the Légion's organizers for the courteous welcome they gave him, but argued that a premature dissolution of the PSF would be detrimental to Vichy's interests, as it would cause resentment among the natural supporters of the National Revolution.[66]

Thus by the winter of 1942 relations between the PSF and the Légion were again at a standstill. PSF federation presidents denounced the Légion at meetings; in Algiers Debay asserted that the organization was "finished." Then in April La Rocque proposed a compromise, stating that he would provide the Légion with lists of potential cadres from among his supporters, provided that these individuals would remain members of the PSF as well. When François Valentin, the head of the Légion, rejected this suggestion and demanded that the cadres quit the PSF, La Rocque responded by insisting that his supporters await his instructions. Fortunately for the PSF, the issue lost much of its potency shortly thereafter when Laval returned as premier, Pucheu was dismissed, and the focus of the Légion's shifted to its paramilitary wing, the Service d'Ordre Légionnaire (SOL), the unruliness of which soon redounded negatively on the Légion itself.[67]

The ongoing feud with the Légion revealed how the PSF viewed itself in relation to Vichy by this time. La Rocque's criticisms of the Légion during his tour pointed to his belief that the PSF was a more ideologically authentic organization; while his own supporters truly identified with the National Revolution, the Légion, he implied, attracted many opportunists. Additional concerns were voiced in the reports La Rocque sent Pétain in 1942. Following his tour of North Africa that February, he composed a detailed analysis of the situation there. He concluded that in Morocco General Noguès was in control, but in

Tunisia and especially Algeria conditions were tenuous. The latter, he suggested, was entering "a decisive phase in its history," with the Muslims increasingly "out of hand." Abuses in housing administration and requisitions partly accounted for the problem, but above all, the authorities were too lenient. Both Muslims and Europeans had the same type of ration cards, and local police were no longer allowed even to *tutoyer* the colonial subjects.[68]

In further reports, written in the autumn of 1942, La Rocque drew similar conclusions regarding conditions in metropolitan France. Though maintaining that Pétain's prestige remained high and that the public had become more understanding about the complex situation Laval faced, he contended that in general the government was increasingly unpopular. Communist activity was on the rise, as were pro-Gaullist sentiments, especially among members of the bourgeoisie who were suffering economically. The *relève* – the drafting of French workers for German factories – was causing increasing resentment, while the black market flourished and more people were getting divorced than ever before. La Rocque recommended that the government cut all ostentatious expenditures and cultivate a spartan image. Propaganda needed to be improved, with fewer "tirades" and more "arguments." The best approach would be to "circulate several simple slogans, from neighbourhood to neighbourhood, village to village, market to market, [and] workshop to workshop." Pétain also needed to make a speech outlining the government's objectives and clarifying the distinction between its policies and those imposed by the Germans.[69]

PSF cadres echoed these criticisms, simultaneously asserting that only their movement could truly renovate France. In the Gard Émile Teyssedre complained that the police were ineffective in responding to "Communist-instigated" food riots, using force to end the demonstrations and making arrests but holding no one. Noting rumours that the local subprefect was a Freemason, Teyssedre went on to criticize the lack of security in the area, concluding that "the National Revolution will not be realized by employing 'persuasion.' In the PSF we are well aware that other, more forceful means are necessary." These comments annoyed the authorities; the departmental prefect, Angelo Chiappe, who knew La Rocque personally, had to intervene to keep Teyssedre out of trouble. Edmond Barrachin also believed the PSF could do a better job than Vichy had. Though he would defect to the Gaullists in the fall of 1942, in March of that year he had a conversation with an American diplomat in Tangier in which he declared, "It was hoped ...

by both de La Rocque and himself that with the death of Pétain or at some other appropriate time of crisis which would provoke an internal revolution in France, the PSF would step in after the initial disorders and gain control and finish what others had begun."[70]

By this time, La Rocque and a number of his colleagues had come to reject one of the government's key policies – collaboration with Germany – to the point where they organized resistance activities in the form of intelligence-gathering. Exactly when this began is unclear. PSF sympathizers claim that La Rocque ordered information to be gathered as early as September 1940 and began transmitting it to the British that December. For his part, Nobécourt concludes that it was not until early 1942 that regular contact was definitively established; the transmissions then continued until November. Machefer is less convinced that earlier intelligence-gathering took place, and he implies that the evidence points to sustained activities of this sort by La Rocque and his followers only after the United States entered the war.[71] The Anglo-French Communications Bureau, which attested to the efforts of the network – named "Klan" – after the war, simply stated that La Rocque furnished the British with information from 1 June 1942 until he was arrested in February 1943 (he was actually arrested in March).[72]

Klan's dangerous work, it seems, was carefully organized. The information it collected came from various sources. The ADP reportedly played an important role, though only a few members were aware of the full significance of their activities. Information also came from PSF supporters inserted into the Bureau des Menées Antinationales, a branch of French army intelligence that monitored "suspect personalities" and the German armistice commission in Paris. Once the material was gathered, La Rocque passed it on to Colonel Georges Charaudeau, head of the Alibi network based in Spain, which cooperated with the British Secret Intelligence Service. As to the nature of the information gathered, after the war PSF activists claimed that it included details about underground aerodromes in Normandy and other installations, and that the Allies had regularly requested further information. They also declared that Klan had been one of the four most important networks in metropolitan France, and they emphasized how La Rocque had remained a public figure while he led it and that its work did not involve Frenchmen fighting one another.[73]

La Rocque tried to be circumspect about these activities, but it seems he had trouble disguising his feelings in meetings with his supporters, and he soon attracted renewed German attention. After

Laval infamously declared in June 1942 that he desired a German victory, La Rocque cautiously observed in *Le Petit Journal* that the head of the government was "authorized to express himself in the name of the Victor of Verdun" and "has promised that our vital interests and honour will be respected." In PSF meetings, however, La Rocque was more critical. At a meeting in Auxerre held in September while he was touring the occupied zone, he revealed himself to be "rather hesitant about the concessions made to the German authorities." The entourage of Otto Abetz, the German ambassador, was alarmed at this news.[74] In October 1942 the Germans cracked down on the PSF in the occupied zone, ensuring that no more meetings were held and denying La Rocque further entry.

In November the Allies invaded French North Africa, and German forces occupied all of France. Increasingly agitated, La Rocque ultimately decided that his task was to guide Pétain and protect France from social and political upheaval. Immediately following the Operation Torch landings, he had written to the marshal and offered to go to North Africa, suggesting that his experience of the region would be useful. But Pétain instead requested that La Rocque continue to report to him on the state of opinion in France. The PSF leader did so without hiding his dismay at what was happening. At meetings he now declared that collaboration, as envisaged by the PSF, was impossible between an occupying power and the occupied country. He also reminded his supporters that they were not to join collaborationist organizations such as the SOL or the PPF, insisting that Doriot still harboured revolutionary ambitions from his Communist days.[75] When Vichy's armistice army was dissolved, La Rocque strongly protested the measure, and days later he sent his most strident letter yet to the marshal. Describing France as being on the threshold of anarchy and noting the defection of senior officers to the Allies, he ended by bluntly stating that "the execution of your decisions and those of the head of your government are accompanied by servile attitudes towards the conqueror on the part of a large number of central officials." He then called on Pétain to form a ministry composed of "ardent patriots" with "respectable private lives," adding that only this measure could ensure the discipline needed to save the country.[76]

La Rocque overestimated the degree of autonomy Pétain retained by the fall of 1942, as well as the marshal's determination to break with Laval over the policy of collaboration.[77] No dramatic change in policy was forthcoming. Undeterred, La Rocque continued to address PSF meetings, write editorials, and "advise" Pétain. His frustration was ever more visible; in *Le Petit Journal* he impatiently wondered, "What is a revolution if not the total, rapid, sudden – perhaps brutal – change of institutions and morals? Where are the changes of this kind in the conduct and thinking of the men appointed as role models and leaders within our national community?" In January 1943, however, he had an audience with the marshal and became convinced that Pétain would listen to him. La Rocque then sent further reports to the head of state and met him on several more occasions, the last on 7 March. By this time, La Rocque later claimed, he had secured Pétain's consent to an accord with the Allies, aimed at "a deliverance of the metropole as much as possible from disorder." Unfortunately, he noted, Pétain had imprudently remarked in front of a group of strangers that he regretted not having listened to La Rocque earlier. Two days later the Gestapo arrested La Rocque at his residence in Clermont-Ferrand. The Germans rounded up a total of 152 PSF activists. Precisely why the series of arrests occurred when it did is unclear, but its timing concurred with German actions against other organizations now deemed to be troublemakers, even if they supported the Vichy regime.[78]

Despite his increasingly obvious opposition to collaboration, La Rocque during these months consistently emphasized the need for loyalty to Pétain and the spirit of the National Revolution, distinguishing between its higher principles and the actions of the current administration. In a pamphlet entitled *France d'aujourd'hui, France de démain*, written at the end of 1942 and intended only for PSF cadres, he declared that Pétain's moral authority remained unshakable, commenting that "his moral status calls to mind those pictures of saints that certain superstitious fishermen dare not remove even if they insult the saint, which they turn against the wall in moments of anger and return to their proper place to request help or sing his praises." La Rocque conceded that the government itself was very unpopular, but added that the PSF still had to "accompany" the marshal: "the only attitude likely to be profitable to the marshal and to the country is to maintain ... [our work] ... in the service of orderly spirit, civic discipline, and public order."[79]

This uneasy balancing act between a continuing endorsement of the National Revolution and a growing rejection of collaboration with the Third Reich was, it seems, also maintained with respect to the persecution of France's Jews. There is some evidence to suggest that some PSF supporters were increasingly disturbed by what was happening. Associates of the movement such as Melchior-Bonnet privately indicated concern about the impact of antisemitic measures. Former PSF militants and friends of La Rocque such as Robert Garric claimed that the movement helped individuals such as the son of La Rocque's physician escape to Switzerland, where a PSF-run hostel provided assistance to other Jews, escaped prisoners, and resisters. It has also been suggested that *Le Petit Journal* employed Jews, who were kept safe with false identity papers at La Rocque's behest, while the PSF leader reportedly expressed his opposition to racial antisemitism in private meetings with German authorities. Certainly, collaborationist newspapers such as *L'Appel* attacked the PSF leader for being pro-Jewish.[80]

But while La Rocque may have disapproved of Vichy's cooperation in carrying out deportations, it is noteworthy that he never reversed his approval of the regime's initial antisemitic measures. In October 1942, after the deportations had begun, he could still comment in a private report to Pétain's cabinet on the unrest ostensibly caused by the involvement of Jewish refugees in the black market, though he recommended that a "humane and rational" way be found to put a stop to these activities, lest they provoke hostility. When the Allies restored political rights to North African Jews after winning control of the region, La Rocque was dismayed: "the restoration of the scandalous privileges granted to the native Jews by the Crémieux law shows an intransigent dogmatism and a lack of psychology that make [one] shudder."[81] While the PSF leader may have been affecting outrage to avoid arousing suspicion and protect the Klan network from scrutiny, the consistency of his hostility to Algeria's Jewish community since the late 1930s suggests otherwise.

In addition, it must be noted that although the PSF's intelligence-gathering efforts indicate the depth of its opposition to collaboration, the Nazi regime was not completely unacceptable to the movement. As Soucy notes, La Rocque in his 1941 book *Disciplines d'action* displayed some admiration for the Nazis, praising "the ardent vitality of the Fascist and Hitlerian regimes."[82] Even more telling are his comments in *France d'aujourd'hui, France de démain*, since it was intended for a closed readership and was written, it seems, after he established contact with the Allies. In it La Rocque regretted the behaviour of the Germans. An opportunity for cooperation between equals – akin to that envisioned by General Ludendorff in 1918, when he reportedly offered to lead German troops against the Bolsheviks under the aegis of Marshal Foch – had been lost. Moreover, as La Rocque contemplated the kind of France he wished to see emerge after the war, he rejected the "Anglo-Saxon" model and maintained that the country had "a lot to learn from the Germans." The Nazis had developed a social cohesion worthy of emulation, at least in some respects: "we must, then, organize a French regime analogous in terms of social development to what could have been established in Germany, but including state and public institutions, private and supervised organizations honouring spiritual forces, developing the personality of the citizens, [and] protecting, encouraging, and disciplining the autonomy of families."[83]

La Rocque evidently saw some contrasts between what the Nazis had constructed and what the PSF desired for France. He expressed concerns about the "pantheistic" and materialist outlook of Nazism, which paralleled Bolshevism and ran contrary to the values of Christian civilization. The vision of France La Rocque outlined instead called for a regime run by an elite respectful of such values, as well as the military, rural life, and the family. There would be no political parties; even the PSF itself would eventually be dissolved. Instead, representation would exist only in the form of an indirectly elected body.[84] In *Le Petit Journal* he praised, as he had before the war, the Iberian dictatorships as models, noting "the patriotic and spiritual formula which Spain offers" and maintaining that "no one disputes th[e] dynamic traditionalism which Salazar, in Portugal, also recommends developing. Therefore, which of us would fear to indicate France's way ahead according to conceptions analogous to those of two peoples so close [to us] in their ethnic origins and Western civilization?"[85] In short, La Rocque offered France a variant of the National Revolution, calling for the installation of an authoritarian but "pluralist" state inspired by the PSF and guided by a paternally minded elite striving for social order.

A MOVEMENT DISPERSED

If the consistency of the PSF leader's political views can be established, tracing the fate of his supporters during the war years is far more difficult. The movement experienced ongoing fragmentation as many members chose to collaborate, to join resistance groups, or to abandon politics altogether. Thus it can be said that the PSF membership shared in the broader experiences of the French people under occupation. More distinctly, the itineraries of some of those who broke with the organization attest to its profound impact on their outlook, showing that its message of national reconciliation could be modified to suit different ends.

A number of former Croix de Feu and PSF supporters found their way into the ranks of collaborationist movements, though in some cases these individuals had broken with La Rocque well before 1940. In the Loiret, for instance, Marcel Déat's Rassemblement National Populaire relied more upon former neo-Socialists for supporters than any other group, but some former PSF members did join up. Within the PPF were a number of former Croix de Feu and PSF supporters, some of whom continued to back Doriot under the occupation. In other cases the shift from supporting La Rocque to collaboration was more complex. Paul Chopine, who had defected from the Croix de Feu in 1935, subsequently denounced La Rocque as a fascist, but a PSF report suggests that he later served in the collaborationist Milice.[86]

There were also those who abandoned the PSF and cooperated more closely with the regime without La Rocque's approval. Félix Olivier-Martin, former editor of *Samedi* and president of the PSF's Vienne federation, became secretary general for youth affairs in 1943.[87] The most prominent individual in this regard was Paul Creyssel, who served as Vichy's secretary general for propaganda from December 1942 to March 1944. Interestingly, though he had separated himself from the PSF soon after the armistice and was fully obedient to Laval, the central themes of his propaganda resonated with the movement's doctrine to a considerable extent. He was disinclined to argue in favour of cooperation with the Germans; instead, his speeches were characterized by a virulent anti-Communism and implored the French people to remain loyal and thus avoid civil war. To be sure, anti-Communism was a staple of countless figures outside the PSF orbit by this time, but among the points that Creyssel emphasized to the French public – reminiscent of La Rocque – was that before the war most "true Communists ... were ardent and sincere militants who believed with all their soul in fighting for bread, peace, and liberty"; it was "the French Communist leaders" who had, "upon Moscow's orders, completely betrayed the entire working class, France, and the cause of peace." Similarly, while Creyssel attacked the same British government that La Rocque secretly aided, his calls for France to avoid civil war were not so different from the PSF leader's concerns about maintaining order and rejecting Gaullism. Eventually the Germans grew convinced that Creyssel was insufficiently sympathetic to their concerns, and he was replaced by

Philippe Henriot, a hardline proponent of collaboration. As compensation, Creyssel became Vichy's minister to Monaco.[88]

At the other end of the spectrum were those who gravitated towards resistance groups against PSF directives. Some of these former PSF supporters even aligned with the left, though the dynamics of that shift could be complex. Jacques Bounin began his break with the PSF in 1941 and eventually joined the *comité directeur* of the Communist-led Front National in the southern zone. But he had initially sought to join the Free French before being approached by the Front National and probably opted for the latter because he saw it as the most effective instrument for opposing the Germans, rather than out of an ideological conversion. By contrast, in her 1950 novel *J'étais au PSF*, Gilette Ziegler describes how a devoted supporter of La Rocque came to endorse Communism. But while the heroine of the novel, Hélène Wetterlé, had contributed to *Le Petit Journal* – as had Ziegler – it is unclear how autobiographical or representative of the attitudes of other "defectors" the book is.[89]

It appears that a greater proportion of former PSF supporters found their way into resistance movements of a conservative-nationalist bent. Certainly, André Mutter, a PSF member whom Barrachin had planned to run as a candidate in 1940, retained a degree of consistency in his political leanings. The Ceux de la Libération movement, which he formed in the occupied zone, focused upon military activities and recruited among conservative nationalists, including disillusioned PSF members. Mutter himself became a member of the Conseil National de la Résistance. General Louis Audibert, a leading figure in the PSF's Loire-Inférieure federation during the 1930s, joined the nationalist-oriented Armée Secrète but was arrested and deported with his entire family to Ravensbruck in March 1944. His wife did not survive; Audibert, however, returned to France and was elected a deputy. He remained very much a figure of the right, but he condemned La Rocque for having adopted an ambiguous stance.[90]

By contrast, some individuals perceived no contradiction in sympathizing with the Free French while remaining affiliated with the PSF, despite La Rocque's constant proclamations to the contrary. For instance, in January 1941 a dozen young men from "good families" associated with the PSF were discovered storing arms in Troyes. They possessed Cross of Lorraine emblems, and two were also carrying photos of La Rocque.[91] However, La Rocque's reaction to the defection of two leading colleagues to the Free French the following year demonstrated his consistent hostility to Gaullism. Though he had played a prominent role in the PSF after the armistice, Charles Vallin went into hiding in the summer of 1942, escaped to Britain, and rallied to de Gaulle; he was soon followed by Edmond Barrachin. Vallin's defection, the movement declared, "contravenes PSF discipline in an unquestionable and infinitely grave manner." For his part, La Rocque felt personally betrayed by the defection of a hitherto close associate; naturally, Barrachin's decision was also condemned.[92]

While his defection obviously represented a complete break with the PSF, Vallin's subsequent activities were controversial and his concerns were not altogether different from La Rocque's. After his defection, some British and Free French officials regarded him as a valuable asset, but others viewed him as a suspicious character and an opportunist. When it was suggested he be named to the French National Committee, objections were raised, especially from the left, and de Gaulle instead sent him on a propaganda tour in Africa. In his speeches Vallin admitted his initial support for Pétain as a man who seemed to incarnate the French spirit and stated that he was hopeful when Laval was dismissed in December 1940. But since then, it had become clear to him that the Vichy regime had adopted a spirit of resignation unfitting of France's glorious past: "I am speaking to Africans. I ask you this question: was it the spirit of Vichy that created the empire? Do you believe that we could conserve it if we retained that spirit of resignation, submission, and passivity?" All patriots now had to unite to deliver the country from the occupier.[93] Dissident from the PSF though he was, Vallin like his former colleagues, felt anguish that was primarily the result of the failure of the National Revolution to ensure French grandeur.

So what of those who remained loyal to the movement? While the PSF's leaders tried to remain optimistic about their prospects, the situation grew increasingly difficult. Some federations claimed to have experienced a revival when demobilized soldiers returned in 1940, and in February 1942 Melchior-Bonnet observed that in Paris the PSF benefited from resentment against the Nazis and collaborationists. In the occupied zone the Germans were convinced that militants remained active despite the ban on political organizations. In the unoccupied zone open activity continued until the movement was suppressed, and there were a few signs of vitality; in early 1943 the police in Brive believed that the PSF was "growing noticeably."[94] Even some supporters who found themselves in POW camps attempted to sustain a sense of PSF camaraderie. In Oflag IV D in Silesia, for example, there were reportedly 250 PSF members out of a total of 8,000 prisoners, and the group held several conferences. But the overall trend – not surprising in light of the conditions of the occupation – was one of decline. As early as October 1941, a member of Pétain's entourage told the American ambassador that the PSF membership totalled 350,000, roughly one-third of its pre-war maximum. While this was still a significant figure, it does suggest considerable fragmentation.[95]

Among those who remained associated with the PSF, there were signs of private dissent from and actions against the Vichy regime, especially during the latter stages of the war. According to Dr Henri Hermann, doyen of the medical faculty in Lyons, Antoinette de Préval gave aid to imprisoned *maquisards* and supported escape attempts while remaining active with the ADP. Stanislas Devaud remained a member of Vichy's Conseil National until July 1943 but then asked to return to his teaching duties. Fernand Robbe furthered the regime's agenda to the point of giving evidence at the Riom trial, but thereafter, he claimed, he supported the resistance. As for Jean Ybarnégaray, following his dismissal from the government in September 1940, he retired to his property in the Basses-Pyrénées. Here, while serving as the mayor of Uhart-Cizé, he was arrested in September 1943 and deported to Germany for helping refugees and resistance volunteers cross into Spain.[96] However, all these former PSF deputies were punished for supporting Vichy, losing their civil status for varying periods of time after the liberation.

Following the arrests of 1943, a new interim PSF leadership obeyed La Rocque's strictures about the need for loyalty to Pétain and avoiding social upheaval, distressed though they were at their colleagues' fate. A group of PSF cadres met with Pétain immediately after the arrests to secure their release, but while the marshal apparently listened with interest and requested documentation that he could show to the Germans, these efforts were to no avail.[97] The presidency in the southern zone ultimately passed to Professor Dodel of Clermont-Ferrand's Academy of Medicine, who had the support of de Préval. Dodel insisted on the need for steadfastness and the importance of maintaining internal order, reflecting a deep-seated fear of a Communist-led revolution: "we will recover painfully [but] securely from the defeat, but not from a civil war." Similarly, in the wake of D-Day he denounced "adventure-seekers," counselling PSF members to carry on with their jobs and "maintain the life of the nation." It appears as though his directives were observed by most of the remaining supporters. While police reports suggest that the membership was angered at the general treatment of the PSF and displayed growing anti-German sentiment – and in a few instances, disillusionment with the marshal himself – most still professed their loyalty to the head of state. In Clermont-Ferrand the PSF reportedly refused "to invest its hopes in the Anglo-Saxons." *Le Petit Journal* continued to be published until August 1944, even though seven of the nine members of its *conseil d'administration* had been arrested. It highlighted activities such as the work of the ADP while paying the required obeisance to the authorities. Reporting on an ADP conference held in September 1943, for instance, the paper was careful to note that in their addresses both de Préval and La Rocque's son Gilles had affirmed the need to support Pétain.[98]

In the meantime, La Rocque and his colleagues endured captivity. A number of them perished; among these were Noël Ottavi and several regional leaders and propaganda delegates.[99] As for the PSF leader himself, after being held briefly in Clermont and then Paris, La Rocque was transferred on 31 August 1943 to Eisenberg prison in Bohemia in the company of other political figures, including Michel Clemenceau, the son of the former prime minister. Frequently restricted to eight hundred calories per day for rations, the PSF leader's health worsened, with wounds sustained from his service in North Africa and during the First World War causing him great discomfort. However, in January 1944 he and Clemenceau were transferred to Itter prison in the Tyrol, where conditions were somewhat better. A number of political notables were detained here, including Édouard Daladier, Paul Reynaud, and CGT leader Léon Jouhaux, as well as Marshal Weygand, General Gamelin, and Jean Borotra, a tennis champion and former member of the Croix de Feu who for a time had been Vichy's *commissaire général* for sport and physical education.[100]

La Rocque remained politically engaged during his incarceration, holding discussion sessions among fellow prisoners in Eisenberg, which postwar testimony suggests had a positive impact on their morale.[101] At Itter, however, controversy erupted. On the day of their arrival, Clemenceau accused La Rocque of writing to Heinrich Himmler and offering the services of the PSF against the Communists if he were released. La Rocque denied the accusation indignantly, and upon consulting the letters, the other prisoners agreed that no such offer had been made. Although Clemenceau conceded that he had not read the letters in question, he nevertheless persisted in accusing La Rocque, suggesting that others existed, which the PSF leader swore was not the case. Daladier effectively brought the dispute to a close by declaring that the accusation was unjustified and that the ongoing dispute in front of the group's German captors – who wished to sow divisions among them – was unseemly.[102]

Thereafter tensions declined somewhat, and La Rocque was free to reflect upon the course of events in France since the First World War, evincing hostility to his captors but also concerns about the future. Other prisoners subsequently depicted him as hapless, even delusional; according to Reynaud, at one point he declared that the Western Allies would soon align themselves with the Germans against the Soviets.[103] He displayed some political and physical courage, however. The captain of the prisoners' ss guard acknowledged that La Rocque refused an offer to be freed if he signed an anti-Communist manifesto. And during the fighting between American and German troops that accompanied the liberation of Itter in May 1945, La Rocque, along with Borotra, Clemenceau, and Reynaud, took up arms and fired upon ss troops, despite his ailing health.[104]

La Rocque's opposition to the Third Reich, however, coexisted with trepidation about France's future in a world where Britain and the United States, countries against which he harboured considerable bitterness, would play a leading role. In a prayer written in 1944 he denounced Woodrow Wilson's peacemaking efforts after the First World War as "pretentious" and untenable. Twenty years later, he argued, France had been abandoned by its allies: "One of them executed its mobilization under the shelter of our forward posts, abandoned the struggle at the critical moment, then constructed its military apparatus behind the rampart of our ruins. The other took two years to acquire the basic means for participation in hostilities." Since his own country had paid such a heavy price for the "follies" of the 1918 peace settlement and the current conflict, La Rocque wondered what would happen when the British and the Americans dominated international affairs: "Must [France] ... be relegated to a secondary rank to work out the [international] order of which she had been the first [nation] at issue and the principal propitiatory victim?"[105]

Despite La Rocque's deep misgivings about the "Anglo-Saxons," it was these countries that spearheaded the liberation of France. As that process got underway, the remnants of the PSF prepared to relaunch the movement, though the effort soon proved abortive. As early as June 1944, EVP members in some areas were instructed to sound out public opinion, and some reported hopefully that La Rocque's deportation had increased sympathy for the PSF. Then in January 1945 the movement's

new vice-president, André Portier, a member of *Le Petit Journal*'s editorial board, announced that the PSF would hold a national congress in
March. While *Le Petit Journal* itself was now banned, a bulletin was circulated which criticized the ban and defended the movement's conduct
during the occupation. Finally, cadres such as Joseph Levet traversed the
country to rejuvenate local organizations.[106] The relaunch, however, was
rapidly cut short. On 9 March, following an attack on the PSF by the
Communist deputy Jacques Duclos in the Constituent Assembly, the
organization was – on dubious grounds, it must be said – pronounced
dissolved on the basis of pre-war judicial decisions. The congress
intended to begin that day was pre-empted, and in at least one case a section meeting was shut down by police. La Rocque himself fared no
better upon his return from captivity two months later, as he was immediately confined to a police barracks in Versailles. Initially told that this
measure was to ensure his own safety against the Communists, La
Rocque was convinced that he had been detained to hinder the revival of
the PSF, and he complained that his confinement only aggravated his
poor health, a concern that some officials came to share.[107]

The new government's treatment of the PSF and its leader was controversial; certainly, the legal underpinnings of the dissolution were
dubious. But it was not the only obstacle to a renaissance of the movement. At this time Barrachin and Vallin, on the strength of their resistance credentials, were building their own political movement, the
Union pour la République, which sought to attract former PSF supporters. Moreover, at the local level it seems that sharp divisions had
emerged and significant disillusionment set in among La Rocque's followers. In the Aude, for example, the local PSF had divided into three
factions by the spring of 1945. One group, estimated as constituting 40
per cent of the membership, were reserving judgment about whether to
continue supporting La Rocque until he accounted for his wartime
stance. A second group of perhaps 35 per cent were totally disenchanted with the movement. Many of them now supported Barrachin
and Vallin; others had joined Mutter's Ceux de la Libération. In fact,
the authorities estimated that only about one-quarter of the total membership remained entirely loyal to La Rocque.[108] If such disaffection is
indicative of the general state of opinion among former PSF supporters,
it seems unlikely that the party could have regained the mass support it
had enjoyed in the 1930s.

In the crucible of war and the ever-changing circumstances surrounding the occupation, the PSF had tried to stake out a distinct posi-

tion. Having made clear its ongoing determination to recast French politics during the "phoney war," thereafter it simultaneously proclaimed its loyalty to Pétain and the ideals of the National Revolution, while eventually opposing the Germans. The PSF's leaders had believed they would benefit from their loyalty to the marshal and hoped that one day they would be in a position to attain power; their gambit failed. It was not that the attitudes of the PSF were unique; more than a few resisters – notably Henri Frenay of Combat – initially hoped that they could combine fidelity to Pétain with opposition to the Nazis. But increasingly, such individuals and groups, including PSF notables such as Vallin, surmised that as conditions in France polarized, this position was impossible.[109] La Rocque and those who remained loyal to him, by contrast, never fully broke with Vichy, even though they tried to distinguish between the marshal and the governments that ruled in his name. Though they may have harboured doubts, to the end they emphasized the need to support the head of state and preserve order. They secretly began to support the Allies but not the Gaullists or internal resistance. They paid dearly for these choices; their move towards resistance brought the full force of the German occupier to bear against them, while after the liberation the PSF's stance towards Vichy condemned it in the eyes of the new authorities.

Like their fellow citizens, PSF supporters had very difficult choices to make. Nor should the courage of those who engaged in resistance activities or the suffering of those who were imprisoned or perished as a result of deportation or other means be minimized. But it remains that the PSF's ambition to realize its visions of France, as developed during the 1930s, continued to determine its conduct during the "phoney war" of 1939–40 and then the occupation. After the defeat of 1940, La Rocque and his supporters consistently presented themselves as authentic, uncompromising proponents of the National Revolution, often demanding that its repressive measures be enacted more firmly. Thus to the end, the PSF partook of a vision of "the Vichy that might have been."[110] It was an image of a united France treated with respect by Germany, rather than a country under Nazi subjugation led by collaborators. But this unity would be achieved through the creation of an authoritarian, exclusionary state. In that sense, unlike the many French women and men who experienced dramatic changes in their status and convictions during this period, La Rocque and his remaining supporters continued to be quite consistent in their outlook.

Epilogue

The story of the PSF itself ends abruptly after the Second World War, with the banning of the party by the new provisional government and La Rocque's death in 1946. Tracing the PSF's legacy is more complex. A successor organization was established, but it never really escaped the political margins. Instead, under the Fourth Republic, former PSF supporters found their way into a range of movements. The best known of these, and the one with which the Croix de Feu and especially the PSF have been sometimes compared, is Charles de Gaulle's Rassemblement du Peuple Français. Yet while there were important continuities between these organizations, to utilize these parallels in order to characterize the PSF as a progenitor of Gaullist democratic conservatism in postwar France is problematic. For in their efforts to promote an exclusionary vision of what it means to be French, parallels can also be drawn between La Rocque's supporters and the contemporary French far right.

La Rocque's detention by the postwar provisional government was both prolonged and questionable. In theory, after his return to France from Itter, he was to be placed in forced residence in Versailles by administrative decree; in fact, without proper orders to this effect, he remained confined to a police barracks, where his health deteriorated. La Rocque required an operation to mend scar tissue that had torn as a result of weight loss during his previous imprisonment, and he suffered attacks of sciatica. He wrote appeals to the prefect of the Seine-et-Oise and to de Gaulle himself requesting release and declaring that he would temporarily refrain from political activity. De Gaulle never replied, but the prefect passed on La Rocque's requests and expressed his concerns about the situation to the Socialist minister of the interior, Adrien

Tixier. Tixier was determined to keep La Rocque in detention while the justice ministry decided whether he would be tried, but in November 1945 a commission for administrative internments visited La Rocque and concluded that he was being wrongfully detained. The following month, though still not released, he was moved to André Portier's residence in Croissy. Thereafter he began to receive proper medical treatment, including an operation for his stomach wounds in late January 1946. Three months later, however, he had to be rushed to Paris after an ulcer developed in his esophagus; he underwent another operation but died on 28 April 1946.[1]

La Rocque had suspected that he was being detained in order to hinder his political activity. His confinement had not prevented him from following political developments with interest, however; nor did it prevent new initiatives. During this time he completed his final book, *Au service de l'avenir*. Furthermore, though La Rocque had hoped that the PSF could still be revived, a number of supporters, with his consent, had formed the Parti Républicain et Social de la Réconciliation Française, generally known as Réconciliation Française (RF), in the summer of 1945. André Portier was its leader, but Joseph Levet seems to have been the driving force in establishing it, tirelessly visiting various departments to put an organization in place. In the opinion of the authorities, the new party's outlook bore a strong resemblance to that of the Croix de Feu and the PSF. RF presented itself as driven by "an ideal, a mystique that is for all those who want to do something, to give of themselves completely for the country," and it characterized its primary goal as the defeat of Communism.[2]

Initially, RF displayed some dynamism – 3,000 people attended a meeting held in Paris in November – but it never came remotely close to emulating the mass appeal of the Croix de Feu or the PSF. At its peak it may have had 10,000 members.[3] There were various reasons for this relatively limited appeal. Certainly, La Rocque's death was a blow to the nascent organization; in the years to come, its members would ceaselessly invoke his memory, though they decided not to re-form the PSF after the ban on the party was lifted in the summer of 1946.[4] RF also found that it was operating in a highly competitive political environment in which the support of former PSF militants could not be taken for granted. Some now favoured the Catholic-oriented Mouvement Républicain Populaire (MRP). Elements of the MRP's platform – the familial vote, better labour-employer relations, a stronger presidency, and an emphasis on reconciling past divisions in the name of a moral revolution – were all themes familiar to former PSF members. And some of the areas where the MRP did well – Alsace, the Manche, the Calvados, and the Nord – had previously been regions of PSF implantation. Indeed, for the national elections of October 1945 La Rocque had reportedly instructed his supporters to vote for MRP lists where necessary in order to block the left, since RF itself had only recently been formed and could not play an appreciable role. It seems plausible that among the former PSF members who supported the MRP, many were never drawn to RF.[5]

The MRP was not the only problem. At the regional level former PSF militants joined a variety of organizations such as the Union Nationale de Rénovation in Alsace and the Union des Républicains du Nord. At the national level in 1945–46 there was a new and serious rival for RF in the form of the Parti Républicain de la Liberté (PRL), which Edmond Barrachin played a leading role in organizing and in which Charles Vallin and André Mutter were also prominent. This organization was to the right of the MRP; its anti-Communism was more vehement and it was a defender of liberal economics. Recruiting extensively among former PSF members (though elsewhere too), the PRL won some forty seats in the National Assembly, doing very well in the Seine, a former bastion of the Croix de Feu/PSF.[6]

Predictably, relations between the PRL and RF were poor. By joining the Gaullists, Barrachin and Vallin had sundered all ties with an embittered La Rocque, and the PRL's president, Michel Clemenceau, was certainly no friend. Above all, the PRL's entry onto the political scene made RF's task of attracting former PSF supporters far more difficult. While he was still alive, La Rocque had refused to countenance any cooperation with it; after his death the leaders of RF declared that "after the Communist party, it is the party of Laniel and Ramarony [two PRL notables] which appears to be the enemy of Réconciliation Française." They proclaimed the PRL to be too sectarian and socially conservative, adding that only under the direst electoral circumstances – namely, if it was a matter of defeating a "Marxist" – would RF members vote for a PRL candidate.[7]

Stymied in its efforts to rebuild the PSF network and facing powerful competition, RF soon found itself engaged in coalition politics, joining the Rassemblement des Gauches Républicaines (RGR) in January 1946. The RGR was a alliance of parties, the most important of which were the Radicals and the new Union Démocratique et Socialiste de la Résistance (UDSR). On the face of it, for the successor to the PSF to align with former enemies such as the Radicals as well as with avow-edly centre-left organizations such as the UDSR was a bizarre arrange-ment. But the alliance had some logic. Though the RGR was widely considered centrist, some of its constituent parties had Pétainist pasts, including Pierre-Étienne Flandin's Alliance Démocratique and Paul Faure's Parti Socialiste Démocratique (both Flandin and Faure had voted power to Pétain in 1940). Indeed, it has been argued that the most salient division between the PRL and the RGR was that the former was composed of resisters while the latter accepted Pétainists into its ranks. Even this split did not to matter very much during the national elections of October 1946, when blocking the Communists was the pri-mary concern of the French right. Réconciliation Française declared it would focus above all on anti-Marxist unity, voting for the RGR, the MRP, or even the PRL if need be. Similarly, though now a leader of the PRL, Edmond Barrachin helped François Mitterrand of the UDSR – for-merly a member of the Volontaires Nationaux and a supporter of Vichy – win a seat in the Nièvre with the support of former PSF cadres.[8] Réconciliation Française remained affiliated with the RGR until 1954; thereafter it joined the right-wing Centre National des Indépendants et Paysans (CNIP).[9] The anointed heir of the PSF thus remained a marginal element within right-wing coalitions, an ironic fate considering La Rocque's reputation for going it alone.

However, an analysis of the postwar legacy of the Croix de Feu/PSF cannot be limited to Réconcilation Française alone. Scholars have also been interested in the links between La Rocque's supporters and Charles de Gaulle's Rassemblement du Peuple Français. Disillusioned with the evolution of the Fourth Republic and desirous of reshaping the French political system according to his own lights, de Gaulle launched the RPF in April 1947. Declaring the parties of the Fourth Republic incapable of rebuilding France and ensuring the national interest in the face of Soviet expansionism, he presented the RPF as a "movement" rather than a traditional party, which patriots of all back-grounds could join. The RPF called for constitutional reform in favour of a stronger executive and better relations between capital and labour, and it was emphatically anti-Communist, denouncing the PCF as "sepa-ratists." Initially it achieved an impressive momentum, winning 40 per cent of the vote in municipal elections in October 1947 and attaining a total membership of 450,000 by 1948. Yet ultimately the RPF was frus-trated in its quest to revise the French constitution; national elections were not held until 1951, and while it won 119 seats that year, this

number was not enough to achieve its goals. By then popular enthusiasm for the movement was waning. Conflict between de Gaulle and his
parliamentarians soon erupted, and in 1953 the parliamentary group
was severed from the movement, which itself disappeared two years
later.[10]

Parallels between the RPF, on the one hand, and the Croix de Feu and
especially the PSF, on the other, are immediately evident, and recent
research has uncovered further links. In its anti-Communism, denunciation of a "weak" political system, and invocation of the need for class
conciliation, the RPF echoed many concerns of the PSF. De Gaulle's
attacks upon "old-style" politicians were severe, and his demands for a
dissolution of the National Assembly after the RPF's success in the
October 1947 municipal elections sounded more than a little like the
PSF's calls for new national elections in 1938. In terms of style, too, RPF
organizers seem to have borrowed from the PSF. They held mass rallies
marked not only by familial imagery, as children in appropriate
regional costume presented the general with flowers, but also by
clashes between Communist protesters and the RPF's *service d'ordre*.
Most generally, as Jean-Paul Thomas has pointed out, "the PSF and RPF
had in common an origin foreign to the world of traditional politics
and a perpetual vision of the sacred union in which all individual pasts
are abolished save for those involving patriotic sacrifice."[11] While the
PSF drew on the myth of the war experience via the Croix de Feu to call
for the regeneration of France, the RPF invoked the legacy of Free
France.

There were also major continuities between the PSF and the RPF in
terms of personnel. At the cadre level the best-known case is Barrachin,
who moved from the PRL (which declined after de Gaulle's entry into
politics) and served on the RPF's executive committee until 1952. But
the links went further than that; of the 119 deputies elected by the RPF
in 1951, approximately 22 had been members or at least sympathizers
of the Croix de Feu and/or the PSF.[12] As for the general membership, it
appears that both the RPF and the movements led by La Rocque relied
heavily on the *classes moyennes* but also tried to reach out to the working class and the peasantry. Both also sought to attract people of varying political outlooks; some were firmly right-wing, while others were
more moderate in outlook, especially insofar as social issues were concerned. With respect to regional implantation, the RPF was very active
in Alsace, the Nord, and the Loire-Inférieure, all of which had been PSF
strongholds. It seems clear that at least in some regions, previous

activity on the part of the PSF made voters more amenable to a message of national unity that transcended party lines.[13]

The affinities between the PSF and the RPF are thus incontestable. But does this resemblance mean that each represents a stage in the evolution of democratic conservatism in France, with the PSF acclimatizing many supporters of the nationalist right to the democratic rules of the game and the RPF continuing the process?[14] On this point, it is worth noting that some former PSF militants questioned the affinities between the two. While Réconciliation Française appreciated the RPF's anti-Communism, its leaders were also quick to point out that de Gaulle had previously cooperated with the PCF. In 1951, when the Communist deputy Jacques Duclos accused de Gaulle of emulating La Rocque, Gilles de La Rocque angrily noted that while his father had sought to reconcile Frenchmen, de Gaulle – "his jailer" – had only widened divisions between them. Only after the former PSF leader's status as a deportee to Nazi Germany was officially recognized in 1961, it seems, was the way cleared for a rapprochement between La Rocque's faithful supporters and the general.[15]

Further distinctions can be made between the Croix de Feu/PSF and postwar Gaullism. Even scholars who stress the parallels between them concede that while both movements emphasized a social conscience as well as nationalist credentials, the RPF did not devote itself to social activism or associational life to the same degree as the PSF had. De Gaulle's priorities, at least at the time of the RPF's inception, were primarily political, focused upon creating new, executive-oriented institutions.[16] Here it might be added that his conception of the relationship between the state and the electorate differed from that of La Rocque. While the general's political style was patrician, he sought to buttress his authority through democratic referenda after achieving power in 1958. La Rocque never had the opportunity to exercise such an option, but the evidence suggests it was an approach he found disdainful. Though he sought to mobilize the masses to achieve the conquest of political power, with respect to exercising that power, he was consistently suspicious of the disruptive implications of universal suffrage.

This outlook remained evident in La Rocque's final work, *Au service de l'avenir*, which appeared after his death in 1946. The book recognized the postwar emphasis upon renovating republican democracy in contrast to the frequent attacks upon it during the 1930s, but it made few concessions to the spirit of the times. La Rocque did claim to favour democracy and denounced the abolition of political parties and the notion of a single party. But he felt that major qualifications had to be placed on universal suffrage: "social improductivity" should lead to exclusion, and he favoured some sort of a two-tiered voting system. Moreover, he still rejected rigid distinctions between democracy and authoritarianism, concluding that "it would be unfounded to take theoretical classifications at face value."[17] In sum, it is doubtful that La Rocque changed his outlook in the final months of his life. He reiterated his desire to restore France to its Christian roots and strove to emphasize the consistency of his thinking. In general, *Au service de l'avenir* shared the hierarchical and organic outlook of the Vichy regime; the book emphasized the importance of collectivities in society and the need to develop solidarity within them and exercise authority over them appropriately.[18] To the end, the PSF's leader remained inspired by a scarcely veiled authoritarian vision.

Any discussion of the continuities between the Croix de Feu/PSF and the RPF must also acknowledge the fact that the RPF itself was controversial. In the late 1940s de Gaulle's harsh anti-Communist rhetoric, the militant style of RPF rallies, and its incursions into Socialist or Communist-dominated areas were reminiscent of precisely the features of the PSF which during the 1930s had seemed so threatening. While accusations on the part of the left that the RPF was fascist were certainly partisan, even more moderate observers such as François Mauriac feared that de Gaulle had risked situating himself on the far right. After he returned to power in 1958, the general appears to have learned some lessons from his time as leader of the RPF. The new Gaullist party, the Union pour la Nouvelle République, avoided an anti-parliamentary demeanour, and de Gaulle himself kept his distance from it. In sum, rather than building successfully upon the legacy of the PSF, postwar Gaullism had to distance itself further from the heritage of authoritarian nationalism to achieve its goals.[19]

There are other, more contemporary movements that can be profitably compared with the Croix de Feu and the PSF, notably Jean-Marie Le Pen's Front National (FN). Launched in 1972 as an umbrella organization for a range of far-right groups, the FN languished for much of the 1970s and early 1980s. But after 1983 it broke through electorally, primarily on the basis of championing racist policies towards immigrants and their descendants, in particular those from the Maghrib, sub-Saharan Africa, and the Caribbean. Since then the FN has regularly won the support of between 10 and 15 per cent of voters in local, parliamentary, and presidential elections. In 2002 Le Pen came in second on the first round of voting in the presidential elections, scoring nearly 17 per cent of the vote, only 2.76 per cent behind the incumbent, Jacques Chirac. Though Chirac went on to defeat Le Pen handily on the second round, the FN's baleful impact on contemporary French politics remains a matter of intense concern.[20]

A brief comparison between the FN and the Croix de Feu/PSF illustrates the degree to which the contemporary far right contrasts with that of the interwar period, but it also suggests some parallels. To be sure, there are critical differences. At the personal level, Le Pen's flamboyant manner contrasts with La Rocque's more formal persona. Unlike the Croix de Feu or the PSF, the FN does not draw upon a myth of wartime unity to mobilize supporters; the drive to reduce the presence of non-white immigrants in French life is at the core of its program, though its doctrine has gradually become more layered. The geography of support for the Croix de Feu and the PSF tended to emulate previous traditions of right-wing support, with particular strength in areas of high Catholic observance and somewhat more presence in northern than in southern France. By contrast, the FN's support is concentrated in the more urbanized, post-industrial eastern half of the country, and it lacks a strong correlation with Catholic observance, though the Catholic fundamentalist group Chrétienté-Solidarité is an important component of the FN coalition.[21] In terms of general context, there can be no doubt that all is not well in contemporary France. High unemployment has afflicted the country for years; the riots in fall 2005, which affected the suburbs of many major cities, and the student protests directed against labour-law reforms in 2006 are indicative of protracted social and economic difficulties.[22] But compared to the 1930s, there is no immediate geopolitical threat equivalent to Nazi Germany, the validity of France's democratic system is not as sharply or openly contested as it was during the interwar years, and the welfare state has served to meliorate social problems somewhat.[23]

Evidently, the two movements are the products of very different times and evince different priorities. Yet some of their concerns are comparable, as are the roles they have played in French politics and society. Le Pen and his colleagues have often claimed to be neither on the left nor on the right, just as La Rocque's supporters did. Le Pen's insistence that the FN is both a "national" and a "social" party recalls La Rocque's emphasis on the need for national renovation and class conciliation. The FN has mobilized women in public life, yet like the Croix de Feu/PSF, it stresses the need to restore traditional familial relations; Le Pen, like La Rocque, has called for the creation of a "family wage" to encourage mothers to stay at home and alleviate the problem of male unemployment.[24] And though it has been suggested that, in contrast to Le Pen, La Rocque accepted immigration so long as newcomers assimilated, this book has argued that xenophobia grew within the Croix de Feu and the PSF as the refugee crisis of the 1930s intensified. In both cases the demonization of enemies as being outside the French nation, whether on political and cultural grounds in the case of the Croix de Feu/PSF or on ethnic grounds in the case of the FN, was intense. Finally, while like the PSF, the FN has repeatedly proclaimed its respect for existing democratic institutions, its emphasis on combatting "disorder" and its hierarchical world view suggest such professions are opportunistic rather than heartfelt.[25]

The FN has not approached the PSF's success in terms of the size of its membership; in the 1990s the party itself claimed 100,000 supporters – a tenth of the PSF's in 1938 – and some observers believe the actual figure is considerably lower than that. But the FN is certainly a party of activists; Le Pen and his followers have created a range of ancillary organizations and a rich associational life. Visiting the FN's Fête Bleu Blanc Rouge in September 1993, the British journalist Jonathan Marcus observed that "the various National Front Circles, associated journals, children's activities and so on, have created a sort of far right counter-culture, almost a mirror image of that created by the Communists, and for very similar reasons. By establishing this web of interlocking organisations, a whole world is created in which the activist can feel at home." While it was actually former members of Doriot's PPF who helped to create the FN's infrastructure, its flanking organizations are certainly broadly reminiscent of those established by the Croix de Feu and the PSF.[26]

This counter-society has helped the FN to achieve something that relatively few movements of the French far right have – longevity. Le Pen and his supporters have endured electoral reversals, defections by former supporters, and various scandals, and have exercised power at the municipal level in cities such as Toulon and Orange, where its officials have sought to enact their discriminatory policies of "national preference" in areas such as welfare and housing. In the process, the FN has had a negative impact on the tenor of political debate in France, particularly with respect to matters of national identity and immigration. Since the 1980s, politicians from the mainstream right have debated how to respond to the Front. While many have rejected electoral cooperation, this has not consistently been the case, especially at the regional and local level. In light of the FN's appeal, various conservative politicians have at one time or another appropriated elements of its rhetoric. In the fall of 1984, for example, future president Jacques Chirac tried to steal some of the FN's thunder by declaring that "if there were fewer immigrants, there would be less unemployment, less tension in certain towns, and lower social costs." On the left, there have been fewer dilemmas concerning the need to compete for voters. But even some Socialist party leaders, such as former prime minister Laurent Fabius, have suggested that while Le Pen was providing the wrong answers, he was asking the right questions. The French Communists, in decline during this period, have also drawn links between immigration and social problems in urban areas, though the party continues to condemn racism. Successive French governments of both the right and the left, while not identical in their approach, have imposed various restrictions and cracked down hard on illegal immigrants. Most have also emphasized their desire to combat racist sentiment yet have conceded that hostility to "foreigners" in France, including the native-born children of immigrants, remains stubbornly high.[27]

The Croix de Feu and the PSF did not have the same opportunity to set down roots and reshape France's political agenda, but the evidence suggests that before 1939 they had begun to do so, and that their desire to recast French political culture in a fundamental way remained fervent. The obstacles in their path were considerable. Not only did the intense opposition of the left pose a threat, but so did competition from other right-wing movements. On the eve of the Second World War La Rocque and his followers faced a new challenge; Daladier's government had begun to co-opt some of "their" policies, making it harder to attack than its predecessors. Yet while the PSF, like its predecessor the Croix de Feu, was most energized when denouncing an impending leftist threat, the party had begun the difficult task of winning over local conservative notables and developing a viable electoral strategy. The way ahead remained uncertain, but compared to rivals such as Doriot, the PSF had proven to be more imposing and durable.

Throughout the 1930s La Rocque and his supporters had held to a vision of a "reconciled" France. For a country that had experienced much suffering in recent years and was beset by vociferous party debates, such a vision could be, and was, beguiling for many people. But for both the Croix de Feu and the PSF the French could only be reconciled by eliding fundamental political and social differences. The future État Social Français was predicated upon autocratic political controls, a conception of France's past that dictated enforced harmony in the present and a stultifying vision of the future adumbrated by its counter-society. Over time, and with the transformation from anti-parliamentary league to political party, there were some changes. But contrary to scholars who have suggested that those shifts amounted to democratic integration, I have argued that they involved defining Frenchness in connection with promoting the nation's Christian identity. Their ideology distinguished both the Croix de Feu and the PSF from Italian Fascism and German Nazism in some respects, but it also located these organizations within the field of authoritarian nationalist movements that poisoned interwar European politics.

As such, the story of the Croix de Feu and PSF is central to understanding the evolution of the Third Republic in its final years. That both the league and the party sometimes invoked republican traditions of freedom of speech and association to denigrate their political opponents and attract followers perhaps testifies to the broad legitimacy the system enjoyed. But the mobilization of hundreds of thousands of people in the service of an intolerant world view also shows that France had not escaped the crisis of interwar European democracy. Tragically, the military defeat of 1940 paved the way for a National Revolution which realized many of the goals of the far right, with disastrous and shameful consequences. It is true that under Vichy itself La Rocque and the PSF were largely excluded from exercising influence and came to oppose the German occupation. But they had nevertheless helped to establish the climate of opinion that made the État Français a possible outcome of catastrophe on the battlefield. The yearning for strong authority, visceral anti-Communism, and exclusionary xenophobia that characterized the opening months of the National Revolution were not only a result of the sudden collapse of 1940; their roots also lie in the political and social evolution of the late Third Republic. While they were not the sole proponents of these sentiments, the Croix de Feu and the PSF had incarnated them to an unprecedented degree.

Notes

AD   Archives Départementales
AN   Archives Nationales, Paris
AP   Archives de Paris
APP   Archives de la Préfecture de Police
BN   Bibliothèque Nationale
CAOM   Centre des Archives d'Outre-Mer
CHEVS   Centre de l'Histoire de l'Europe au Vingtième Siècle
FO   Foreign Office
NA   National Archives, Kew (previously Public Record Office)
RG   Record Group
USNA   United States National Archives

INTRODUCTION

1 Daladier, *Prison Journal*, 247–50, 261, entries for 11 January, 6 February 1944.
2 Brumeaux, *La Rocque citoyen*; Rudaux, *Croix de Feu*; La Rocque and La Rocque, *La Rocque tel qu'il était*.
3 Rémond, *Droites en France*, 212–14.
4 On the influence of Rémond's interpretation, see Bingham, "Defining French Fascism, Finding Fascists in France." Regional studies include Prévosto, "Fédération du Nord"; Chouvel, "Croix de Feu et le PSF en Haute-Vienne"; Ferragu, "Croix de Feu et le PSF en Indre-et-Loire"; Florin, "Des Croix de Feu au Parti Social Français"; Gabillard, "Viticulteurs angevins et le Mouvement Croix de Feu–PSF." Weng, "Historique et la doctrine du PSF" focuses on ideology.

5 Machefer's publications include "Autour du problème algérien en
   1936–1938"; "Sur quelques aspects"; "Union des droites"; "Croix de Feu";
   "Parti Social Français en 1937–1937"; "Tardieu et La Rocque"; "Fusillade
   de Clichy," in *Presse et Politique*; *Ligues et fascismes en France*; "Presse et
   politique dans les années trente" (with Fred Kupfermann); "Parti Social
   Français," in Rémond and Bourdin, eds., *France et les Français*; "Action
   Française et le PSF"; "Croix de Feu devant l'Allemagne," in *La France et
   l'Allemagne, 1932–1936*; and "Syndicats Professionnels Français." See also
   his two articles published in *Le Monde*, 29 April 1976, 11 August 1982.

6 Anderson, *Conservative Politics in France*, 201–9; Howlett, "Croix de
   Feu."

7 Nobécourt, *Colonel de La Rocque*, 966.

8 Kéchichian, "D'une Association d'anciens combattants à un mouvement de
   mobilisation morale," in Andrieu, Le Béguec, and Tartakowsky, eds., *Associations et champ politique*; Thomas, "Effectifs du Parti Social Français."

9 Thomas, "Parti Social Français."

10 Soucy, "French Fascism and the Croix de Feu"; *French Fascism: The Second
    Wave*, esp. 104–203; and "Functional Hating."

11 Irvine, "Fascism in France."

12 Goodfellow, *Between the Swastika and the Cross of Lorraine*; Sternhell, *Ni
    droite ni gauche*, 83–92.

13 Passmore, "French Third Republic"; "Croix de Feu"; "Boy Scouting for
    Grown-Ups?"; *From Liberalism to Fascism*; "Planting the Tricolor"; and
    "Croix de Feu and Fascism," in Arnold, ed., *Development of the Radical
    Right in France*.

14 Irvine, "Fascism in France," 294; Passmore, "Planting the Tricolor," 816.

15 Dobry, "Thèse immunitaire face aux fascismes," in Dobry, ed., *Mythe de
    l'allergie française*, quotation on 67. For an earlier presentation of his views,
    see Dobry, "Février 1934 et la découverte de l'allergie"; a translation of this
    article is available in Jenkins, ed., *France in the Era of Fascism*, 129–50.

16 Leschi, "Étrange cas La Rocque," in Dobry, ed., *Mythe de l'allgerie française*,
    155–94.

17 Jenkins, "Conclusion: Beyond the Fascism Debate," in Jenkins, ed., *France in
    the Era of Fascism*, 213–15.

18 Paxton's views were first outlined in "Five Stages of Fascism," a revised ver-
    sion of which appears in Jenkins, ed., *France in the Era of Fascism*, 105–28.
    His approach is fully developed in *Anatomy of Fascism*.

19 Paxton, *French Peasant Fascism*, esp. 154–64.

20 Blinkhorn, "Introduction," in Blinkhorn, ed., *Fascists and Conservatives*;
    Payne, *History of Fascism*, 14–19; Mann, "Contradictions of Continuous

Revolution," in Kershaw and Lewin, eds., *Stalinism and Nazism*; Levy, "Facism, National Socialism and Conservatives in Europe."

21 On the conception of fascism as revolutionary, see Mosse, *Fascist Revolution*, 30–4. See also Burrin, *Fascisme, nazisme, autoritarisme*, 49–71.

22 Weber, *Hollow Years*, 119–20; Nobécourt, *Colonel de La Rocque*, 599–661.

23 This is the term used by Rymell in "Militants and Militancy."

24 These include Machefer, "Syndicats Professionels Français"; Passmore, "Planting the Tricolor"; and Kennedy, "Croix de Feu, the Parti Social Français, and the Politics of Aviation."

25 Rymell, "Militants and Militancy," 2.

26 Payne, *History of Fascism*, 291–2.

27 Paxton, *French Peasant Fascism*, 162–4.

28 Irvine, "Fascism in France," 275.

29 Passmore, *From Liberalism to Fascism*, 250–1.

30 Jackson, *France: The Dark Years*, 102–4.

31 Berstein, "France des années trente allergique au fascisme"; see also Rémond, *Droites en France*, 214.

32 Nord, *Republican Moment*, 245–54.

33 Sherman, *Construction of Memory in Interwar France*.

34 Lindenberg, *Années souterraines*; Hellman, *Communitarian Third Way*.

35 Roberts, *Civilization without Sexes*.

36 On French identity, see Lebovics, "Creating the Authentic France," in Gillis, ed., *Commemorations*; Peer, "Peasants in Paris," in Ungar and Conley, eds., *Identity Papers*. See also Noiriel, *Origines républicaines de Vichy*.

CHAPTER ONE

1 Rémond, *Droites en France*, argues that the leagues continued the Bonapartist tradition into the twentieth century, while Sternhell, "Political Culture of Nationalism," in Tombs, ed., *Nationhood and Nationalism*, 27, contends that the new nationalism of the 1880s was distinctive in crucial ways. For a discussion of the waning of the Bonapartist movement, see Rothney, *Bonapartism after Sedan*.

2 See Rutkoff, *Revanche and Revision*.

3 Tombs, *France, 1814–1914*, 447–53; see also Mazgaj, "Origins of the French Radical Right," 291–6, and Irvine, *Boulanger Affair Reconsidered*.

4 For a provocative overview, see Birnbaum, "Affaire Dreyfus, culture catholique et antisémitisme," in Winock, ed., *Histoire de l'extrême droite*, 87–98.

5 See Weber, *Action Française*, as well as Tannenbaum, *Action Française*; Winock, "L'Action française," in Winock, ed., *Histoire de l'extrême droite*,

125–56. For its activities after the First World War, see Jenkins, "Action Française à l'ère du fascisme," in Dobry, ed., *Mythe de l'allergie française*, 107–54.

6 See Goyet, "'March sur Rome,' version originale sous-titré," and Jenkins, "Action Française à l'ère du fascisme," in Dobry, *Mythe de l'allgerie française*, 93–4, 139.

7 For a detailed account, see Soucy, *French Fascism: The First Wave*, chaps. 2–3, which argues that the various leagues of the 1920s were fascist. By contrast, Plumyène and LaSierra, *Fascismes français 1923–1963*, chap. 1, argues that while all of the leagues were authoritarian and nationalist, only some were fascist.

8 Soucy, *French Fascism: The First Wave*, chaps. 4–5; see also Douglas, *From Fascism to Libertarian Communism*.

9 McMillan, "Catholicism and Nationalism in France," in Tallett and Atkin, eds., *Catholicism in Britain and France*.

10 For an account of the infighting of the 1920s, see Soucy, *French Fascism: The First Wave*, chap. 6.

11 Servent, *Mythe Pétain*, 121–34, 175–9. See also Becker, *Guerre et la foi*.

12 Pollard, *Reign of Virtue*, 9–41.

13 Young, *France and the Origins of the Second World War*, 7–24; Adamthwaite, *Grandeur and Misery*, 131–9, 189–93.

14 Noiriel, *Origines républicaines de Vichy*, 96–8.

15 Dard, *Années 30*, 12–15, 21; Paxton, *French Peasant Fascism*, 13–15; Weber, *Hollow Years*, 33–5, 53–4; Berstein, *France des années 30*, 24–33, 47–51; Jackson, *France: The Dark Years*, 68–72.

16 Passmore, *From Liberalism to Fascism*, 116–62; Monier, *Années 20*, 171–9; Dard, *Années 30*, 41–4, 54–7.

17 Jackson, *France: The Dark Years*, 43–55.

18 Relevant works include Touchard, "Esprit des années 1930," in Michaud, ed., *Tendances politiques dans la vie française*; Loubet del Bayle, *Nonconformistes des années trente*; Lindenberg, *Années souterraines*; Hellman, "Communitarians, Non-conformists, and the Search for a New Man," in Fishman et al., eds., *France at War*, 91–4. On the debate over French intellectuals and fascism, see, among others, Sternhell, *Ni droite ni gauche*; Simard, "Intellectuels, fascisme et antimodernité"; and Wohl, "French Fascism, Both Right and Left."

19 Weber, *Hollow Years*, 131–7.

20 Soucy, *French Fascism: The Second Wave*, 59–103; Paxton, *French Peasant Fascism*, 62.

21 See Nobécourt, *Colonel de La Rocque*, 91–124.

22 *Le Flambeau*, November 1929; Prost, *Anciens combattants*, 3: 119.

23 Howlett, "Croix de Feu," 58.

24 *Le Flambeau*, December 1929, January 1930; Machefer, "Croix de Feu devant l'Allemagne," in *La France et l'Allemagne*, 112–20.

25 Howlett, "Croix de Feu," 57–62; Nobécourt, *Colonel de La Rocque*, 170–7.

26 See Nobécourt, "'Affaire La Rocque' en 1899," though he claims that La Rocque was not heavily influenced by his father.

27 La Rocque and La Rocque, *La Rocque tel qu'il était*, 20. On de Foucauld see Porch, *Conquest of the Sahara*, 277–89.

28 La Rocque and La Rocque, *La Rocque tel qu'il était*, 21–2.

29 Howlett, "Croix de Feu," 45–6; Nobécourt, *Colonel de La Rocque*, 26–30.

30 AN 475AP 289, La Rocque to Lyautey, 5 May 1930.

31 Nobécourt, *Colonel de La Rocque*, 126–37.

32 On Catholic activism, see Nord, "Catholic Culture in Interwar France," and McMillan, "France," in Buchanan and Conway, eds., *Political Catholicism in Europe*.

33 Clément, "Épiscopat," 106–7; AN 475AP 289, La Rocque to Lyautey, 5 May 1930.

34 La Rocque, testimony in Chambre des Députés, *Rapport fait au nom de la commission d'enquête*, annexes, 2: no. 3383, 1569, session of 13 April 1934; Chopine, *Six ans chez les Croix de Feu*, 46–70.

35 Association des Amis de La Rocque, *Pour mémoire*, 6; Nobécourt, *Colonel de La Rocque*, 120–4; Howlett, "Croix de Feu," 69–76, presents a convincing account.

36 *Le Flambeau*, November 1929, April, December 1930, July, October 1931.

37 *Le Flambeau*, October, November, 11 November 1931.

38 Howlett, "Croix de Feu," 97–100; Nobécourt, *Colonel de La Rocque*, 197–8.

39 APP B/a 1901, reports, 4, 31 March 1931; Weng, "Historique et la doctrine," 22–3; Howlett, "Croix de Feu," 109–10; *Le Flambeau*, December 1933; Machefer, "Croix de Feu devant l'Allemagne," in *La France et l'Allemagne*, 119–20.

40 *Le Flambeau*, April 1930, March 1931, June 1932; Millman, "Croix de Feu et l'antisémitisme," 51–2.

41 Lyautey, *Du rôle social de l'officier*; *Le Flambeau*, September 1934.

42 Lindenberg, *Années souterraines*, 194–202; Lambelet, "Frenchmen into Spaniards?"; Amdur, "Paternalism, Productivism, Collaborationism," 139, 142; Kuisel, *Ernest Mercier*, 105–9; Singer, "Lyautey: An Interpretation of the Man," 133–4, 136.

43 *Le Flambeau*, February, January, April 1930, April, January, March 1932.

44 Irvine, *French Conservatism in Crisis*, 114–15; *Le Flambeau*, May 1931.

45 AN 324AP 79*bis*, La Rocque to Tardieu, 27 April 1931, 16 June 1932, de Préval to Tardieu, 17 April 1932.

46 Howlett, "Croix de Feu," 101–5; Machefer, "Tardieu et La Rocque," 11–21; Nobécourt, *Colonel de La Rocque*, 214–19; Monnet, *Refaire la République*, 449–60.

47 *Le Flambeau*, December 1929, July 1930, March 1932.

48 *Le Flambeau*, April, September, 11 November 1931, February, April 1932; APP B/a 1901, report, 22 March 1931.

49 CHEVS LR1, file II.B.1, letters from Georges Bonnefous, 1 May 1932, Frederic Pic, 14 April 1932, report by president of 9th section to La Rocque, 22 April 1932; CHEVS LR2, file II.B.5, La Rocque to M. Denais, 6 June 1932, report, Meurthe-et-Moselle section, 28 March 1932.

50 *Le Flambeau*, May 1932.

51 Nobécourt, *Colonel de La Rocque*, 211–12, 223–5.

52 Chopine, *Six ans chez les Croix de Feu*, 77–8, 146–7; APP "Ligues/Croix de Feu," dossier on Croix de Feu, April 1936, 99, 102; *Le Flambeau*, March 1932, March 1933, April 1934.

53 Vallat, *Nez de Cléopâtre*, 137; Hautecloque, *Grandeur et decadence des Croix de Feu*, 24–6; Petit, *De La Rocque est-il un chef?* 17; Popelin, *Arènes politiques*, 35–6. De Préval and Ottavi described their roles to the authorities in AP 212/69/1, article 155, depositions dated 20 and 24 November 1936 respectively.

54 *Le Flambeau*, January 1930.

55 AN BB18 3048/2, Commissaire Divisionnaire Guillaume, transmitting report by Brigadier Schmitt and Inspector Valentini, 31 July 1936. On the Regroupement, see La Rocque's testimony in Chambre des Deputés, *Rapport fait au nom de comission d'enquête*, annexes, 2: no. 3383, 1616, dated 13 April 1934.

56 *Le Flambeau*, February 1930, March 1932, March 1933; AN 451AP 81, "Note aux chefs de section," 11 September 1933; AN BB18 3048/2, Brigadier Schmitt and Inspector Valentini to Juge d'Instruction Bru, 31 July 1936, 18–20.

57 Howlett, "Croix de Feu," 76–7, 117–18; Nobécourt, *Colonel de La Rocque*, 141–2.

58 Nobécourt, *Colonel de La Rocque*, 140; Weng, "Historique et la doctrine," 10–13; Howlett, "Croix de Feu," 59–60.

59 *Le Flambeau*, October 1932, provides a list of Croix de Feu sections and office addresses.

60 Nobécourt, *Colonel de La Rocque*, 1017n46; Howlett, "Croix de Feu," 90–1, 113; Passmore, *From Liberalism to Fascism*, 219.

61 Figures from Nobécourt, *Colonel de La Rocque*, 142–8, 984–5.

62 Rymell, "Militants and Militancy," 94–9.

63 Jankowski, *Communism and Collaboration*, 47; Florin, "Fédération du Nord," 238–9.

64 AN 451AP 81, Malicet to La Rocque, 5 May 1930; *Le Flambeau*, January 1932; Ferragu, "Croix de Feu et le PSF en Indre-et-Loire," 1–2.

65 AN 451AP 81, Chevassu to La Rocque, 28 July 1930; CHEVS LR2, file II.C.1., Schwerer to La Rocque, 17 March 1934.

66 AD Hérault 1M 1118, commissaires spéciaux (Sète, Montpellier), 25 February, 3 March 1934; CAOM B3 522, sûreté départementale (Constantine), 19 November 1930.

67 *Le Flambeau*, July 1930.

68 *Le Flambeau*, December 1932.

69 *Le Flambeau ardennais*, February 1936; *Le Flambeau*, June 1930, December 1932, July 1933.

70 *Le Flambeau*, July 1930, July 1932, January, March, May, July 1933; AN 451AP 82, Croix de Feu recruiting poster, n.d.

71 *Le Flambeau*, June 1930, 25 May 1935. For the contestation of Joan of Arc's memory, see Gildea, *Past in French History*, 154–65.

72 *Le Flambeau*, January, February, July 1933.

73 Chambre des Députés, *Rapport fait au nom de la commission d'enquête*, annexes, 2: no. 3383, 1598–9, testimony by La Rocque on 13 April 1934.

74 *Le Flambeau*, October 1933 (passage emphasized in original).

75 *Le Flambeau*, November 1933; AN 451AP 81, "Instruction urgente au sujet de l'activité générale de l'association," 25 April 1933, "Note très secrète," 22 May 1933; *Le Flambeau*, December 1933.

76 Chopine, *Six ans chez les Croix de Feu*, 106–8.

77 Jankowski, "Stavisky and His Era," 59–60; for a detailed account, see the same author's *Stavisky*.

78 Weber, *Action Française*, 322–40; Hoisington, "Toward the Sixth of February," 65; USNA RG59 851.00/1319, Strauss to Secretary of State, 27 March 1934. For La Rocque's musings, see his testimony in Chambre des Députés, *Rapport fait au nom de la commission d'enquête*, annexes, 1: no. 3383, 294–6, session of 9 March 1934.

79 Du Réau, *Édouard Daladier*, 119–21, 126–7; Hoisington, "Toward the Sixth of February," 65; Monnet, *Refaire la République*, 261–9.

80 *Le Flambeau*, February, March 1934; Howlett, "Croix de Feu," 124–5.

81 Howlett, "Croix de Feu," 122–3; *Le Flambeau*, February 1934; CHEVS LR2, file II.C.1, La Rocque to Richard, 18 April 1934.

82 Howlett, "Croix de Feu," 123–8, 136–8; Daladier, *Prison Journal*, 247–50, entry for 8 January 1944; on the joint meetings see Chambre des Députés, *Rapport fait au nom de la commission d'enquête*, annexes, 2: no. 3383, 1558, testimony by M. Bourdon, commissaire spécial, chef du service, Cherbourg, 13 April 1934.

83 Chambre des Députés, *Rapport fait au nom de la commission d'enquête*, annexes, 1: no. 3384, 2–6; AN 451AP 81, circular by La Rocque, 5 February 1934.

84 Weber, *Action Française*, 335–40; Howlett, "Croix de Feu," 131–4; Rymell, "Militants and Militancy," 196; Nobécourt, *Colonel de La Rocque*, 262–3.

85 CHEVS LR 2, file III.B.I, reports of the 9th Section, 12 February 1934, 25th Section, 15 February 1934; 50th Section, 13 February 1934, 55th Section, n.d.. For the accusations and denials of drunkenness, see AN 72AJ 1821, note, 6 February 1934, and Chambre des Députés, *Rapport fait au nom de la commission de l'enquête*, annexes, 1: no. 3383, 98, general report by the commission.

86 Passmore, "Boy-Scouting for Grown-Ups?" 532–3; Howlett, "Croix de Feu," 137; Nobécourt, *Colonel de La Rocque*, 266–9.

87 Passmore, "Boy-Scouting for Grown-Ups?" 533; Daladier, *Prison Journal*, 259–60, entry for 6 February 1944.

88 Chambre des Députés, *Rapport fait au nom de la comission d'enquête*, annexes, 1: no. 3383, 52–3, 100–3, general commission report of MM. Dormann and Salette.

89 *Le Flambeau*, March 1934; Berstein, *France des années 30*, 75; Monnet, *Refaire la République*, 271.

90 USNA RG 59 851.00/1309, Strauss, 23 February 1934. See also Weber, *Action Française*, 341–2, though he concludes La Rocque benefited "simply because he did not move at all."

CHAPTER TWO

1 The membership of the Croix de Feu will be examined more fully in the next chapter.

2 Popelin, *Arènes politiques*, 37; Clément, "Épiscopat," 109.

3 AN F7 13241, prefect (Moselle), 15 June 1935.

4 *Le Flambeau*, October, December 1934, 13 April 1935.

5 Chambre des Députés, *Rapport fait au nom de la commission d'enquête*, annexes, 2: no. 3383, 1640, testimony by Pozzo di Borgo, 16 April 1934.

6 Roussellier, "André Tardieu et la crise du constitutionalisme libéral," 67–9; *Le Flambeau*, November 1934.

7 *Le Flambeau*, November, December 1934, AD Gard 1M 715, commissaire spécial (Nîmes), 3 December 1934; Soucy, *French Fascism: The Second Wave*, 112.

8 APP "Ligues/Croix de Feu," Croix de Feu dossier, April 1936, 71–2.

9 Wileman, "Alliance Républicaine Démocratique," 248–60; AN 451AP 118, La Rocque to Flandin, 2 March 1935; directeur du cabinet to La Rocque, 4 March 1935; chef du sécretariat (Croix de Feu) to directeur du cabinet, 5 March 1935; présidence du conseil, président to La Rocque, 7 March 1935; La Rocque to Flandin, 13 March 1935; *Le Flambeau*, 2 March, 1 February, 23 March, 1 June 1935.

10 Werth, "French Fascism," 146; Soucy, *French Fascism: The Second Wave*, 124, 126.

11 *Le Flambeau*, 30 November, 21 December 1935; Cointet, *Pierre Laval*, 176–202.

12 *Le Flambeau*, 17 August, 28 December 1935, 1 February 1936.

13 APP B/a 1901, report, 12 March 1936; *Le Flambeau*, 14 March 1936. For other accusations along these lines, see AD Gard 1M 715, commissaire spécial (Nîmes), 20 January 1936.

14 Chambre des Députés, *Rapport fait au nom de la commission d'enquête*, annexes, 2: no. 3385, 20; *Le Flambeau*, 9 May 1936; Kuisel, *Ernest Mercier*, 110–11.

15 Irvine, *French Conservatism in Crisis*, 117, 123–4, 114–15; AD Loire-Atlantique 1M 470, commissaire spécial (Saint-Nazaire), 21 August 1935.

16 Howlett, "Croix de Feu," 138–40; Soucy, *French Fascism: The Second Wave*, 66–7; Nobécourt, *Colonel de La Rocque*, 273–84.

17 CHEVS LR2, file II.C.1, Schwerer to de La Rocque, 17 March 1934, sécretaire général (Croix de Feu) to Schwerer, 24 March 1934.

18 AD Hérault 1M 1118, commissaire spécial (Montpellier), 13 March 1936; USNA RG 59 851.00/1420, Warrington Dawson, 28 June 1935.

19 APP B/a 1902, report, 16 June 1936; CAOM B3 323, sûreté départementale (Constantine), 11 March 1935.

20 AD Nord 68J 68, "Circulaire de service générale pour les chefs de section Croix de Feu et Volontaires Nationaux," Paris, 30 September 1935.

21 Nobécourt, *Colonel de La Rocque*, 283.

22 AD Loire-Atlantique 1M 470, prefect, 14 October 1935.

23 APP B/a 1901, report, 1 June 1934; Guerrin, *Croix de Feu?* 12.

24 La Rocque, *Service public*, 22–3, 80, 49, 76–7.

25 Ibid., 144–5.

26 Ibid., 164–8.

27 Ibid., 180.

28 Ibid., 123, 137, 126.

29 Ibid., 31–3, 78–80, 112, 216, 224–6.

30 Nobécourt, *Colonel de La Rocque*, 350; La Rocque, *Service public*, 196–216, 71; Passmore, "Croix de Feu," 76–7. On the 1848 constitution, see Pilbeam, *Republicanism in Nineteenth-Century France*, 220–2; on the family vote, see Smith, *Feminism and the Third Republic*, 90, 95–6.

31 *Sept*, 28 December 1934; Clément, "Épiscopat," 106–9.

32 CAOM 1K26, sûreté départementale (Algiers), 11 January 1935; CAOM B3 707, prefect (Constantine), 9 August 1935; Cantier, *Algérie sous le régime de Vichy*, 230.

33 AN 451AP 85, secretary (Philippeville) to La Rocque, 20 June 1932; CAOM B3 522, sûreté départementale (Constantine), 5 July 1934; CAOM Oran 466, sûreté départementale (Oran), 14 November 1935; CAOM Oran 2413, commissaire central (Tlemcen), 29 October 1935; Millman, "Croix de Feu et l'antisémitisme," 52–6.

34 Mayeur, "Catholicisme intransigeant," in Mayeur, *Catholicisme social*, 17–38; Nord, "Three Views of Christian Democracy."

35 For more on Rageot, especially his views regarding gender and pro-natalism, see Roberts, *Civilization without Sexes*, 7, 35–6, 103–4, 125–6, 223n34.

36 *Le Flambeau*, February 1934, 9 March 1935; AD Nord 68J 79, Section Lilloise, *Compte-Rendu in extenso de la grande réunion privée du 28 avril 1934*, 10–13.

37 AN 451AP 135, "Collaborateurs ayant donné des articles depuis le mois de Mars 1936," 30 January 1936; the date referred to in the document is probably meant to be March 1935.

38 *Le Flambeau*, June 1934, 2 March, 6 April 1935; Passmore, "Planting the Tricolor," 843–5.

39 *Le Flambeau*, 20 April, 16 March 1935, 25 January 1936; Passmore, "Planting the Tricolor," 843–4; AN 451AP 83, Colette Yver, "Pourquoi j'adhère au Regroupement National du Croix de Feu," in a brochure entitled *Comment les hommes de la victoire sauveront la paix française* (n.d.).

40 Micaud, French Right and Nazi Germany, 240; Keylor, Jacques Bainville, 158.

41 *Le Flambeau*, October 1934.

42 *Le Flambeau*, 1 June, 21 September 1935.

43 *Le Flambeau*, 7 September, 12 October 1935.

44 *Le Flambeau*, 9, 30 May 1936.

45 *Le Flambeau*, 28 March, 9 May 1936. On this trend, see Micaud, *French Right and Nazi Germany*, 85–106.

46 *Le Flambeau*, 14 March 1936.

47 Hellman, "Communitarians, Non-conformists and the Search for a 'New Man,'" in Fishman et al., eds., *France at War*, 92; Nobécourt, *Colonel de La Rocque*, 350–1; Maud'huy, "French National Revival," 626.

48 Kalman, "Vers un ordre économique nouveau," 263–6.

49 Hellman, *Communitarian Third Way*, 110–12; CHEVS LR2, file IV.C.4, Branellec to La Rocque, 12 July, Ottavi to Branellec, 13 July 1935.

50 De Maud'huy quoted in Pinol, "Temps des droites," in Sirinelli, ed., *Histoire des droites*, 1: 319; AN F7 13241, reports, 17, 26 June 1935; Nobécourt, *Colonel de La Rocque*, 351–5; CAOM 1K26, sûreté départementale (Algiers), 22 July 1935.

51 NA FO 432/1, part II, no.7, C 4861/125/17, Clerk to Simon, 18 July 1934; Hermann, preface to Chopine, *Six ans chez les Croix de Feu*, 13–15.

52 Rémond, *Droites en France*, 213–14; Nobécourt, *Colonel de La Rocque*, 292–6, 300–3.

53 APP "Ligues/Croix de Feu," "Au sujet de l'activité Croix de Feu," October 1935, 18–19.

54 Irvine, "Fascism in France," 275.

55 Prost, "Manifestations du 12 février en province," in Bouvier, ed., *France en mouvement*, 12–30; AN F7 12969, report, 19 May 1934; APP B/a 1901, report, 4 August 1934; USNA RG 59 851.00/1351, Marriner, 19 July 1934; AD Bouches-du-Rhône M6 8288, prefect of Vaucluse to prefect of Bouches-du-Rhône, 6 September 1934, enclosing Croix de Feu circular dated 18 July 1934.

56 Passmore, "Boy-Scouting for Grown-Ups?" 545; USNA RG 59 851.00/1365, Strauss, 9 October 1934; *Le Flambeau*, September 1934.

57 Howlett, "Croix de Feu," 156–7; La Rocque and La Rocque, *La Rocque tel qu'il était*, 294; AD Gard 1M 715, commissaire spécial (Nîmes), 3 December 1934; AN 451AP 81, "Circulaire urgent," 11 January 1935; AP 212/69/1, article 155, "Pieces déposées a l'appui de l'interrogatoire de La Rocque," circular, 14 November 1934.

58 AD Oise Mp 5132, commissaire de police (Senlis), 3 March 1935; AN F7 13241, reports, 17, 28 June, 24 July, 26 August 1935.

59 *Le Flambeau*, 20 April 1935. Nobécourt, *Colonel de La Rocque*, 320–2, argues that while some members were involved in the affair, they were disobeying the movement's directives.

60 *Le Flambeau*, 22 June 1935; CAOM 1K26, prefect (Algiers) to governor general of Algeria, 13 June 1935.

61 For an example of aggression against the Croix de Feu, see CAOM Oran 466, sûreté départementale, 14 November 1935; for the incidents in Affreville, see CAOM 1K26, commissaire de police (Affreville), 30 September 1935.

62 Passmore, "Boy-Scouting for Grown-Ups?" 545–6.

63 Passmore, "Boy-Scouting for Grown-Ups?" 548–50; Rymell, "Militants and Militancy," 198–9. Nobécourt, *Colonel de La Rocque*, 327–8, emphasizes the confusion of the situation.

64 Berstein, *Histoire du Parti Radical*, 2: 392–6; Larmour, *French Radical Party*, 174–5.

65 USNA RG 59 851.00/1462, Dawson, 3 December 1935.

66 *Le Flambeau*, 22 October, 23, 30 November 1935.

67 USNA RG 59 851.00/1462, Dawson, 3 December 1935.

68 *Le Flambeau*, 12, 19 October, 23, 30 November 1935; CHEVS LR2, file IV.A, pamphlet entitled *La Dissolution des Croix de Feu?* Kéchichian, "D'une Association d'anciens combattants à un mouvement de mobilisation morale," in Andrieu, Le Béguec, and Tartakowsky, eds., *Associations et champ politique*, 321.

69 USNA RG 59 851.00/1475, report, 11 January 1936; the report's suggestion that the offer was brokered by Laval is disputed by Nobécourt, *Colonel de La Rocque*, 357–64.

70 Passmore, "Croix de Feu and Fascism," in Arnold, ed., *Development of the Radical Right*, 109.

71 USNA RG 59 851.00/1470, attaché's report, 16 December 1935.

72 *Le Temps*, 8 December 1935; AD Moselle BH 5220, pamphlet by the Abbé Ritz entitled *Réflexions d'un Lorrain sur le Mouvement Social Français des Croix de Feu*; AD Aisne 1M 20, prefect, 4 February 1936.

73 See the commentary in *Le Temps*, 8 and 9 December 1935.

74 AN 451AP 81, "Statuts des Croix de Feu et Briscards," n.d., "Statuts du Mouvement Social Français des Croix de Feu," n.d.; AP 212/69/1, article 155, "Perquisition chez M. Jean Chatelard à Senlis," circular "Mouvement Croix de Feu," 22 January 1936.

75 APP "Ligues/Croix de Feu," dossier on Croix de Feu, April 1936, 193 (the paragraph in question has been crossed out).

76 BN, *Croix de Feu, Parti Social Français: Tracts politiques*, document nos. 9, 16 (emphasis in original).

77 AN F7 13983, report, 7 May 1936.

78 AN 451AP 82, posters, n.d.; BN, *Croix de Feu, Parti Social Français: Tracts politiques*, document no. 5; *Le Flambeau*, 7 September 1935.

79 CHEVS LR2, file II.B.2 (a), "Circulaire préparatoire à la période des élections municipales," n.d.; *Le Flambeau*, 27 April 1935; CAOM B3 323, chef de la sûreté (Constantine), 22 March, 11 July 1935, commune mixte (Maadid), 12 July 1935, subprefect (Batna), 17 July 1935.

80 *Le Flambeau*, 21 December 1935, 11 January 1936; AN 451AP 91, La Rocque, "Les Croix de Feu devant le problème des élections," n.d. but late 1935–early 1936. The following paragraphs are an analysis of this document; unless otherwise indicated, direct quotations come from it.

81 For this suggestion, see AP 212/69/1, article 155, "Perquisition chez M. Jean Chatelard à Senlis," circular, "Mouvement Croix de Feu," 22 January 1936.

82 Howlett, "Croix de Feu," 171–9; Nobécourt, *Colonel de La Rocque*, 376–7; Passmore, "Croix de Feu and Fascism," in Arnold, ed., *Development of the Radical Right*, 103–7. Soucy emphasizes how the document highlights La Rocque's opportunism in "Functional Hating," 166.

83 *Manifeste Croix de Feu*, 6–7.

84 Nobécourt, *Colonel de La Rocque*, 377–81; *Le Canard enchaîné*, 8 April 1936.

85 Pinol, "Temps des droites," in Sirinelli, *Histoire des droites*, 1: 315; Shennan, "Parliamentary Opposition to the Front Populaire," 680–3.

86 *Manifeste Croix de Feu*, 14–15.

87 *Le Flambeau*, 22, 29 February, 7, 14, 21 March 1936. These writings were collected and published in a pamphlet entitled *Autour des élections* (copy in AN 451AP 81).

88 AD Nord 68J 68, "Participation des membres du Mouvement Croix de Feu aux réunions électorales," 8 April 1936; APP B/a 1902, report, 1 April 1936; AD Aisne 4Z 7, commissaire de police (Hirson), 31 March 1936; AD Oise Mp 5233, prefect, 25 April 1936.

89 CHEVS, LR2, file II.B.3, circular, 8 April 1936.

90 AD Aisne 4Z 7, commisaire de police (Hirson), 14 March 1936; AD Oise Mp 5233, prefect, 25 April 1936; AD Gard 1M 715, commissaire special (Nîmes), 14 April 1936.

91 AN 317AP 85, de Kerillis to Marin, 29 May 1936.

92 Nobécourt, *Colonel de La Rocque*, 391–2; CAOM B3 522, sûreté départementale (Constantine), 5, 23 February, 15 March 1936.

93 AD Hérault 1M 1118, commissaire spécial (Sète), 23 April 1936; AD Oise Mp 5233, subprefect (Senlis), May 1936.

94 CHEVS LR2, file II.B.3, notes, n.d.; AN F7 13983, report, 14 May 1936.

95 Nobécourt, *Colonel de La Rocque*, 385, 391; Weng, "Historique et la docrine," 43; Irvine, *French Conservatism in Crisis*, 126n43.

96 AN F7 13983, reports, 4, 5, 8, 27, 29 May 1936; APP "Ligues/Croix de Feu," dossier on Croix de Feu, April 1936, 271–4; APP B/a 1902, report, 2 June 1936; *Le Flambeau*, 30 May, 6, 13 June 1936; AP 212/69/1, article 155, "Perquisition chez M. Émile Plocque [president of the 17th section]," "Note

sur les renseignements donnés aux délégués par M. Ottavi du Comité Directeur Croix de Feu," n.d.

97 NA FO 432/2, part 5, no. 108, C 4553/1/17, Clerk to Eden, 22 June 1936; APP B/a 1902, report, 14 May 1936; AD Aisne 4Z 7, commissaire spécial (Hirson), 20 June 1936; AD Yvelines 4M2 66, commissaire de police (Pontoise), 21 June 1936.

98 CHEVS LR1, file I.A.4, "Conseil d'administration du 25 juin 1936"; APP B/a 1901, report, 27 June 1936.

99 NA FO 432/1, part 4, no.5, C 5313/33/17, Clerk to Hoare, 8 July 1935; Weber, *Hollow Years*, 119–20.

100 Paxton, *French Peasant Fascism*, 161–3.

101 USNA RG 59 851.00/1542, Dawson, 8 June 1936. Similar remarks were made by La Rocque at a meeting in Perpignan; see *La Flamme catalane*, 1 June 1936.

102 Jackson, *Popular Front*, 42–6; see also Wolikow, *Front Populaire*, 83.

103 See, for example, AN F7 14817, minister of interior, 29 August 1935, commissaire de police mobile, 31 August 1935.

104 APP "Ligues/Croix de Feu," directeur des renseignements généraux, 25 February 1936.

105 Nobécourt, *Colonel de La Rocque*, 410–11.

106 *Manifeste Croix de Feu*, 14.

CHAPTER THREE

1 On the challenges of working with such sources, see Paxton, *French Peasant Fascism*, 6–8.

2 Nobécourt, *Colonel de La Rocque*, 141–2, 640, 984–5nn11–13, 1061nn8–9; see also Weng, "Historique et la doctrine," 10–12.

3 APP "Ligues/Croix de Feu," dossier, April 1936, 64; USNA RG 59 851.00/1420, Warrington Dawson, 28 June 1935; AN F7 13241, report, 3 July 1935.

4 This figure is suggested by Milza, "Ultra-droite des années trente," in Winock, ed., *Histoire de l'extrême droite*, 165, and Howlett, "Croix de Feu," 180–1.

5 Weng, "Historique et la doctrine," 13–19; Goodfellow, *Between the Swastika and the Cross of Lorraine*, 141.

6 APP "Ligues/Croix de Feu," dossier, April 1936, 32–3.

7 *Croix de Feu du Gard*, 15 May 1936; AN F7 13030, prefect of Alpes-Maritimes, 25 September 1935.

8 APP "Ligues/Croix de Feu," note, 18 February 1935.

9 APP "Ligues/Croix de Feu," dossier, April 1936, 64.

10 This information comes from various reports in AD Aisne 1M 20 and 4Z 7, and AD Hérault 1M 1118.

11 AN F7 13033, prefect (Drôme), 25 November, 24 December 1935; AD Aube SC15 856, subprefect (Nogent-sur-Seine), 19 October 1935, 8 April 1936.

12 AD Gard 1M 715, prefect, 12 May 1934, commissaire spécial (Nîmes), 10 July 1935.

13 CAOM B3 323, commissaire de police (Djidjelli), 6 July 1935. On the complexities of social status in Algeria, see Prochaska, *Making Algeria French*, 167–8, 170, 172–3.

14 Milza, *Fascisme français*, 138 (using data provided by Janine Bourdin). Other local studies bear this estimate out. See, for example, Ferragu, "Croix de Feu et le PSF en Indre-et-Loire," 3; Florin, "Des Croix de Feu au Parti Social Français," 245, 247, 266n83; and Gabillard, "Viticulteurs angevins," 489.

15 Müller, "French Fascism and Modernization," 84–8.

16 AN F7 12969, report, 14 April 1934; APP B/a 1902, report, 4 August 1934; AN F7 13241, report, 1 August 1935. On the economic crisis, see Paxton, *French Peasant Fascism*, 11–50.

17 Soucy, *French Fascism: The Second Wave*, 132; Weng, "Historique et la doctrine," 103–4.

18 AD Hérault 1M 1118, prefect, April–May 1936.

19 AD Aisne 4Z 7, subprefect (Vervins), 9 July 1935, 16 April 1936; AD Aisne 1M 20, prefect, 21 April 1936; Paxton, *French Peasant Fascism*, 124–5.

20 AD Oise Mp 5132, subprefect (Senlis), 24 June 1935, commissaire de police (Beauvais), 29 June 1935; CAOM B3 323, administrator(Maadid), 12 July 1935.

21 AD Hérault 1M 1118, commissaire spécial (Sète), 18 December 1935.

22 AD Aisne 1M 20, prefect, 21 April 1936; AD Yvelines 4M2 66, commissaire de police (St-Germain-en-Laye), 23 April 1936.

23 AD Hérault 1M 1118, prefect, April–May 1936; AD Gard 1M 715, commissaire spécial, 14 April 1936; AD Oise Mp 5233, subprefect (Compiègne), 2–8 December 1935.

24 Passmore, *From Liberalism to Fascism*, 239–42.

25 Jeanneney, "Fédération Républicaine," in Rémond and Bourdin, eds., *France et les Français*, 349–50.

26 Irvine, *French Conservatism in Crisis*, 42.

27 Goodfellow, *Between the Swastika and the Cross of Lorraine*, 140; see also the report of the meeting of the Vittel (Vosges) section in November 1934 in *Le Flambeau*, December 1934.

28 AD Vendée 4M 413, commissaire de police (Luçon), 1 April 1936, prefect, 18 October 1935.

29 Gabillard, "Viticulteurs angevins," 488.

30 Chouvel, "Croix de Feu," 32–3; AD Loire-Atlantique 1M 470, subprefect (Nazaire), 26 March 1934, commissaire divisionnaire (Nantes), 1 October 1934, commissaire central, 29 May 1935; AD Gard 1M 715, commissaire spécial (Nîmes), 10 August 1935, prefect, 16 October 1935, 14 April 1936; *Le Flambeau du Gard*, October 1937.

31 On the military, see Thomas, "Parti Social Français et le monde militaire," in Forcade, Duhamel, and Vial, eds., *Militaires en République*, 417–29; *Le Flambeau*, 25 May 1935; AN F7 13241, report, 18 June 1935; APP B/a 1901, report, 31 October 1935; AD Aisne 1M 20, prefect, 30 October 1935.

32 Clément, "Épiscopat," 109–10; Péan, *Une Jeunesse française*, 35, 40–1.

33 CAOM B3 323, chef de la sûreté départementale, 11 July 1935; Goodfellow, *Between the Swastika and the Cross of Lorraine*, 145.

34 Nobécourt, *Colonel de La Rocque*, 282–3, 358–62; AN F7 13241, report, 28 September 1935; CAOM 1K26, sûreté départementale (Algiers), 2 March 1935.

35 AD Loire-Atlantique 1M 470, prefect, 13 June 1935; AD Hérault 1M 1118, inspecteur principal, 22 January 1936.

36 *Le Flambeau des Bouches-du-Rhône* 6, 31 March 1936; AD Gard 1M 715, Capitaine Sanguinetti, 29 September 1935.

37 AN F7 13033, commissaire spécial (Brest), 1 August 1934; commissaire spécial (Quimper), 5 July 1934, 7 December 1935; AD Yvelines 4M2 66, commissaire spécial, 30 March 1936.

38 AN F7 13241, report, 1 August 1935.

39 Ferragu, "Croix de Feu et le PSF en Indre-et-Loire," 3; AD Yvelines 4M2 66, commissaire spécial, 9 April 1936.

40 *Le Flambeau des Bouches-du-Rhône*, 31 March 1936; AD Aisne 4Z 7, subprefect (Vervins), 23 January, 30 June 1935; AD Loire-Atlantique 1M 470, commissaire central (Nantes), 29 May 1935.

41 Machefer, "Croix de Feu," 34; Howlett, "Croix de Feu," 140–4, 152–3, 160–2; Nobécourt, *Colonel de La Rocque*, 358–62, 366.

42 AN F7 13983, report, 29 May 1936.

43 AD Hérault 1M 1118, *Bulletin des sections Croix de Feu du département de l'Hérault*, n.d. but probably December 1935; prefect, 12 December 1935, inspecteur principal, 22 January 1936.

44 AD Hérault 1M 1118, prefect, 18 February 1936, commissaire spécial (Sète), 25 February, 4, 9 March, 17 April 1936.

45 Rymell, "Militants and Militancy," 95; Jankowski, *Communism and Collaboration*, 50–1; AD Gard 1M 715, commissaire spécial, 13 December 1935; *Croix de Feu du Gard*, 15 March, 15 April 1936.

46 Roberts, *Civilization without Sexes*, 1–16.

47 *Manifeste Croix de Feu*, 13; for a case study, see Koos, "Fascism, Fatherhood, and the Family."

48 McMillan, "Women, Religion and Politics," 355–64; and Sarti, *Ligue Patriotique des Françaises*. On women in the nationalist leagues, see Koos and Sarnoff, "France," in Passmore, ed., *Women, Gender and Fascism*.

49 See Passmore, "Femininity and the Right," 60.

50 La Rocque, *Service public*, 76–7. For an example of a Croix de Feu militant supporting votes for women, see CAOM B3 522, commissaire de police (Batna), 27 January 1936.

51 AN 451AP 87, "Allocution de Mlle de Préval," 26 October 1936; *Le Flambeau*, March 1934.

52 *Le Flambeau*, April, June, July, September, December 1934; AN F7 13241, report, 23 September 1935; Ferragu, "Croix de Feu et le PSF en Indre-et-Loire," 4; AD Gard 1M 715, commissaire spécial (Nîmes), 29 January 1936.

53 APP B/a 1901, report, 2 June 1936; *Le Flambeau*, 2 November 1935; *Le Flambeau des Bouches-du-Rhône*, 31 January 1936. For the extent to which other political parties mobilized women, see Smith, *Feminism and the Third Republic*, chap. 2.

54 AN 451AP 87, report, "Oeuvre Sociale Croix de Feu/Section Féminine du Mouvement Social des Croix de Feu," n.d.; Passmore, "Planting the Tricolor," 824.

55 AN 451AP 87, report, n.d.; AD Loire-Atlantique 1M 470, prefect, 29 November 1935.

56 AN 451AP 87, report, "Oeuvre Sociale Croix de Feu/Section Féminine du Mouvement Social des Croix de Feu," n.d.

57 CAOM F405, commissaire de police (commune d'Hussein-Day), 26 November 1935; AD Yvelines 4M2 66, prefect, 22 April 1936.

58 AN 451AP 87, "Rapport sur l'activité du centre de Saint-Ouen (Oct. 1935 – Juin 1936)"; AN F7 12965, report, 17 March 1936.

59 Passmore, "Planting the Tricolor," 831–6, 847.

60 Green, "Gender, Fascism and the Croix de Feu," and "Bouboule Novels," in Hawthorne and Goslan, eds., *Gender and Fascism in Modern France*.

61 *Le Flambeau*, February, 5 October 1935; AN 451AP 87, "Allocution de Mlle de Préval," 26 October 1936; "Allocution de M. Ottavi," 26 October 1936; "Allocution de Mlle Marochetti," 28 October 1936.

62 CAOM B3 522, commissaire central (Bône), 9 March 1936; AN 451AP 87, "Rapport trimestriel, janvier-avril 1936."

63 AD Hérault 1M 1118, *Bulletin des sections Croix de Feu de l'Hérault, de l'Aude et de l'Aveyron*, 1 April 1936.

64 AN 451AP 87, "Rapport trimestrial janvier–avril 1936," commissaire-général du Mouvement Social, 7 January 1936.

65 AN 451AP 87, "Cours élementaires de formation sociale," n.d. but early 1936; *Le Flambeau*, 29 February 1936.

66 Coutrot, "Youth Movements in France in the 1930s"; Alexander, "Duty, Discipline and Authority," in Atkin and Tallett, eds., *Right in France*, 131–4; Hoisington, *Lyautey and the French Conquest*, 1–20; Atkin, *Church and Schools in Vichy France*, 18–20; Halls, *Youth of Vichy France*, 7–11.

67 La Rocque, *Service public*, 117–18; *Le Flambeau*, 30 March, 11 May 1935.

68 *Le Flambeau*, November 1932, May 1933.

69 *Le Flambeau*, 25 May 1935, 16 May 1936; AN F7 13983, report, 7 May 1936.

70 *Le Flambeau*, February 1930, September 1931, March 1932, March, August 1933, July 1934; Howlett, "Croix de Feu," 116.

71 APP B/a 1902, report, 26 December 1935; CAOM F405, commissaire de police (Arba), 30 December 1935. See also *Le Flambeau*, January 1934, 11 January 1936.

72 *Le Flambeau*, March 1933; AN F7 13983, report, 6 May 1936; *Le Flambeau morbihannais*, 5 June 1933.

73 *Le Flambeau*, March, August 1933, January, July 1934.

74 *Le Flambeau*, 1 February, 9 March, 2 November, 14 December 1935, 11 January 1936; AN F7 13983, report, 21 May 1936; Péan, *Une Jeunesse française*, 33–4.

75 *Le Flambeau*, September 1931, June, July, September 1932, June, August 1933, April 1934.

76 *Le Flambeau*, 23, 30 March, 6 April, 25 May, 8 June, 2 November 1935, 30 May, 20 June 1936.

77 Downs, "Municipal Communism and the Politics of Childhood," quotation on 218.

78 *Le Flambeau*, July 1932, reproduces the regulations for the Plainfaing *colonie*; the 18 May 1935 issue suggests that little had changed three years later.

79 Downs, "Municipal Communism and the Politics of Childhood," 230–3.

80 *Le Flambeau*, September 1931, 27 April 1935.

81 *Le Flambeau*, February 1930, March 1932, March 1933; CHEVS LR1, file I.B.3, "Organisation du service d'Entr'aide," région parisienne, 20 December 1935; AN 451AP 81, "Note aux chefs de section," 11 September 1933.

82 AN BB18 3048/2, Brigadier Schmitt and Inspector Valentini to Juge d'instruction Bru, 31 July 1936, 18–20; AD Nord 68J 68, report, 14 May 1936, AD Nord 68J 167, "Directives générales à donner aux bureaux d'études syndicales pour la formation des syndicats professionels," n.d.

83 APP B/a 1902, report, 1 December 1935; AN BB18 3048/2, report, 31 July 1936, 21–5; AD Aisne 1M 20, prefect, 21 April 1936.

84 APP B/a 1902, report, 14 February 1936.

85 *Le Flambeau*, 11, 18, 25 May 1935.

86 AD Alpes-Maritimes 5M 541, commissaire spécial (Breil), 13 May 1935; AN F7 13983, report, 24 May 1936; *Le Flambeau*, 30 May 1936.

87 *Le Flambeau*, 5, 26 October 1935, June 1934 (first passage emphasized in original).

88 *Le Flambeau*, May, November 1934, 20 July 1935.

89 Nord, *Republican Moment*, 229–32; see also Mosse, *Image of Man*, 155–80.

90 Gildea, *Past in French History*, 161–2; AN F7 13983, report, 14 May 1936; *Le Flambeau*, 16 May 1936.

91 Rymell, "Militants and Militancy," 226–30; *Le Flambeau*, June 1934, 22 June, 7 December 1935.

92 AP 212/69/1, article 146, Brigadier Schmitt, 24 October 1936. For a detailed account of Mermoz's career, see Chadeau, *Mermoz*.

93 For more information, see Kennedy, "Croix de Feu," 377–82.

94 On this point, see Chadeau, *Mermoz*, 243–8.

95 Rymell, "Militants and Militancy," 231; AP 212/69/1, Brigadier Schmitt, 24 October 1936; APP B/a 1901, report, 31 March 1936; AN F7 13241, report, 3 August 1935; *Le Flambeau*, 30 May 1936.

96 AN F7 12965, report, 31 March 1936; *Le Flambeau*, 9 May, 4 April 1936.

97 AN 451AP 91, La Rocque, "Croix de Feu devant le problème des élections"; AN 451AP 84, "Institut Royal des Affaires Internationales, conférence du Lieutenant-colonel de La Rocque," 19 February 1935.

98 For recent examples of these contrasting approaches, see Mosse, *Fascist Revolution*, 1–44 (though he notes that the fascist revolution was to be "respectable"), and Paxton, *Anatomy of Fascism*. For a recent discussion of trends in the historiography, see Griffin, "Primacy of Culture."

99 On this point, see Mann, *Fascists*, 14–16.

100 On the evolution of the membership of the Fascist and Nazi movements, see Lyttelton, *Seizure of Power*, esp. 42–76, and Childers, *Nazi Voter*. Fritzsche, *Germans into Nazis*, sees the Nazis as successful in generating a cross-class appeal.

101 For a brief discussion of the Nazis and Fascists in this regard, see De Grand, *Fascist Italy and Nazi Germany*, 57–68.

102 Passmore, "Boy Scouting for Grown-ups?" 528–30. Mann, *Fascists*, 16–17, also emphasizes the centrality of paramilitarism.

103 Griffin, "Primacy of Culture," 21–43; but see also Roberts, "Comments on 'The Primacy of Culture,'" 259–63.

104 Mosse, *Fascist Revolution*, 30–3; Knox, *Common Destiny*, 78–95.

105 Paxton, "Five Stages of Fascism," 14–21.

106 Jackson, *France: The Dark Years*, 43–64.

107 Burrin, *Fascisme, nazisme, autoritarisme*, 258.

108 On the cult of the *union sacrée*, see Sherman, *Construction of Memory in Interwar France*, 296–301.

109 Knox, *Common Destiny*, 59–78.

110 *Le Flambeau*, 1 January 1935.

111 Burleigh, *Third Reich*, 115–16.

112 See Kallis, "To Expand or Not to Expand."

113 Cullen, "Leaders and Martyrs."

114 Eatwell, "Towards a New Model of Generic Fascism," 189; Cullen, "Leaders and Martyrs," 424–7.

115 *Le Flambeau*, 22 June 1935.

116 Knox, *Common Destiny*, 68.

117 See Sternhell, *Ni droite, ni gauche*; on the shift in Sternhell's views regarding the Croix de Feu, see Jenkins, "Contextualizing the Immunity Thesis," in Jenkins, ed., *France in the Era of Fascism*, 9.

118 Passmore, "Croix de Feu," 74; *Le Flambeau*, 27 June 1936.

119 Soucy, "Nature of Fascism in France," 50–2; Tucker, *Fascist Ego*, 247; Soucy, *Fascist Intellectual*, 80–1.

120 Linz, "Authoritarian Regime," in Allardt and Rokkan, eds., *Mass Politics*, 251–83; Paxton, *Anatomy of Fascism*, 215–18. Mann, *Fascists*, 43–8, provides a useful discussion of the varieties of right-wing authoritarianism, though he focuses on regimes.

121 *Manifeste Croix de Feu*, 6.

122 CAOM F405, commissaire de police (Mascara), 26 October 1935.

123 For commentary on this problem, see Soucy, "Problematizing the Immunity Thesis," in Jenkins, ed., *France in the Era of Fascism*, 85–90.

124 Here my views differ somewhat from those of Passmore, "Croix de Feu," 71, 92, and Mann, *Fascists*, 16–17, who stress the centrality of paramilitarism to defining fascism.

125 Mann, "Contradictions of Continuous Revolution," in Kershaw and Lewin, eds., *Stalinism and Nazism*, 140–1; see also Levy, "Fascism, National Socialism, and Conservatives."

126 Preston, *Politics of Revenge*, 3–29.

CHAPTER FOUR

1 AP 212/691, article 151, commissaire de police (Moulins) to prefect of the Allier, 23 September 1936. This and the following paragraph are based upon this report.

2 PSF: *Bulletin de la section de Lunéville*, 29 November 1936; AD Nord 68J 104, "Équipes Volontes de Propagande," n.d.; AP 212/69/1, article 149, PSF local committee for Paris's 18th arrondissement to La Rocque, 5 October 1936; Howlett, "Croix de Feu," 210–11; Machefer, "Parti Social Français," 74. The PSF's growth and its organizational evolution will be discussed in more detail in chapter 6.

3 Rémond and Bourdin, "Forces adverses," in Bourdin, ed., *Léon Blum, chef de gouvernement*, 137–59; Irvine, *French Conservatism in Crisis*, 84–95; Shennan, "Parliamentary Opposition"; Wileman, "P.-É. Flandin and the Alliance," 153–4; Delbreil, *Centrisme et démocratie-chrétienne*, 293–5.

4 *Le Flambeau*, 25 July 1936.

5 *Le Flambeau*, 8 August 1936 (emphasis in original).

6 Parry, "Articulating the Third Republic," 172–6.

7 AN BB18 3004/2, procureur de la République (Clermont-Ferrand), 17 August 1936, procureur général, 25 August 1937, report on press commentary, 21 August 1936. Nobécourt, *Colonel de La Rocque*, 451–65, provides a detailed account of the episode, strongly condemning the left-wing press.

8 AN 451AP 108, "Parti Social Français – réunion du 15 Septembre 1936 (Lyon): discours de M. Vallin."

9 CAOM B3 635, sûreté départementale (Constantine), 14 August 1936.

10 AP 212/69/1, article 151, La Rocque, communiqué, 8 September 1936, appended to directeur de la police judiciaire to procureur de la République, 10 September 1936; CAOM F405, sûreté départementale (Algiers), 18 September 1936.

11 AN F7 14817, inspecteurs principaux de police mobile (Saint-Brieuc), 25 October 1936.

12 CAOM B3 707, gendarmerie nationale (Constantine), 30 June 1936; AN BB18 3048/2, directeur de la police judiciaire, 6 July 1936; AD Hérault 1M 1119, minister of interior, 11 September 1936; AD Aube SC15 656, Chef d'Escadron Dupuis, 24 November 1936, commandant (Nogent-sur-Seine), 27 November 1936.

13 AN F7 14817, commissaire divisionnaire (Rennes), 19 October 1936.

14 AN BB18 3048/2, procureur de la république (Oran), 14 September, 15 October 1936; CAOM 3CAB 25, procureur général (Oran), 7 July 1937; Koerner, "Extrême droite en Oranie," 569–78.

15 AN BB18 3048/2, commissaire divisionnaire, chef de la 10ème brigade régionale de police mobile, 1 October 1936; AP 212/69/1, article 149, perquisition Désobliaux, seal no. 13, "Région parisienne – liaisons"; AN F7 14817, inspecteur de police mobile, 17 October 1936.

16 Blatt, "Cagoule Plot," in Mouré and Alexander, eds., *Crisis and Renewal in France*; Parry, "Counter-Revolution by Conspiracy," in Atkin and Tallett, eds., *Right in France*.

17 Daladier, *Prison Journal*, 263–5, entry for 7 February 1944; Nobécourt, *Colonel de La Rocque*, 543–69.

18 AP 212/69/1, article 152, Danner to Varin (head of the EVP), 23 September 1936.

19 AP 212/69/1, article 152, search of PSF headquarters; seal no. 2, Danner to Varin, 22 September 1936; seal no. 19, Edmond Barrachin, "Point de vue personnel sur la position politique du part à ce jour et l'attitude qu'il lui convient d'adopter dans les circonstances présents," n.d.

20 *Le Flambeau*, 10 October 1936; Howlett, "Croix de Feu," 223–4. Bourne and Watt, eds., *British Documents*, 22: doc. 88, 349–50, Clerk to Eden, 30 January 1937, gives a figure of 1,400 arrests.

21 USNA RG 59 851.00/1664, report by Bullitt, 14 April 1937.

22 *Le Flambeau*, 10 October 1936; AD Gard 1M 715, prefect of Var, 20 January 1937; see also AD Alpes-Maritimes 4M 542, directeur de police d'état, 17 December 1936.

23 See, for example, AD Yvelines 4M2 66, première brigade régionale de police mobile, 30 January 1937.

24 AD Hérault 1M 1119, subprefect (Béziers), 10 October 1936; AD Yvelines 4M2 66, prefect, 24 December 1936; CAOM B3 327, arrondissement de Philippeville, 10 November 1936.

25 APP B/a 1952, reports, 25, 26 September 1936; AN F7 12820, report, 23 March 1937; *L'Heure française*, 23 January 1937; AN F7 12819, report, 6 February 1937.

26 AD Nord 68J 104, supplement to PSF *Bulletin d'informations*, no. 67, "Instructions générales à suivre en cas d'agression."

27 *Le Flambeau*, 3, 17, 24 October 1936, 6 March, 1 May 1937.

28 AN F7 13985, report on Clichy incident, 25 March 1937; see also Howlett, "Croix de Feu," 240–1; Rymell, "Militants and Militancy," 201–2; and Machefer, "Fusillade de Clichy," in *Presse et Politique*.

29 *Le Flambeau*, 20, 27 March 1937.

30 *Le Flambeau*, 27 March 1937; USNA RG 59 851.00/1661, report by Wilson, 6 April 1937.

31 USNA RG 59 851.00/1662, "Political Riots at Clichy," March 1937.

32 See, for example, AD Marne 30M 144, commissaire spécial (Reims), 19 March 1937.

33 AN BB18 3048/2, procureur de la République, 5 April 1937.

34 *Le Flambeau*, 19 June 1937.

35 AD Oise Mp 5233, subprefect (Senlis), 4 November 1936; AD Hérault 1M
    1119, subprefect (Béziers), 5, 10 October 1936; AD Loire-Atlantique 1M 470,
    subprefect (Châteaubriant), 31 December 1936, 6 April 1937; AD Aisne 4Z 6,
    commissaire de police (Hirson), 28 January 1938; CAOM B3 327,
    Philippeville, 10 November 1936.

36 Machefer, "Action Française et le PSF"; Irvine, *French Conservatism in Cri-
    sis*, 132–3.

37 Koerner, "Extrême Droite en Oranie," 574–7; CAOM 1K26, sûreté
    départementale (Algiers), 10 August 1936.

38 AD Vendée 4M 413, prefect, 14 September 1936.

39 AP 212/69/1, article 151, circular, 16 July 1936; *Le Flambeau*, 8 August 1936
    (emphasis in original).

40 AP 212/69/1, La Rocque to Goy, 5 October 1936; AN 451AP 116, La Rocque,
    "Circulaire du service général," 28 October 1936; AN F7 14817, circular by
    La Rocque, 3 November 1936; *La Volonté bretonne*, 5 November 1936; AN
    451AP 121, memo, "cooperation," n.d.

41 CAOM B3 327, commissaire de police (Batna), 6 December 1936; AN 451AP
    120, letter to La Rocque, 26 June 1936; Irvine, *French Conservatism in Cri-
    sis*, 131–4; AN 451AP 120, Vallat to La Rocque, 23 November 1936; *Le
    Flambeau*, 21 November, 5, 12 December 1936, 20 February, 13 March
    1937; Jeanneney, *François de Wendel en République*, 567–8.

42 *Le Flambeau*, 21 November 1936.

43 Irvine, *French Conservatism in Crisis*, 137–44; Howlett, "Croix de Feu,"
    244–7.

44 *Le Volontaire '36*, 4 June 1937; AN 451AP 120, Pierre Taittinger to E.
    Nicolle, 27 April 1937; *Le Flambeau*, 24 April 1937; PSF: *Bulletin
    d'informations*, nos. 31, 33 (11, 25 May 1937).

45 Desgranges, *Journal d'un prêtre-député*, 81–3, 114–15, entries for 29 Decem-
    ber 1936 and 23 April 1937.

46 AP 212/69/1, article 152, "Résumé d'un conversation avec X," n.d. but likely
    fall 1936.

47 CAOM Oran 70, sûreté départementale, 3 December 1936; AD Hérault, 1M
    1119, inspecteur principale (Montpellier), 5, 18 September, 30 December
    1936; AD Alpes-Maritimes 4M 542, commissaire divisionnaire de police
    spéciale, 1 October 1936, commissaire spécial (Cannes), 15 October 1936.

48 CAOM F405, sûreté départementale (Algiers), 24 September 1936; CAOM B3
    327, sûreté (Constantine), 7 December 1936; Koerner, "Extrême Droite en
    Oranie," 580–1.

49 Howlett, "Croix de Feu," 232–4; NA FO 432/2, part VI, no. 6, C4952/1/17,
    Clerk to Eden, 6 July 1936; USNA RG 59 851.00/1561, report by Dawson, 3

August 1936; *Le Canard enchaîné*, 24 June 1936; USNA RG 59 851.00/1661, report by Wilson, 6 April 1937.

50 *L'Émancipaton nationale*, 11 July 1936; Brunet, *Jacques Doriot*, 219–25; Jouvenel, "Parti Populaire Français"; Soucy, *French Fascism: The Second Wave*, 256–68.

51 AD Hérault 1M 1119, commissaire spécial (Sète), 4 January 1937.

52 AD Gard 1M 715, commissaire spécial (Nîmes), 30 December 1936, 6 January 1937; CAOM B3 635, commissaire spécial (Bône), 27 February 1937.

53 AD Alpes-Maritimes 4M 542, commissaire divisionnaire de police spéciale, 1 October 1936; AD Alpes-Maritimes 4M 543, directeur de la police d'état, 9 October 1936, prefect, 27 January 1937.

54 AN F7 14817, report, January 1937; *L'Emancipation nationale*, 12 December 1936; AD Alpes-Maritimes 4M 543, commissaire divisionnaire de police spéciale (Nice), 28 May 1937.

55 Machefer, "Union des droites," 118; Brunet, *Jacques Doriot*, 269.

56 Howlett, "Croix de Feu," 248–50. See also La Rocque's column and his comments at the regional congress for the Franche-Comté, both in *Le Flambeau*, 8 May 1937.

57 *Gringoire*, 21 May 1937.

58 Robbe, *Parti Social Français et le Front de la Liberté*; *Le Flambeau*, 22, 29 May, 12 June 1937; AN 451AP 116, memo, "Direction province," 18 June 1937; Brunet, *Jacques Doriot*, 273–4.

59 AD Somme 99M 165, commissaire de police, 1 June 1937; AN 451AP 120, Barrachin to Faucherre (president of Hérault PSF), 30 April 1937, note by Sète section, 3 June 1937.

60 Nobécourt, *Colonel de La Rocque*, 573–80; *Le Petit Journal*, 19 January 1938.

61 Dobry, "Thèse immunitaire face aux fascismes," in Dobry, ed., *Mythe de l'allergie française*, 54–5.

62 PSF: *Bulletin d'informations*, nos. 31, 33, 34 (11, 25 May, 1 June 1937); CAOM Oran 70, sûreté (Oran), 2 June 1937; AN 451AP 116, "Direction province," 18 June 1937, "Extraits du discours prononcé par le colonel de La Rocque au congrès de l'Auvergne, le 3 Octobre 1937," "Élections cantonales – centralisation des résultats," 4 October 1937; *Le Petit Journal*, 2 September 1937.

63 *Le Petit Journal*, 26 October 1937 (which gives a figure of 299); Weng, "Historique et la doctrine," 84–7; Rudaux, *Croix de Feu*, 244–5; Howlett, "Croix de Feu," 265–9, 330–1.

64 Koerner, "Extrême Droite en Oranie," 584–8; Florin, "Des Croix de Feu au Parti Social Français," 247; Austin, "Conservative Right and Far Right," in

Blinkhorn, ed., *Fascists and Conservatives*, 190; PSF: *Bulletin d'informations*, no. 49 (20 September 1937); Ferragu, "Croix de Feu et le PSF en Indre-et-Loire," 32–3.

65 Machefer, "Tardieu et La Rocque," 14; Kupferman and Machefer, "Presse et politique dans les années trente," 25–31.

66 Boulic and Lavaure, *Henri de Kerillis*, 144–7; Howlett, "Croix de Feu," 251–8, quotation on 257; Monnet, *Refaire la République*, 449, 454–8; Machefer, "Tardieu et La Rocque," 14–15.

67 AN AJ 1822, "L'Affaire La Rocque vu par la presse," vol. 1, clipping from *Choc*, 15 July 1937.

68 Howlett, "Croix de Feu," 255–7; see also Nobécourt, *Colonel de La Rocque*, 583–5; Kupferman and Machefer, "Presse et politique dans les années trente," 40–3; and Daladier, *Prison Journal*, 265, entry for 7 February 1944.

69 AN AJ 1822, vol.1, clipping from *L'Action française*, 1 August 1937, vol.2, clippings from *L'Action française*, 11 August 1937, and *La Liberté*, 8 August 1937; vol. 3, clipping from *Le Jour*, 21 August 1937.

70 *Le Flambeau*, 31 July 1937.

71 AN AJ 1822, vol.1, clippings from *L'Oeuvre*, 27 July 1937, and *Le Journal*, 4 August 1937.

72 Nobécourt, *Colonel de La Rocque*, 611–12; *Le Temps*, 28 October 1937; see also Howlett, "Croix de Feu," 258–60; Machefer, "Action Française et le PSF," 125; and Monnet, *Refaire la République*, 450–4.

73 AN AJ 1822, vol. 7, clipping from *L'Action française*, 14 December 1937; see also *Le Jour*, 14 December 1937.

74 *Le Temps*, 28 October, 17 November 1937; Monnet, *Refaire la république*, 450–3; Howlett, "Croix de Feu," 263; Machefer, "Tardieu et La Rocque," 16–17.

75 *Le Temps*, 18, 30 November, 1 December 1937, 3 January 1938; Howlett, "Croix de Feu," 263–4.

76 Leschi, "Étrange cas La Rocque," in Dobry, ed., *Mythe de l'allergie française*, 179; AD Yvelines 4M2 66, commissaire divisionnaire, 27 July 1937, commissaire spécial (Versailles), 30 July 1937; Prévosto, "Fédération du Nord," 31–5.

77 AD Oise Mp 5133, commissaire de police (Chantilly), 18 November 1937; AD Marne 30M 144, commissaire spécial (Châlons-sur-Marne), 22 November 1937.

78 Thomas, "Effectifs du Parti Social Français," 70; AD Alpes-Maritimes 4M 542, commissaire divisionnaire de police spéciale, 28 August 1937; AN 324AP 79, Perret to Tardieu, 8 November 1937. See chapter 6 for more on the PSF's growth.

79 *Samedi*, 6 November 1937; AN AJ 1822, vol. 3, clippings from *L'Époque*, 28 August 1937, and *Candide*, 18 November 1937.

80 Howlett, "Croix de Feu," 262–3; Daladier, *Prison Journal*, 279–80, entry for 23 June 1944.

81 Irvine, *French Conservatism in Crisis*, 149–51; APP B/a 1952, note, 2 December 1937.

82 See Paxton, *French Peasant Fascism*, 159–64.

83 Vallin, "Parti Social Français"; *Le Flambeau*, 2 January 1937; *PSF: Bulletin d'informations*, no. 28 (20 April 1937), supplement: "Schema de conférence – nous ne sommes pas fascistes."

84 Passmore, "Boy-Scouting for Grown-Ups?" 554–6; Bourne and Watt, eds., *British Documents*, 23: doc. 28, Phipps to Eden, 24 January 1938. For a threat of violence, see CAOM Oran 70, commissaire de police (Mostanagem), 13 December 1936.

85 AD Yvelines 4M2 66, minister of interior, memorandum, 20 August 1936.

86 AN F7 14817, Paris prefect of police, 26 January 1937, with report dated January 1937 attached; AN BB18 3048/2, directeur de la police judiciaire, 30 October 1936, procureur de la république (Oran), 15 October 1936.

87 AN BB18 3048/2, direction criminelle, note for the garde des scéaux, 24 November 1936; note for the cabinet, 5 December 1936.

88 Howlett, "Croix de Feu," 203–6; AP 212/69/1, article 149, "Projet: Désobliaux," n.d.; "Région parisienne – liaisons," n.d.; AP 212/69/1, article 153, unsigned letter to Franck Cognat (Valence), 5 August 1936.

89 USNA RG 59 851.00/1760, report by Wilson, 27 December 1937; Bourne and Watt, eds., *British Documents*, 23: doc. 28, Phipps to Eden, 24 January 1938; Nobécourt, *Colonel de la Rocque*, 611–12.

90 USNA RG 59 851.00/1664, report, 14 April 1937.

91 Nobécourt, *Colonel de La Rocque*, 447–8, 471–83.

92 Weber, *Action Française*, 387; Brunet, *Jacques Doriot*, 275–81; NA FO 432/4, no. 4, C 102/102/17, Phipps, 6 January 1938; Paxton, *French Peasant Fascism*, 135–8.

93 Irvine, *Boulanger Affair Reconsidered*, 4, 125.

94 Irvine, "Fascism in France," 275.

95 See, for example, Berstein, "De la démocratie plébiscitaire au gaullisme," in Berstein, ed., *Cultures politiques en France*, 151, and Thomas, "Parti Social Français," 42–3.

96 Barrachin had served as a deputy for the Ardennes in 1934–36, succeeding Etienne Riché, who had died in 1934 and who was the brother of Georges Riché, the Croix de Feu's treasurer. Barrachin lost the seat in the 1936 election. See Le Béguec, "Premiers rassemblements," 27–8; Thomas, "Parti Social

Français," 38, 43–4; Vallat, *Nez de Cléopâtre*, 140. Vallat is admittedly biased, but his characterization of Barrachin accords with his conduct in the PSF.

97 AP 212/69/1, article 152, Barrachin, "Point de vue personnel sur la position politique du parti à ce jour," n.d.

98 AP 212/69/1, article 152, Vallin, "Note pour les orateurs du siège (2)," 16 July 1936.

99 Lacretelle, *Qui est La Rocque?* 9, 13–14, 22, 24, 30, 47; see also Alden, *Jacques de Lacretelle*, 218–22; Barrachin in *Le Flambeau*, 29 May 1937. The lecture was later published as *Parti Social Français devant le pays*.

100 APP B/a 1952, report, 29 December 1937.

101 *Le Petit Journal*, 9 February, 9 May 1938.

102 *Parti Social Français: Une mystique, une programme*, 4–5; *Le Flambeau*, 23 January 1937 (passage emphasized in original).

103 *Le Petit Journal*, 8 January 1938.

104 *Le Flambeau*, 1 May 1937; *L'Alliance Démocratique*, 11 June, 9 July 1937; *Le Petit Journal*, 13 November 1937.

105 PSF: *Bulletin d'informations*, no. 49 (20 September 1937); Delbreil, *Centrisme et démocratie-chrétienne*, 334–6.

106 PSF: *Bulletin d'informations*, no. 3 (27 October 1936); *Le Flambeau*, 6, 13, 20 February 1937; Larmour, *French Radical Party*, 171, 183, 220. It should be noted that Lamoureux had at first cautiously endorsed the Popular Front.

107 PSF: *Bulletin d'informations*, no. 24 (24 March 1937) (passage emphasized in original).

108 AN 451AP 120, "Le PSF et les Radicaux," n.d.; the document is almost entirely reproduced in Howlett, "Croix de Feu," 359–62. While it is not certain that Barrachin authored the document, his official duties and other recommendations about adopting a more democratic veneer point strongly in that direction. See Nobécourt, *Colonel de La Rocque*, 1063n53.

109 PSF: *Bulletin d'informations*, no. 37 (24 June 1937); *Le Flambeau*, 3 July 1937; Machefer, "Parti Social Français," in Rémond and Bourdin, *France et les Français*, 308–11.

110 *Le Petit Journal*, 8, 29 January 1938; Berstein, *Histoire du Parti Radical*, 2: 471–2, 495–7; AD Gard 1M 715, commissaire central, 7 July 1937.

111 AN 451AP 120, "Le PSF et les Radicaux."

112 For this interpretation, see Machefer, "Parti Social Français," in Rémond and Bourdin, eds., *France et les Français*, 326; Nobécourt, *Colonel de La Rocque*, 647–51.

113 *Sept*, 26 February 1937. Nobécourt, *Colonel de La Rocque*, 347–8, suggests that the interview was "ghosted" by a PSF journalist, but believes that it still accurately depicted La Rocque's views at the time.

114 Passmore, *From Liberalism to Fascism*, 269; Clément, "Épiscopat,"
    111–13.
115 AN F7 14817, commissaire divisionnaire (Rennes), 23, 28 October 1936;
    Réalité, 19 February 1938. On the varying political attitudes among Catho-
    lics during this period, see McMillan, "France," in Buchanan and Conway,
    eds., *Political Catholicism*, 40–54.
116 *Le Flambeau*, 22 August 1936.
117 *Le Flambeau*, 14 November 1936, 10 April 1937. For the theme of sexual
    immorality in French antisemitic discourse, see Birnbaum, *Un Mythe
    politique*, 209–24.
118 Jackson, *Popular Front in France*, 250–1; *Le Petit Journal*, 23 January 1938.
119 *La Flamme du Midi*, 14 May 1937.
120 Millman, *Question juive*, 264–5; CAOM Oran 70, sûreté, 23 February 1937.
121 For an overview, see Tostain, "Popular Front and the Blum-Viollette Plan,"
    in Chafer and Sackur, eds., *French Colonial Empire and the Popular Front*,
    218–29.
122 CAOM B3 635, sûreté (Constantine), 14 August 1936; CAOM F405,
    commissaire de police (Affreville), 20 October 1936; Machefer, "Autour du
    problème algérien."
123 *Sept*, 26 February 1937; *Le Flambeau*, 26 December 1936.
124 *Le Flambeau*, 22 August 1936.
125 AN F7 14817, inspecteur de police mobile (Saint-Brieuc), 23 October 1936;
    CAOM Oran 70, commissaire divisionnaire (Oran), 25 April 1939; CAOM B3
    635, commissaire de police (Saint-Arnaud), 19 April 1939. See also Koerner,
    "Extrême Droite en Algérie," 590–2.
126 See Micaud, *French Right and Nazi Germany*, chap. 7.
127 *Le Flambeau*, 24 October 1936, 6 February 1937.
128 *Le Flambeau*, 6 February 1937.
129 *Le Flambeau*, 12 June 1937; *Le Petit Journal*, 17 July 1937.
130 For the PSF's position in comparison to the rest of the French right, see
    Micaud, *French Right and Nazi Germany*, 123–5, 130–1.
131 Thomas, "Effectifs du Parti Social Français," 71–2.
132 For a case study, see Conway, "Extreme Right in Inter-War Francophone
    Belgium."

CHAPTER FIVE

1 Werth, *Twilight of France*, 204.
2 AD Loire-Atlantique 1M 470, prefect, 25 May 1938; CAOM 1K75, police
    spéciale (Algiers), 9 April 1938.

3 AD Gard 1M 715, prefect, 27 January 1938; AD Somme 99M 165, commissaire spécial (Amiens), 29 June 1938, *Journal d'Amiens*, 2 July 1938, report by capitaine Holleville, 5 July 1938.

4 *Le Flambeau d'Indochine*, 1 February 1939; PSF *Bulletin d'informations*, nos. 68, 77–9, 100 (21 February, 29 June, 7, 14 July 1938, 29 June 1939).

5 There is a good overview in Dard, *Années 30*, 184–92.

6 Berstein, *Histoire du Parti Radical*, 2: 538–58.

7 Jackson, *France: The Dark Years*, 97–111.

8 Machefer, "Parti Social Français," in Rémond and Bourdin, eds., *France et les Français*, 310–13; *Le Petit Journal*, 11, 13, 17 April 1938; *Samedi*, 16 April 1938.

9 Machefer, "Le Parti Social Français," in Rémond and Bourdin, eds., *France et les Français*, 313.

10 Ibid., 313; *Le Petit Journal*, 14 October 1938; PSF *Bulletin d'informations*, no. 88 (17 October 1938).

11 AD Loire-Atlantique 1M 470, commissaire central, 23 December 1938.

12 *Le Petit Journal*, 16, 19 November 1938; Machefer, "Parti Social Français," in Rémond and Bourdin, eds., *France et les Français*, 318–19; PSF: *Bulletin d'informations*, no. 92 (16 January 1939).

13 Nobécourt, *Colonel de La Rocque*, 648; Howlett, "Croix de Feu," 307–8.

14 *Je suis partout*, 15, 22, 29 July, 5, 12, 19, 26 August, 2 September 1938. Compared to some other right-wing papers, *Je suis partout* was not quite so hostile to the PSF. This outlook may have been due to Paul Creyssel's links to some of its staff; see Dioudonnat, *Je suis partout*, 90, 179–84.

15 AD Marne 30M 147, commissaire divisionnaire (Reims), 20 January, commissaire central, 19 May 1939.

16 AN 451AP 127, "Rapport sur la fédération de Tunisie," n.d. but late 1938 – early 1939; "Opinion des musulmans tunisiens sur le PSF," 12 January 1939

17 *Le Petit Journal*, 16 February, 28 March 1939.

18 Berstein, *Histoire du Parti Radical*, 2: 584; AD Somme 99M 165, commissaire spécial, 17 April 1939; commissaire de police, 27 March 1939; La Rocque, *Paix ou guerre?* 3.

19 Machefer, "Parti Social Français," in Rémond and Bourdin, eds. *France et les Français*, 320–1; Berstein, *Histoire du Parti Radical*, 2: 584. Daladier later claimed that he had tried to contact La Rocque; see Daladier, *Prison Journal*, 261–2, entry for 6 February 1944.

20 Machefer, "Parti Social Français," in Rémond and Bourdin, eds., *France et les Français*, 308–9; Howlett, "Croix de Feu," 307–8; Berstein, *Histoire du Parti Radical*, 2: 472, 583–4.

21 *Le Petit Journal*, 28 July 1939.

22 *Le PSF montcellin*, June 1939 (emphasis in original).

23 *Le PSF creusotin*, 1 April, 15 July 1939; PSF, *Fédération de la Loire: Bulletin fédéral de la documentation*, 27 March 1939; AD Aisne 1M 19, commissaire spécial (Laon), 27 May 1939.

24 Jackson, *Popular Front in France*, 220; Thomas, "Effectifs du Parti Social Français," 70–1.

25 Jackson, *Popular Front in France*, 219–20; Bourne and Watt, eds., *British Documents*, 23: 282, doc. 102, Phipps to Halifax, 13 March 1939; *Agir*, May 1939.

26 *Le Flambeau*, 6, 13 March, 15 May 1937; Howlett, "Croix de Feu," 324–6; Goguel, "Élections législatives," in Rémond and Bourdin, eds., *Édouard Daladier, chef de gouvernement*, 48. See also Austin, "Conservative Right and the Far Right," in Blinkhorn, ed., *Fascists and Conservatives*, 184–8.

27 AN 451AP 120, "Le PSF et les Radicaux."

28 *L'Action française*, 11 May, 12, 23/24 December 1938; Petit, *De La Rocque est-il un chef?*

29 Brunet, *Jacques Doriot*, 289–90; PSF: *Bulletin d'informations*, no. 71 (23 March 1938); *L'Émancipation nationale*, 16 July 1938; *Le Petit Journal*, 17 May 1938; CAOM Oran 70, commissaire divisionnaire (Oran), 11 May 1938; AD Alpes-Maritimes 4M 543, commissaire divisionnaire (Nice), commissaire central (Cannes), 8 May 1938; AD Alpes-Maritimes 5M 542, directeur de la police d'état, 29 March 1938.

30 Passmore, "Boy-Scouting for Grown-Ups?" 555–6.

31 Irvine, *French Conservatism in Crisis*, 150–1, 154–5; AN 451AP 120, Barrachin to Ottavi, 24 February 1939.

32 AD Alpes-Maritimes 4M 542, directeur de la police d'état, 13 November 1938; Howlett, "Croix de Feu," 327–9; Thomas, "Parti Social Français et le monde militaire," in Forcade, Duhamel, and Vial, eds., *Militaires en République*, 423–4.

33 *Le Flambeau des Vosges*, June 1939.

34 AN 451AP 120, Barrachin to Ottavi, 24 February 1939; Burrin, *Dérive fasciste*, 272.

35 AD Alpes-Maritimes 4M 542, directeur de la police d'état, 7 January, 3 March 1939; Schor, "Parti Populaire Français," 120; AN 451AP 119, note, 10 July 1939.

36 Goguel, "Élections législatives," in Rémond and Bourdin, eds., *Edouard Daladier, chef de gouvernement*, 51–2, 284, though Goguel does not note that Bounin's victory benefited the PSF.

37 AN 451AP 120, Barrachin to Ottavi, 24 February 1939. Information on the 1936 elections can be found in *Le Temps*, 28 April, 5 May 1936.

38 AN 451AP 120, Barrachin to Ottavi, 24 February 1939.

39 Howlett, "Croix de Feu," 324–6; Weng, "Historique et la doctrine," 88–9.

40 AN 451AP 120, Barrachin to Ottavi, 24 February 1939; AP D3 M2 17, election poster.

41 Burrin, *Dérive fasciste*, 274–5.

42 For information, see Jolly, *Dictionnaire des parlementaires français*; Larmour, *French Radical Party*; and Berstein, *Histoire du Parti Radical*.

43 AN 451AP 120, Barrachin to Ottavi, 24 February 1939. Information on these deputies comes from Jolly, *Dictionnaire des parlementaires*; Irvine, *French Conservatism in Crisis*; and Wileman, "Alliance Républicaine Démocratique," 384–6.

44 AN 451AP 120, Barrachin to Ottavi, 24 February 1939.

45 Tixier-Vignancour, *Des Républiques, des justices et des hommes*, 275, gives the incredible estimate of nearly 200 seats. See also Howlett, "Croix de Feu," 335.

46 Peyrefitte, "Premières sondages d'opinion," in Rémond and Bourdin, *Édouard Daladier, chef du gouvernement*, 276–7; Howlett, "Croix de Feu," 335.

47 AN 451AP 120, Barrachin to Ottavi, 24 February 1939.

48 Paxton, *French Peasant Fascism*, 54–5.

49 *Le Petit Journal*, 29 June, 8, 9 August 1939. For the significance of La Rocque's decision not to run in elections, see Leschi, "Étrange Cas La Rocque," in Dobry, ed., *Mythe de l'allergie*, 176–7.

50 *Parti Social Français: Une mystique, une programme*, 3–4.

51 *Le Petit Journal*, 12 September 1937.

52 *Parti Social Français: Une mystique, une programme*, 19–21.

53 Ibid., 19–20 (passage emphasized in original), 39–41; Kalman, "Vers un ordre économique nouveau," 263.

54 AN 451AP 124, Louis Escande and Pierre Kula, "Organisation de la profession: ce qui a été fait dans l'industrie du bâtiment et des travaux publics," December 1937, 35 pp., quotation on 30.

55 *Le Flambeau*, 2 January, 20 March, 22 May 1937.

56 *L'Ouvrier libre*, May 1938; *Le Flambeau* 2 January, 13 March, 24 April 1937; *Le Petit Journal*, 21 February 1938.

57 *Le Flambeau*, 26 Sept 1936; *Le Paysan sauvera la France avec le PSF*, 16–18, 27–9.

58 AD Nord 68J 216, pamphlet by de Nadillac, *Conseils sur la propagande électorale dans les milieux agricoles*, 3–4.

59 Barrachin, *Le PSF devant le pays*; PSF: *Bulletin d'informations*, no. 19 (16 February 1937) (passage emphasized in original).

60 PSF, *Bulletin d'informations*, no. 81 (1 July 1938), supplement, schéma de conférence: "Le PSF et le problème du chomage"; Caron, "Antisemitic

Revival in France in the 1930s," 42n63, 44n73; *Le Flambeau*, 31 October 1936; *Le Petit Journal*, 28 June 1939.

61 Passmore, *From Liberalism to Fascism*, 270–4; AN 451AP 124, "Note concernant l'aide morale à apporter aux campagnes et l'action du PSF dans les milieux paysans," n.d.

62 See Kalman, "Vers un ordre économique nouveau," 266–8; for the quotation, see *Parti Social Français: Une mystique, une programme*, 9.

63 *Parti Social Français: Une mystique, une programme*, 31–2 (passage emphasized in original); for a discussion of the incident, see *La Volonté bretonne*, 5 February 1938.

64 *Parti Social Français: Une mystique, une programme*, 33–4.

65 *Le Flambeau du Sud-Ouest*, 17 July 1937.

66 Vallin, *Aux Femmes du PSF* (passage emphasized in original); *Parti Social Français: Une mystique, une programme*, 38–9; *Le Flambeau*, 1, 22, 29 May 1937.

67 *La Liberté du Maine*, April 1938.

68 PSF, *Bulletin d'informations*, no. 70 (14 March 1938), supplement, "Schéma des conférences – la retour de la mère au foyer."

69 AN 451AP 133, Casanova to de Préval, 31 July 1939.

70 *La Flamme des Deux-Sèvres*, April 1939; *Le Petit Journal*, 13 May 1939.

71 AD Gard 1M 715, commissaire de police, 1 July 1939.

72 *Le Petit Journal*, 28 February 1938.

73 *Le Petit Journal*, 4 December 1938 (emphasis in original); the report had been prepared by Stanislas Devaud.

74 *Le Petit Journal*, 11 November 1937, 8 July, 1 March 1938.

75 AN 451AP 114, *L'Étudiant social* no.6 (October 1938); *Le Petit Journal*, 8 July, 4 December 1938; AN 451AP 115, Jean Daujat, "L'Université dans l'État Social Français," report to the national congress of PSF students, 27–28 February 1938; *L'Étudiant social* no.10 (February 1939).

76 See Lebovics, *True France*.

77 *Le Petit Journal*, 6 March 1938; PSF: *Bulletin d'informations*, no. 18 (9 February 1937).

78 *Le Flambeau de l'Isère*, 18 February 1938; *La Volonté bretonne*, 5 March 1939; Goodfellow, *Between the Swastika and the Cross of Lorraine*, 140–2.

79 *Le Flambeau*, 11 July 1936.

80 CAOM B3 635, police spéciale (Constantine), 23 October 1938; *Le Flambeau*, 13 March, 5 June 1937.

81 *Le Petit Journal*, 13 February 1938. For a study of interwar colonial ideology, see Conklin, *Mission to Civilize*.

82 CAOM Oran 70, commissaire divisionnaire (Oran), 22 April 1938; CAOM B3 635, police spéciale (Constantine), 23 October 1938.

83 Millman, *Question juive*, 258–64; AD Oise Mp 5134, subprefect (Senlis), 15 October 1938.

84 Millman, *Question juive*, 259; Caron, *Uneasy Asylum*, 276–7; *Le Petit Journal*, 23 April 1939; *Journal officiel*, sessions of 10, 14 March 1939, 902–4, 955–7.

85 PSF: *Bulletin d'informations*, no. 81 (1 July 1938), "Schema de conférence no. 10 – le PSF et le problème du chomage."

86 Caron, "'Jewish Question,'" in Alexander, ed., *French History*, 186–7; PSF: *Bulletin d'informations*, no. 90 (22 November 1938).

87 Taguieff, *Illusion populiste*, 107–45; Winock, "Populismes français," though Winock's characterization of the PSF is somewhat different from the one offered here.

88 *Le Petit Journal*, 28 February 1938; Veuillot, *La Rocque et son parti*, 61, 86–93.

89 AD Loire-Atlantique 1M 470, commissaire central (Nantes), 23 December 1938; *Le Petit Journal*, 5 March 1939.

90 Veuillot, *La Rocque et son parti*, 88–93; see also La Rocque's editorial in *Le Petit Journal*, 10 August 1939.

91 AN 3W 138, dossier on Paul Creyssel, 29 June 1946, 6.

92 Quoted in Micaud, *French Right and Nazi Germany*, 139 (Micaud's translation).

93 *Le Petit Journal*, 27 February, 20 March 1938.

94 *Le Petit Journal*, 11 September 1938.

95 *Le Petit Journal*, 26 May, 8 July 1938; AN 451AP 107, "Documentation des propagandistes – le problème tchéchoslovaque," 1 October 1938.

96 *Le Petit Journal*, 30 September 1938.

97 *Samedi*, 12 February 1938; *Le Petit Journal*, 19 July 1938.

98 *Le Petit Journal*, 25 March, 30 July 1939.

99 *La Flamme*, 31 March 1939; *Le Petit Journal*, 15 July, 2 August 1939.

100 *Le Petit Journal*, 5 January 1939.

101 *Le Petit Journal*, 30 July 1939. While the quotation does not specify what sort of accords might be signed, in a speech given in April 1939 La Rocque had declared that an economic agreement with the Soviets was the only arrangement he considered feasible; see La Rocque, *Paix ou guerre?*

102 *Le Petit Journal*, 23, 28 August, 18 September 1939.

103 For the criticism of Mandel, see *Le Petit Journal*, 8 July 1938; for the reaction to Flandin, see CAOM Oran 70, commissaire divisionnaire (Oran), 4 November 1938.

104 Micaud, *French Right and Nazi Germany*, 205–7.

105 *Le Petit Journal*, 16 May 1939.

106 *Le Petit Journal*, 5 February 1939.

107 *Le Petit Journal*, 31 August 1937.

108 *Le Petit Journal*, 10 February, 13 August 1939.

109 CAOM B3 635, commissaire de police (Saint-Arnaud), 19 April 1939; *Le Petit Journal*, 18 June 1939.

110 *Le Petit Journal*, 22 July 1939.

111 *Le Petit Journal*, 11 August 1939.

112 Berstein, *Histoire du Parti Radical*, 2: 588.

CHAPTER SIX

1 *Le Petit Journal*, 9 August 1937.

2 *Le Volontaire '36*, 16 July 1937, 1 June 1938; Passmore, *From Liberalism to Fascism*, 249.

3 For an analysis of these materials, see Thomas, "Effectifs du Parti Social Français."

4 In the Doubs, for example, the PSF was slow to get underway; see AN F7 13033, prefect (Doubs), 25 November. For Algeria see, for example, CAOM B3 327, sûreté (Constantine), 7, 20 July 1936.

5 Thomas, "Effectifs du Parti Social Français," 69–70.

6 Howlett, "Croix de Feu," 210–11; Machefer, "Parti Social Français en 1936–1937," 74; USNA RG 59 851.00/1661, report by Wilson, 6 April 1937.

7 Howlett, "Croix de Feu," 286–9; Thomas, "Effectifs du Parti Social Français," 71–2. Nobécourt, *Colonel de La Rocque*, 386, suggests a total of 1.5–2 million, though how he arrives at this figure is unclear.

8 SFIO membership reached 200,000 in June 1936; the Communists surpassed it with 320,000 the following year. See Wolikow, *Front Populaire en France*, 159–60.

9 *La Flamme vendéenne*, 1/15 August 1939; Prévosto, "Fédération du Nord," 15–16, 63–4.

10 Thomas, "Effectifs du Parti Social Français," 75–6.

11 *Le Flambeau*, 21 November 1936; Howlett, "Croix de Feu," 236–7.

12 *Le Flambeau*, 13 July 1937, shows that six of the PSF's first seven departmental congresses were held in northern and eastern France.

13 Jankowski, *Communism and Collaboration*, 21; Cantier, *Algérie sous le régime de Vichy*, 230; *La Flamme* (Algiers), 10 March 1939; AN 451AP 120, Barrachin to Ottavi, 24 February 1939.

14 Thomas, "Effectifs du Parti Social Français," 75–6; Chouvel, "Croix de Feu," 235–43; Machefer, "Parti Social Français en 1936–1937," 74; Florin, "Des Croix de Feu au Parti Social Français," 243–4.

15 *La Volonté du Centre*, 23 October 1937.

16 See, for example, AD Alpes-Maritimes 4M 542, directeur de police d'état (Nice), 30 January 1939; a similar observation appears in AD Marne 30M 146, commissaire spécial (Châlons-sur-Marne), 8 February 1938.

17 AN F7 14817, prefect of police (Paris), report, January 1937; AD Marne 30M 146, commissaire central (Reims), 19 December 1938; AD Alpes-Maritimes 4M 542, commissaire divisionnaire de police spéciale, 4 March 1938; Machefer, "Tardieu et La Rocque," 18–19; Prévosto, "Fédération du Nord," 52–4, 63–4; Florin, "Des Croix de Feu au Parti Social Français," 245–7.

18 *Le Flambeau*, 5 December 1936, 9 January, 27 February, 17 April 1937.

19 AD Alpes-Maritimes 4M 542, commissaire spécial (Cannes), 21 July 1937, commissaire divisionnaire, 28 August 1937, 29 March 1938; AD Hérault 1M 1119, directeur de la police d'état, 13 January 1938; commissaire spécial (Sète), 4 January 1937; Chouvel, "Croix de Feu et le PSF en Haute-Vienne," 83–6.

20 Paxton, *French Peasant Fascism*, 158–9; *La Volonté bretonne*, 20 April 1937; Chouvel, "Croix de Feu et le PSF en Haute-Vienne," 220–1; Prévosto, "Fédération du Nord," 51–2; AD Gard 1M 715, commissaire de police (Beaucaire), 13 April 1937.

21 Passmore, *From Liberalism to Fascism*, 277–89.

22 Howlett, "Croix de Feu," 283–5; Thomas, "Parti Social Français et le monde militaire," in Forcade, Duhamel, and Vial, eds., *Militaires en République*, 417–24.

23 AN F7 14817, inspecteurs de police mobile (Saint-Brieuc), 21 October 1936; Thomas, "Parti Social Français et le monde militaire," in Forcade, Duhamel, and Vial, eds., *Militaires en République*, 425.

24 This information is derived from the *Dictionnaire des parlementaires français*.

25 Chouvel, "Croix de Feu et le PSF en Haute-Vienne," 216–17; Prévosto, "Fédération du Nord," 45–6; Thomas, "Effectifs du Parti Social Français," 66.

26 Passmore, "Class, Gender, and Populism," in Atkin and Tallett, eds., *Right in France*, 190–1; CHEVS LR4, Vernon *fichier* (figures compiled by Gilles de La Rocque).

27 AD Loire-Atlantique 1M 470, commissaire central, 29 June 1938; AP 212/69/1 article 152, "Perquisition au journal *Le Flambeau*," seal no. 2, "Bordereaux des adhésions PSF," 7, 9, 10, 16, 17, 18 July 1936; Prévosto, "Fédération du Nord," 41; AD Alpes-Maritimes 4M 542, commissaire spécial (Cannes), 21 July 1937; Ferragu, "Croix de Feu et le PSF en Indre-et-Loire," 18; Thomas, "Droites, les femmes et le mouvement associatif," in Andrieu, Le Béguec, and Tartakowsky, eds., *Associations et champ politique*, 527–8.

28 Vallin, "Parti Social Francais," 212–13; AP 212/69/1, article 153, deposition by Octave Cornet, December 1936; *Samedi*, 19 June 1937.

29 Thomas, "Parti Social Français," 42–5; Nobécourt, *Colonel de La Rocque*, 430–2, 437–8, 483; Howlett, "Croix de Feu," 210–11.

30 AD Marne 30M 146, commissaire central, 19 December 1938; Austin, "Conservative Right and the Far Right," in Blinkhorn, ed., *Fascists and Conservatives*, 190.

31 AD Marne 30M 144, commissaire divisionnaire (Reims), 20 February 1937.

32 This was perceived to be the case in Algeria, for example. See Koerner, "Extrême Droite en Oranie," 593–4.

33 AD Hérault 1M 1119, commissaire spécial (Sète), 4 January 1937; AD Alpes-Maritimes 4M 542, commissaire spécial (Cannes), 21 July 1937; directeur de la police d'état, 13 January 1938; commissaire divisionnaire, 4, 29 March 1938.

34 Prévosto, "Fédération du Nord," 15–16; Florin, "Des Croix de Feu au Parti Social Français," 243–4; AN F7 14817, prefect of police (Paris), January 1937.

35 CAOM B3 327, sûreté (Constantine), 7 July 1936; AD Oise Mp 5299, commissaire spécial (Beauvais), 20 January 1939; AD Vendée 4M 413, commissaire de police (Fontenay-le-Comte), 21 October 1936.

36 AD Aisne 4Z 6, commissaire de police (Guise), 12 February 1937; Goodfellow, *Between the Swastika and the Cross of Lorraine*, 144–5; AD Yvelines 4M2 66, prefect (Seine-et-Oise), 20 January 1937.

37 Machefer, "Tardieu et La Rocque," 18.

38 Leleu, *Géographie des élections françaises*, 216, map 8; Barral, *Département de l'Isère*, 335, 512–17; Chouvel, "Croix de Feu et le PSF en Haute-Vienne," 51–7, 62–3, 74–8; *Le Flambeau*, 13 March 1937.

39 APP B/a 1952, report, 10 February 1938.

40 CAOM F405, sûreté départementale (Algiers), 14 September 1936; CAOM 1K75, sûreté départementale (Algiers), 10 June 1937; AD Loire-Atlantique 1M 470, subprefect (Saint-Nazaire), 2 April 1938.

41 See Kershaw, *Hitler 1889–1936*, 380–91.

42 PSF: *Bulletin de la section de Lunéville*, 29 November 1936; AD Nord 68J 104, "Équipes Volantes de Propagande," n.d.; AP 212/69/1, article 149, PSF local committee for Paris's 18th arrondissement to La Rocque, 5 October 1936; AN F7 15284, "Note sur l'existence légale du PSF," 17 May 1945.

43 Howlett, "Croix de Feu," 208–9.

44 Ibid., 207–9; AN 451AP 116, copy of pamphlet *Union Interfédérale du Parti Social Français: Statuts*; Nobécourt, *Colonel de La Rocque*, 641–2.

45 For a breakdown of attendees of the first congress, see CHEVS LR3, minutes notebook no. 1, 19–25.

46 BN, *Croix de Feu, Parti Social Français: Tracts politiques, 1934–1939*, doc. no. 33, *Parti Social Français section de Versailles-Montreuil: Bulletin de liaison*, no. 3 (January 1939).

47 APP B/a 1952, note, 11 December 1938; Howlett, "Croix de Feu," 188–90; Passmore, *From Liberalism to Fascism*, 277–8.

48 AN 451AP 116, comité exécutif, 3 February 1938; AN F7 12966, report, 29 June 1938; AN 451AP 106, circular, 21 June 1939; AP 212/69/1, article 151, commissaire central (Rouen), 5 December 1936; CAOM 1K75, police spéciale (Algiers), 17 March 1938; Howlett, "Croix de Feu," 293–5.

49 CAOM Oran 70, commissaire divsionnaire (Oran), 5 November 1938; AN 451AP 120, letter from A.A. Bachy, September 1938; "Note pour M. Barrachin," 14 April 1939; Bachy, "Ristourne des fédérations," 10 May 1939.

50 AN 451AP 87, secrétaire générale pour l'Action Sociale, 14 September 1936.

51 AN 451AP 87, "Allocution de Mlle de Préval," 26 October 1936; AD Nord 68J 107, circular by Garrigoux, 1 April 1937; AD Nord 68J 164, circular, 24 April 1937.

52 AN 451AP 135, memorandum, 29 June 1939; Garrigoux, *Parti Social Français et l'Action Sociale*, 6.

53 AN 451AP 131, reports on section activities for Clermont-Ferrand, 20 December 1938, and Pau and Colmar, both n.d. but probably fall 1938; AN 451AP 133, Danner to de Préval, 25 April 1938; Rymell, "Militants and Militancy," 78–81.

54 Garrigoux, *Parti Social Français et l'Action Sociale*, 7–9; Passmore, "Planting the Tricolor," 833–5; see also AN 451AP 134, Mlle Fouché, "Extraits du rapport sur le rôle de l'auxiliaire sociale," presented at the PSF's social congress, 16–17 May 1939.

55 PSF: *Bulletin d'informations*, no. 52 (14 October 1937).

56 For speeches by Casanova, see *L'Heure française*, 15 December 1936; AD Gard 1M 715, commissaire central (Nîmes), 7 July 1937; commissaire de police, 1 July 1939; AD Alpes-Maritimes 4M 542, police d'état, 19 October 1936, 31 January, 25 April 1938.

57 *La Liberté du Maine*, June 1937; *Le Flambeau des Vosges*, July 1939; Rymell, "Militants and Militancy," 76–85; PSF: *Bulletin d'informations*, no. 52 (14 October 1937), no. 59 (9 December 1937).

58 AN 451AP 133, Casanova to de Préval, 31 July 1939.

59 Ibid.

60 AD Nord 68J 163, Fédération du Nord to Marcel Clairin, 24 June 1939; AD Nord 68J 216, *Service social*, no. 11 (May–June 1939), "Organisation de l'Action Civique," n.d. but probably 1939.

61 AN 451AP 135, memorandum, 29 June 1939.

62 AD Nord 68J 164, "Groupes d'Action Sociale: règlement," [n.d.]; Rymell, "Militants and Militancy," 183.

63 AN 451AP 131, Groupe Féminin d'Action Sociale (Pau), "Rapport sur l'activité du Groupe du 1 Octobre 1937 au 30 September 1938"; AN 451AP 133, PSF, Service Social: Travail-Famille-Patrie, no. 10 (March–April 1939).

64 BN, Croix de Feu, Parti Social Français: Tracts politiques, 1934–39, doc. no. 33, PSF, section de Versailles-Montreuil: Bulletin de liaison, no. 3 (January 1939).

65 Le PSF Creusotin, 15 July 1939.

66 Le Flambeau, 26 June 1937; Weng, "Historique et la doctrine," 93–4; Le Flambeau des Vosges, August 1939; AD Nord 68J 164, "Colonies de vacances PSF été 1937"; "Colonies de vacances 1938."

67 AN 451AP 131, Garrigoux to déléguées regionales et fédérales, 7 April 1938.

68 Prévosto, "Fédération du Nord," 133; AD Nord 68J 164, "Colonies de vacances PSF été 1937"; "Colonies de vacances 1938"; "Colonies de vacances," 1 May 1939.

69 Le Flambeau, 24 October, 5, 12 December 1936; Rymell, "Militants and Militancy," 37–40, 43, 47, 59; Le Flambeau de l'Isère, 1 June 1939.

70 L'Étudiant social, April–May 1938; Pourquoi s'en faire? August–September 1937.

71 AD Nord 68J 216, pamphlet, Deuxième congrès national des étudiants PSF; Pourquoi s'en faire, March 1938.

72 Le Flambeau, 15 February 1936; Rymell, "Militants and Militancy," 41–3, 55–8, for the survey, though my conclusions differ from his; Caron, "Antisemitic Revival in France," 33, 37, 41–9.

73 Coutrot, "Youth Movements," 29–35; Jeal, Baden-Powell, 409–23. There is a more critical assessment in Rosenthal, Character Factory.

74 Ory, Belle illusion, 783–4.

75 Machefer, "Syndicats Professionnels Français," 104–9; AD Nord 68J 167, "Directives générales à donner aux bureaux d'études syndicales pour la formation des syndicats professionnels."

76 AD Nord 68J 167, Bureau d'Études Syndicales, 13 November 1936, "Propagande et controverse," 7 October 1937; "Le Syndicalisme," 18 November 1936; Syndicats professionnels: Bulletin d'information de la section locale de Tourcoing, no. 2 (February 1939), no. 3 (March–April 1939).

77 Machefer, "Syndicats Professionnels Français," 91–4; AD Nord 68J 167, "Élections des délégués du 15 au 31 mai 1937," 7 June 1937. Zdatny, "Collaboration or Resistance," 755, argues that the SPF grossly exaggerated its strength.

78 Machefer, "Syndicats Professionnels Français," 93–6, 98–100, 102–4; Ferragu, "Croix de Feu et le PSF en Indre-et-Loire," 39; Chouvel, "Croix de

Feu et le PSF en Haute-Vienne," 130; Howlett, "Croix de Feu," 218; AD
Marne 30M 146, commissaire général (Reims), report, 20 June 1938.

79 Machefer, "Syndicats Professionnels Français," 96–8; Prévosto, "Fédération
du Nord," 153–4; Chouvel, "Croix de Feu et le PSF en Haute-Vienne," 130;
Howlett, "Croix de Feu," 220.

80 Passmore, *From Liberalism to Fascism*, 284–95; Rudaux, *Croix de Feu*, 193;
L'Ouvrier libre, 12 March 1939.

81 AD Oise Mp 5133, commissaire de police (Senlis), 16 March 1937; AD Alpes-
Maritimes 4M 542, police d'état (Nice), 13 January 1938.

82 AN 451AP 124, report by Louis Escande and Pierre Kula, "Organisation de la
profession: ce qui a été fait dans l'industrie du bâtiment et des travaux
publics," December 1937; "Profession organisée," 14 January 1938;
Groupements professionels du bâtiment et des travaux publics de la région
parisienne, "Ordre du jour," 19 March 1938.

83 AD Nord 68J 168, Étienne Motte-Flipo, Centre d'Information et de
Propagande PSF dans les Milieux Patronaux, Intellectuels et Bourgeois, 3
December 1938; Motte, circular, 17 December 1938, délégué du groupement
patronal to Georges Petit, 3 June 1939.

84 *Le Petit Journal*, 20 May 1939.

85 Howlett, "Croix de Feu," 216; AD Yvelines 4M2 67, sûreté, 11 December 1937.

86 Ferragu, "Croix de Feu et le PSF en Indre-et-Loire," 40; Machefer, "Syndicats
Professionnels Français," 102–4, 111.

87 AN BB18 3048/2, Brigadier Schmitt and Inspector Valentini, report, 31 July
1936.

88 Rymell, "Militants and Militancy," 179–81; Passmore, "Planting the Tricolor," 836–7.

89 AN 451AP 135, memorandum, 29 June 1939; Rymell, "Militants and Militancy," 181–3.

90 AD Marne 30M 146, commissaire divisionnaire (Reims), 20 December 1938;
Murray, "French Workers' Sports Movement"; *Le Flambeau*, 22 May 1937;
La Volonté du Centre, 25 March 1939.

91 AN 451AP 87, "Allocution de Mlle de Préval," 26 October 1936; Garrigoux,
Centres sociaux, 14–15.

92 Holt, *Sport and Society in Modern France*, 208–10.

93 Ory, *Belle Illusion*, 743–7; Reynolds, *France between the Wars*, 72–5.

94 *Le Flambeau*, 18, 25 July, 10, 31 October, 21 November 1936.

95 *Le Flambeau*, 8 August, 10 October 1936; AD Nord 68J 171, circular by
Mermoz, 10 October 1936.

96 *Gringoire*, 25 December 1936; see also Nobécourt, *Colonel de La Rocque*,
629–30.

97 *Le Flambeau*, 12, 26 December 1936, 16 January 1937; Mermoz, *Mes Vols*, 222–5; AN 451AP 99, circular by La Rocque, 26 March 1937; *Le Petit Journal*, March, 25 June, 8 December 1938.

98 *Marianne*, 16 December 1936; *Le Figaro*, 31 December 1936; *L'Humanité*, 10 December 1936.

99 Chadeau, *Mermoz*, 297–301; Facon, "Image des aviateurs," 96–8; Mortane, *Mermoz*, 12, 20, 71–4, 92–4.

100 Wohl, "Par la voie des airs," 54–5; Chadeau, *Mermoz*, 310–14; Kessel, *Mermoz*, 230–1, 310, 407, 414, 416–17.

101 AN 451AP 100*bis*, *Le Démocrate de l'Aisne*, 26 July 1939.

102 Rudaux, *Croix de Feu*, 207–8; *Le Flambeau*, 12 June 1937; *Samedi du Poitou*, 18 June 1938; Reynolds, *France between the Wars*, 73.

103 AN 451AP 99, "Rapport de Chateland, Casanova et Lebatteux sur le fonctionnement et l'activité des aéro-clubs et de la Fédération Jean-Mermoz," n.d.; "Notes sur la comptabilité de la Fédération Jean Mermoz," 16 June 1938.

104 AN 451AP 99, "Constitution de la Fédération Jean Mermoz," n.d.; "Buts de la Fédération Jean Mermoz," n.d.; confidential report to PSF executive comittee, 8 March 1937; *Le Flambeau*, 6 March, 12 June 1937.

105 APP B/a 1952, report, 15 November 1938; Nobécourt, *Colonel de La Rocque*, 659–60.

106 Nobécourt, *Colonel de La Rocque*, 659–60; PSF: *Bulletin d'informations*, no. 98 (19 May 1939).

107 *Le Petit Journal*, 3, 7 May 1939.

108 *Le Petit Journal*, 14 July 1939. For more on right-wing views of this event, see Tumblety, "Civil Wars of the Mind," 406–7.

109 *Le Petit Journal*, 14 July 1939.

110 Passmore, *From Liberalism to Fascism*, 258–61; Paxton, *Anatomy of Fascism*, 70–1; Jackson, *France: The Dark Years*, 78.

111 See *Le Petit Journal*, 10 April, 29 June, 4, 9 July 1939.

112 *Le Petit Journal*, 28 August 1939.

113 Jackson, *France: The Dark Years*, 43–64.

114 Burrin, *Dérive fasciste*, 291–312; Wileman, "P.-E. Flandin and the Alliance," 163; Berstein, *Histoire du Parti Radical*, 2: 588.

115 Jackson, *France: The Dark Years*, 112–13.

CHAPTER SEVEN

1 Bédarida, "Vichy et la crise de la conscience française," in Azéma and Bédarida, eds., *Le Régime de Vichy*, 93–4; see also Hoffmann, *Decline or*

Renewal? 3–25; Munholland, "Wartime France," 810–21; Peschanski, "Vichy Singular and Plural," in Fishman et al., eds., *France at War*, 107–24; and Burrin, "Ideology of the National Revolution," in Arnold, ed., *Development of the Radical Right*, 135–52.

2 Irvine, "Domestic Politics and the Fall of France," in Blatt, ed., *French Defeat of 1940*, 87–92.

3 CHEVS LR3, notebook no. 1, "Conseil national extraordinaire du 22 Avril 1939," 137.

4 Rossi-Landi, *Drôle de guerre*, 16–18.

5 La Rocque and La Rocque, *La Rocque tel qu'il était*, 168–9; Nobécourt, *Colonel de La Rocque*, 668–71.

6 La Rocque and La Rocque, *La Rocque tel qu'il était*, 168; AD Nord 68J 107, La Rocque, circular, 13 February 1940.

7 AN 451AP 134, prefect of Seine to president of ADP, 18 September 1939; AN 451AP 123, "Les filiales sociales du PSF," n.d. but late 1944–early 1945; AD Gard 1M 715, H. du Moulin to La Rocque, 8 December 1940.

8 *Le Petit Journal*, 18 September 1939; *Journal officiel*, 14 December 1939, 2302.

9 AN 451AP 118, La Rocque to Daladier, 8 November 1939 [the date of the report itself is 4 November]; AN 451AP 118, La Rocque to Lebrun, Clapier, Gamelin et al., 7 December 1939.

10 Crémieux-Brilhac, *Français de l'an 40*, 1: 212–15. For the voting records of the PSF deputies (though Jacques Bounin is incorrectly described as non-PSF), see Rossi-Landi, *Drôle de guerre*, annex 5B, 213–25.

11 See, for example, Young, *France and the Origins*, 133–4, 136–7.

12 *Journal officiel*, 14 December 1939, 2278–84; *Le Petit Journal*, 11 December 1939.

13 Imlay, *Facing the Second World War*, 174–5.

14 Crémieux-Brilhac, *Français de l'an 40*, 1: 346–60, 385–92; Jackson, *France: The Dark Years*, 113–18.

15 Imlay, *Facing the Second World War*, 178–81; see also Crémieux-Brilhac, *Français de l'an 40*, 1: 215, 223–5, 241–4, and Irvine, *French Conservatism in Crisis*, 205–6.

16 Crémieux-Brilhac, *Français de l'an 40*, 1: 223, 225–6, 241–2; *Le Petit Journal*, 10 January 1940; APP B/a 1952, report, 22 February 1940.

17 AN 451AP 127, "La Rocque en Finlande," n.d.; *La Documentation mensuelle du PSF*, 11 May 1940.

18 For evidence of the dislocation caused by the onset of war, see Melchior-Bonnet, *Lettres du temps de guerre*, 44, entry for 14 December 1939; on the funding drive, see AD Nord 68J 107, PSF Service Financier, "La souscription

du patron," 8 March 1940; on claims that activity was vibrant, see *La Documentation mensuelle du PSF*, 6 April 1940.

19 AN 451AP 127, La Rocque, "Le gouvernement français et l'affaire finlandaise," n.d.; Rossi-Landi, *Drôle de guerre*, 43, 51–5; see also Imlay, *Facing the Second World War*, 176.

20 Imlay, *Facing the Second World War*, 181–4, quotation on 182.

21 Nobécourt, *Colonel de La Rocque*, 676–7.

22 Crémieux-Brilhac, *Français de l'an 40*, 1: 253–5; APP B/a 1952, report, 6 April 1940; CHEVS LR3 notebook no. 1, "Conseil national extraordinaire du 7 Avril 1940," 144–5; APP B/a 1952, report, 1 April 1940.

23 Imlay, *Facing the Second World War*, 183–5.

24 AN 451AP 118, La Rocque to Reynaud, 8 May 1940; Nobécourt, *Colonel de La Rocque*, 680–1.

25 La Rocque and La Rocque, *La Rocque tel qu'il était*, 172–7; Jeanneney, *Journal politique*, 61–2, 73–4, entries for 3, 16 June 1940; Nobécourt, *Colonel de La Rocque*, 683–9.

26 Nobécourt, *Colonel de La Rocque*, 685–96, 699–701; Machefer, "Sur quelques aspects," 37–8.

27 On the Bergery declaration, see Irvine, *French Conservatism in Crisis*, 208; Jackson, *France: The Dark Years*, 143. Wieviorka, *Orphelins de la République*, 109–39, provides a detailed analysis of the dynamics behind the right-wing vote.

28 APP B/a 1952, report, 23 April 1940.

29 Wieviorka, *Orphelins de la République*, 33.

30 Melchior-Bonnet, *Lettres du temps de guerre*, 71–2, entry for 9 July 1940.

31 For evidence of pro-British sentiment among some PSF supporters, see CAOM 1K75, police spéciale (Algiers), 5 July 1940; for the concerns of the Parisian leadership, see APP B/a 1952, report, 23 October 1940.

32 In 1938 the PSF had 20,000 members in the Rhône and 13,000 in Marseilles; see Passmore, *From Liberalism to Fascism*, 249, and Jankowski, *Communism and Collaboration*, 67.

33 Melchior-Bonnet, *Lettres du temps de guerre*, 121–2, 138–40, entries for 3 November, 23 December 1940.

34 AN 451AP 128, circular by La Rocque, 24 July 1940; AD Alpes-Maritimes 4M 542, copy of circular by La Rocque, 2 November 1940.

35 AN 2AG 449, directeur du cabinet civil, "Note pour le service de censure," 8 October 1940.

36 AN 2AG 449, La Rocque to Pétain, 6 December 1940; APP B/a 1952, report, 23 October 1940; AD Gard 1M 715, circular, December 1940.

37 AN 2AG 449, report, 22 November 1940; AD Gard 1M 715, report, 2 January 1941.

38 Melchior-Bonnet, *Lettres du temps de guerre*, 136–8, entry for 28 November 1940; CHEVS LR3, notebook no. 1, 148–51, minutes of PSF permanent administrative commission meeting, 23 February 1941.

39 AN 2AG 449, La Rocque, "Aux présidents de fédération et de sections," 16 September 1940; AN F7 15287, "Au sujet du Comte de La Rocque Casimir," 16 August 1941.

40 *Le Petit Journal*, 1 October 1940.

41 AN 2AG 449, La Rocque to General de Laurencie, 12 December 1940; de Laurencie to La Rocque, 13 December 1940; La Rocque to du Moulin, 28 February 1941.

42 Melchior-Bonnet, *Lettres du temps de guerre*, 78–9, entries for 21, 22 July 1940; see also Cointet, "Marcel Déat et le parti unique," 1–16.

43 AN 2AG 449, La Rocque to Pétain, 5 May 1941; Cointet, *Conseil National de Vichy*, 98, 103; Bidussa and Peschanski, eds., *France de Vichy*, 221–2.

44 AN 2AG 449, La Rocque, "Aux presidents," 16 September 1940; Jackson, *France: The Dark Years*, 259; for local examples, see Jankowski, *Communism and Collaboration*, 197n7; Sweets, *Choices in Vichy France*, 65; Zaretsky, *Nîmes at War*, 128–9.

45 AN 2AG 449, "Rapport sur la réunion de La Rocque à Lyon," 22 November 1940; AD Gard 1M 715, report, 3 March 1941.

46 Nobécourt, *Colonel de La Rocque*, 702–6; La Rocque, *Disciplines d'action*, 75–6, 107–8; *Le Petit Journal*, 1 April 1941 (emphases in original).

47 *Le Petit Journal*, 7 January 1941.

48 For this argument, see Passmore, "Croix de Feu and Fascism," in Arnold, ed., *Development of the Radical Right*, 114–15; for La Rocque's emphasis upon the centrality of elites, see *Le Petit Journal*, 4 November 1940.

49 *Le Petit Journal*, 20, 27 October 1940.

50 AN F7 15497, "Renseignements sur le Colonel de La Rocque," 7 November 1945; Machefer, "Sur quelques aspects," 41. For La Rocque's stance, see *Le Petit Journal*, 5, 10, 18 October 1940. On Vichy's antisemitic legislation, see Zuccotti, *The Holocaust, the French*, 51–64, and Marrus and Paxton, *Vichy France and the Jews*, xvii, 3–21, and 83–95.

51 AN 2AG 449, La Rocque to Pétain, 29 April 1941 (emphasis in original). Responding to La Rocque on 5 May, Pétain was polite but found the report overly pessimistic.

52 AN 2AG 449, La Rocque, "Note pour ma famille PSF de la zone occupée," 1 August 1940; *Le Petit Journal*, 31 October 1940.

53 AN 2AG 449, circular, 17 December 1940; La Rocque, *Disciplines d'action*, 78–9; AN F7 15287, notes, 23 October, 20 November 1940; Nobécourt, *Colonel de La Rocque*, 789.

54 Melchior-Bonnet, *Lettres du temps de guerre*, 181–2, entries for 16, 18 March 1941; AN F7 15284, note, n.d. but probably June 1941; *Le Petit Journal*, 25 May 1941.

55 *Le Petit Journal*, 27 July 1941, 11 March 1942.

56 AN 2AG 449, "Aide-mémore sur les relations actuelles du PSF avec le gouvernement," 12 June 1941.

57 AD Nord 68J 159, La Rocque's closing speech to PSF congress, 29 June 1941 (passage emphasized in original).

58 Jackson, *France: The Dark Years*, 158–61, 174–6, 178–85, 213–15.

59 On this concept, see Kedward, *Resistance in Vichy France*, 209, and Jackson, *France: The Dark Years*, 343.

60 AN 2AG 449, La Rocque to Pétain, 7 August 1941; AN F7 15327, note, October 1941; Cointet, *Légion Française*, 151–4; Nobécourt, *Colonel de La Rocque*, 748–53.

61 Cointet, *Légion Française*, 198–9; AN 2AG 449, "Aide-mémoire," 12 June 1941, La Rocque to du Moulin, 22 October 1941; NA FO 371/32116, Z 7754/6248/17, Steward to Stirling, 16 October 1942.

62 AN 451AP 123, "Les Filiales sociales du PSF," n.d.; Diamond, *Women and the Second World War in France*, 67; Le Crom, "L'Association refuge du politique," in Andrieu, Le Béguec, and Tartakowsky, eds., *Associations et champ politique*, 332.

63 Melchior-Bonnet, *Lettres du temps de guerre*, 86–7, 184–5, entries for 25 September 1940, 25 March 1941; *Le Petit Journal*, 25, 26 October 1942, 8/9 May, 26 September 1943; Passmore, "Planting the Tricolor," 850–1.

64 AN F7 15284, report on ADP, 6 September 1943; note on ADP, 18 July 1944.

65 USNA RG 59 851.00/2385, report by Leahy, 3 October 1941.

66 AN 2AG 449, La Rocque to General Laure, 10 October 1941; "Note au sujet des tournées départementales du lt.-col. de La Rocque," 3 November 1941; La Rocque to du Moulin, 19 March 1942; AN 2AG 604, Valentin, letter to Légion cadres, 15 October 1941.

67 CAOM 5CAB59, note, n.d.; Cointet, *Légion Française*, 196–201; Azéma, "Milice"; Jackson, *France: The Dark Years*, 277–8.

68 AN 2AG 449, La Rocque, report on North Africa, 1 February 1942.

69 AN 2AG 618, La Rocque to Ménétrel, 4/5 September 1942, note, 8 October 1942.

70 AD Gard 1M 715, Teyssedre to La Rocque, 22 January 1942 [intercepted 24 January 1942]; note by prefect, 7 February 1942; Zaretsky, *Nîmes at War*, 178–83, 136; *Le Petit Journal*, 16 November 1942; USNA RG 59, 851.00/2698, 851.00/2928, reports by J. Rives Childs (Tangier), 18, 25 March 1942.

71 Brumeaux, *La Rocque citoyen*, 53; Association des Amis de La Rocque, *Pour mémoire*, 19–20; Nobécourt, *Colonel de La Rocque*, 820–2; Machefer, "Sur quelques aspects," 49–51.

72 AN F7 15287, A.I. Thomas, Anglo-French Communications Bureau, attestation, 11 June 1945. For the members of the Alibi network – though these lists do not appear to include members of Klan – see NA HS 6/459, "Note pour le directeur du cabinet du ministre," "Réseau Alibi, list des lettres de remerciements"; HS 6/468, "France: cross reference list of British and French agents."

73 Nobécourt, *Colonel de La Rocque*, 820–4; Paillole, *Services spéciaux*, 224–369; AN F7 15284, note, 7 July 1945; AN F7 15287, note, 16 June 1945.

74 *Le Petit Journal*, 25 June 1942; AN 2AG 449, note, 14 September 1942.

75 AN 2AG 618, La Rocque to Pétain, 4, 8 November 1942; AN 2AG 449, notes, 8 October 1942, 6 January, 25 February 1943.

76 *Le Petit Journal*, 9 November 1942; AN 2AG 449, La Rocque to Pétain, 14 November 1942.

77 For an overview of the situation, see Atkin, *Pétain*, 157–85.

78 *Le Petit Journal*, 3 February 1943; La Rocque and La Rocque, *La Rocque tel qu'il était*, 191–2. Nobécourt, *Colonel de La Rocque*, 876–84, suggests that it was a denunciation by the Milice that led to the move against the PSF.

79 La Rocque, *France d'aujourd'hui, France de démain*, 11–12.

80 Melchior-Bonnet, *Lettres du temps de guerre*, 209, 229, entries for 19 December 1941, 16 January 1942; Nobécourt, *Colonel de La Rocque*, 806–12; AN F7 15287, report, 16 August 1941 with clippings from *L'Appel*, 29 May, 5 June 1941.

81 AN 2AG 618, note, 8 October 1942; *Le Petit Journal*, 16/17 January 1943.

82 Soucy, *French Fascism: The Second Wave*, 119–20.

83 La Rocque, *France d'aujourd'hui, France de démain*, 5–6.

84 Ibid., 5–6, 16–18, 25.

85 *Le Petit Journal*, 16 December 1942.

86 Gordon, *Collaborationism in France*, 122, 199; AN 451AP 126, "Nouveaux cadres de la Révolution Nationale en Oise-Sud," n.d.

87 Paxton, *Vichy France*, 252.

88 Lévy and Veillon, "Propagande et modelage des esprits," in Azéma and
   Bédarida, eds., *Le Régime de Vichy et les Français*, 191–3, 197; Jeanneney,
   Journal politique, 488n14; Creyssel, *Un Complot contre la France*, 6; see also
   Creyssel, *Temps de la colère*.

89 Nobécourt, *Colonel de La Rocque*, 850; Ziegler, *J'étais au PSF*.

90 Vinen, *Bourgeois Politics in France*, 116; Thomas, "Parti Social Français et le
   monde militaire," in Forcade, Duhamel, and Vial, eds., *Militaires en
   République*, 427–9; and Gildea, *Marianne in Chains*, 358, who describes
   Audibert as having been deported to Buchenwald rather than Ravensbruck.

91 AD Aube 110J 10, prefect's report, 30 January 1941.

92 Nobécourt, *Colonel de La Rocque*, 824–51; AD Nord 68J 185, PSF Nord federation bulletin, no. 41 (5–12 October 1942).

93 NA FO 371/32116, Z 7410/6248/17, telegram from Rooker, 30 September
   1942; Z 7754/ 6248/17, Steward to Stirling, 16 October 1942; Crémieux-
   Brilhac, *France libre*, 389–90; Vallin, *Seul Combat*, 10–11, 53–4.

94 *Le Volontaire '36*, July 1940; AD Aisne 1M 19, feldkommandant to prefect, 8
   May; depositions by Carette, Susini, and Flabat, 14 May; commissaire spécial
   (Laon), 15 May; prefect to feldkommandanteur, 19 May 1941; Melchior-
   Bonnet, *Lettres du temps de guerre*, 236–9, entry for 20 February 1942; AN
   F7 15327, note, 22 February 1943.

95 Nobécourt, *Colonel de La Rocque*, 770–1; USNA RG 59 851.00/2385, report
   by Leahy, 3 October 1941.

96 AN 451AP 102, letter by Henri Hermann, 5 October 1946; *Dictionnaire des
   parlementaires français*, 3: 327, 342; *Journal officiel … Lois et décrets*, 7
   October 1945, 6321; AN 3W 346, préfecture de police, cabinet de M.
   Mathieu, 2 October 1945. For Ybarnégaray's brief career as a minister, see
   Pollard, *Reign of Virtue*, 103–5, 224n24.

97 AN 451AP 123, "Les dirigeants du Progrès Social Français," n.d.; AN 3W 290,
   minutes of meeting between Pétain and PSF, 18 March 1943; Le Tanneur to
   Pétain, 21 March 1943.

98 AN F7 15497, "Enquête à Clermont-Ferrand sur les incidences de
   l'arrestations du Colonel de La Rocque par les autorités allemandes," 15
   April 1943; notes, 29 May, 4 August, 27 October 1943; *Le Petit Journal*, 26
   September; see also 6/7 November 1943, 10/11 June 1944.

99 Nobécourt, *Colonel de La Rocque*, 817, gives a fuller list.

100 Ibid., 890–911; Bankwitz, *Maxime Weygand and Civil-Military Relations*,
    354–5. François-Poncet, *Carnets d'un captif*, 13–81, discusses conditions at
    Itter before La Rocque's arrival.

101 See the testimonies reproduced in La Rocque and La Rocque, *La Rocque tel
    qu'il était*, 203–21.

102 Three accounts of the incident are Daladier, *Prison Journal*, 250–5, entries for 9, 10, 11 January 1944; Reynaud, *Carnets de captivité*, 309–12, entries for same dates; and Léon-Jouhaux, *Prison pour hommes d'état*, 69–75.

103 Reynaud, *Carnets de captivité*, 361, entry for 10 March 1945.

104 Léon-Jouhaux, *Prison pour hommes d'état*, 74, 154–5.

105 Préval, *Deux prières de La Rocque déporté*, 18–21.

106 AN 451AP 126, note, 11 June 1944; AN 451AP 128, *PSF: Bulletin d'information*, February 1945; AN F7 15284, report, 25 January 1946.

107 AN 451AP 128, circular, 6 September 1945; Coston, ed., *Partis, journaux et hommes politiques*, 78; AD Aube 110J 10, commissaire divisionnaire (Châlons-sur-Marne), 19 March 1945; Lottman, *People's Anger*, 188–93.

108 AN F7 15284, note, n.d. but 1945; report, 7 July 1945; AD Aube 110J 10, note, 20 February; commissaire de police (Troyes), March 1945.

109 See Jackson, *France: The Dark Years*, 413–17, 456–60, 509–11.

110 For a case study of another organization faced with comparable dilemmas, see Hellman, *Knight-Monks of Vichy France*.

EPILOGUE

1 Lottman, *People's Anger*, 188–93; Nobécourt, *Colonel de La Rocque*, 912–27.

2 AN F7 15284, report, 25 January 1946.

3 AN F7 15284, report, 25 January 1946; Vinen, *Bourgeois Politics in France*, 177.

4 AN F7 15284, renseignements généraux, 6 August 1946, 24 March 1947.

5 Shennan, *Rethinking France*, 80–5; Bichet, *Démocratie chrétienne en France*, 57; Leleu, *Géographie des élections françaises*, 238, map 30; AN F7 15287, renseignements généraux, 16 March 1946.

6 Thomas, "Parti Social Français," 52–3; Vinen, *Bourgeois Politics in France*, 115–36.

7 AN F7 15287, renseignements généraux, 16 March 1946; AN F7 15284, renseignements généraux, 6 August 1946.

8 Vinen, *Bourgeois Politics in France*, 174–80; Duhamel, "Parti Radical et le RGR," in Le Béguec and Duhamel, eds., *Reconstruction du Parti Radical*, 137–8, 147n37; *La Réconciliation Française: cahiers d'information intérieur: "Fidélité"* [n.d.], *"Organisation"* [n.d.], *"Ralliement"* [n.d.]; Péan, *Une Jeunesse française*, 523–7.

9 *Le Flambeau de la Réconciliation Française*, 5 November 1950, 27 May, 24 June 1951, November 1954, December 1956, November 1957; Vinen, *Bourgeois Politics in France*, 234–51; Coston, "Des Croix de Feu à la Réconciliation Française," in Coston, *Partis, journaux*, 80.

10 There is a useful overview of the RPF in Shennan, *De Gaulle*, 56–73; for more depth, see the edited collection published by the Fondation Charles de Gaulle, *De Gaulle et le Rassemblement du Peuple Français.*

11 Shennan, *De Gaulle*, 63–5; Thomas, "Parti Social Français," 54–60.

12 On Barrachin's defection, see Lacouture, *De Gaulle, 2: Le Politique*, 384–7; on the deputies, see Le Béguec, "Antécédents politiques des députés RPF," in Fondation Charles de Gaulle, *De Gaulle et le Rassemblement du Peuple Français*, 339.

13 Vinen, *Bourgeois Politics in France*, 218–23; Charlot, *Gaullisme d'opposition*, 86–9, 180–91; Thomas, "Parti Social Français," 71; Thomas, "Effectifs du Parti Social Français," 82–3.

14 See Thomas, "Parti Social Français," 51. This connection is also implied in Berstein, "De la démocratie plebiscitaire au gaullisme," in Berstein, ed., *Cultures politiques.*

15 *Le Flambeau de la Réconciliation Française: Cahiers intérieures de l'information*, second series, no. 3 (n.d.), no. 23 (22 March 1948); *Le Flambeau de la Réconciliation Française*, 16 January 1949, 27 May 1951; Nobécourt, *Colonel de La Rocque*, 959–61; La Rocque and La Rocque, *La Rocque tel qu'il était*, 251–2.

16 Thomas, "Parti Social Français," 57–61.

17 La Rocque, *Au service de l'avenir*, chapter 5, 85–112, quotation on 87.

18 Ibid., chapters 2 and 3, 21–7, 29–45.

19 Shennan, *De Gaulle*, 60–1, 68–70; Watson, "Internal Dynamics of Gaullism, 1958–1969," in Atkin and Tallett, eds., *Right in France*, 255.

20 Useful introductions to the FN include Perrineau, "Front National: 1972–1994," in Winock, ed., *Histoire de l'extrême droite*, 243–99; Marcus, *National Front and French Politics*; Simmons, *French National Front*; Fysh and Wolfreys, *Politics of Racism in France*. On the 2002 elections, see Atkin and Tallett, "Towards a Sixth Republic?," in Atkin and Tallett, eds., *Right in France*, 293–304.

21 Marcus, *National Front and French Politics*, 100–30, 35–8, 176–9.

22 For brief but useful commentary on these events, see Pfaff, "French Riots" and "France: The Children's Hour."

23 For comparisons of the interwar far right with contemporary movements, see Paxton, *Anatomy of Fascism*, 175–88, and Prowe, "'Classic' Fascism and the New Radical Right."

24 Marcus, *National Front and French Politics*, 111–14; Passmore, "Feminity and the Right," 63–7.

25 Nobécourt emphasizes the differences between the FN and the Croix de Feu/PSF in *Le Monde*, 9 May 1988; on the FN's authoritarianism, see Simmons, *French National Front.*

26 Marcus, *National Front and French Politics*, 1–5, 27–51, quotation on 3–4; Wolfreys, "Neither Right nor Left," in Atkin and Tallett, eds., *Right in France*, 269–71.

27 Marcus, *National Front and French Politics*, 131–58, quotation on 136.

Bibliography

ARCHIVAL SOURCES

Archives Départementales

Aisne: 1M 19, 1M 20, 4Z 6, 4Z 7
Alpes-Maritimes: 4M 541, 4M 542, 4M 543
Aube: 110J 10, SC15 856, SC17 551
Bouches-du-Rhône: M6 8288
Gard: 1M 715
Hérault: 1M 1118, 1M 1119
Loire-Atlantique: 1M 470
Marne: 30M 144, 30M 145, 30M 146, 30M 147, 30M 161, 2Z 156
Moselle: BH 5220, 26Z 18, 26Z 19
Nord: 68J: PSF Tourcoing federation, cartons 67–8, 79, 104–9, 159, 163–4,
    167–8, 171, 187, 206–8, 216
Oise: Mp 5299, Mp 256/2, Mp 5132, Mp 5133, Mp 5134, Mp 5233
Somme: 99M 109, 99M 149/2, 99M 165
Vendée: 4M 413
Yvelines: 4M2 66, 4M2 67

Archives Nationales, Paris

PRIVATE PAPERS
451AP: François de La Rocque
475AP: Hubert Lyautey
317AP: Louis Marin
324AP: André Tardieu

GOVERNMENT DOCUMENTS

2AG: Philippe Pétain Papers

3W: Postwar Trials

72AJ 1821: Press clippings on 6 February riots

72AJ 1822: Press Clippings on the La Rocque–Tardieu controversy

BB18: Ministry of Justice

F7: General Police

Archives de Paris

212/69/1: Trial records of PSF leaders for reconstituting the Croix de Feu

D3 M2 17: Paris by-election, 1938

Archives de la Préfecture de Police, Paris

"Ligues/Croix de Feu": Unnumbered dossier on Croix de Feu

B/a 1901: Reports on Croix de Feu

B/a 1902: Reports on Croix de Feu/PSF

B/a 1952: Reports on PSF

Bibliothèque Nationale, Paris

Croix de Feu, Parti Social Français: tracts politiques, 1934–1939

Centre des Archives d'Outre-Mer, Aix-en-Provence

Governor-General of Algeria
2CAB3, 3CAB25, 5CAB59
Archives Départementales
Algiers: 1K26, 1K75, F405
Constantine: B3 323, B3 327, B3 522, B3 635, B3 707
Oran: 70, 466, 2413

*Centre de l'Histoire de l'Europe au Vingtième Siècle,
Archives d'Histoire Contemporaine, Paris*

Fonds de La Rocque (LR), cartons 1–4

National Archives, Kew

FO 371: Reports on France

FO 432: Confidential print, France
HS 6: Special Operations Executive, reports relating to France

United States National Archives, College Park, Maryland

RG 59 851.00: Reports on France

CROIX DE FEU/PSF NEWSPAPERS AND BULLETINS

Agir (1939)
Bulletin des Associations Croix de Feu du département d'Alger (1935)
Bulletin des Sections Croix de Feu de l'Hérault, de l'Aude et de l'Aveyron
   (1936)
Bulletin mensuel PSF Saint-Étienne (1937)
Croix de Feu du Gard (1936)
Les Croix de Feu de Rouen et de Normandie (1935)
La Documentation mensuelle du PSF (1940)
L'Espoir lorrain (1937)
L'Étudiant social (1938–39)
Le Flambeau (1929–37)
Le Flambeau ardennais (1936)
Le Flambeau des Bouches-du-Rhône (1936)
Le Flambeau de Bourgogne (1937–38)
Le Flambeau de Cannes (1938)
Le Flambeau de Flandre-Artois-Picardie (1938–39)
Le Flambeau de Franche-Comté et territoire de Belfort (1938)
Le Flambeau du Gard (1936–37)
Le Flambeau d'Indochine (1938–40)
Le Flambeau de l'Isère (1937–39)
Le Flambeau marocain (1938)
Le Flambeau morbihannais (1933–34)
Le Flambeau normand (1938)
Le Flambeau de la Réconciliation Française (1946–57)
Le Flambeau du Sud-Ouest (1937–39)
Le Flambeau des Vosges (1939)
La Flamme (1936–39)
La Flamme catalane (1936)
La Flamme des Deux-Sèvres (1939)
La Flamme du Midi (1937)
La Flamme tourangelle (1938–40)

La Flamme vendéenne (1938–39)

Le Français du Centre-Ouest (1937)

L'Heure française (1936–38)

La Liberté du Maine (1937–39)

L'Ouvrier libre (1937–39)

Le Petit Journal (1937–44)

Pourquoi s'en faire? (1937–38)

PSF: Bulletin d'information (1945)

Le PSF creusotin (1939)

Le PSF montcellin (1939)

Parti Social Français: Bulletin de la Fédération des Deux-Sèvres (1938)

Parti Social Français: Bulletin d'informations (1936–39)

Parti Social Français: Bulletin de la section de Lunéville (1936)

*Parti Social Français, Fédération de la Loire: Bulletin fédéral de
    documentation* (1939)

Parti Social Français: Fédération de la Moselle (1940)

Parti Social Français, section de Versailles-Montreuil: Bulletin de liaison (1939)

Parti Social Français: Section du canton de Maronne (1938)

Le Ralliement du Nord de la France (1937)

Réalité (1938)

La Réconciliation Française: Bulletin d'information (1945)

La Réconciliation Française: Cahiers d'information intérieur (1946)

La Relève: Feuille de liaison des Croix de Feu de la Section du Rhône (1930–31)

Samedi (1937–38)

Samedi du Poitou (1938)

Service sociale: Travail-Famille-Patrie (1939)

*Syndicats Professionels: Bulletin d'information de la section locale de
    Tourcoing* (1939)

Le Volontaire '36 (1936–42)

La Volonté bretonne (1936–40)

La Volonté du Centre (1937–40)

OTHER NEWSPAPERS AND PERIODICALS

L'Alliance démocratique (1937–39)

Le Canard enchaîné (1936)

L'Émancipation nationale (1936–39)

Le Figaro (1936)

Gringoire (1936–37)

L'Humanité (1936)

Je suis partout (1938–39)
Le Jour (1937)
Marianne (1936)
Sept (1934–37)
Le Temps (1935–37)

OTHER PUBLISHED SOURCES

Adamthwaite, Anthony. *Grandeur and Misery: France's Bid for Power in Europe, 1914–1940*. London: Edward Arnold, 1995.

Alden, Douglas. *Jacques de Lacretelle: An Intellectual Itinerary*. New Brunswick, NJ: Rutgers University Press, 1958.

Alexander, Martin, ed. *French History since Napoleon*. London: Arnold, 1999.

Allardt, Erik, and Stein Rokkan, eds. *Mass Politics: Essays in Political Sociology*. New York: Free Press, 1970.

Amdur, Kathryn. "Paternalism, Productivism, Collaborationism: Employers and Society in Interwar and Vichy France." *International Labor and Working-Class History* 53 (1998): 137–63.

Anderson, Malcolm. *Conservative Politics in France*. London: Allen and Unwin, 1974.

Andrieu, Claire, Gilles Le Béguec, and Danielle Tartakowsky, eds. *Associations et champ politique: La Loi de 1901 à l'épreuve du siècle*. Paris: Publications de la Sorbonne, 2001.

Arnold, Edward, ed. *The Development of the Radical Right in France: From Boulanger to Le Pen*. New York: St. Martin's Press, 2000.

Association des Amis de La Rocque. *Pour mémoire ... La Rocque, les Croix de Feu et le Parti Social Français*. Auteuil: Imprimerie des Orphelins Apprentis d'Auteuil, 1985.

Atkin, Nicholas. *Church and Schools in Vichy France, 1940–1944*. New York: Garland, 1991.

– *Pétain*. London and New York: Longman, 1998.

Atkin, Nicholas, and Frank Tallett, eds. *The Right in France: From Revolution to Le Pen*. 2nd ed. London: I.B. Tauris, 2003.

Aucouturier, Marcel. *Au service du Parti Social Français: Réponses à 45 questions et objections*. Charleville: P. Anciaux, 1938.

– *Programme du Parti Social Français: Pour la reconstruction de l'État Social Français*. Charleville: P. Anciaux, 1938.

Autour des élections: Principes d'arbitrage du Mouvement Croix de Feu. Paris: Le Flambeau, 1936.

Azéma, Jean-Pierre. "La Milice." *Vingtième siècle* 28 (1990): 83–105.

Azéma, Jean-Pierre, and François Bédarida, eds. *Le Régime de Vichy et les Français*. Paris: Fayard, 1992.

Bankwitz, Philip. *Maxime Weygand and Civil-Military Relations in Modern France*. Cambridge, Mass.: Harvard University Press, 1967.

Bard, Christine. *Les Filles de Marianne: Histoire des féminismes 1914–1940*. Paris: Fayard, 1995.

Barrachin, Edmond. *Le Parti Social Français devant le pays*. Paris: SEDA, 1937.

Barral, Pierre. *Le Département de l'Isère sous la Troisième République*. Paris: Armand Colin, 1962.

Becker, Annette. *La Guerre et la foi: De la mort à la mémoire 1914–1930*. Paris: Armand Colin, 1994.

Berstein, Serge, ed. *Les Cultures politiques en France*. Paris: Seuil, 1999.

– *La France des années 30*. 2nd ed. Paris: Armand Colin, 1993.

– "La France des années trente allergique au fascisme: À propos d'un livre de Zeev Sternhell." *Vingtième siècle* 2 (1984): 83–94.

– *Histoire du Parti Radical*. Vol.2, *Crise du radicalisme*. Paris: Presses de la FNSP, 1982.

Bichet, Robert. *La Démocratie chrétienne en France: Le Mouvement Républicaine Populaire*. Besançon: Jacques et Demontrand, 1980.

Bidussa, David, and Denis Peschanski, eds. *La France de Vichy: Archives inédites d'Angelo Tasca*. Milan: Feltrinelli, 1996.

Bingham, John. "Defining French Fascism, Finding Fascists in France." *Canadian Journal of History* 29 (1994): 525–43.

Birnbaum, Pierre. *Un Mythe politique: La "république juive."* Paris: Fayard, 1988.

Blatt, Joel, ed. *The French Defeat of 1940: Reassessments*. New York: Berghahn, 1998.

Blinkhorn, Martin, ed. *Fascists and Conservatives: The Radical Right and the Establishment in Twentieth-Century Europe*. London: Unwin Hyman, 1990.

Bonnefous, Édouard. *Histoire politique de la Troisième République*. Vols. 4–7. Paris: Presses Universitaires de France, 1959–67.

Boulic, Jean-Yves, and Anne Lavaure. *Henri de Kerillis 1889–1958: L'absolu patriote*. Rennes: Presses Universitaires de Rennes, 1997.

Bourdin, Janine, ed. *Léon Blum, chef de gouvernement 1936–1937*. Paris: Armand Colin, 1967.

Bourne, Kenneth, and D.C. Watt, eds. *British Documents on Foreign Affairs*. Part II, series F, vols. 22, 23, *France 1936–1939*. Ed. Anthony Adamthwaite. Bethesda: University Publications of America, 1993.

Bouvier, Jean, ed. *La France en mouvement 1934–1938*. Seyssell: Champ Vallon, 1986.

Brumeaux, Jean. *La Rocque citoyen*. Saint-Étienne: n.p., n.d.

Brunet, Jean-Paul. *Jacques Doriot: Du communisme au fascisme*. Paris: Éditions Balland, 1986.

Buchanan, Tom, and Martin Conway, eds. *Political Catholicism in Europe, 1918–1965*. Oxford: Oxford University Press, 1996.

Burleigh, Michael. *The Third Reich: A New History*. New York: Hill and Wang, 2000.

Burrin, Philippe. *La Dérive fasciste: Doriot, Déat, Bergery 1933–1945*. Paris: Seuil, 1986.

– *Fascisme, nazisme, autoritarisme*. Paris: Seuil, 2000.

Cantier, Jacques. *L'Algérie sous le régime de Vichy*. Paris: Odile Jacob, 2002.

Caron, Vicki. "The Antisemitic Revival in France in the 1930s: The Socioeconomic Dimension Reconsidered." *Journal of Modern History* 70 (1998): 24–73.

– *Uneasy Asylum: France and the Jewish Refugee Crisis, 1933–1942*. Stanford: Stanford University Press, 1999.

Chadeau, Emmanuel. *Mermoz*. Paris: Perrin, 2000.

Chafer, Tony, and Amanda Sackur, eds. *The French Colonial Empire and the Popular Front: Hope and Disillusion*. New York: St. Martin's Press, 1999.

Chambre des Députés. *Rapport fait au nom de la commission d'enquête chargée de rechercher les causes et les origines des évènements du 6 février 1934 et jours suivants*. n.p., n.d.

Charlot, Jean. *Le Gaullisme d'opposition 1946–1958: Histoire politique du Gaullisme*. Paris: Fayard, 1983.

Childers, Thomas. *The Nazi Voter*. Chapel Hill: University of North Carolina Press, 1984.

Chopine, Paul. *Six ans chez les Croix de Feu*. Paris: Gallimard, 1935.

Chouvel, Marie-Anne. "Les Croix de Feu et le PSF en Haute-Vienne et sur la bordure occidentale du Massif Central." Mémoire de maîtrise, Université de Paris X – Nanterre, 1971.

Clément, Jean-Louis. "L'Épiscopat, les démocrates-chrétiens et les Croix de Feu, 1930–1936." *Revue historique* 603 (1997): 103–13.

Cohen, William. "The Colonial Policy of the Popular Front." *French Historical Studies* 7 (1972): 368–93.

Cointet, Jean-Paul. *La Légion Française des Combattants 1940–1944: La tentation du fascisme*. Paris: Albin Michel, 1995.

– "Marcel Déat et le parti unique (été 1940)." *Revue d'histoire de la Deuxième Guerre Mondiale* 23 (1973): 1–16.

– *Pierre Laval*. Paris: Fayard, 1993.

Cointet-Labrousse, Michèle. *Le Conseil National de Vichy 1940–1944*. Paris: Amateurs de livres, 1989.

– *Vichy et le fascisme*. Brussels: Éditions Complexe, 1987.

Conklin, Alice. *A Mission to Civilize: The Republican Idea of Empire in France and West Africa, 1895–1930*. Stanford: Stanford University Press, 1997.

Conway, Martin. "The Extreme Right in Inter-War Francophone Belgium: Explanations of a Failure." *European History Quarterly* 26 (1996): 267–92.

Costa Pinto, Antonio. "Fascist Ideology Revisited: Zeev Sternhell and His Critics." *European History Quarterly* 16 (1986): 465–83.

Coston, Henry, ed. *Partis, journaux et hommes politiques d'hier et d'aujourd'hui*. Paris: Lectures françaises, 1960.

Coutrot, Aline. "Youth Movements in France in the 1930s." *Journal of Contemporary History* 5 (1970): 23–35.

Crémieux-Brilhac, Jean-Louis. *Les Français de l'an 40*. Vol.1, *La Guerre oui ou non?* Paris: Gallimard, 1990.

– *La France libre: De l'appel du 18 juin à la Libération*. Paris: Gallimard, 1996.

Creyssel, Paul. *Un Complot contre la France et la paix*. Mâcon: X. Perroux et fils, n.d.

– *Le Temps de la colère: Allocution prononcée à la radio par Monsieur Paul Creyssel, le jeudi 16 décembre 1943*. Paris: Imprimerie JEP, n.d.

Cullen, Stephen. "Leaders and Martyrs: Codreanu, Mosley and José Antonio." *History* 71 (1986): 408–30.

Daladier, Édouard. *Prison Journal, 1940–1945*. Trans. Arthur D. Greenspan. Boulder: Westview Press, 1995.

Dard, Olivier. *Les Années 30*. Paris: Librairie Générale Française, 1999.

De Grand, Alexander. *Fascist Italy and Nazi Germany: The "Fascist" Style of Rule*. London: Routledge, 1995.

Delbreil, Jean-Claude. *Centrisme et démocratie-chrétienne en France: Le Parti Démocrate Populaire des origines au M.R.P. (1919–1944)*. Paris: Publications de la Sorbonne, 1990.

Desgranges, Jean-Marie. *Journal d'un prêtre-député, 1936–1940*. Paris: La Palatine, 1960.

Diamond, Hanna. *Women and the Second World War in France, 1939–1948: Choices and Constraints*. Harlow: Pearson Education, 1999.

Dictionnaire des parlementaires français: Notices biographiques sur les parlementaires français de 1940 à 1958. Vols. 1–3. Paris: La Documentation Française, 1988–94.

Dioudonnat, Pierre-Marie. *Je suis partout, 1930–1944: Les maurrassiens devant la tentation fasciste*. Paris: La Table Ronde, 1973.

La Dissolution des Croix de Feu? n.p.: Publications L.P., 1935.

Dobry, Michel. "Février 1934 et la découverte de l'allergie de la société française à la 'révolution fasciste.'" *Revue française de sociologie* 30 (1989): 511–33.

– ed. *Le Mythe de l'allergie française au fascisme*. Paris: Albin Michel, 2003.

Douglas, Allen. *From Fascism to Libertarian Communism: Georges Valois against the Third Republic*. Berkeley: University of California Press, 1992.

Downs, Laura Lee. "Municipal Communism and the Politics of Childhood: Ivry-sur-Seine, 1925–1960." *Past and Present* 166 (2000): 205–41.

Du Réau, Elisabeth. *Édouard Daladier 1884–1970*. Paris: Fayard, 1993.

Eatwell, Roger. "Towards a New Model of Generic Fascism." *Journal of Theoretical Politics* 4 (1992): 161–94.

Facon, Patrick. "L'Image des aviateurs à travers l'oeuvre de Jacques Mortane." *Revue historique des armées* 183 (1991): 93–102.

Ferragu, Martine. "Les Croix de Feu et le PSF en Indre-et-Loire." *Cahiers de l'Institut d'histoire de la presse et de l'opinion publique* 1 (1973): 2–42.

Fishman, Sarah, et al., eds. *France at War: Vichy and the Historians*. Oxford: Berg, 2000.

Florin, J.-P. "Des Croix de Feu au Parti Social Français: Une mutation réussie? L'exemple de la fédération du Nord (1936–1939)." *Revue du Nord* 59 (1977): 233–71.

Fondation Charles de Gaulle and Centre Acquitain de Recherches en Histoire Contemporain. *De Gaulle et le Rassemblement du Peuple Français (1947–1955)*. Paris: Armand Colin, 1998.

Forcade, Olivier, Eric Duhamel, and Philippe Vial, eds. *Militaires en République 1870–1962: Les officiers, le pouvoir et la vie publique en France*. Paris: Publications de la Sorbonne, 1999.

La France et l'Allemagne 1932–1936. Paris: Éditions du CRNS, 1980.

François-Poncet, André. *Carnets d'un captif*. Paris: Fayard, 1952.

Fritzsche, Peter. *Germans into Nazis*. Cambridge, Mass.: Harvard University Press, 1998.

Fysh, Peter, and Jim Wolfreys. *The Politics of Racism in France*. 2nd ed. Houndmills: Palgrave Macmillan, 2003.

Gabillard, Philippe. "Les Viticulteurs angevins et le Mouvement Croix de Feu–PSF (1935–1939)." *Annales de Bretagne et des Pays de l'Ouest* 90 (1983): 483–94.

Garrigoux, Jeanne. *Les Centres sociaux*. Sceaux: René Papier, 1939.

– *Le Parti Social Français et l'Action Sociale: Rapport présenté au deuxième congrès nationale du PSF*. Paris: n.p., 1937.

Gildea, Robert. *Marianne in Chains: In Search of the German Occupation of France*. London: Macmillan, 2002.

– *The Past in French History*. New Haven: Yale University Press, 1994.

Gillis, John, ed. *Commemorations: The Politics of National Identity*. Princeton: Princeton University Press, 1994.

Goodfellow, Samuel. *Between the Swastika and the Cross of Lorraine: Fascisms in Interwar Alsace*. Dekalb: Northern Illinois University Press, 1999.

Gordon, Bertram. *Collaborationism in France during the Second World War*. Ithaca and London: Cornell University Press, 1980.

Green, Mary Jean. "Gender, Fascism and the Croix de Feu: The 'Women's Pages' of *Le Flambeau*." *French Cultural Studies* 8 (1997): 229–39.

Griffin, Roger. "The Primacy of Culture: The Current Growth (or Manufacture) of Consensus within Fascist Studies." *Journal of Contemporary History* 37 (2002): 21–43.

Guerrin, Henry. *Croix de Feu?* Paris: n.p., April 1934.

Guiol, Patrick. *L'Impasse sociale du Gaullisme: Le RPF et l'action ouvrière*. Paris: Presses de la FNSP, 1985.

Halls, W.D. *The Youth of Vichy France*. Oxford: Oxford University Press, 1981.

Hautecloque, F. de. *Grandeur et decadence des Croix de Feu*. Paris: La Bourdonnais, 1937.

Hawthorne, Melanie, and Richard J. Goslan, eds. *Gender and Fascism in Modern France*. Hanover: University Press of New England, 1997.

Hellman, John. *The Communitarian Third Way: Alexandre Marc and Ordre Nouveau, 1930–2000*. Montreal and Kingston: McGill-Queen's University Press, 2002.

– *The Knight-Monks of Vichy France: Uriage, 1940–1945*. 2nd ed. Montreal and Kingston: McGill-Queen's University Press, 1997.

Hoffmann, Stanley. *Decline or Renewal? France since the 1930s*. New York: Viking, 1974.

Hoisington, William. *Lyautey and the French Conquest of Morocco*. New York: St. Martin's Press, 1995.

– "Toward the Sixth of February: Taypayer Protest in France, 1928–1934." *Historical Reflections* 3 (1976): 49–67.

Holt, Richard. *Sport and Society in Modern France*. London: Macmillan, 1981.

Howlett, Gareth. "The Croix de Feu, the Parti Social Français and Colonel de La Rocque." DPhil dissertation, Oxford University, 1985.

Imlay, Talbot. *Facing the Second World War: Strategy, Politics, and Economics in France, 1938–1940*. Oxford: Oxford University Press, 2003.

Irvine, William D. *The Boulanger Affair Reconsidered: Royalism, Boulangism, and the Origins of the Radical Right in France*. New York: Oxford University Press, 1989.

– "Fascism in France and the Strange Case of the Croix de Feu." *Journal of Modern History* 63 (1991): 271–95.

– *French Conservatism in Crisis: The Republican Federation of France in the 1930s*. Baton Rouge: Louisiana State University Press, 1979.

Jackson, Julian. *France: The Dark Years, 1940–1944*. Oxford: Oxford University Press, 2001.

– *The Popular Front in France: Defending Democracy, 1934–1938*. Cambridge: Cambridge University Press, 1988.

Jankowski, Paul. *Communism and Collaboration: Simon Sabiani and Politics in Marseille, 1919–1944*. New Haven: Yale University Press, 1989.

– *Stavisky: A Confidence Man in the Republic of Virtue*. Ithaca: Cornell University Press, 2002.

– "Stavisky and His Era." *French Politics & Society* 10 (1992): 39–65.

Jeal, Tim. *Baden-Powell*. London: Hutchinson, 1989.

Jeanneney, Jean-Noël. *François de Wendel en République: L'argent et le pouvoir 1914–1940*. Paris: Seuil, 1976.

Jeanneney, Jules. *Journal politique: septembre 1939–juillet 1942*. Ed. Jean-Noël Jeanneney. Paris: Armand Colin, 1972.

Jenkins, Brian, ed. *France in the Era of Fascism: Essays on the French Authoritarian Right*. New York: Berghahn Books, 2005.

Jolly, Jean, ed. *Dictionnaire des parlementaires français: Notices biographiques sur les ministres, députés et sénateurs français de 1889 à 1940*. 7 vols. Paris: Presses universitaires de France, 1960–77.

Journal officiel de la République française: Débats parlementaires. Chambre des Députés. 1936–40.

Journal officiel de la République française: Lois et decrets. 1945.

Jouvenel, Bertrand de. "Le Parti Populaire Français." *Sciences politiques* 52:4 (1937): 363–70.

Kallis, Aristotle. "To Expand or Not to Expand? Territory, Generic Fascism and the Quest for an 'Ideal Fatherland.'" *Journal of Contemporary History* 38 (2003): 237–60.

Kalman, Samuel. "Vers un ordre économique nouveau: Conflict between the Traditional and the Modern in the Croix de Feu/Parti Social Français Economic Vision." *Proceedings of the Western Society for French History* 27 (2001): 261–71.

Kedward, H.R. "Patriots and Patriotism in Vichy France." *Transactions of the Royal Historical Society* 32 (1982): 175–92.

– *Resistance in Vichy France: A Study of Ideas and Motivations in the Southern Zone, 1940–1942.* Oxford: Oxford University Press, 1978.

Kennedy, Sean. "The Croix de Feu, the Parti Social Français, and the Politics of Aviation, 1931–1939." *French Historical Studies* 23 (2000): 373–99.

Kershaw, Ian. *Hitler, 1889–1936: Hubris.* London: Allen Lane, 1998.

Kershaw, Ian, and Moshe Lewin, eds. *Stalinism and Nazism: Dictatorships in Comparison.* Cambridge: Cambridge University Press, 1997.

Kessel, Joseph. *Mermoz.* Paris: Gallimard, 1938.

Keylor, William R. *Jacques Bainville and the Renaissance of Royalist History in Twentieth-Century France.* Baton Rouge: Louisiana State University Press, 1979.

Knox, MacGregor. *Common Destiny: Dictatorship, Foreign Policy, and War in Fascist Italy and Nazi Germany.* Cambridge: Cambridge University Press, 2000.

Koerner, Francis. "L'Extrême Droite en Oranie (1936–1940)." *Revue d'histoire moderne et contemporaine* 20 (1973): 568–94.

Koos, Cheryl. "Fascism, Fatherhood, and the Family in Interwar France: The Case of Antoine Rédier and the Légion." *Journal of Family History* 24 (1999): 317–29.

Kuisel, Richard. *Ernest Mercier: French Technocrat.* Berkeley: University of California Press, 1967.

Kupferman, Fred, and Philippe Machefer. "Presse et politique dans les années trente: Le cas du *Petit Journal.*" *Revue d'histoire moderne et contemporaine* 22 (1975): 7–51.

Lacouture, Jean. *De Gaulle.* Vol.2, *Le Politique, 1944–1959.* Paris: Seuil, 1985.

Lacretelle, Jacques de. *Qui est La Rocque?* Paris: Flammarion, 1937.

Lambelet, André. "Frenchmen into Spaniards? Army Officers, Political Ideology, and Education, 1936–1940." *Proceedings of the Western Society for French History* 24 (1997): 267–77.

Larmour, Peter. *The French Radical Party in the 1930s.* Stanford: Stanford University Press, 1964.

La Rocque, Édith de, and Gilles de La Rocque. *La Rocque tel qu'il était.* Paris: Fayard,1962.

La Rocque, François de. *Au service de l'avenir: Réflexions en montagne.* Paris: SEDA,1946.

– *Autour des élections: Principes d'arbitrage du Mouvement Croix de Feu.* Paris: Éditions du *Flambeau,* 1936.

– *Disciplines d'action*. Clermont-Ferrand: Éditions du *Petit Journal*, 1941.
– *France d'aujourd'hui, France de demain*. Pamphlet for party cadres, 1 January 1943. (Copy in AN 451AP 102; much of this pamphlet is now reproduced in Dobry, ed., *Mythe de l'allergie française*, 416–25.)
– *Paix ou guerre?* Paris: SEDA, 1939.
– *Service public*. Paris: Grasset, 1934.
Le Béguec, Gilles. "Premiers rassemblements d'objectifs: Le Mouvement Quatrième République et l'Union pour la Nation." *Cahiers de la Fondation Charles de Gaulle* 4 (1997): 23–38.
Le Béguec, Gilles and Eric Duhamel, eds. *La Reconstruction du Parti Radical 1944–1948*. Paris: L'Harmattan, 1993.
Lebovics, Herman. *True France: The Wars over Cultural Identity, 1900–1945*. Ithaca: Cornell University Press, 1992.
Lefebvre, Jean, ed. *Laon 1936: Front Populaire et action municipale: Essai de synthèse et catalogue d'exposition*. Laon: Bibliothèque Municipal de Laon, 1986.
Leger, Bernard. *Les Opinions politiques des provinces françaises*. Paris: Recueil Sirey, 1936.
Leleu, Claude. *Géographie des élections françaises depuis 1936*. Paris: Presses Universitaires de France, 1971.
Léon-Jouhaux, Augusta. *Prison pour hommes d'état*. Paris: Denoël Gonthier, 1973.
Levy, Carl. "Fascism, National Socialism, and Conservatives in Europe, 1914–1945: Issues for Comparativists." *Contemporary European History* 8 (1999): 97–126.
Lindenberg, Daniel. *Les Années souterraines 1937–1947*. Paris: La Découverte, 1990.
Lottman, Herbert. *The People's Anger: Justice and Revenge in Post-Liberation France*. London: Hutchinson, 1986.
Loubet del Bayle, Jean-Marie. *Les Nonconformistes des années trente: Une tentative de renouvellement de la pensée politique française*. Paris: Seuil, 1969.
Lyautey, Hubert. *Du Rôle social de l'officier*. Paris: R. Julliard, 1946.
Lyttelton, Adrian. *The Seizure of Power: Fascism in Italy, 1919–1929*. 2nd ed. London: Weidenfeld and Nicolson, 1987.
Machefer, Philippe. "L'Action Française et le PSF." *Études maurrassiennes* 4 (1980): 125–33.
– "Autour du problème algérien en 1936–1938: La doctrine algérienne du PSF: Le PSF et le projet Blum-Violette." *Revue d'histoire moderne et contemporaine* 10 (1963): 147–56.

– "Les Croix de Feu (1927–1936)." *L'Information historique* 34 (1972): 28–34.
– "Le Parti Social Français en 1936–1937." *L'Information historique* 34 (1972): 74–80.
– "Sur quelques aspects de l'activité du colonel de La Rocque et du Progrès Social Français pendant la seconde guerre mondiale." *Revue d'histoire moderne et contemporaine* 57 (1965): 35–56.
– "Les Syndicats Professionnels Français (1936–1939)." *Le Mouvement social* 119 (1982): 91–112.
– "Tardieu et La Rocque." *Bulletin de la Société d'histoire moderne* 15 (1973): 11–21.
– "L'Union des droites: Le PSF et le Front de la Liberté, 1936–1937." *Revue d'histoire moderne et contemporaine* 17 (1970): 12–26.
– ed. *Ligues et fascismes en France 1919–1939*. Paris: Presses Universitaires de France, 1974.
McMillan, James F. "Women, Religion and Politics: The Case of the Ligue Patriotique des Françaises." *Proceedings of the Annual Meeting of the Western Society for French History* 15 (1988): 355–64.
Malherbe, Henri. *La Rocque: Un chef, des actes, des idées*. Paris: Plon, 1934.
Manifeste Croix de Feu: Pour le peuple, par le peuple. Supplement to *Le Flambeau*, 11 April 1936.
Mann, Michael. *Fascists*. Cambridge: Cambridge University Press, 2004.
Marcus, Jonathan. *The National Front and French Politics: The Resistible Rise of Jean-Marie Le Pen*. New York: New York University Press, 1995.
Marrus, Michael, and Robert Paxton. *Vichy France and the Jews*. Stanford: Stanford University Press, 1995 [1981].
Maud'huy, Bertrand de. "The French National Revival." *Foreign Affairs* 12:4 (1934): 622–28.
Mayeur, Jean-Marie. *Catholicisme social et démocratie chrétienne: Principes romains, expériences françaises*. Paris: Éditions du Cerf, 1986.
Mazgaj, Paul. "The Origins of the French Radical Right: A Historiographical Essay." *French Historical Studies* 15 (1987): 287–315.
Melchior-Bonnet, Christian. *Lettres du temps de guerre 1939–1942*. Ed. Alain Melchior-Bonnet. Paris: Éditions Imago, 1999.
Mermoz, Jean. *Mes Vols*. 2nd ed. Paris: Flammarion, 1986.
Micaud, Charles. *The French Right and Nazi Germany, 1933–1939: A Study of Public Opinion*. Durham, NC: Duke University Press, 1943.
Michaud, Guy, ed. *Tendances politiques dans la vie française depuis 1789*. Paris: Hachette, 1960.

Millman, Richard. "Les Croix de Feu et l'antisémitisme." *Vingtième Siècle* 38 (1993): 47–61.

– *La Question juive entre les deux guerres: Ligues de droite et antisémitisme en France.* Paris: Armand Colin, 1992.

Milza, Pierre. *Fascisme français: Passé et présent.* Paris: Flammarion, 1987.

Monier, Frédéric. *Les Années 20.* Paris: Librairie Générale Française, 1999.

Monnet, François. *Refaire la République: André Tardieu, une dérive réactionnaire (1876–1945).* Paris: Fayard, 1993.

Mortane, Jacques. *Mermoz.* Paris: Plon, 1936.

Mosse, George. *The Fascist Revolution: Toward a General Theory of Fascism.* New York: Howard Fertig, 1999.

– *The Image of Man: The Creation of Modern Masculinity.* New York: Oxford University Press, 1996.

Mouré, Kenneth, and Martin Alexander, eds. *Crisis and Renewal in France, 1918–1962.* New York: Berghahn, 2002.

Le Mouvement Croix de Feu au secours de l'agriculture française. n.p., 1935.

Le Mouvement Croix de Feu et l'ordre social. Montrouge: n.p., 1935.

Müller, Klaus-Jürgen. "French Fascism and Modernization." *Journal of Contemporary History* 11 (1976): 75–100.

Munholland, Kim. "Wartime France: Remembering Vichy." *French Historical Studies* 18 (1994): 810–21.

Murray, W.J. "The French Workers' Sports Movement and the Victory of the Popular Front in 1936." *International Journal of the History of Sport* 4 (1987): 203–30.

Nadillac, Joseph de. *Conseils sur la propagande électorale dans les milieux agricoles.* Paris: n.p., September 1937.

Nobécourt, Jacques. "Une 'Affaire La Rocque' en 1899: Avant le PSF, Justice-Égalité?" *Revue d'histoire moderne et contemporaine* 47 (2000): 505–24.

– *Le Colonel de La Rocque 1885–1946, ou les pièges du nationalisme chrétien.* Paris: Fayard, 1996.

Noiriel, Gérard. *Les Origines républicaines de Vichy.* Paris: Hachette, 1999.

Nord, Philip. "Catholic Culture in Interwar France." *French Politics, Culture and Society* 21 (2003): 1–20.

– *The Republican Moment: Struggles for Democracy in Nineteenth-Century France.* Cambridge, Mass.: Harvard University Press, 1995.

– "Three Views of Christian Democracy in *Fin de Siècle* France." *Journal of Contemporary History* 19 (1984): 713–27.

Ory, Pascal. *La Belle Illusion: Culture et politique sous le signe du Front Populaire 1935–1938.* Paris: Plon, 1994.

Paillole, Paul. *Services spéciaux (1935–1945)*. Paris: La Table Ronde, 1975.

Parry, D.L.L. "Articulating the Third Republic by Conspiracy Theory." *European History Quarterly* 28 (1998): 163–88.

Le Parti Républicain et Social de la Réconciliation Française. n.p., August 1945.

Le Parti Social Français et la semaine de 40 heures. Paris: n.d.

Le Parti Social Français: Une mystique, une programme. n.p., n.d.

Passmore, Kevin. "Boy Scouting for Grown-Ups? Paramilitarism in the Croix de Feu and Parti Social Français." *French Historical Studies* 19 (1995): 527–57.

– "The Croix de Feu: Bonapartism, National Populism or Fascism?" *French History* 9 (1995): 67–92.

– "Femininity and the Right: From Moral Order to Moral Order." *Modern and Contemporary France* 8 (2000): 55–69.

– "The French Third Republic: Stalemate Society or Cradle of Fascism?" *French History* 7 (1993): 417–49.

– *From Liberalism to Fascism: The Right in a French Province, 1928–1939*. Cambridge: Cambridge University Press, 1997.

– "Planting the Tricolor in the Citadels of Communism: Women's Social Action in the Croix de Feu and Parti Social Français." *Journal of Modern History* 71 (1999): 814–52.

Passmore, Kevin, ed., *Women, Gender and Fascism in Europe, 1919–45*. New Brunswick: Rutgers University Press, 2003.

Paxton, Robert. *The Anatomy of Fascism*. New York: Alfred A. Knopf, 2004.

– "The Five Stages of Fascism." *Journal of Modern History* 70 (1998): 1–23.

– *French Peasant Fascism: Henry Dorgères's Greenshirts and the Crises of French Agriculture, 1929–1939*. New York: Oxford University Press, 1997.

– *Vichy France: Old Guard and New Order, 1940–1944*. New York: Columbia University Press, 2001 [1972].

Payne, Stanley. *A History of Fascism, 1914–1945*. Madison: University of Wisconsin Press, 1995.

Le Paysan sauvera la France avec le PSF. Paris: n.d.

Péan, Pierre. *Une Jeunesse française: François Mitterrand 1934–1947*. Paris: Fayard, 1994.

Petit, Jacques. *De La Rocque est-il un chef?* Paris: Société de Librairie et d'Éditions, 1938.

Pfaff, William. "France: The Children's Hour." *New York Review of Books* 53 (11 May 2006): 40–3.

– "The French Riots: Will They Change Anything?" *New York Review of Books* 52 (15 December 2005): 88–9.

Pilbeam, Pamela. *Republicanism in Nineteenth-Century France, 1814–1871.* London: Macmillan, 1995.

Plumyène, Jean, and Raymond LaSierra. *Les Fascismes français, 1923–1963.* Paris: Seuil, 1963.

Pollard, Miranda. *Reign of Virtue: Mobilizing Gender in Vichy France.* Chicago: University of Chicago Press, 1998.

Popelin, Claude. *Arènes politiques.* Paris: Fayard, 1974.

Porch, Douglas. *The Conquest of the Sahara.* New York: Knopf, 1984.

Presse et politique: Actes du Colloque de Nanterre (mars 1973). Houilles: CEREP, 1973.

Preston, Paul. *The Politics of Revenge: Fascism and the Military in 20th Century Spain.* London: Routledge, 1990.

Préval, Antoinette de. *Deux prières de La Rocque déporté.* n.p.: Imprimerie des Tournelles, 1947.

– *In Memoriam: Conférence du 6 octobre 1946.* n.p., n.d.

Prévosto, Jacques. "La Fédération du Nord du Parti Social Français, 1936–1939." Mémoire de maîtrise, Université de Paris x – Nanterre, 1971.

Prochaska, David. *Making Algeria French: Colonialism in Bône, 1870–1920.* Cambridge: Cambridge University Press, 1990.

Prost, Antoine. *Les Anciens Combattants et la société française, 1914–1939.* 3 vols. Paris: Fondation Nationale des Sciences Politiques, 1977.

Prowe, Diethelm. "'Classic' Fascism and the New Radical Right in Western Europe: Comparisons and Contrasts." *Contemporary European History* 3 (1994): 289–313.

Rémond, René. *Les Droites en France.* 2nd ed. Paris: Aubier Montaigne, 1982.

Rémond, René, and Janine Bourdin, eds. *Édouard Daladier, chef de gouvernement, avril 1938–septembre 1939.* Paris: Presses de la FNSP, 1977.

– eds. *La France et les Français en 1938–1939.* Paris: Presses de la FNSP, 1978.

Reynaud, Paul. *Carnets de captivité 1941–1945.* Paris: Fayard, 1997.

Reynolds, Siân. *France between the Wars: Gender and Politics.* London: Routledge, 1996.

Ritz, Charles. *Réflexions d'un Lorrain sur le Mouvement Social Français des Croix de Feu.* Metz: Éditions le Lorrain, 1935.

Robbe, Fernand. *Et maintenant? ... après douze mois de gouvernement de Front Populaire.* Paris: SEDA, 1937.

– *Le Parti Social Français et le Front de la Liberté.* Paris: SEDA, 1937.

Roberts, David D. "Comments on 'The Primacy of Culture.'" *Journal of Contemporary History* 37 (2002): 259–63.

Roberts, Mary Louise. *Civilization without Sexes: Reconstructing Gender in Postwar France, 1917–1927.* Chicago: University of Chicago Press, 1994.

Rosenthal, Michael. *The Character Factory: Baden-Powell and the Origins of the Boy-Scout Movement.* New York: Pantheon Books, 1986.

Rossi-Landi, Guy. *La Drôle de guerre: La vie politique en France, 2 septembre 1939 – 10 mai 1940.* Paris: Armand Colin, 1971.

Rothney, John. *Bonapartism after Sedan.* Ithaca: Cornell University Press, 1969.

Roussellier, Nicholas. "André Tardieu et la crise du constitutionnalisme libéral." *Vingtième siècle* 21 (1989): 57–70.

Rudaux, Philippe. *Les Croix de Feu et le PSF.* Paris: Éditions France-Empire, 1967.

Rutkoff, Peter. *Revanche and Revision: The Ligue des Patriotes and the Origins of the Radical Right in France, 1882–1900.* Athens: Ohio University Press, 1981.

Rymell, John. "Militants and Militancy in the Croix de Feu and Parti Social Français: Patterns of Political Experience on the French Far Right (1933–1939)." PhD dissertation, University of East Anglia, 1990.

Sarti, Odile. *The Ligue Patriotique des Françaises, 1902–1933: A Feminine Response to the Secularization of French Society.* New York: Garland, 1992.

Schor, Ralph. "Le Parti Populaire Français dans les Alpes-Maritimes (1936–1939)." *Cahiers de la Mediterranée* 33–4 (1986–87): 99–125.

Section lilloise des Croix de Feu et Briscards. *Compte-rendu in extenso de la grande réunion privée du 28 avril 1934.* Lille: Nouvelliste-Dépêche, 1934.

Servent, Pierre. *Le Mythe Pétain: Verdun ou les tranchées de la mémoire.* Paris: Payot, 1992.

Shennan, Andrew. *De Gaulle.* New York: Longman, 1993.

– "The Parliamentary Opposition to the Front Populaire and the Elections of 1936." *Historical Journal* 27 (1984): 677–95.

– *Rethinking France: Plans for Renewal, 1940–1946.* Oxford: Clarendon Press, 1989.

Sherman, Daniel. *The Construction of Memory in Interwar France.* Chicago: University of Chicago Press, 1999.

Simard, Marc. "Intellectuels, fascisme et antimodernité dans la France des années trente." *Vingtième siècle* 18 (1988): 55–75.

Simmons, Harvey. *The French National Front: The Extremist Challenge to Democracy.* Boulder: Westview Press, 1996.

Singer, Barnett. "Lyautey: An Interpretation of the Man and French Imperialism." *Journal of Contemporary History* 26 (1991): 131–57.

Sirinelli, Jean-François, ed. *Histoire des droites en France*. 3 vols. Paris: Gallimard, 1992.

Smith, Paul. *Feminism and the Third Republic: Women's Political and Civil Rights in France, 1918–1945*. Oxford: Oxford University Press, 1996.

Soucy, Robert. *Fascist Intellectual: Drieu La Rochelle*. Berkeley: University of California Press, 1979.

– "French Fascism and the Croix de Feu: A Dissenting Interpretation." *Journal of Contemporary History* 26 (1991): 158–88.

– *French Fascism: The First Wave, 1924–1933*. New Haven and London: Yale University Press, 1986.

– *French Fascism: The Second Wave, 1933–1939*. New Haven and London: Yale University Press, 1995.

– "Functional Hating: French Fascist Demonology between the Wars." *Contemporary French Civilization* 23 (1999): 158–76.

– "The Nature of Fascism in France." *Journal of Contemporary History* 1 (1966): 27–55.

Sternhell, Zeev. *Ni droite ni gauche: L'idéologie fasciste en France*. 3rd ed. Brussels: Éditions Complexe, 2000.

Sternhell, Zeev, with Mario Snajder and Maia Asheri. *The Birth of Fascist Ideology*. Trans. David Maisel. Princeton: Princeton University Press, 1994.

Sweets, John. *Choices in Vichy France: The French under Nazi Occupation*. New York: Oxford University Press, 1986.

Taguieff, Pierre-André. *L'Illusion populiste*. Paris: Berg, 2002.

Tallett, Frank, and Nicholas Atkin, eds. *Catholicism in Britain and France since 1789*. London: Hambledon Press, 1996.

Tannenbaum, Edward. *The Action Française: Die-Hard Reactionaries in Twentieth-Century France*. New York: Wiley, 1962.

Thomas, Jean-Paul. "Les Effectifs du Parti Social Français." *Vingtième siècle* 62 (1999): 61–83.

– "Le Parti Social Français." *Cahiers de la Fondation Charles de Gaulle* 4 (1997): 39–77.

Tixier-Vignancour, Jean-Louis. *Des Républiques, des justices et des hommes*. Paris: Albin Michel, 1976.

Tombs, Robert. *France, 1814–1914*. London: Longman, 1996.

– ed. *Nationhood and Nationalism in France: From Boulangism to the Great War, 1889–1918*. London: Harper Collins, 1991.

Tucker, William. *The Fascist Ego: A Political Biography of Robert Brasillach*. Berkeley: University of California Press, 1975.

Tumblety, Joan. "Civil Wars of the Mind: The Commemoration of the 1789 Revolution in the Parisian Press of the Radical Right, 1939." *European History Quarterly* 30 (2000): 389–429.

Ungar, Steven, and Tom Conley, eds. *Identity Papers: Contested Nationhood in Twentieth-Century France.* Minneapolis: University of Minnesota Press, 1996.

Union Interfédéral du Parti Social Français: Statuts. Lyon: Imprimerie C. Roure, 1938.

Vallat, Xavier. *Le Nez de Cléopâtre: Souvenirs d'un homme de droite (1919–1944).* Paris: Éditions les Quatre Fils Aymon, 1957.

Vallin, Charles. *Aux Femmes du PSF: Conférénce faite aux déléguées des groupes d'Action Sociale du PSF (région parisienne).* n.p., n.d.

– "Le Parti Social Français." *Sciences politiques* 52 (1937): 211–24.

– *Un Seul Combat pour une seule patrie.* Algiers: Edmond Charlot, 1943.

Veuillot, François. *La Rocque et son parti comme je les ai vus.* Paris: Plon, 1938.

Vinen, Richard. *Bourgeois Politics in France, 1945–1951.* Cambridge: Cambridge University Press, 1995.

Weber, Eugen. *Action Française: Royalism and Reaction in Twentieth-Century France.* Stanford: Stanford University Press, 1962.

– *The Hollow Years: France in the 1930s.* New York: W.W. Norton, 1994.

Weng, Ting-Lung. "L'Historique et la doctrine du Parti Social Français." Thèse de droit, Université de Nice, 1970.

Werth, Alexander. *France in Ferment.* New York: Harper and Brothers, 1935.

– "French Fascism." *Foreign Affairs* 15 (1936): 141–54.

– *The Twilight of France, 1933–1940.* Ed. D.W. Brogan. New York: Howard Fertig, 1966 [1942].

Weygand, Maxime. *La Rocque: Conférence faite à Paris le 21 mars 1952.* n.p., n.d.

Wieviorka, Olivier. *Les Orphelins de la République: Destinées des députés et sénateurs français (1940–1945).* Paris: Seuil, 2001.

Wileman, Donald. "L'Alliance Républicaine Démocratique: The Dead Centre of French Politics, 1901–1947." PhD dissertation, York University, 1988.

– "P.-É. Flandin and the Alliance Démocratique, 1929–1939." *French History* 4 (1990): 139–73.

Winock, Michel, ed. *Histoire de l'extrême droite en France.* Paris: Seuil,1993.

– "Populismes français." *Vingtième siècle* 56 (1997): 77–91.

Wohl, Robert. "French Fascism Both Right and Left: Reflections on the Sternhell Controversy." *Journal of Modern History* 63 (1991): 91–8.

– "Par la voie des airs: L'entrée de l'aviation dans le monde des lettres françaises 1909–1939." *Le Mouvement social* 145 (1988): 41–64.

Wolikow, Serge. *Le Front Populaire en France*. Brussels: Éditions Complexe, 1996.

Young, Robert. *France and the Origins of the Second World War*. New York: St. Martin's Press, 1996.

Zaretsky, Robert. "Neither Left, nor Right, nor Straight Ahead: Recent Books on Fascism in France." *Journal of Modern History* 73 (2001): 118–32.

– *Nîmes at War: Religion, Politics and Public Opinion in the Gard, 1938–1944*. University Park: Pennsylvania State University Press, 1995.

Zdatny, Steven. "Collaboration or Resistance? French Hairdressers and Vichy's Labor Charter." *French Historical Studies* 20 (1997): 737–72.

Ziegler, Gilette. *J'étais au PSF*. Paris: Les Éditeurs Français Réunis, 1950.

Zuccotti, Susan. *The Holocaust, the French, and the Jews*. New York: Basic Books, 1993.

Index